Royal Fever

Royal Fever

THE BRITISH MONARCHY IN CONSUMER CULTURE

Cele C. Otnes and Pauline Maclaran

UNIVERSITY OF CALIFORNIA PRESS

University of California Press, one of the most distinguished university presses in the United States, enriches lives around the world by advancing scholarship in the humanities, social sciences, and natural sciences. Its activities are supported by the UC Press Foundation and by philanthropic contributions from individuals and institutions. For more information, visit www.ucpress.edu.

University of California Press
Oakland, California

Library of Congress Cataloging-in-Publication Data

Otnes, Cele, author.
    Royal fever : the British monarchy in consumer
culture / Cele C. Otnes and Pauline Maclaran. — First edition.
        pages   cm
    Includes bibliographical references and index.
    ISBN 978-0-520-27365-8 (cloth : alk. paper)
    ISBN 978-0-520-27366-5 (pbk. : alk. paper)
    ISBN 978-0-520-96214-9 (ebook)
    1. Windsor, House of—Public opinion.   2. Windsor, House
of—Marketing.   3. Royal houses—Great Britain—Public opinion.
    4. Royal houses—Great Britain—Marketing.   I. Maclaran, Pauline,
author.   II. Title.   III. Title: British monarchy in consumer culture.
    DA28.35.W54O88 2015
    929.7′2—dc23
                                                    2015024080

Manufactured in the United States of America

24 23 22 21 20 19 18 17 16 15
10 9 8 7 6 5 4 3 2 1

In keeping with a commitment to support environmentally responsible and sustainable printing practices, UC Press has printed this book on Natures Natural, a fiber that contains 30% post-consumer waste and meets the minimum requirements of ANSI/NISO Z39.48–1992 (R 1997) (*Permanence of Paper*).

CONTENTS

FIGURES AND TABLES

FIGURES

TABLES

PREFACE

What would British consumer culture—or for that matter, global consumer culture—be like if its Royal Family had never existed? At various times throughout the thousand-plus-year history of the monarchic clan, millions of people have sought to experience its pomp, pageantry, and peccadilloes, enmeshing themselves in the life stories of individual family members, or in the saga of the lineage as a whole. The invention of the telegraph and cheap printing techniques in the mid-nineteenth century enabled rapid-fire transmission of images and information, spurring the growth of royal fever on the global stage. Of late, computer-based and cellular communication modes have helped the British Royal Family (hereafter, the Royal Family) to once again achieve a successful reputational turnaround.

One long-standing way to consume the Royal Family is to delve into any number of books (or entire genres) devoted to them. When we began this project, Hilary Mantel's *Bring Up the Bodies,* the second volume in her historical fiction trilogy about Henry VIII's court, had just won the United Kingdom's Man Booker prize for fiction (its precursor, *Wolf Hall,* did so in 2009). But books on the topic are not always literary; they are academic, architectural, artistic, biographical, commemorative, cultural, fictional, historical, humorous, pop-cultural, and even pop-up.[1] Quite reasonably, a reader might ask, "Why do we need another book on the Royal Family?" Our answer is that as researchers of consumer behavior, we focus on how people engage in and with contemporary consumption practices and the goods, services, and experiences associated with this particular monarchy. In short, this book focuses both on what people buy or do when they engage in royal-related consumption and why they feel compelled to do so.

We became intrigued by this topic as we noticed the seemingly endless links between the marketplace and past and present royal personages in commemoratives, fashion, films and television, historic sites, media products, and touristic experiences, to name but a few arenas. As our appendix explains, we officially began our fieldwork with a weeklong immersion in England that culminated in the wedding of Prince Charles and Camilla Parker Bowles in April 2005. We technically concluded our fieldwork with another immersion of the same length in March 2014. But even as we were finalizing the details of this book, the royal-memorabilia marketplace was gearing up for yet another merchandising opportunity—namely, celebrating the birth of Princess Charlotte, the second child of the Duke and Duchess of Cambridge.

Although our ethnographic approach emphasizes contemporary aspects of royal production and purchasing, we also delve into the deeply rooted history of this phenomenon, which predates both the creation of market-oriented economies and a global contemporary consumer culture. As many historians observe, long before high-quality goods and services were available to their subjects, monarchs enjoyed the finest offerings that artisans, chefs, and craftsmen could produce. Even as consumption has become more democratized, kings, queens, and their families around the globe still occupy the top of the human social hierarchy. Consequently, most typically enjoy unfettered access to customized and luxurious goods, services, and experiences.

During our nine years of work on this book, we witnessed the receding and resurgence of what many now call the Royal Family "brand."[2] In June 2000, the British newspaper the *Guardian* reported that support for the Royal Family was at its lowest level in modern times, with only 44 percent of those polled believing Britain would be worse off without a monarchy. Furthermore, more people indicated indifference to the Royal Family's existence than had done so in the early 1990s, "when only 5% to 10% said they did not have a view."[3] But just twelve years later (a mere drop in the bucket for the over-thousand-year lineage), and prior to the Queen's Diamond Jubilee celebrations in 2012, another *Guardian* poll showed the Royal Family enjoying record popularity, with 69 percent of respondents agreeing Britain would be worse off if the monarchy was to be disbanded.[4]

Even when interest in the Royal Family in Britain was at its nadir, "St. James's Palace" (the moniker for the monarchy's publicity department, housed in that residence) continued to emphasize the need for brand visibility. For example (and as chapters 7 and 8 explore), in 1993 the Queen agreed for the first time to open Buckingham Palace to the public. Since then, it has become one of the more popular royal sites in London. In the summer of 2011, a record 600,000 visitors traipsed through its rooms and corridors, a 50 percent increase from the year before. No doubt, the visitor count was spurred by the palace's exhibit of the wedding gown that Catherine Middleton wore when she married Prince William in April of that year.[5]

To be clear about our own stance, neither of us entered into this project because we collect or consume Royal Family phenomena beyond any average touristic sense. Yet we understand the appeal of many aesthetic and experiential elements contained within the royal consumption smorgasbord. We can appreciate Andy Warhol's diamond-dusted portraits of the Queen, admire the way *The King's Speech* was cast and crafted, and enjoy the haute-couture gowns designed for women in the Royal Family. At the same time, we recognize that the monarchy is not everyone's cup of Earl Grey tea. In short, our goal is to shine the spotlight on how the British monarchy has wielded, and continues to wield, its influence in the marketplace. We hope to unpack the myriad reasons consumers and creators of royal-related products, services, and experiences find themselves drawn to these entities, and why they devote their money, creative energy, and leisure time to the intersection of the British monarchy and consumer culture.

Proponents of the institution often argue that the Royal Family exerts a great deal of economic and cultural significance not only in Britain, but also within a growing global consumer culture. Yet these sentiments often encounter rancorous resistance from critics who label the institution archaic and elitist. Such divisiveness, coupled with the controversies often surrounding (and sometimes spurred by) the Royal Family over the dynasty's long tenure, provide compelling reasons for a book that focuses on how and why people continue to devote themselves to consuming (and producing; see chapters 6 and 7) all things royal. And as we also demonstrate, engaging in such practices is an increasingly popular pastime across the globe.

The summary of recent activity within the Royal Family in "Key Events in the British Royal Family since 1981" (p. xxiv) depicts the monarchy's myriad milestones and transitions in recent decades. Moreover, there is no doubt that other events of equal or greater magnitude will occur in the near future. Given the Queen's robust health and the fact that her mother lived to be 101, it is likely that on September 9, 2015, Elizabeth II will become the longest-reigning monarch in British history, surpassing Victoria's reign of sixty-three years, seven months, and three days (or 23,226 days, 16 hours, and

23 minutes). More of the Queen's grandchildren are likely to marry and have children in the next decade, and a royal funeral or two seems inevitable. We predict these events will contribute to increased cultural and consumer-oriented interest in the British monarchy.

Winnowing our choice of the types of royal-related consumption and production to explore proved challenging, given the seemingly infinite array of options. In the end, we decided to try and capture a fairly wide representation of experiences. Several key figures who emerge in this book assisted us with our goal. One is Margaret Tyler, known in Britain and beyond as a prolific, self-described eccentric collector of royal memorabilia. Nevertheless, because the Royal Family cuts such a wide swath across the global-commercial landscape, we did minimize or omit several key topics. Probably the one receiving the shortest shrift pertains to historical and current commentaries on royal food consumption and production. However, several excellent resources discuss the pivotal role of banquets and food practices among the contemporary family, and others offer perspectives on royal gastronomic rituals during specific historical periods.[6] Nor do we devote as much space as is deserved to the Royal Family's patronage of the arts (including their support of artists, authors, composers, and dramatists). Again, several excellent resources exist on this topic.[7]

The introduction that follows offers a basic overview of the origins, structure, and past and present roles of monarchies in the world—but primarily in Britain. Chapter 1 explores the pervasiveness of the Royal Family as a cultural and global entity, and presents our arguments for understanding the brand as a phenomenon that we label the Royal Family Brand Complex (RFBC). In chapter 2, we examine what we identify as the key internal and external support systems that enable the RFBC to retain its prominence in global consumer culture. Chapter 3 introduces the reader to the world of Margaret Tyler, royal collector extraordinaire—now a media celebrity in her own right—and discusses how such passionate preservers of the British monarchy contribute to its value and visibility.

In chapter 4, we describe how the public commoditized and consumed the now-iconic Diana, Princess of Wales, who came to dominate the global discourse surrounding the British monarchy during her lifetime. In chapter 5, we review the ways film, television, and theater have portrayed and popularized the Royal Family. Chapter 6 explores the ways the RFBC intersects with various aspects of the marketplace. It explores how the Royal Warrant makes visible the monarchy's patronage of goods and services, and how the RFBC leverages the marketplace to serve its own commercial and cultural interests. We also delve into how advertisers depict the Royal Family, sometimes in ways that skirt established standards. In chapter 7, we discuss the history and management of royal touristic practices, delving into the strategic activities of Historic Royal Palaces, a charity responsible for the day-to-day operations of six royal residences. Chapter 8 continues our focus on royal sites by offering a case study of Windsor, England. Located just twenty-three miles from London, it is home to the venerable Windsor Castle and is the Queen's favorite weekend getaway. We explore the locale as the site of many key events in royal history.

No book on royal consumer culture would be complete without exploring the two most recent monumental events occurring within the British monarchy—the wedding of Prince William to Catherine Middleton on April 29, 2011, and the birth of their son, Prince George, on July 22, 2013. In chapter 9, we review the extravagance, fashion, luxury, and opulence (and occasional reining in and resistance) associated with these events, and how they contribute to the RFBC. Chapter 10 offers our reflections on the future trajectory of the RFBC and the issues we believe it will face as it tries to maintain its appeal in Britain and the world.

Finally, we would like to explain two of our stylistic choices. First, regarding our titular reference to Queen Elizabeth II, it is standard practice for some stakeholders (e.g., the British monarchy's official website, Historic Royal Palaces) to always refer to Her Majesty as "The Queen," (with a capital *T*), regardless of where her title appears in a sentence. (Note that the British Parliament's official website does not follow this convention.) With no disrespect intended, we follow the lead of most scholars and authors, who use a lowercase *the* in her title. Second, with respect to our usage of *royal* versus *Royal,* we use the uppercase version only when it appears as part of a proper noun (e.g., Royal Ascot). As protocol dictates, we now bow out of this preface, without turning our back to the Queen. We hope readers find the topic of how the RFBC intersects with British and global consumer culture as engaging to read about as we have found it to explore.

Cele Otnes, University of Illinois at Urbana-Champaign
Pauline Maclaran, Royal Holloway University of London
May 2015

ACKNOWLEDGMENTS

The number of people whom we wish to thank for their assistance and moral support over the many years we spent preparing this book could fill up the Clock Courtyard at Hampton Court Palace. First, we are especially grateful to Margaret Tyler, who allowed us into her life for almost a decade, entertained and educated us with her deep knowledge of the Royal Family and its myriad consumer-culture proliferations, and introduced us to many producers and consumers of the Royal Family.

We are grateful to members of the staff at Historic Royal Palaces for their time and insights—including Michael Day, Deirdre Murphy, and Alexandra Kim. We thank both Robert Lower and John Pym, the owner and the manager of the former commemorative store Hope and Glory, who talked to us at length about royal commemorative memorabilia and introduced us to many of their customers. We thank those who took the time to discuss their collections and other types of royal-related passions with us, as well as members of the media who allowed us to interview them, and the fans we met at the Making of a Monarchy for the Modern World conference at Kensington Palace in 2012. They include Theodore Harvey, whose encyclopedic knowledge of the monarchy and role as a consultant to the manuscript is much appreciated. Thanks also to Andrew Lannerd, who was extremely helpful in correcting and offering facts, figures, and nuances pertaining to the manuscript, and who shared aspects of his collection with us.

We thank our academic departments and universities for their financial, intellectual, and moral support in helping us to produce and disseminate this work. Our many academic friends and colleagues have been supportive. Two in particular—Eileen Fischer of York University and Elizabeth Crosby of the University of Wisconsin LaCrosse—coauthored with us on related pieces of the royal consumption saga, and helped us to remain relevant and engaged in our academic community while we juggled the overwhelming aspects of book authorship. We thank Mike Robinson, director of the Ironbridge International Institute for Cultural Heritage, and Helaine Silverman and Paul Kapp, director and associate director of the Collaborative for Cultural Heritage Management and Policy at the University of Illinois, respectively, for their feedback on various presentations of this work. We appreciate all of the royal tidbits sent to our e-mail inboxes and Facebook pages, and the enthusiasm and suggestions for this project from our academic friends and colleagues, including Catherine Alington, Fleura Bardhi, Stephen Brown, Giana Eckhardt, Christina Goulding, Deborah Owen, Andy Prothero, Aric Rindfleisch, Shona Rowe, Julie Ruth, Sharon Shavitt, Madhu Viswanathan, Tiffany White, Linda Tuncay Zayer, and our faculty colleagues in our respective departments. Tony Farr gave us great feedback on various draft chapters. Kent Drummond and Ashleigh Logan shared wonderful insights on their personal experiences of royal events. Kimberly Sugden shared her perspective as an American "expat" in England and kindly allowed us to reproduce several photos of royal-related activities. We thank Paul Kapp, Ashleigh Logan, John F. Sherry, Jr., and Ekant Veer for allowing us to use their photographs. Thanks also to the staff at the Rare Book & Manuscript Library at the University of Illinois, and everyone who bestowed royal memorabilia and ephemera on us (including resistant versions; in that vein, thanks to Alan Bradshaw).

We appreciate the contributions of our former students or assistants who assisted with presentations, book chapters, and vital compilations for the book, especially Caitlin Carson, Joseph Evertz, Julian Hartman, Ben Lee, Jonathan Philippe, and Elaina Shapiro. Thanks to other undergraduate and graduate students from the University of Illinois and beyond who worked for us for money or academic credit: Lauren Bonvallet, Garrett Burger, Jackie Ceglinski, Johanna Kephart, Lilian Mehta, Emily Otnes, Gina Puntini, Leonard Schloer, Adam Sidor, Tammy Stern, Carlos Uribe, and Ye Sun. Julian Hartman deserves special mention for being immersed in the royal trenches for almost a year, and for spearheading many excellent finds for the chapters. Doctoral-level research assistants at Illinois who helped us with this project include Robert Arias, Sydney Chinchanachokchai, Elizabeth Crosby, Erin Ha, Behice Ece Ilhan, Mina Kwon, Atul Kulkarni, and Srinivas Venugopal. Samiya Khan, a student at Royal Holloway University of London, also collected data for us. We take full responsibility for any omissions or errors.

Finally, we are extremely grateful to our acquisitions editor, Reed Malcolm, as well as Rachel Berchten, Leslie Davisson, Stacy Eisenstark, Elena McAnespie, and other members of the editorial, production, and marketing teams at the University of California Press for their patience, enthusiasm for, and faith in this project. We thank Elizabeth Berg for her detailed copyediting. We are also especially grateful to those who reviewed the book for the Press and made suggestions for improvement. Most of all, we thank our families for their continual support (and Mark Otnes for his assistances with graphics, as always), for learning more than they probably thought they would ever learn about the Royal Family, and for sharing material and even eyewitness accounts of some of the relevant events they witnessed.

PROCLAIMED ENGLISH/BRITISH
MONARCHS: 1066–PRESENT*

HOUSE OF NORMANDY

William I (the Conqueror)	1066–1087
William II	1087–1100
Henry I	1100–1135

HOUSE OF BLOIS

Stephen	1135–1154

HOUSE OF ANJOU

Henry II	1154–1189†
Richard I	1189–1199
John	1199–1216

* Three others ruled for very short periods, but their claims to the throne were disputed: Matilda (1141), Louis VIII of France (1216–17), and Lady Jane Grey (1553).

† Following French tradition, Henry II had his son crowned co-ruler in 1170. But "Henry the Young King" predeceased his father, so typically he is not included in the line of succession.

HOUSE OF PLANTAGENET

Henry III	1216–1272
Edward I	1272–1307
Edward II	1307–1327
Edward III	1327–1377
Richard II	1377–1399

HOUSE OF LANCASTER

Henry IV	1399–1413
Henry V	1413–1422
Henry VI	1422–1461
	1470–1471 (restored)

HOUSE OF YORK

Edward IV	1461–1470
	1471–1483 (restored)
Edward V	1483*
Richard III	1483–1485

HOUSE OF TUDOR

Henry VII	1485–1509
Henry VIII	1509–1547
Edward VI	1547–1553
Mary I	1553–1558†
Elizabeth I	1558–1603

* Never crowned.

† Upon his marriage to Mary in 1554, Philip II of Spain was declared King of England by an Act of Parliament, but lost his claim to the throne when she died in 1558.

HOUSE OF STUART

James I   1603–1625
Charles I   1625–1649

THE INTERREGNUM (NO MONARCH)

1649–1660

HOUSE OF STUART (RESTORED)

Charles II   1660–1685
James II   1685–1688
William III and Mary II   1689–1694
William III   1694–1702
Anne   1702–1714[*]

HOUSE OF HANOVER

George I   1714–1727
George II   1727–1760
George III   1760–1820
George IV   1820–1830
William IV   1830–1837
Victoria   1837–1901

HOUSE OF SAXE-COBURG AND GOTHA

Edward VII   1901–1910
George V   1910–1917

[*] The Acts of Union in 1706 and 1707 united the Kingdoms of England and Scotland as "Great Britain"; thereafter, Anne became Queen of Great Britain and Ireland.

HOUSE OF WINDSOR

George V	1917–1936
Edward VIII	1936*
George VI	1936–1952
Elizabeth II	1952–present

* Never crowned.

KEY EVENTS IN THE BRITISH
ROYAL FAMILY SINCE 1981

1981	Prince Charles marries Lady Diana Spencer
1982	Prince William, their son, is born
1984	Prince Henry ("Harry"), their son, is born
1986	Prince Andrew marries Sarah Ferguson ("Fergie")
1988	Princess Beatrice, their daughter, is born
1990	Princess Eugenie, their daughter, is born
1992	Princess Anne and Mark Phillips divorce
	Princess Anne marries Timothy Laurence
	Windsor Castle suffers £37 million ($62 million) in fire damage
	The Queen declares 1992 her "Annus Horribilis"
1993	The Queen opens Buckingham Palace for public tours
1995	Martin Bashir interviews Princess Diana on the BBC television program *Panorama*
1996	Charles and Diana divorce
	Andrew and Sarah divorce
1997	Diana dies in a car accident
	Diana's funeral is held in Westminster Abbey
	HMY *Britannia* is decommissioned
	Windsor Castle renovation is completed
1998	HMY *Britannia* opens for public tours in Edinburgh
1999	Prince Edward marries Sophie Rhys-Jones
2000	The Queen Mother celebrates her hundredth birthday
2002	The Queen celebrates her Golden Jubilee
	Princess Margaret, the Queen's sister, dies
	The Queen Mother dies
2005	Charles marries Camilla Parker Bowles

2007	The Queen and Prince Philip celebrate their sixtieth wedding anniversary
	The Queen becomes Britain's oldest reigning monarch
2011	Prince William marries Catherine Middleton
	Prince Philip celebrates his ninetieth birthday
2012	The Queen celebrates her Diamond Jubilee
	Kensington Palace reopens after a £12 million ($19 million) renovation
	London hosts the 30th Summer Olympic Games
	William and Catherine announce first pregnancy
2013	The bones of Richard III (r. 1483–1485) are found in Leicester, England
	Prince George, son of William and Catherine, is born
2014	Richard III Visitor Centre opens in Leicester
	Scotland's referendum on independence is defeated
	William and Catherine announce second pregnancy
	Blood Swept Lands and Seas of Red is exhibited at the Tower of London
2015	Richard III is reinterred at Leicester Cathedral
	Princess Charlotte, daughter of William and Catherine, is born
	Elizabeth II becomes the longest-reigning English/British monarch (Sept. 9)

The Politics and Business
of Monarchy

During a hectic two-week period in early 2013, those who follow the goings-on of monarchies around the world found themselves with news aplenty to pique their interest. On January 28, Queen Beatrix of the Netherlands announced she was giving up the throne to make way for her forty-five-year old son to become the first Dutch king since 1890. Exactly one week later, archaeologists at Britain's University of Leicester confirmed through DNA testing that a skeleton located in the ruins of Greyfriars Church below a "car park" in that city belonged to King Richard III. In 1485, he was the last English king to die in battle, and his body was thought to have been irretrievably lost. Finally, on February 11, Pope Benedict XVI announced his resignation after eight years as pontiff. The pope is ruler of the Catholic Church, and Vatican City is considered a monarchy, so his decision was as much an abdication as "Queen Bea's" two weeks before. Worldwide, each event spurred conversations about royalty, rulers, and renewal—and they also provide an excellent starting point from which to pose the question: in contemporary global society, why are monarchies still so compelling to millions of people around the world?

As we note in the preface, our book focuses on why and how consumers and producers invest their time, money, energy, and other resources engaging with the Royal Family. Given the sheer scope of these activities, we discuss to a lesser extent why some resist engaging in them. To ground our discussion, in this introduction we offer a brief overview of what monarchy means in the current global landscape. In so doing, we set the stage to explore why the Royal Family has endured for over one thousand years, when many (in truth, most) monarchic dynasties have been disbanded or disrupted, or have disappeared altogether.* Put simply, the institution of monarchy is on the downslide; although it was the most popular form of government in the nineteenth century, only forty-four nations recognize monarchs today—and sixteen of these, known as the Commonwealth Realms, share Queen Elizabeth II as head of state. After we discuss the basic configurations of monarchy, we turn our attention to the Royal Family in particular, exploring issues pertaining to their genetic connections, the evolution of their duties and powers, and the financing of their luxurious (or, in their critics' eyes, ludicrously lavish) lifestyles.

We begin by addressing a seemingly straightforward question: What is a monarchy? The simple answer is that it is the form of government that concentrates political power in one ruler (or occasionally in joint ones, as exemplified by William III and Mary II of England). This concentration of sovereignty is what distinguishes a monarchy from the other broad category of government—the republic—in which multiple political leaders are elected or appointed to lead, rather than inheriting the responsibility. In short, the distinguishing characteristic of a republic is that it is *not* headed by a monarch. Moreover, when a sovereign's subjects say they advocate republicanism, this does not mean they necessarily share political leanings with the U.S. political party of the same name. Instead, they are expressing their desire for the monarchy to end altogether.

The process of assuming the throne is known as "accession," rather than the often misused term "ascension" (as one Royal-retailer we interviewed quipped, "Only Jesus had an ascension").[1] But, to confuse matters, once accession occurs, it is typical parlance to describe a monarch as "ascending the throne." Technically, the title passes to the successor immediately after the previous monarch dies or is deposed; no ceremony is required to enact the change of power, although in Britain the new monarch meets with the Accession Council for a formal proclamation of succession. Many countries mark the transition with a simple inaugural blessing or benediction. But in the United Kingdom and some Asian countries, new monarchs participate in public and often extremely elaborate coronation ceremonies. These cultural events often occur months after a monarch's accession, not only because

---

* Even the Queen's husband, Prince Philip, fell victim to such cataclysms; as a baby, he was smuggled out of Greece in a fruit crate on a British freighter when his uncle King Constantine I of Greece was deposed.

they require time to plan but because it is considered inappropriate to conduct anything celebratory so close to the recent death of the previous monarch. Of course, these events can also be extremely expensive; merely decorating the streets of London for the Queen's coronation in 1953 cost £36 million ($61.6 million in today's dollars). These ceremonies also typically feature a mélange of micro-rituals, such as the anointing of the monarch with holy oil as a sign of divine endorsement, somber processions of nobility and important political figures, an impressive guest list brimming with foreign leaders and dignitaries, and attendees (especially the new ruler) bedecked in special jewels, robes, and symbols.

Monarchs are known by many honorifics around the world, including *King/Queen, Emperor/Empress, Czar/Czarina* (from the word *Caesar*), *Sultan*, and (more rarely, given the paucity of women rulers in Muslim countries) *Sultana*. These are often followed by a slew of royal "styles and titles" that capture the scope of the monarch's dominion. The Queen's most recognized style and title is short and simple, considering the size of her realm: "Elizabeth II, by the Grace of God, of the United Kingdom of Great Britain and Northern Ireland and of her other Realms and Territories, Queen, Head of the Commonwealth, Defender of the Faith." Yet her actual style and title depends on which area of the world is addressing her. In short, she possesses a different honorific within each of the sixteen Commonwealth realms.

Another key aspect of monarchy is that it is typically understood as a job for life, which is why Queen Beatrix's abdication was noteworthy to many royal-watchers around the world. (Her own subjects may not have been very surprised; she was actually the third Dutch monarch in a row to abdicate.) In contrast, even as she approaches her ninetieth birthday on April 21, 2016, Elizabeth II is highly unlikely to relinquish her crown, since British monarchs typically "keep hanging on, until death parts them from the throne."[2] Should the Queen emulate her mother and live to be 101, Prince Charles—already Britain's longest-serving heir apparent—will be close to eighty when he accedes.

In sum, the monarchic system typically relegates ruling power to one individual, who often, but not always, retains the throne until death. Yet the real-world configurations of monarchies are much more complex than this definition implies. Understanding the global variations requires unpacking issues such as how succession is determined and how (if at all) a monarch wields power.

Historically, royal succession has typically been the most critical issue rulers must face. At times in history when succession policies have been ambiguous—as when monarchs waited until breathing their last to name their successors—the consequences have been monumental and disastrous. In fact, the Royal Family's entire lineage is traceable to a succession dispute that began in 1066 between Harold II and William of Normandy. Harold, who had no hereditary claim to the throne, was elected king by the Witan, a council of Anglo-Saxon rulers of England's regional territories, after Edward the Confessor died without naming a successor. William, on the other hand, was Edward's actual blood relative. When he defeated Harold at the Battle of Hastings and united several disparate kingdoms, William became the common ancestor of all subsequent kings and queens of England (after 1707, the Kingdom of Great Britain).

For hundreds of years after William's reign, the wars English rulers funded and fought were almost as likely to be internal fights for the Crown as they were reactions to foreign threats. The financial and human costs of such crises eventually became too great to sustain, even for medieval kings, whose popularity and power depended as much on their skill with a sword as on their ability to craft foreign diplomacy. As political and legal systems became increasingly bureaucratized during the eighteenth and nineteenth centuries, monarchies found their paths to perpetuation codified into laws. The most common outcome was stipulating a hereditary route to succession—but here again, definitions of what constitutes an heir still vary widely across monarchies. For example, one common version of "male primogeniture" dictates that the crown and title must pass to the monarch's firstborn son, and then to any heirs this son produces, regardless of their sex. If the firstborn son has no children, this procedure is repeated with the second son and so on, until a son or grandchild of the original monarch ultimately is selected.

Other countries follow a much stricter version of this law, stipulating that only the male children of male heirs are eligible to succeed. Under that system, a monarch with no male heirs will find his daughters and any of their children passed over. Rights to the crown then pass to the closest eligible male relative, even one living in another region or foreign country (who might not even speak the language of his new subjects). Historically, it has often been the case that as the biological and geographic distance between blood relatives increased, claims to the throne became thornier—and the chances of conflict over succession more likely.

Until very recently, the British system followed a more liberal form of male primogeniture, allowing daughters of monarchs to accede if no other *legitimate* male heirs existed. This distinction was critical given the number of illegitimate children sired by English kings (Charles II reputedly had fourteen to seventeen, by perhaps as many as eight different mistresses). Ironically, this rule led to the situation where Queen Victoria, who was both female and the longest-reigning monarch in British history, had to pass over her firstborn daughter, Princess Victoria, in favor of her firstborn son, Prince Albert Edward. The Queen's second-oldest child, Princess Anne, also has moved several places down the line of succession due to male primogeniture. When Anne was born, she was second in the line of succession. At present, she is now twelfth in line behind her three brothers, all of their male and female children, and the children of Prince William and his wife, Catherine, Duchess of Cambridge.

Especially for critics of the monarchy, it may have seemed that the stone walls encasing the institution within such an inherently sexist succession system were virtually impenetrable. But in April 2013, Parliament passed the Succession to the Crown Act, which states that heirs to the throne will now be determined according to the more liberal rule of "absolute primogeniture." Effectively, this means that if Prince William and Catherine's first child had been a girl, she would have been the first female in British history to not have become queen simply because no eligible male relatives could be found.

Both biological sex and birth order seem to dictate relatively straightforward succession guidelines. To make matters more complicated, however, some hereditary monarchies layer additional stipulations onto these criteria. For example, British law still excludes Catholics from inheriting the throne, a vestige of the Act of Settlement in 1701. At that time, after Queen Anne's death, over fifty of her Catholic heirs were bypassed in the quest for a successor. George Louis, who ruled the German state of Hanover, made an uncontested bid for the throne, although he was not the only candidate who could claim blood ties. In 1714, at age fifty-four, he arrived for the only the second time on the shores of England and was crowned George I, even while retaining his Hanoverian title.[3]

In contrast to hereditary systems, some countries elect monarchs after delegates debate the merits of potential nominees and cast votes. Sometimes the candidate pool consists of the current ruler's relatives, who (perhaps not surprisingly) often elect a member of their own family to succeed. In these situations, both elected and hereditary succession procedures come into play. The most visible elected monarchy is that of Vatican City. In March 2013, after Pope Benedict XVI's resignation, the 115 Catholic cardinals who were under age eighty convened in the Sistine Chapel, discussing nominees and proceeding through several rounds of voting, until two-thirds of them had cast their ballots for Cardinal Jorge Bergoglio of Argentina, who took the name Pope Francis upon his election.

Types of monarchies also can be delineated according to the source and amount of the ruler's power. Two categories exist, with the constitutional option much more common than the alternative, which is absolute rule. As implied by the name, in absolute monarchies rulers wield total and complete power over their subjects, typically with guidance from trusted advisers. Only six absolute monarchies exist today. Five—Brunei, Oman, Qatar, Saudi Arabia, and Swaziland—are also hereditary; the sixth is the elected papacy.

Constitutional monarchies exist within the confines of laws drawn up by larger governing bodies. As more diverse and less monarchic forms of government took hold throughout Europe from the eighteenth to the twentieth century, a common pattern emerged: either authoritarian monarchs subjected themselves to the policies put forth by constitutional (or communist) rule or they faced dire consequences, such as banishment or execution. Often, people felt deep ambivalence about deposing such a visible cultural symbol, one who had represented their cultural values and their nation's visibility on the world stage. In France, where the opulence of the royal court had become morally reprehensible to so many living in poverty, this ambivalence showed itself in a series of stutter-steps to abolish the monarchy. After the decade-long French Revolution began in 1789, the monarchy was not abolished until 1792. It was then resurrected in 1814, only to be abolished again in 1848. But even today, the "Royalistes de France" gather every January 21, the date Louis XVI was beheaded, "not just to pay homage ... but to mourn the death of the French monarchy."[4]

Constitutional monarchies specify not only rules pertaining to succession but also the duties and limits of the ruler's power. Although Britain ostensibly adheres to this system, in truth the nation has no formal written constitution. Instead, members of Parliament (or MPs) debate and craft laws, Acts of Parliament, and unwritten conventions. Collectively, this legislation serves as the ratified body of work that directs and guides policy in Britain—and that its monarchs must respect.

Worldwide, two main forms of constitutional monarchies exist. First, executive constitutional monarchies feature rulers who are still subject to laws but remain visibly and actively involved in determining the political activities of their country. For instance, Prince Albert of Monaco exercises joint rule over his (three-quarter-square-mile) realm with a minister of state whom he selects. This minister both acts as Albert's counsel and adviser, and oversees two legislative councils that debate and enact laws. In contrast, a ceremonial constitutional monarchy typically is stripped of any true authority. Although a ceremonial monarch may be recognized as titular head of state, typically an elected politician assumes the responsibilities of running the government on a day-to-day basis. In Britain and Japan, for example, the prime minister (or PM) takes on this role, functioning much like the president of the United States, by wielding executive power and working with the legislative branch to formulate and implement policy.

"Monarchists," or those who support the institution in its various forms, often argue that Royal families represent important symbolic and emotional links to national heritage. In Britain, historically both Parliament and the citizenry have supported its monarchy through financial and social means, in myriad ways. In line with the pervasive "norm of reciprocity" that typifies many social relationships, however, supporters also expect monarchs and their families to willingly play roles in significant and visual cultural rituals, national holidays, and global events. When they choose not to, the reputation of the monarchy can suffer, lending cultural credence to calls for republicanism. For example, after her husband, Prince Albert, died in 1861 at age forty-two, Queen Victoria entered a ten-year phase of deep mourning and almost total seclusion, earning the nickname "the Widow of Windsor." Although eventually cajoled into increasing her public appearances, her "protracted privacy ... cast a gloom over high society[,] deprived the populace of its pageantry, [and harmed] the dressmaking, millinery, and hosiery trades."[5]

Having explained the various permutations of monarchy, we can now describe the British variant in just three words: hereditary, constitutional, and ceremonial. But it is also worth exploring who exactly has inherited the English (and later British) crown.* Every monarch in the current line of

* The term *British* is used for monarchs ruling after the Acts of Union joined the England and Scotland in 1707 and 1708.

succession claims a blood tie to William the Conqueror. Many historians declare him to be the first "real" king of England, because he successfully united the various fiefdoms that riddled the large island landmass under one rule. As the list of British monarchs that precedes this introduction indicates, thirty-five kings and seven queens have been proclaimed rulers of England or Britain. The list also includes two rightfully named king but never crowned. Edward V acceded in 1483 at age twelve after his father Edward IV's death. But before he could be crowned, he likely was murdered in the Tower of London after his uncle (who then declared himself King Richard III) seized power (see chapter 7). In addition, Lady Jane Grey, whom Edward VI had named in his will as his successor, was technically queen only for nine days in 1553. At that time, Edward's sister Mary won her claim to the throne and subsequently saw Jane declared a traitor and beheaded.

That some British monarchs enjoyed long reigns is evident when we compare their number to U.S. presidents: forty-two in 947 years, versus forty-four in 225 years. Yet disentangling the genetic cocktail of the Royal Family is not nearly as straightforward as this relatively small number may imply. Two issues explain why the Royal line of succession "has bent and buckled many times in the course of a thousand years."[6] First, the monarchs' ability to produce successors has varied widely. Perhaps surprisingly, given both their perceived potential as wealthy, powerful mates and the criticality of producing an heir, eleven kings or queens in the lineage—over one-fourth of the total—bore no legitimate children at all. One of the great ironies within the monarchic metanarrative is that while Henry VIII's ruthless (and some would say, murderous) pursuit of legitimate progeny resulted in three legitimate children, their inability or unwillingness to produce heirs brought the tumultuous Tudor dynasty to a screeching halt after a relatively short 118 years.* Likewise, a second metanarrative—Queen Victoria's reign— never would have occurred if her uncle William IV's two legitimate daughters had lived past infancy, or if any of his ten illegitimate children had been eligible to rule.

Although prohibited from making a claim to the throne, monarchs often acknowledged blood ties to illegitimate children by granting them a sur-

---

* Henry's son, Edward VI, was fifteen when he died; Mary I experienced a false pregnancy at age thirty-eight but bore no children; Elizabeth I chose to never marry, to the consternation of her advisers.

name that began with the designation *Fitz,* which means "son of." Yet from its onset, the discourse about legitimate and "Fitz" children was both ironic and hypocritical, considering that the Conqueror (also known as William the Bastard) was himself the illegitimate son of the unmarried Robert I, Duke of Normandy, and his mistress Herleva. But as was often the case with the warrior kings, prowess on the battlefield often trumped blood claims. Especially in the medieval era, those who coveted their relatives' thrones often engaged in myriad unethical and immoral strategies—declaring vulnerable legitimate heirs to be illegitimate, killing their own siblings, and even sparking civil wars in an attempt to wrest the throne from relations.

In contrast to those monarchs who bore no legitimate children, several British kings and queens managed to see many offspring live to adulthood. This feat was especially notable during the Middle Ages. Complications during childbirth, childhood diseases, and sweeping medical tragedies—such as the Black Death, which killed over one-third of Continental Europeans in the 1300s—were commonplace. Progeny-prolific rulers thus often contributed enormously to the longevity and stability of the British monarchy, as many royal children were subsequently promised at young ages for monarchic marriages across the European continent. Seven of Queen Victoria's nine children married into Royal families—and another succeeded her on the British throne. Many of her forty-two grandchildren (as well as her great-grandchildren) also joined royal houses on the Continent, earning Victoria the nickname "the grandmother of Europe." Given this sweeping genetic dispersal across the Continent, it is not surprising that Elizabeth II, herself a great-great-granddaughter of Victoria, married a member of European royalty who was a great-great-grandson of the matriarch. In fact, the Queen and Prince Philip are third cousins through one branch of the family tree and second cousins once removed through another.[7]

In addition to the Conqueror, six other monarchs each produced nine legitimate children—and James II and George III sired an impressive fifteen apiece. Of course, lack of a legitimate heir to the throne could mean the end of a dynastic line and the rise of another "Royal house," or strain of the Royal Family still related (albeit sometimes through half-relations) by blood. The names of many British houses—Norman, Plantagenet, Hanover—clearly illuminate the European roots of the Royal Family and the fact that genetically, "English monarchs are also usually something else."[8] In fact, the current Royal moniker, House of Windsor, which George V adopted by Royal

Proclamation in July 1917, could rightly be cited by marketers today as a clear example of strategic "brand repositioning." The King was concerned that the Germanic surname "Saxe-Coburg and Gotha" might cause bitter feelings among British subjects locking forces with Kaiser Wilhelm II (himself a grandson of Queen Victoria) during World War I.

Royal intermarriage among very close kin, until recently a common practice, means the Queen also can claim blood ties to ancient nobles of Saxony, Scotland, Ireland, and even to the Danish king Sweyn Forkbeard—acknowledged by some scholars as the first "king of the English in 1013."[9] A traceable bloodline of over fifty generations—one of the longest in the Western world—is often touted as evidence of the "heritage value" of the British monarchy and as one reason to preserve the institution.*

Moving beyond the roots of the Royal Family, it is important to address another key question with respect to the monarchy—namely, what duties do the Queen (and her family) actually fulfill? Earlier, we alluded to the fact that through the medieval era and a bit beyond, male monarchs were expected to train as soldiers and lead troops onto the battlefield. As early as the 1500s, however, most were also more likely to act as autocratic rulers than soldiers. Beginning with the Act of Settlement in 1701 and throughout the eighteenth century, parliamentary rules continually stripped British monarchs of their powers. So if warriors, tyrants, and empire builders are no longer apt metaphors for its kings and queens, which ones are more suited to illuminating the duties and roles of the modern British monarchs?

As noted, the Queen (with her family) now occupies a largely ceremonial and symbolic place in British culture, even as she wields no official political power. But it is also true that she, as well as her son and successor Prince Charles, can veto legislation that could affect their "hereditary revenues, personal property or personal interests of the Crown."[10] In fact, a twenty-eight-page parliamentary publication titled "Queen's or Prince's Consent" outlines the procedures for acquiring consent from the monarch or her son, primarily if legislation intersects or could affect their interests in the Duchies of Lancaster or Cornwall. Moreover, while not often acting in an official political capacity, the Queen spends much of her time reviewing important

---

* As dynastic bloodlines go, however, the British lineage pales when compared to that spawned by Confucius; his line is traceable from his birth in 551 B.C. through 2,550 years and 85 generations.

documents and state papers transported to her via the famous "red boxes," to prepare herself for her typically weekly consultations with her PM.

In terms of her myriad ceremonial roles, the Queen also carries out a specific set of royal duties perceived as symbolically supportive of the political system. For instance, she officially invites any newly elected PM to form a government in her name, officiates over the annual ceremony of the State Opening of Parliament, and serves as the "fount of honour," or the only person allowed to confer all honorary titles, such as peerages, knighthoods, and recognitions for gallantry. As the British monarchy has transitioned from a governing to a symbolic institution, those occupying the throne likewise have withdrawn from "exposed political positions [and a] gradual adoption of a posture of neutrality."[11] But in her advisory role to the PM, the Queen takes full advantage of exercising the three rights constitutional historian Walter Bagehot identifies as those the monarch possesses: the right to be consulted, the right to encourage, and the right to warn.[12] In over sixty years on the throne, she has advised twelve PMs, beginning with the venerable Winston Churchill and including the only female to occupy that position, Margaret Thatcher. She has also consulted with 145 PMs in the Commonwealth nations.

Furthermore, many of the Queen's ceremonial activities serve as unofficial acts of diplomacy. In that role, she and many of her family members often act as ambassadors across the world in general and in the Commonwealth nations in particular (like Australia and New Zealand, sites of the 2014 goodwill tour; see chapter 9). The Commonwealth is a consortium of fifty-four nations with a combined population of over two billion people. All except Mozambique and Rwanda are former UK colonies and vestiges of the former British Empire, which at its peak was the largest in history. The Commonwealth has its roots in Canada's declaration of dominion from Britain in 1867. This document led to the appointment of Canada's PM and the country's transition to independence, while enabling it to retain political and emotional ties to Britain.

The Commonwealth grew rapidly during the twentieth century, even as wars, diplomatic concessions and decolonization eroded the British Empire. Although the countries are ostensibly connected by mutual interests in economic development, democracy, and racial equality, the Royal Family has found it increasingly important to make regular goodwill tours to Commonwealth members, to retain visibility and promote British business interests.

A third ceremonial role of the Queen and her family is in the arena of philanthropy. Since George II first voiced his support to the Society of Antiquaries in 1751, members of the Royal Family have lent their endorsements and energies to many charitable organizations in the United Kingdom and beyond.[13] The Queen is now a named patron of over six hundred charities. Likewise, her only daughter, Princess Anne (the Princess Royal), is known as a tireless philanthropist, typically fulfills more charitable engagements per year than other members of her family, and has earned the title of "the hardest-working Royal." Princess Diana was also known for her charity work and for taking on controversial or even dangerous causes.

A fourth role the Queen and her family maintain is to serve as what we term "cultural conservationists." In a very real sense, the micro- and macro-pageants embedded and enacted regularly (even daily; consider the Changing of the Guard at Buckingham Palace) help preserve the history of the nation and enhance Britain's appeal to domestic and foreign tourists. From the annual "Trooping the Colour" ceremony that marks the Queen's birthday* to less frequent but often fervently (and maybe even feverishly) anticipated occasions, such as Royal weddings, funerals, and coronations, these events allow the public to view the Royal Family at the height of their aesthetic glory. Of course, people's actual encounters with the Royal Family often are limited; many onlookers are content to observe the pageantry from behind barricades. But in fact, savvy followers seeking a brush with royal greatness know they can access the Court Circular—the Royal Family's list of official engagements—either in a newspaper or on the British monarchy's official website.† With such information in hand, it is relatively easy to view senior members of the Royal Family up close—much easier, in fact, than seeing the president or vice president of the United States.

The Royal Family's roles of cultural preservation and propagation include not only these relatively fleeting ritual experiences but also more prolonged efforts of acquiring, protecting, and providing access to historic and cultural treasures. As we will discuss, the Royal Collection Trust oversees an unsurpassed trove of priceless works of art and literature by some of the world's

---

* The Queen's actual birthday is April 21. But because the weather is usually less predictable at that time of year, Trooping the Colour usually occurs on a Saturday in June. Dates of her official birthday celebrations vary throughout the Commonwealth, sometimes even within the same country (e.g., Australia).

† The official website for the British monarchy is located at www.royal.gov.uk.

great masters. It also houses some of the world's most famous jewels, musical instruments, stamps, coins, antiquities, and contemporary creations.

Finally, the Queen has publicly averred that she believes her Royal duties include upholding cultural values such as patriotism, religious faith, and support for the nuclear family. But in truth, the role of the monarch as a moral compass is relatively new within the dynasty. It is often traced to Victoria and Albert's dedication to family, as well as to social and cultural stability and reform.[14] In fact, William IV and George IV, the kings immediately preceding Victoria, often were satirized as symbols of debauchery, gluttony, and buffoonery. Many regard as admirable Elizabeth II's determination to never put a foot wrong. But as Her Majesty (and the world) has discovered, dedicating one's life to serving as a moral barometer is one thing, and convincing family members to follow suit is quite another.

Given the ways monarchs' duties have evolved, perhaps the most appropriate description for those who will rule Britain in the twenty-first century is that of global and national goodwill ambassador. Yet these duties often involve elaborate entertaining in addition to exchanging gifts with dignitaries, participating in state visits as guests or hosts, and traveling the world. So the final questions we explore in this introduction are these: how much does the Royal Family cost, and who foots the bill?

In addressing this question, a remark made by the Queen's father that "we are not a family; we are a firm" is an illuminating starting point.* It aptly captures the fact that the financial dimension of the monarchy is merely one aspect that requires management. In 2013, the British Monarchy's website reported that the Crown employed 1,200 staff—and that taxpayers absorbed the cost for (only) 450 of them. In addition, the Royal Household comprises people with specific skills in areas such as "catering and hospitality, gardening, finance, secretarial, media relations, marketing, human resources, IT [Information Technology], property surveying and maintenance, equine management, visitor management and retail, furniture restoration, curatorship, and strategic planning and research."[15] Furthermore, public ceremonies, goodwill tours, and other occasions often require additional temporary employees, particularly in the area of security—costs that taxpayers bear as well. The cost for security at the 2011 royal wedding was estimated to be half

---

* Prince Albert (later George VI) apparently made this remark after being rebuked for smoking in academic dress at Cambridge and being told his conduct was especially heinous for a member of the Royal Family.

the total for the event, or $35 million. This figure funded 5,000 police, 200 mounted police, and 35 sniffer dogs. Furthermore, because the wedding day was declared a public holiday, all (except, presumably, the dogs) were paid overtime.[16]

So who foots the bill for the Royal Family? In 2013, the answer to this question changed dramatically. In 1990, when the British populace was at its most apathetic about the monarchy, the Queen agreed to curtail finances previously allocated to some within the monarchy's inner circle (e.g., titled cousins and other aristocrats with kin ties). In the past, arguments supporting such allowances were rooted in the fact that these relatives often stood in for the Queen or Prince Philip at charity and cultural events. The famous and much criticized "Civil List," which specified allocations for various areas in the Royal Household, included allowances for specific members of the Royal Family. In 2013, the Civil List system was completely supplanted by the new Sovereign Grant, which is based on 15 percent of the royalties of the Crown Estate, or the monarchy's revenues from its real-estate investments and farming output. The Queen is sole grantee of these funds, with the remaining 85 percent directed to Parliament. The Crown's allocation is then dispersed to cover expenses related to staff, residential upkeep, travel, and allowances to individuals. In essence, the fund is intended to cover all costs related to the monarchy, except for the extra security required for public ceremonies and events. This solution is regarded as "elegant in its simplicity and pragmatic in its consequences. . . . [I]t also removes the need [for the monarchy] to periodically negotiate a payment plan with Parliament."[17] Put simply, the strategy conceptualizes the Royal Family as essentially self-sufficient.

However, the Sovereign Grant system still does not address criticisms that the amount of money the Royal Household receives is excessive. In fact, for two years in a row, the Grant rose by £5 million (with the Queen receiving £40 million [$68.5 million] in 2014), due to record profits by the Crown Estate.[18] Furthermore, critics are quick to point out that the reason the Crown can generate these profits is because the Royal Family engaged in land-grabbing practices for hundreds of years.

We have alluded to other assets that the Royal Family also holds. Yet in truth, the Queen's individual net worth, estimated recently by *Forbes* to be $500 million, is relatively paltry compared to the wealthiest royal in the world, King Bhumibol Adulyadej of Thailand, who is worth $30 billion.[19] Of course, the Queen's defenders often point out that most of the assets at her disposal are held in trust for the monarchy and will pass to her successor.[20]

In sum, monarchy is a diverse and often complex form of government—especially when considering issues such as succession and power distribution. The number of people actually ruled by sovereigns in the world is at an all-time low, and the days of new monarchies being created may be over. Nevertheless, ceremonial forms of the institution still remain, and are even vibrant, in many countries.

FIGURE 1. Solar Queens. Courtesy of Ekant Veer.

ONE

The Magnetism of the Monarchy

It is a typical cool, slightly rainy mid-May week in London, 2012. Seemingly out of nowhere, hundreds of images begin to appear of an eighty-six-year-old great-grandmother whose sartorial choices tend toward colorful dyed-to-match ensembles from hat to hem, her ubiquitous Launer leather handbag on her arm. Under British law, she exceeded the legal retirement age for women over two decades earlier, but this octogenarian-in-overdrive still spends many of her days cutting ceremonial ribbons, shaking hands, hosting large garden parties for people she has never met, or entertaining dignitaries from around the world.

Regardless of how people feel about her or her family, they would be hard-pressed to avoid her image in London—and in much of the world—during the late spring of 2012. From an optician's window on Kensington High Street, she appears encased in an ornate gold frame and surrounded by signs proclaiming a £50 discount, adorned by a bright silver tiara and sporting an oversized pair of baby-blue-rimmed sunglasses, pink lipstick, and a satisfied smile (figure 2). She also stands in cardboard-cutout form in a dress-shop window on Regent Street, next to a pouty mannequin in Union Jack leggings.

A few hundred feet away, on Piccadilly Circus, she beams at window shoppers from a seemingly endless mélange of photos taken at different stages of her life that adorn souvenir shortbread tins, coffee mugs, tea towels, and miscellaneous tchotchkes. In high-end department stores like Peter Jones and Liberty, discerning collectors can choose more elegant representations of her visage, forgoing items that bear "happy snaps."* Yet the pervasive references to this matriarch are not always blatantly linked to commercial gains; many appear as

* A term for low-resolution images silkscreened onto typically inexpensive ceramics.

FIGURE 2. The Queen in a London optician's ad, June 2012. Photo by Cele Otnes.

indicators of respect, reverence, or restraint. Across the street from the Russell Square tube station, a sidewalk sandwich board sponsored by the quick-casual chain Au Bon Pain reminds passengers to "Keep it Clean" for her.

Six weeks later, she spectacularly trumps her own triumphant turnaround in popular opinion, in what seems destined to become her most beloved and blogged-about consumer-culture cameo. In a teleskit embedded in the opening ceremony of the London Olympics, watched live by 900 million people around the world, she plays herself delivering secret orders to the British spy James Bond (Daniel Craig), then proceeds to "parachute jump" with him, via a stunt double, into Olympic Stadium. But even had she never participated in that event, and could only savor the official four-day celebration of her sixty years on the throne, the outcome would still have been the same. For in 2012—during the "Summer of London"[1]—Britain's Queen Elizabeth II became an icon of cool.[2] For a tweed-skirted persona whose image serves as cultural shorthand for conservative and correct manner and mode, and whose younger relatives often have done her image no favors in recent decades, such a turnaround in public sentiment was nothing short of miraculous.[3]

Yet even when some members of the Royal Family are criticized and even skewered for their decidedly unregal actions, their foibles and failings nonetheless still attract the interest of many people around the world. Tabloid-fueled British society and the increasing international outreach of online and social media mean royal missteps and debacles often are dispensed with gleeful immediacy around the globe and prove as or more compelling than their triumphs. In fact, contrary to Oscar Wilde's observation that "the only thing worse than being talked about is not being talked about," at times the risk to the monarchy of becoming laughingstocks, scapegoats, or cultural afterthoughts seems quite high.

Of course, since oral and written forms of cultural expression originated, depictions of rulers have ranged from fawning and flattering to borderline traitorous to outright seditious. But as more sophisticated mass media forms developed over the centuries, some modes—political cartoons, for example—became expected and accepted forms of (often devastating) commentary, especially in Britain.[4] Furthermore, in recent years, other types of media offerings, such as opinion polls, have contributed to perceptions that the Royal Family's appeal to the British populace was becoming more and more tenuous. After Prince Charles and Princess Diana divorced in 1996, one newspaper survey reported that "46 percent of respondents believed Charles was unfit to be king, an increase of 13 percent in two years."[5]

Certainly the Royal Family has not been alone among monarchies in its vulnerability. Since the beginning of the twentieth century, the world has seen a marked decline in the number of crowned heads, especially in Europe. In 1900, for example, monarchs ruled over almost every country on the continent. But by 2012, only ten of fifty European countries featured hereditary monarchs recognized as legitimate by their governing bodies. As we note in our introduction, at the end of the twentieth century, a prorepublican discourse seemed to be gaining strength in Britain, with public commentary increasingly expressing apathy, anger, and downright nastiness toward the Royal Family. One result of this outcry was that the Queen agreed to pay income taxes (as had some of her forbearers),[6] give up some historic entitlements, and even relinquish her beloved royal yacht, the HMY *Britannia*. (Supposedly, one of the few times she has cried in public was at its decommissioning ceremony in 1997). Furthermore, the outcry over the diminishing relevance of the monarchy has resulted in "the Firm" mounting a continuous and controlled campaign of image management from within. Margaret Tyler, known as an über-fan of the Royal Family, observes, "The Royals now know they have to win us over. They're not daft."[7]

This campaign for people's attention and interest around the world has certainly been spurred by global gains in consumer culture, media saturation, and a heightened interest in luxury and aesthetics. Given how these phenomena dovetail with perceptions of royal lifestyles, plenty of people continue to vote with their credit cards and valorize past, present, and even future aspects of the British monarchy. To some extent, the institution has become an entity that people can purchase and possess in some fashion, producing enjoyable benefits in the process.

Of course, over its lifespan, the British monarchy often has proved contentious for a variety of reasons—especially when rulers still wielded political power. Indeed, the early warrior kings often habitually and irrevocably uprooted the lives of ordinary citizens within and beyond the boundaries of the British Isles. Furthermore, some monarchs' decisions to defy powerful cultural institutions and place their personal goals above their subjects' welfare often led to shattering and irrevocable social and cultural changes. Consider, for example, Henry VIII's decision in 1534 to effectively dissolve the Catholic Church in England and appoint himself head of the Anglican Church, so he could divorce his first wife and eventually enter into a quintet of future marriages.

In this book, we explore how and why the Royal Family maintains the level of fascination they do for many people around the world, given that scholars and subjects alike typify some British monarchs (and their heirs apparent) in the lineage as bloodthirsty, extravagant, foppish, immoral, reactionary, selfish, and even (often justifiably) criminal. Furthermore, given the numerous price points of entry into the world of royal consumption, and the choices of how best to tangibilize these representations, people are able to deftly customize their experiences while shielding themselves from aspects they find less desirable. For example, they might choose to immerse themselves solely in royal "dark tourism,"[8] such as the lore and gore associated with the Tower of London or, more recently, with the tragic events surrounding Princess Diana's death. Regardless of people's particular proclivities, we address these general questions: What do consumers gain by consuming the British Royal Family? What factors contribute to the viability and vividness of royal consumption experiences?

Before we focus on these questions in more contemporary times, it is worthwhile to remember that "royal-watching" has historically compelled much of the citizenry in what is now known as Great Britain. Until the broad-scale development of mass media in the late nineteenth century, people typically learned about activities through proclamations "nailed on the market cross, read aloud by a sheriff or other local official, or circulated and reported in village or alehouse."[9] Until recently, many royal rituals were regarded as private and sometimes secretive affairs of state rather than occasions for public cultural celebration. But as more citizens migrated to London and its environs, they created chronicles of their increasing presence at the processionals that preceded coronations, funerals, and triumphal civic pageants celebrating victories over enemies on the battlefield, such as that described below:

> When Henry V returned from Agincourt in 1415 he saw two gigantic figures
> ... upon the entrance to London Bridge; on the bridge itself were "innumerable boys representing the angelic host, arrayed in white, with glittering wings." ... On the King's approach ... "sparrows and other small birds" were set free ... an image of the Sun, "which glittered above all things," was placed on the throne and around it ... angels [sang and played] all kinds of musical instruments." ... "The city of London might, at that time, have been termed a *stage.*"[10]

Yet the concept of royal-watching has not always referred to adopting the presumably pleasurable stance known as the "tourist gaze."[11] From 1066 until 1743, when George II was the last king to fight in battle, the British were involved in over fifty wars. During much of this "warrior king" era (aptly named since all English monarchs after William the Conqueror were male until 1553), royal watching often meant watching *out* for monarchs or, in particular, their armies. Kings and queens were under constant pressure to replenish their royal treasuries and to rouse and replace lost troops, equipment, and transportation. Citizens resigned themselves to sacrificing crops, livestock, mounts, sons, and other resources to their authoritarian rulers to serve as militia and materiel for battle. Often these requests took the form of seizures and even midnight raids, with compensation coming only in the "satisfaction" of fulfilling one's duty to the Crown. Of course, failure to offer up these resources could result in punishments as severe as those rained down onto the enemy.

With warrior kings often as likely to plunder their own subjects as to protect them, the notion of engaging in any kind of royal-themed touristic experiences, or of collecting souvenirs or traveling to seek royal encounters, would have been unfathomable to both rural and urban folk. As we discuss later in this book, the British economy was primarily based on agrarian and cottage-based industries until the Industrial Revolution, which began in Britain in the late eighteenth century and completely changed the socioeconomic structure of the nation, and then the world. Before that seismic occurrence, royal commemorative items were limited in type and number— although during the Tudor era, monarchs did leverage seals, medals, coins, paintings, and even illustrations in best-selling books (including the Bible) to perpetuate and promote their own images.[12] Coins bearing royal visages were actually issued for kings ruling various sections of Britannia before William the Conqueror united the regions, and began to appear regularly by 800 A.D.[13] But until the rise of an industrialized and urbanized Britain, "for many people, the king's image on coins was the only likeness of the monarch which they were likely to see in their lifetimes."[14]

After 1688, the British Parliament began to abate the power of the monarchy through increasing constitutional restrictions. At the same time, two other key factors reshaped the nature of "royal watching." First, the role of the warrior king waned by the end of the eighteenth century; the metaphor was displaced by the decidedly more passive role of the monarch as diplomat (if the monarchs took much interest in ruling at all). Second, a structured and stable class system arose. Its most distinctive characteristic was the aristocratic class or landed gentry throughout England, Wales, Ireland and Scotland, which reached its heyday prior to World War I.

Throughout the reigns of most of Britain's monarchs, royal-watching for the lower classes who lived outside of London typically involved lining the hedgerows along Britain's village roads, where proclamations (and later, newspapers) reported that monarchs and their entourages would be traveling. Within the aristocracy, however, a more formal and demanding type of interaction, which involved extravagant consumption, emerged. During the nineteenth and part of the twentieth centuries, the peak era of Britain's great country houses, the most important families in society were expected to extend invitations to elaborate weekend parties and resign themselves to members of royalty inviting themselves as well. Of course, most families regarded snaring members of the ruling class for their country weekends, or even overnight, as a great social coup. In probably one of the most expensive examples of anticipatory consumption, many owners of Britain's great houses even commissioned the building of ornate "royal beds." These cost thousands of pounds and were created to the aesthetic standards fit for the monarch, although most aristocrats never even knew if a royal visit would come to pass.[15] Sometimes, however, the situation evolved into a classic example of being careful what one wished for. In the late nineteenth century, Prince Albert Edward's (later Edward VII) lavish tastes meant entertaining him during a house party often cost his hosts £5,000– £10,000 per weekend.* It was rumored that Lord Suffield was so desperate to be relieved of the duty and expense that he burned down his own home, Gunton Park.[16] Later, when Edward VII's daughter-in-law became Queen Mary, she was known for admiring treasures at people's homes until her host and hostess got the hint and offered her the items as gifts. As a result, she acquired a reputation for winding "her way round the country houses of England vacuuming up the Meissen."†[17]

Between the two world wars, the British aristocracy was gradually but irrevocably felled by the perfect storm of a global depression, a decline in demand for British goods around the world, the battlefield deaths and horrific injuries incurred during World War I by many sons and heirs of the great houses, and crippling changes in estate taxation laws. As a result, many of the finest families were forced to sell not only their country homes but their city residences as well—often complete with priceless works of art, jewels, and furnishings. Liquidating these assets also meant curtailing weekend house parties or eliminating them completely. Consequently, by World War II large weekend house parties had died out, shifting the sites of the Royal Family's entertainment to their own palaces and to events such as the annual presentation of upper-class debutantes at court.[18]

---

* Conservatively, £5,000 in 1890 would be equivalent to more than £450,000 ($708,000) in 2014; www.measuringworth.com.

† Since 1710, a German manufacturer of very expensive porcelain.

The decline of the aristocracy also meant that the British upper class began to interact with the Royal Family at events that members of the lower social classes could also attend. At significant sporting events, such as Wimbledon and Royal Ascot, for example, tickets are available to the general public. Distinctions in the ways the social classes interact are still maintained even at these more democratically accessible events, but sometimes class boundaries disappear completely around their fringes. In 2005, after the wedding of Prince Charles and Camilla Parker Bowles in Windsor, many wedding guests in their tails, top hats, and "fascinators"* dined at the bistro chain Café Rouge in Windsor & Eton Central train station at tables alongside more plebian spectators who had stood behind the barricades, waving as the couple's limousine sped off after the ceremony.[19]

These days, spectacle-laden public activities typically signify important milestones for the Royal Family. But for the people whose passions involve following members of that particular gene pool, these occasions also provide an opportunity to commemorate the continuation of a well-chronicled, historical lineage. Of course, some family milestones clearly differ from those the average citizenry experience in their own families. After all, only royal personages can be the central figures of events like coronations, or even "lesser" ceremonies, such as Charles's investiture as the Prince of Wales at Caernarfon Castle in 1969.

In sum, on both the interpersonal and commercial fronts, the ability to engage with the Royal Family has become increasingly democratic. Collectors from all income and societal levels can own whatever types of commemoratives from whatever eras they desire, as long as they have the time, energy, and money required to acquire them. Of course, as is true with any constellation of consumption activities, people's engagement with the Royal Family depends on who they themselves are, what they value, and how they believe their involvement with the monarchy, or the individuals within the institution, contributes to or reflects their own identities.

The variety of choices royal consumers can make in the marketplace is almost staggering, and the ways people can engage with the British monarchy within a global consumer culture range from mainstream to downright eccentric. For example, some people choose only to skim the cream and participate in the most elite and expensive royal-related offerings. "Thomas," a successful American stockbroker and self-professed Anglophile, had gar-

---

* Decorated headpieces, often featuring feathers and beads.

nered enough income to retire by his late forties.[20] He spends four months of each year in London, indulging his passion for English history and adding to his high-end collection of gilded and crested royal commemoratives. He reports that his favorite pieces to collect are those produced by Minton (a famous English pottery brand until the postwar era), that often cost thousands of pounds. During another four months of the year, he lives in Cape Town, South Africa, where he immerses himself in a social group composed largely of Anglophiles.[21] He spends the remaining months in the United States, where much of his collection resides in his closets and china cabinets.

On the other side of the coin are collectors more concerned with quantity than quality, and who may not be as discriminating (or in fact, discriminating at all) in terms of the items they possess. Their collections might include pieces that would be described as royal kitsch, or even more critically, "tat," a British term for tacky or tasteless items. Collector extraordinaire Margaret Tyler, to whom we devote an entire chapter, identifies one piece she owns as "the ugliest thing I've got. . . . I know it's supposed to be Charles and Diana, but they look like the Everly Brothers. . . . I thought it was a vase, but it's got a hole in the back."[22]

Unlike Margaret, who allows this piece to commingle with higher-end items, some collectors find themselves drawn to kitsch, particularly the vulgar variants. Often, however, they separate these from more reverential commemorative varieties. "John" began our tour of his home by proudly discussing the items in large glass cabinets filled with gilded commemoratives produced by many of Britain's stalwart potteries. Toward the end of the tour we ventured into a small upstairs office, where he proudly showed off a set of Diana "matryoshka," or Russian-style wooden nesting dolls (figure 3). The largest was of Princess Diana, and the other male figures, in descending size and importance, represented those with whom she had been romantically involved.*[23] Yet even collectors who do not venture into raunchier realms still can opt for a display that is more silly than sacred, by acquiring items such as a mug displaying a sketch of Prince Charles with his ear forming the handle, William and Catherine wedding toilet paper, or a caricature of the Royal Family on motorcycles in racy, revealing leather outfits.

A key reason to understand this full spectrum of royal representations is that doing so highlights the differences in consuming the *British* Royal

---

* John then related the tasteless logic behind this nesting set, noting that all the men had "been in Diana."

FIGURE 3. Diana, Princess of Wales nesting dolls. Photo by Cele Otnes.

Family versus other monarchies around the globe. For example, Thailand is not considered an absolute monarchy, but it is nevertheless illegal to speak ill of its Royal Family, and being caught doing so can result in jail time. So it is highly unlikely any Thai retailer would risk offering, say, a coffee mug that pokes even gentle fun at King Bhumibol Adulyadej's extreme wealth or his world record as the longest-reigning monarch.[24] Furthermore, googling the terms *Oman Royal Souvenirs* or *Saudi Royal Souvenirs* results only in pictures of British Royal Family memorabilia that shops in those countries offer.

It might be assumed that the few remaining monarchies in Europe would be motivated to tailor their royal-related merchandise to a broad array of touristic tastes. Here too, however, the range of royal-themed goods, services, and experiences on the Continent in no way approaches what can be acquired in Britain. Even with a spate of recent royal weddings in these countries, the range of monarchic merchandise is decidedly narrow. When

Prince Albert of Monaco married his longtime girlfriend, Charlene Wittstock, in 2011, the press reported that just days prior to the ceremony, she had tried to board a plane and return to her native South Africa. At the time, rumors were swirling that Albert recently had fathered his third illegitimate child. Commenters on stories appearing online offered up such advice as "If she had had any doubts whatsoever, she should have bolted," or they mentioned Prince Albert's two other illegitimate children, the couple's age difference (Charlene was thirty-three to his fifty-three when they married), or his receding hairline. Yet souvenirs for the event did not reflect such pointed commentary. Instead, shops in Monte Carlo offered only official and more refined (code to collectors of royal kitsch for "bland") commemorative coins, postage stamps, fans, and ceramics.

Contrast this muted mercantile response with the types of artifacts people can find in Britain to satisfy the "curious psychological need for royal narratives and for imagined participation in royal lives."[25] Even when Charles and Diana divorced and the resulting negative public sentiment led many to assume that the future of the monarchy was tenuous, manufacturers responded with commemoratives of that event. One piece even satirized the divorce by leveraging one of the most traditional forms of commemorative—the souvenir plate—depicting an image of the couple with a large black crack down the center.

Some European countries feature monarchies whose members also make themselves accessible to their subjects, and who, one might assume, would be open to whimsical or even critical retail representations. But even in countries like Norway, where marketers eagerly offer tourists a plethora of moose- and troll-related souvenirs, the few royal items and touristic experiences available are both bland and respectful (when they exist at all).

In short, marketplace representations of the British Royal Family run the gamut from what anthropologist Helaine Silverman labels "portable royalty" (e.g., teaspoons, thimbles, coffee mugs, and key chains) to large-scale, expensive choices. These include refrigerators boasting full-size William and Catherine engagement photo decals, and replicas of royal housewares and jewelry made of gold, silver, porcelain, and other fine materials priced in the thousands of pounds. Furthermore, items can satisfy any level of taste and immersion desired. Yet such a range also reveals and reinforces a clear ambivalence about the role of the monarchy in Britain, supporting the fact that for many people, the institution reflects the "glamour of backwardness."[26] Even consumers at opposite ends of the spectrum of royal consumption seem comfortable with this cultural ambivalence, often finding support in brand communities or "tribes"[27] that help resolve any inconsistencies within experiences. If the Royal Family often is interpreted as a mixed bag with respect to its contemporary cultural relevance, people still reward the pervasiveness and persistence of the institution, and of the members within it, by voting with their wallets at souvenir kiosks, ticket counters at royal residences, retail shops, antique stores and flea markets, theaters, and online outlets.

Placing this mixed-bag metaphor under deeper scrutiny on a cultural level, it can be argued that for some, the Royal Family represents contested territory. Simply put, it often serves as a source of pride during certain times in history, and a source of shame during others. For many republicans in Britain and those whose loyalties lie more with their roots in Scotland, Northern Ireland, and Wales, the Royal Family often represents an underlying source of irritation that during key events in history expands in importance, or rather, "gets inflamed, like an appendix."[28] Some people, like artist Lydia Leith, even use their entrepreneurial skills to create souvenirs reflecting people's ambivalence, displeasure, or fatigue with the Royal Family. Prior to the 2011 royal wedding, she invented the "Throne Up" sick bag, ostensibly to be used by those standing in the London streets to observe the event. After sales outpaced her expectations, she extended her merchandise line to include Diamond Jubilee and royal baby sick bags as well.

Disentangling people's feelings about the British monarchy is a complex process, since so many of the cultural narratives that apply to the Royal Family are inextricably linked to deeply entrenched, iconic aspects of national identity and heritage. Consider, for example, the visuals associated with English/British heritage: bucolic castles with heraldic flags fluttering from their turrets, the material culture based on chivalry and knighthood, gracious and elegant gardens, rolling landscapes and moors, and sedate rivers that have seen many stately processions of royal barges. Furthermore, another key element of Britain's brand stable since the 1500s is William Shakespeare, who wrote ten plays about English kings, as well as others about real and fictional noble and royal figures. A mixed bag the Royal Family may be, but it seems indisputable that engaging with them in the marketplace contributes greatly to tourists' affinity for England (and to a lesser extent, for Scotland as well). Furthermore, the salience of the Royal Family among tourists as icons of British consumer culture may be gaining in importance as cultural practices and touristic experiences that are understood as quintessentially British, such as high tea and visits to revered sites like Stonehenge,* become threatened with extinction.

We are certainly not the first authors to discuss the Royal Family as an object of consumer, or even touristic, gaze—as the recently published *Royal Tourism* attests.[29] Nor are we even the first to conceptualize it as a brand. In recent years, it has become apparent that St. James's Palace, the administrative arm that handles image management and public relations for the Royal Family, understands the value of applying and executing sophisticated branding and positioning techniques. Increasingly, journalists also have latched onto the concept of the British-monarchy-as-brand, both when it seems to be in favor and when it is struggling. In 2001, an essay in Britain's *New Statesman* described the Royal Family as "just another brand which happens, like Marks & Spencer† ... to look somewhat tarnished and outdated."[30] Ten years later, the French journalist Julie Guérineau observed that Prince William's marriage to Catherine Middleton would help modernize "the image of one of the oldest British brands"[31] and result in over £200 million ($337 million) in memorabilia sales.

But to understand what people mean when they bandy about the term *brand* to describe the British Royal Family, it is important to revisit the roots of the word. An analysis of over one hundred articles by two marketing scholars determined that *brand* actually describes twelve distinct concepts.[32] These were further classified as pertaining either to "input" (aspects of the brand managed and delivered by the company) or "output" (those aspects that consumers and other stakeholders contribute). Ultimately, they argued, a brand can be understood as a complex value system for a product that a firm creates, communicates, and manages. Marketing scholar Marie-Agnès Parmentier offers a specific definition of a brand as "a repository of meanings fueled by a combination of marketers' intentions, consumers' interpretations, and numerous sociocultural networks' associations."[33]

Extensive work by the British scholar John Balmer and his colleagues focuses on the types of values managers of monarchic brands should attend to, in order to maintain relevance and resonance with stakeholders. Balmer argues that a monarchy is a "corporate heritage brand," one coalescing around a core promise that links consumers to a "material testimony [and] a set of

* Two major highways have been built in close proximity to the landmark.
† A middle-market chain, also known as "Marks" or "M&S." In 1998, it became the first British retailer to earn a pretax profit of £1 billion.

practices concerned with the continuity, persistence and substantiality of collective identity in the past, present and future."[34] Basing their research on actual interactions with members of the Swedish Royal Family, he and his coauthors identify eight *R*s that monarchies need to manage to preserve the royal corporate-heritage identity: royal, religious, regal, ritual, relevant, respected, responsive, and regulation."[35] An important point is that these eight dimensions emanate from their focus on marketing strategy: that is, they reflect recommendations emanating from study of the monarchy itself with respect to successfully maintaining and managing its repository of meanings. In other words, referring to a distinction we noted above, the strategic perspective on monarchic branding focuses on the input from the corporate entity itself.

We recognize the value and importance of the work by Balmer and his colleagues. Yet we believe that understanding the Royal Family as a brand requires exploring output elements as well, or those aspects consumers and other stakeholders identify as important and desirable. One would hope and expect that what the "Firm" considers critical to its success would overlap to some degree with what other stakeholders seek from it. Our nine-year immersion into the brand supports that assumption to some degree. Our intention is to complement and expand the "input" perspective and in no way diminish the importance of Balmer and his colleagues' work. We believe our exploration of the experiences of consumers and stakeholders, coupled with our deep dive into the literature on branding, tourism, and related topics, enables us to provide a well-rounded understanding of the Royal Family brand.

Based on the perspectives of parties outside the corporation, we present our conceptualization of the Royal Family as a composite of five types of brands—an entity we will refer to as the Royal Family Brand Complex (henceforth, the RFBC; see figure 4). Furthermore, we believe that each brand component within the RFBC contributes one or more unique dimensions that enable it to retain its allure and to support the key narratives used to coproduce goods, services, and experiences related to the brand. These core brand elements, and the fundamental benefits of each, contribute separately or in combination to the many different ways people experience and enjoy the RFBC.

The first type of brand we discuss is the *global brand*. We have already alluded to the popularity of the British monarchy in terms of viewership levels of royal-related activities. In the ensuing chapters, we will continually

FIGURE 4. The Royal Family Brand Complex. Courtesy of Mark Otnes.

demonstrate the popularity of the RFBC on the global stage. Balmer notes that because the Queen is the sovereign of the United Kingdom and fifteen other realms (not to mention head of the Commonwealth of Nations), she is "*de facto*, sixteen Queens rolled into one."[36] Furthermore, the increasing appeal of the consumer-culture ethos around the world, which touts the belief that goods, services, and experiences are central to achieving life's goals (and perhaps to an extent constitute its meaning), has led to a corresponding increase in interest in the RFBC.

In particular, the growth of the middle class in the BRIC countries (Brazil, Russia, India, and China), which encompass 25 percent of the world's landmass and 40 percent of its population, has opened up new opportunities for consumers to enjoy discretionary purchases such as global leisure travel. Shopping is often touted as one of the most popular touristic activities in the world, and gift giving is even more important within most Asian cultures than in Western ones. As a result, many royal-themed retailers and touristic sites have experienced an upsurge in retail sales as the reservoir of global tourists to Britain expands.

Of course, there will likely always be a subset of global consumers to whom the Royal Family means little or nothing. Those who have no access to media infrastructures or global representations of consumer culture obviously come to mind. Countries with histories that have long been intertwined with Britain (such as India or former African colonies within the British Empire), huge subsets of people subsist at the bottom of the pyramid. Even if they are aware of the Royal Family, it is doubtful they follow them with much commercial or cultural fervor. Furthermore, others within and outside Britain may adopt a decidedly "semi-detached"* posture—preferring to ignore the monarchy on an everyday basis but entering into the cultural conversation when it seems the socially appropriate thing to do.

The key dimension of the RFBC experience that aligns most closely with its global-brand component is the *fairy tale*. This literary genre is understood by sociolinguists to be a subset of the folktale, itself a universal form of narrative. Like other folktales, fairy tales began as orally transmitted narratives and have been found all over the world, dating from as early as 100–200 C.E. in the Roman Empire and the third century C.E. in India.[37] Traditionally, these stories are laced with heroes and heroines, fanciful creatures who assist these protagonists with overcoming obstacles in their quests, and a happy ending that depicts the hero or heroine fulfilling his or her quest and destiny. It is important to note that neither fairies nor animal helpers are required in contemporary versions of fairy tales, but all still share the central thematic motif of the underdog proving his or her worth through trials, and then gaining his or her heart's desire. The fairy tale is thus essentially one of character trumping all—with the hero or heroine expected to possess the traits of compassion, cleverness, creativity, and persistence (as captured by Catherine Middleton's nickname of "Waity Katie" during her prolonged courtship with Prince William prior to their 2011 wedding).

In fact, the centrality of the fairy tale to the RFBC surfaces most visibly in the discourse surrounding recent royal weddings. It would be impossible to account for the appeal of the weddings of Charles and Diana, William and Catherine, and even that of the Queen and Prince Philip, without drawing parallels to the romantic stories in this genre.† But besides romances, other types of fairy tales also exist in the royal canon. Most recently (as the recent film *The King's Speech* portrays), George VI initially was the shy, stammering "spare" whose brother's abdication forced him onto the throne. Hampered by a serious speech impediment, he sought assistance from Lionel Logue, who helped the new King through rigorous training and practice. George VI rewarded his "helper" (as Logue would be understood in the fairy tale genre) by awarding him the title of Commander of the Royal Victorian Order in 1944.

The global aspect of the fairy-tale dimension of the RFBC has received huge support from that great creator and disseminator of fairy tales, the

---

* A "semi-detached," or a "semi," is the British term for a duplex.

† Although a member of both the Greek and Danish royal families, Philip essentially was an impoverished suitor, as his family had been forced to flee Greece in 1922.

Walt Disney Company. Disney's first feature film, *Snow White and Seven Dwarves,* released in 1937, was royal themed, and the studio has released ten movies in which plots revolve around underdogs gaining the hands of princes or princesses. In the past few decades, the biggest change in the way people consume films and television programs is their ability to watch them ad infinitum at their leisure. In other words, viewers' experiences are no longer restricted by the length of cinematic runs or the number of times programs air on television. Furthermore, the development of transmedia consumption, or the delivery of similar or related content across a variety of media platforms,[38] means that children all over the world can now dress up in Disney costumes, watch Disney films, peruse Disney storybooks, and watch the Disney Channel on a variety of high-tech devices all at the same time. The importance of royal characters to the Disney oeuvre is reinforced by visits to the Disney theme parks, now located in five countries, or by vacations on Disney cruise ships. All of this prince-and-princessing bolsters the idea that royalty and its trappings are worthy of being idolized around the world. The stories reinforce the message that, especially for a girl, life in a castle with a bona fide Prince Charming is the happiest ending she can wish for (never mind how problematic feminists find this interpretation).

That the heir apparent to the British throne and his successor both chose commoner wives now makes royal fairy tales seem even more attainable across the globe.* This aspect of the RFBC has received support from the European royal families who have seen their members marry commoners as well. In 2010, for instance, Crown Princess Victoria of Sweden married her personal trainer, Daniel Westling. Prior to her marriage, Crown Princess Mette-Marit of Norway not only was a commoner, but also was a single mother who admitted to a rebellious past.

The second brand component that helps define the RFBC is the *human brand.* Of late, there has been much interest in marketing circles in making distinctions between brands containing inanimate objects and those composed of people. Matthew Thomson, who has researched human brands, notes that one important distinction between these brands and their nonhuman counterparts is that consumers typically form much stronger and more permanent emotional bonds with human brands. He found that people claimed to form emotional connections and to experience more meaningful

---

* Lady Diana Spencer wed Prince Charles in 1981; Camilla Parker Bowles wed Prince Charles in 2005; Catherine Middleton married Prince William in 2011.

lives with "actors, comedians, models, directors, radio personalities, writers, singers, athletes, musicians, politicians, and royalty."[39]

Even the most autocratic, tyrannical members of the RFBC still meet the basic definition of a human brand—that is, they were alive for a period of time. Yet it was not until very recently that the monarchs or their relatives even felt the need to make themselves accessible to their subjects. Some, like Victoria, simply did not grasp the importance of adding an accessible (or even visible) human touch to the brand. Many credit Diana, Princess of Wales, for reinforcing the lesson that "in the context of human brands, it is not just quantity [of interaction] but also quality that matters."[40] Nevertheless, curtsying to the Queen or other members of the Royal Family and shaking hands across the barricades are likely to be the only kinds of activities most consumers can expect when engaging with the RFBC, given the strict rules of royal protocol. For example, although bowing and curtsying to the Royal Family are no longer mandatory, rules like "Do not speak unless spoken to," "Don't touch the Queen," and if eating a meal with her, "Don't go to the loo . . . for the love of God"[41] demonstrate that the RFBC (or at least, its handlers) still supports the manufacture of distance from some stakeholders.*

We believe the human-brand dimension that contributes most to the viability of the RFBC is the fiasco. From the perspective of human-brand management, the biggest challenge stems from the fact that royal personages are, indeed, human. Unlike the box of washing powder Prince Charles refused to be compared to when the subject of crafting his image arose, human beings often are quite unpredictable—and often negatively so. In contrast to tragedies, which we label as sad and unexpected events (e.g., Prince Albert's death at age forty-two), or to events enmeshed in political intrigue (e.g., the deaths of kings in wars or Charles I's execution), fiascos are outcomes that reflect the Royal Family members' lapses or failures in judgment and may require reputational repair. Since the 1990s, the younger members of the Royal Family have served as the sources of most fiascos. Although many of these "human brands" are no longer in the familial fold, Prince Harry's antics (wearing a Nazi uniform at a Halloween party or, as recently as 2012, enjoying nude strip billiards in Las Vegas) have served

---

* Dickie Arbiter, the Queen's former press secretary, disputes these rules, noting that only one is actually obligatory. Upon first addressing the Queen, one should refer to her as "Your Majesty," after which it is permissible to use "Ma'am, as in ham."

as a source of entertainment for those who enjoy rubbernecking during the unfolding of royal missteps. Furthermore, as depicted in *The Queen,* many people regarded Elizabeth II's inability to recognize how much her subjects wished her to act as the public face of mourning after Diana's death as a fiasco as well.*

Fiascos make important contributions to the RFBC in at least two ways. First, they provide an added entrée into consuming the monarchy for those claiming to be less interested in its material aspects and more attuned to its historical dimensions. Many people (including academics, who have built entire careers doing so) immerse themselves in understanding the RFBC's less desirable decisions and actions because of the ways these changed history. Although Henry VIII's tumultuous reign often comes to mind, decisions of other monarchs, or those in their entourages, have had similarly devastating consequences. The irony, of course, is that a plethora of material culture (e.g., books, tours, and videos) supports the interests of those who claim interest in RFBC's history rather than its commercial aspects.

A second reason fiascos support the RFBC is that they help make the family and institution objects of empathy, as ordinary people can relate to the consequences incurred after lapses in judgment. The distance is reduced between monarchs—whose coronations hint at links to divinity and perhaps even immortality—and the "mere mortals" who seek to know about them. Fiascos help reinforce what marketing scholar Stephen Brown and his colleagues describe as the desirable aspect of "brand ambiguity."[42] Such ambiguity stems from three dimensions within a brand's overarching narrative: (1) confusions (e.g., why Edward VIII would renounce his birthright for a twice-divorced American woman who admitted she was "nothing to look at"); (2) contradictions (e.g., Edward VII's reputation upon death as the "people's king," when as Albert Edward, Prince of Wales, it was claimed that his lecherous and gluttonous ways brought "the monarchy to the verge of destruction");[43] and (3) cumulations—or multiple meanings (consider how the saga of Henry VIII's six wives has been spun in myriad mediated forms).

A third brand component of the RFBC—one that also shares some overlap with the human brand—is the *family brand.* Although all family brands

---

* Royal fiascos are as old as the lineage itself. When William the Conqueror was crowned on Christmas Day 1066, he ordered his army to suppress any protests. Jittery guards mistook the crowd's enthusiasm inside Westminster Abbey as signs of an impending riot and set fire to the surrounding houses.

are human, the reverse is not true; family brands are human brands composed of kinship networks. As such, family brands typically offer those engaged with them two distinct types of touch points—the personalities of the individual family members and the narratives that highlight relational dynamics within the kinship circle.* (An example from the United States illustrates this point nicely. A recent article about Chelsea Clinton observes that she is "the product of two of the most powerful brands in the world. Now she's finally carving out her own identity—by joining the family business.")[44] Given the ubiquity of the family as a key social structure throughout the world, the global commercial appeal of such entities as the Beckhams, the Coppolas, and the Kardashians or the dynastic power of the Bushes, the Gandhis, and the Kennedys should not be too surprising.

Obviously, a family dynasty preoccupied with its own succession and propagation offers a potentially rich template for narratives that enhance or detract from the brand. Germane to the RFBC complex, however, is the fact that family brands, which are "imbued with cultural resonance . . . that is, rich symbolic and functional meanings, tend to hold stronger positions in the marketplace, even when their meanings are contested."[45] While we recognize the tautological aspect of this statement, the most significant dimension we believe the family brand contributes to the RFBC is, quite simply, family. In truth, the idea of kings or queens touting themselves as heads of a Royal Family is relatively new to the dynasty. Some monarchs actually downplayed their relationships with family members—especially those who were close to them in the line of succession. Often, they would banish members from court, exile them to faraway locations, lock them away in prison, or even have them killed.

Free from troublesome relatives, monarchs could then focus on shaping their own images as charismatic individuals rather than members of kin networks. Kevin Sharpe argues that Henry VIII was the first monarch who understood the concept of crafting an individual personal brand for himself, centuries before marketers honed the concept. Focusing on his "personal monarchy—adult, male, strong, brave, decisive, authoritarian," Henry was clearly a human brand who chose to downplay the family aspects of his persona (perhaps for obvious reasons, given his marital history and rocky relationships with his daughters).[46]

---

* A third aspect of the RFBC's family brand component is that it reinforces the thousand-plus-year blood ties of the entire Royal lineage—lending it not only cultural and historical credence but also much rarer biogenetic clout.

Almost three hundred years after Henry VIII's reign, Queen Victoria's husband, Prince Albert, began to shift the paradigm of the Royal persona from one focused heavily on the monarch to one that was decidedly more family-friendly. Albert purportedly was one of the first to use the phrase "Royal Family," reinventing the unit as "a beacon of bourgeois domesticity. Using the new medium of photography, he projected an image of queen and consort as adoring couple, surrounded by obedient, subdued children."[47] Of course, having nine children, almost all of whom married royalty themselves, certainly enhanced the family feel of the lineage. All future British monarchs, except for Edward VIII, who was unmarried while he reigned, subsequently supported and enhanced this family-brand image. Some, like the Queen's father, George VI, even contributed their own "slogans" to the family brand; he was fond of calling himself, his wife, and his two daughters "us four." The Queen and Prince Philip also have contributed to the family-brand dimension, not only by producing four children, but also through their long marriage, and close relationships both with her sister, Princess Margaret, and with the Queen Mother.

The family-brand dimension of the RFBC was once again brought into high relief during the 1990s and early 2000s, when three of the Queen's children divorced and the Queen Mother and Princess Margaret passed away. Again, because family brands are also human ones, these interludes provided people with opportunities to experience empathy and extend sympathy. By the mid-1990s, one-third of all marriages in Britain were dissolving before their fifteenth anniversaries. Our key royal informant, Margaret Tyler, even observed, "Charles and Camilla . . . are role models in a way for divorced families who are making second marriages . . . because it's happening all the time. But if people see it happening in the Royal Family, it makes them feel better."[48]

We noted earlier that our perspective on royal branding overlaps a bit with Balmer's more strategically-oriented conceptualization. It is this next component of the RFBC, the *heritage brand,* where this overlap is most obvious. Balmer and his colleagues offer five characteristics of heritage brands that connect them to key points in their own and others' history: a track record, or the ability to deliver value over a long period of time; longevity (although this alone does not guarantee success); core values that guide policies and actions; the use of symbols; and a history important to their own identity.[49]

With respect to heritage branding, we believe one key dimension the RFBC contributes to that component is fanfare. For consumers and critics alike, probably no activities stoke emotional linkages to the British monarchy more than its public rituals, many of which are rooted in ancient customs. Even routine, repetitious, and relatively low-key rituals like the Changing of the Guard at Buckingham Palace or Windsor Castle are laden with highly aesthetic material elements, such as brightly colored regimental uniforms, beautifully groomed animals, musicians, and of course, a palatial backdrop. Each activity is carefully planned and enacted by practiced professionals who take their work very seriously, and each is observed by onlookers with no role other than enjoying the artifacts, scripts, performance roles, and the presence of an audience—all of which are required for rituals to retain their cultural vitality.[50]

One of the most lavish royal rituals is the coronation of a new monarch. These events predate William the Conqueror, because the various kings who ruled over sections of England held crowning ceremonies before he united much of the landmass under a single rule.* In addition to the processions of monarchs and dignitaries that mark the occasion as a truly global recognition of the British Crown, the coronation ceremony incorporates scriptures, hymns, and anointment by oil to affirm that the new monarch has been chosen by God. This aspect of the event has its roots in the divine right of kings—a doctrine asserting that monarchs are not required to answer to human authority.[51] The anointing was considered the most sacred aspect of the service—so sacred, in fact, that the Queen did not allow that part of her coronation to be filmed.

The fact that many royal cultural rituals stem from ancient (or at least old) practices does not preclude them from adapting to the times when doing so seems prudent. In fact, some modernization even seems incongruous and contributes to the RFBC's ambiguity. These adaptations include incorporating the themes from *Star Wars* and *Game of Thrones* into the repertoires of the bands playing at the Changing of the Guard, or the Royal Artillery Band's rendition of Stevie Wonder's "Isn't She Lovely" during the military salute to the newborn Princess Charlotte in May 2015. But sometimes, spontaneous decisions during these rituals seem welcome and newsworthy—as when Prince William kissed his new bride Catherine not once but twice during the Royal Family's appearance on the balcony of Buckingham Palace after their wedding.

---

* The liturgy was originally devised by St. Dunstan for the coronation of King Edgar, which took place in Bath in 973 C.E. Dunstan's service still forms the basis for the modern ceremony.

Finally, we argue that the last brand component of the RFBC is the *luxury brand*. Once the purview of the extreme upper echelons of society and protected by sumptuary laws that dictated the types of fabrics and colors people could own, the market for luxury brands has been expanding since the turn of the nineteenth century. During that period, philosophical and political shifts toward democratization, improvements in standards of living, increased globalization, and forms of communication made luxury goods familiar and even accessible to many in the middle class. But the Royal Family still enjoys two kinds of luxury that cannot be bought— namely, the luxuries of *exception* and *exemption*. Simply put, the Queen is afforded the privilege of opting out of many routine cultural norms required for all other people. She is the only driver in Britain whose cars do not require license tags, nor does she require a passport to travel. She celebrates her birthday on different days in different continents. She can even take liberties with luxury brands that other consumers cannot: "The royal mascots [of St. George poised over a slain dragon] are the only exceptions that Rolls-Royce will allow to replace their own Spirit of Ecstasy on the hood of their cars."[52]

In the twenty-first century, the marketplace for luxury brands continues to skyrocket. In 2007, their global value was estimated at $263 billion, a 31 percent increase over the previous five years,[53] Contributing to this growth are the demands within the rapidly increasing middle classes in Asia, the Middle East, and South America, which crave the elite status that luxury brands can convey. Jean-Noël Kapferer, who has written extensively about luxury goods and brands, defines them as multisensory, highly aesthetic, and possessing a strong "human content" (that is, they are handmade or produced by services rendered by a human). Furthermore, he notes, a luxury product is rooted in a culture: "In buying a Chinese luxury product (silk, let's say), you are buying not just a piece of material but a little bit of China as well."[54]

In addition to the standard luxury-brand houses, such as Cartier, Chanel, and Dior, we add the House of Windsor (the moniker of the current Royal Family since 1917) and the House of Tudor, particularly when Henry VIII and Elizabeth I reigned. Furthermore, we assert that the royal-luxury brand dimension receives support from two key sources. The first of these is fashion. Recent royal-watchers could not be blamed for associating fashion almost exclusively with Princess Diana, because her elevation to superstardom was based on her mediated persona as one part supermom, one part supermodel, and one part supersaint. But as noted above, fashion was a fixture within the monarchy long before Diana joined the family. Elizabeth I, herself a clever seamstress of her own brand, purportedly owned three thousand gowns, which grew "increasingly elaborate with the passing years. . . . [They] asserted her wealth and power [and featured] images and symbols of the representation of the Virgin Queen."[55] Some monarchs were specifically known as clothes horses or even dandies. George IV (r. 1820–1830), for example, was reputed to be "a man of style, a man of taste . . . determined to create palaces that would rival any in Europe." Furthermore, he "did not follow fashions, he set them . . . [abandoning] multi-colored 'peacock' fashions in favor of . . . smart, black, sombre dress pioneered by George and [Beau] Brummell in the 1790s."[56] Furthermore, Edward VII was known to be extremely particular about dress; he even dictated to his mistresses (and their family members) what they were to wear on certain occasions.

Even those kings and queens who did not perceive clothing or décor to be essential to their identities were still monarchs, after all, so they typically sported apparel made of the choicest fabrics and with the highest level of craftsmanship. Most readers probably perceive the Queen as a middle-aged or even elderly woman whose interests lie more with colts and corgis than with couture. Yet it is worth remembering that as a princess and a young monarch, she was turned out for affairs of state in gowns by the leading designers of her day, including her favorite, Norman Hartnell. Although not considered an arbiter of high fashion, the Queen possesses her own style, which centers on achieving maximum visibility when among the public. As such, she typically wears bright but tasteful ensembles, and always carries a clear umbrella so her face can be seen even in the rain.*

These days, both traditional and social media take for granted that the fashion choices of younger members of the Royal Family are of interest to their readers and viewers. Usually extensive coverage of the topic focuses on the women's choices—with extra column inches and footage devoted to controversial ones and to rapidly disseminating copycat buying surges. Of course, the luxury items associated with the RFBC extend well beyond the realm of clothing, as the tourists who troop through lushly decorated royal residences laden with priceless armor, art, ceramics, and tapestries can attest.

* In 2014, the retailer Hammacher Schlemmer advertised "Her Majesty's Umbrella," made by Fulton for the Queen, for $49.95. The ad featured a Queen look-alike under the umbrella, sporting "her" trademark tasteful monochrome ensemble.

The second key aspect associated with the luxury-brand component of the RFBC is fortune. The Royal Family does not crack the top ten in terms of the wealthiest monarchies in the world; the three richest are those of Thailand, Brunei, and Saudi Arabia, in that order. Nevertheless, the Queen's net worth is estimated at half a billion dollars. When the wealth of the Crown (the institution of the British monarchy) is figured in, the picture changes dramatically. *Forbes* estimates that it possesses over £6 billion ($10 billion) in art, real estate, rare books and manuscripts, and royal swans, among other assets.[57] Some of these may be impossible to appraise, but a recent assessment valued Buckingham Palace alone at close to £1 billion ($1.68 billion).[58]

There are two key ways these assets impact consumers of the RFBC. First, the monarchy provides access to many of the rarities in its possession so the public can enjoy them. For example, the Queen's Gallery at Buckingham Palace regularly stages themed art exhibits that consist of items from the Royal Collection. Likewise, the Round Tower at Windsor Castle houses the most comprehensive group of drawings by Leonardo da Vinci in the world, and these are regularly rotated, and even toured, for public viewing. Thus the monarchy makes much of its assets visible—and therefore accessible and open to consumption by tourists and British citizenry alike—through patronage, preservation, and presentation.

Second, the immediate members of the Royal Family possess the means to live a lifestyle of unfettered consumption if they so choose. Within the inner circle, however, different family members exhibit very different standards with respect to embracing opulence. Royal biographer Sally Bedell Smith claims that the Queen "knows what everything costs and economizes when necessary. Guests at routine Buckingham Palace receptions are served wine, potato chips and nuts, while at [Charles's parties at] Clarence House they get gourmet hors d'oeuvres . . . floral displays and theatrical lighting."[59] Regardless, people's vicarious consumption of the RFBC lifestyle, especially through television programs, films, and other visual phenomena, accounts for much of the appeal of the monarchy.

We acknowledge that for many, the RFBC holds no appeal whatsoever, and in fact may be antithetical to their interests or values. We recognize that even during times when the popularity of the Royal Family seems to drown out criticism, there are still plenty of people who align with anti-monarchists (those against the institution of monarchy itself), anti-royalists (who oppose certain or all members of the current family), or those critical of the

FIGURE 5. Resisting at Trooping the Colour, 2012. Photo by Cele Otnes.

monarchy or its personages on aesthetic, ideological, or other grounds. Sometimes these protestors make themselves visible, even during highly celebrated rituals such as the Queen's Trooping the Colour parade (figure 5). Visit any website reporting on a recent royal event and inevitably a consistent stable of critical themes emerges: the Royal Family is a waste of taxpayers' money and lacks gainful employment; the young royals are trussed-up bimbos (if female) or embarrassments with no sense of propriety or self-restraint (e.g., Prince Harry); they are painful reminders of a class system that fosters an unequal society; or perhaps worst of all, they are not even (or are barely) English.

People have voiced their opposition to the monarchy as long as records have been kept of its existence. But as the power of British monarchs continued to recede and the monarchy moved to a reign-versus-rule model, criticism began to focus more on how much the institution costs to maintain, rather than on specific political concerns. Our intention is neither to enter into a debate about whether the Royal Family is worth what it costs, nor to weigh in on whether the monarchy represents negative vestiges of colonialism and patrician rule. We are fully aware that these issues are real and raw for some but have set our own views aside to explore the influence and interaction that the RFBC exerts within consumer culture.

As pp. xxiv–xxv show, the three-plus decades following the marriage of Prince Charles and Princess Diana represent a particularly dynamic period in the life of the British monarchy. During that period, cultural and commercial events, along with developments in global and mobile communication technologies, have increased people's access to the Royal Family and, for many, increased its relevance as well. These events range from the decisions to open to tourists both Buckingham Palace and the HMY *Britannia,* to renovations of several key palaces, and even to the choice of London as the site for the 2012 Summer Olympics.

In the remainder of this book, we demonstrate how aspects of the RFBC, and the dimensions of the five brand components that compose it, shape consumer experiences and producer offerings in realms such as collecting, commemorating, and mediated and touristic experiences. We discuss how those responsible for orchestrating these activities weave many (sometimes all) of these facets into their offerings. We do not limit our discussion to these five brand components, or to the key aspects associated with each, but unpack other relevant aspects of royal consumption and production as specific contexts require. In so doing, we affirm our assertion that the RFBC offers consumers and other stakeholders potent, prolific opportunities and outlets through which to experience consumer culture. It is this combination of compelling brand facets that makes the RFBC unique, intriguing, enticing, and even addictive for many around the globe.

TWO

The Roots of Royal Fever

In May 2013, almost one year after the Queen's Diamond Jubilee celebration, one of us stood on the grounds of the Royal Palace in Oslo, Norway, located at the crest of its main street, Karl Johans Gate. After being immersed in the RFBC for years, it seemed fitting to see how the official home of the Queen's second cousin, King Harald V, compared to hers. Norway's population of slightly over five million is less than one-twelfth that of Britain's. So the relative modesty of the Norwegian palace (173 rooms, compared to 775 at Buckingham Palace) was not surprising. But two other aspects of the Norwegian royal experience were almost jarring when compared to the British version.

First, visitors roam freely around the parklike grounds of Oslo's Royal Palace with the three sentries on duty, keeping close to their guardhouses. Security personnel at Britain's royal residences clearly are instructed not to interact with visitors, but the Norwegian guards chat and even pose for pictures. But even more bizarre to the experienced British-royal watcher is this fact: although Karl Johans Gate is awash in tourist shops and global retailers like the Hard Rock Café, the average number of royal souvenirs found in establishments along the street is essentially zero. In fact, not one ceramic plate, mug, tea towel, thimble, T-shirt, or even a high-end commemorative could be had. (A few days later, we did find a few postcards bearing portraits of the Norwegian Royal Family at the Viking Ship Museum, miles from the palace.) It isn't that Norwegian retailers spare their visitors kitsch; their shops are stuffed with sacred to silly varieties of moose, reindeer, Vikings, Laplanders, and a bevy of trolls. But two weeks exploring tourist and antique shops in Norway's interior and on its coastline revealed that royal merchandise is essentially an invisible blip on the country's retail radar.*

We offer the Norwegian example to pick up a point made in the previous chapter—that no monarchy comes close to achieving the level of commercial and cultural success the RFBC enjoys. In this chapter, we examine the factors that bolster the commercial uniqueness and appeal of the British variant of monarchy, many of which are supported by discourses that feed or tap into the growth of consumer culture. We organize our discussion around five internal characteristics (e.g., those emanating from some aspect of the British Crown), and five external ones, pertaining to some aspect of British, global, or consumer culture that do not stem from the monarchy itself.

We begin with the internal trait of *longevity*. Previously, we described the British lineage as traceable back to at least William the Conqueror's crowning in 1066—an impressive fact, even if the skills and accomplishments of individual monarchs have varied widely over the ensuing centuries.† Recently, two key trends in contemporary consumer culture have bolstered the fascination with royal (and human) longevity. First, people are increasingly consuming their own roots. Worldwide, in 2012 an estimated $2.3 billion was spent on genealogy-related products and services.[1] One article recently noted, "'Who's Your Daddy?' is now a $1.6 billion question," reflecting the amount that the private equity firm Permira paid for the website Ancestry.com.[2] Much of this growth is fueled by advances in genetic testing, which allow people to more accurately and completely trace their ethnic origins. Until such technologies were available, only those with notorious or noteworthy relations could reliably trace back their ancestors for more than a few generations, typically through written documents. The valorization of celebrity (along with the increasing fascination with human and family brands) also means people often hope to discover links to greatness in their family trees and leverage any resulting newfound fame in the present.

* Theodore Harvey, whom we introduce later in the chapter, reports that the same is true in Amsterdam, with tourist souvenirs "emphasiz[ing] sex and drugs, even though the Netherlands has a wonderful (and generally popular) royal family."

† William often is described as the first king of England because he united disparate kingdoms in the region. Yet the Royal Family's roots are reliably traceable to the Anglo-Saxon English kings, beginning with Egbert (r. 802–839 A.D.).

Germane to our focus, the website Thegenealogist.com offers to help people determine if they are related to royalty. Likewise, the American Association of Retired Persons (AARP), which boasts over 38 million members, noted recently that Catherine Middleton has American relatives, so she "can help you get into the 'Related to Royals' club, too."[3] Of course, fascination with royal genealogy is nothing new; during Victoria's reign, a large genealogical chart titled "Coronation Stone" claimed to trace the Queen's roots "by an unbroken series of 124 generations from our FIRST PARENTS," Adam and Eve.[4]

The second trend bolstering the salience of longevity is that people are increasingly hungry to discover, reimagine, and reappropriate family narratives. Stories have always been an integral part of human existence. In an increasingly mediated and text-rich society where people's best tales are retweeted, shared, liked on Facebook, e-mailed, or incorporated into fan fiction, narratives are no longer the purview of master storytellers or best-selling authors. Reality television programs—especially those about people with ordinary lives or jobs—contribute to the increased visibility and valuation of narratives in everyday life. Most people's lineages may never yield stories worth sharing, or perhaps that should be shared. Yet tales such as the revelation that the American comedienne Ellen DeGeneres is Catherine Middleton's fifteenth cousin reinforce the value of seeking out real-life compelling genealogical sagas.

As a brand laden with compelling narratives that run the gamut from virtuous to vengeful, the RFBC is difficult to top. Consider just a few story lines emanating from the lineage, all of which also figure prominently in enhancing the brand's consumer-culture connections:

- A young woman with no childhood friends, whose mother shared her bedroom until she was eighteen, grows up to be Britain's longest-reigning queen, ruler of the world's largest empire, and mother to nine children whose descendants populate the thrones of Europe.

- A shy twenty-year-old kindergarten assistant marries the Prince of Wales, gives birth to "an heir and a spare," divorces him, becomes one of the most glamorous and photographed women of the twentieth century, and dies in a car accident at thirty-six.

- A handsome but tyrannical king divorces his first wife (formerly married to his brother) so he can remarry, irrevocably changing the religious landscape of his entire kingdom in the process. He orders his second wife beheaded after three years and remarries four more times.

- A king who dies in battle in 1485 and whose body is thought to be irretrievably lost is found in the ruins of a church in Leicester, England, in 2013.

As some of these narratives attest, longevity and stability within the Royal Family are not always consistent bedfellows. Moreover, the monarchs' own stances toward stability often vacillated greatly from one generation to the next—and sometimes during their own lifetimes. Queen Victoria's son, who after acceding was known as "fat King Edward," was described as flamboyant and self-indulgent—but was also generally regarded as effective and credited with restoring pomp and public visibility to the monarchy. He was succeeded by his son, George V, and Queen Mary, whose tenure at court was described not only as stable but as downright dull: "More often than not, [the couple] would dine frugally alone together at the Palace, he in white tie and tails and the Order of the Garter, she in majestic evening dress, and be punctually in bed by eleven fifteen."[5]

It may therefore seem paradoxical that we offer *stability* as the second internal factor that bolsters the RFBC. The Hanoverian kings who ruled in the eighteenth and part of the nineteenth century were regarded within and without the Royal Household as deeply flawed; the last three (George III, George IV, and William IV) were understood to be respectively gravely ill or insane, a debauched bigamist, and "excitable, undignified [and] frequently absurd."[6] This situation changed dramatically when Victoria married Albert in 1840 and they publicly dedicated themselves to portraying a virtuous and idyllic family life. Since Victoria's accession in 1837, only six monarchs have reigned in Britain, with either Victoria or Elizabeth II on the throne for over two-thirds of that time. In short, for the last 177 years—with two short-lived exceptions whose reigns totaled about a decade—Britain's monarchs have consistently preached the values of duty, family, and morality.

Probably the most recognized exception to this assertion was the highly dramatic (or, more accurately, melodramatic), saga of Edward VIII and the twice-divorced American Wallis Simpson, and his decision to abdicate in 1936 so he could marry her. Yet many historians agree that in the long run, the fallout from Edward VIII's decision actually enhanced the Crown's resiliency. This event, as well as the Royal Family's stoic demeanor during World War II, proved that like their subjects, the monarchy was made of gritty stuff and could "Keep Calm and Carry On." Queen Elizabeth (later the Queen Mother) successfully epitomized empathy with her subjects.

After German bombs rained down on Buckingham Palace, she remarked, "I'm glad we've been bombed. It makes me feel I can look the East End in the face."

But no matter how much monarchs may value stability, history has demonstrated that they cannot control their family members' actions or attitudes. The Queen's current family situation mirrors that of many her subjects, as she has had to accept her children's affairs, divorces, and remarriages. Yet her consistency in carrying out her duties, charity commitments, civic rituals, and calendrical cycle of life at her Royal residences reinforces the Queen's desired image as a bedrock of constancy after over sixty years on the throne.

A third factor inherent within the Crown that contributes to the RFBC is the *British Commonwealth*. The birth of this consortium of nations is rooted in the Statute of Westminster that Parliament passed in 1931, which established independent legislative rule for former British territories that were already essentially self-governing. The growth of the Commonwealth was spurred by decolonialization after World War II, because many independent nations, most notably India and Pakistan, wished to retain ties with Britain. From its inception with eight countries, its fifty-three nation-states now contain one-fourth of the world's population. Commonwealth nations do not have to pay homage to the sovereign in any formal manner, but voluntarily affiliate themselves with Britain, and with each other, through mutually beneficial activities that serve their social and economic interests.

Certainly, the diversity and global dispersion of Commonwealth nations contributes to the visibility of the RFBC. But even more important is the fact that the Royal Family often acknowledges its relationship with Commonwealth members through a pivotal activity laden with high-end, symbolic consumption—the royal tour. Since the Queen's accession in 1952, she has undertaken over 180 tours, visiting every Commonwealth nation but Cameroon and Rwanda. She was the first reigning monarch to travel around the world, prompting Winston Churchill, her first PM, to compare her to Sir Francis Drake, who circumnavigated the globe.[7] Commonwealth tours originally were strategic ventures designed to foster economic relations, but this has been less true since the European Union eased trade barriers. The Royal Family has also used tours for its own ends: George VI took his wife and daughters on an important four-month goodwill tour to South Africa and Rhodesia in 1947. Although tackling a full ambassadorial agenda, the King also hoped it would take Princess Elizabeth's mind off her burgeoning romance with Prince Philip of Greece. (The strategy did not work; six months after the tour ended, the couple were married.)

The Royal Family does not limit its travels to Commonwealth countries; fully two-thirds of the Queen's global travels have been to unaffiliated nations, for the purpose of maintaining Britain's presence on the global stage. The Queen's former press agent Dickie Arbiter notes that such visits help the government further its "current diplomatic relations ... promote British exports, or as part of a programme of cultural or educational exchanges."[8] More recently, foreign travel has helped the Royal Family engage in reputational repair as they try to manage the human dimension of the RFBC. In May 2013, Prince Harry's trip to the United States included stops at several Armed Forces facilities. Many interpreted the tour as an attempt to defuse the negative attention arising over his trip in August 2012, when photos of the naked prince playing "strip billiards" in a Las Vegas hotel room were beamed around the world.

Not inconsequentially, such tours also bring to the fore luxurious aspects of the RFBC that many people vicariously enjoy. Most feature elaborate ceremonies, exhibitions, and parades. Such visits allow host countries to parade their assets as well: when the Queen and Prince Philip arrived in Tonga for the first time, "Queen Salote was waiting ... with a London cab she had ordered during her coronation visit [to England]."[9]

Two other aspects of tours further highlight the luxury dimension of the RFBC. First, the wardrobes created for the events often demonstrate a sophisticated understanding of the political semantics of fashion. Meticulously planned garments and accessories typically pay homage to key symbols of the host countries. The Queen's courtier must "consider the colors of the insignia [in] the country.... [D]resses and insignia [should] not clash, and fabrics are carefully selected to [account] for the climate.... Hats must be neat and the brims 'off the face' to ensure that the Queen is visible at all times."[10] On her first (and longest, at seven months) tour in 1953–54, and again on a tour to Canada in 1957, the Queen wore her coronation gown by the designer Norman Hartnell. Its intricate embroidery featured symbols of every nation in the Commonwealth.

More recently, on her historic visit to the Republic of Ireland in 2011, the first ever by a British monarch since the Irish Free State was established in 1922, the Queen began her tour duties "resplendent in a cloak of emerald green and a dress of St. Patrick's blue."[11] Likewise, when William and Catherine visited Canada in 2011, the Duchess disembarked from the airplane in a lace dress by Canadian designer Erdem Moralioğlu and, later on the tour, sported a red maple-leaf hat and gold maple-leaf brooch on loan from the Queen.

Gifts received by the Queen represent a second significant luxury-laden aspect of royal tours. These range from meticulously-fashioned pieces of jewelry (often depicting a country's trademark flora or fauna) to uniquely crafted items. In advance of the tours, the Queen's private secretary typically dispatches a six-thousand-word document specifying the requirements for the visit; one instruction notes that gifts of animals are not welcome. However, "touring the Gambia in 1961 the Queen was offered a baby crocodile in a biscuit tin. It had to spend the night in the bath of [assistant private secretary] Sir Martin Charteris."[12] A 2009 exhibit of gifts and fashions acquired during royal tours included elaborate Maori feather cloaks symbolizing chieftainship that the Queen and Prince Philip wore on subsequent visits to New Zealand, totem poles, and a whale's tooth from Fiji.

Elite modes of transportation—most notably, royal yachts—also add luster to royal tours. Charles II received the first of these, a fifty-foot version of a man-of-war called *Mary,* from the Dutch East India company in 1660.[13] Presumably, the HMY *Britannia,* which served the Royal Family from 1953 to 1997, will be the last unchartered ship to serve the monarchy. Described as a country house at sea, it was furnished with items from its predecessors. These included an innovative table designed prior to the invention of ship stabilizers; it used weights to ensure that "a gin and tonic [could] be safely left on its surface [during] a Force Eight gale without spilling a drop."[14] In addition to providing private and relaxed accommodations for tours, *Britannia* served as a venue for entertaining dignitaries at home and abroad.

Estimates of the cost to refurbish *Britannia* made its continued use infeasible, so the decision was made to sell her for her scrap value, making way for the buyer to have her refurbished and restored. Four cities competed to provide *Britannia* a new home, and in April 1998, Edinburgh's Port of Leith was chosen. *Britannia* opened as a tourist attraction in October 1998 and in slightly over fifteen years has seen over 4.2 million visitors.

Much to the delight of journalists and royal-watchers, goodwill tours often provide ripe opportunities for some members of the RFBC to demonstrate their all-too-human dimensions. In particular, Prince Philip has revealed his (in)famous tactlessness so often on tours that the website aardvarkmap.net offers a world map highlighting the locations of his most notorious gaffes. He once asked members of two former rival Aboriginal tribes who now jointly oversee a national park in Australia, "Do you still throw spears at each other?" (About two thousand miles away, on an island in the Vanuatu chain, he is revered as a god; the tribe's most prized possessions are signed photos of him.)[15]

The fourth factor internal to the RFBC that has helped to maintain and increase its commercial and cultural resonance is its *use of professional marketing strategies and tactics*. Until the nineteenth century, prior to the full-blown development of mass media and the relentless British tabloid industry, goings-on at court were not necessarily fodder for everyday discussion outside of castle walls. In fact, news about royalty typically spread through postings at central places in towns or through court gossip, and was often limited to what the monarchs wanted known. Such control even extended into the mass media era; in 1936, few people in Britain knew that Edward VIII and the press had reached a "gentleman's agreement" allowing photographers to record his Balkan vacation as long as the published pictures contained no trace of his then-mistress, Wallis Simpson.

Early autocratic English monarchs often did not focus on crafting unique personas for themselves.* This situation began to change with the Tudors. Henry VIII in particular leveraged paintings, images, arms, and medals to reaffirm his power and authority, and to disseminate a masculine, powerful image throughout his realm. Kevin Sharpe, in *Selling the Tudor Monarchy*, argues that the first monarch who truly understood the importance of creating a positive and political image was Elizabeth I. She was assisted by social and economic changes in the sixteenth century, including "the emergence of a market economy and consumer culture which brought about changes in the modes . . . forms . . . and responses to royal representations."[16]

One genre that became extremely popular was the illustrated book. *Containing the True Portraiture of the Countenances and Attires of the Kings of England,* published in 1597, was the first to include carefully-drawn pictures of all monarchs since William the Conqueror. It is credited with spurring the public's desire to acquire and own royal images.[17] Elizabeth's reign spawned what could be considered the first royal porcelain souvenir; it bears her image and a short motto, and is on display at the Museum of London.[18]

---

* Some early monarchs did adopt and disperse personal symbols: Richard II (r. 1377–1399) distributed badges with his "White Hart" (*hart* is an archaic term for mature stag) emblem to those loyal to the Crown.

Nobles also wore other items that bore her image, including cameo pins, as a way to curry Elizabeth's favor.

To distract her advisers and subjects from her decision not to marry, and from the sometimes seemingly unrelenting religious persecutions occurring at her behest, Elizabeth carefully crafted her image as Gloriana, "the strong, wise and good Virgin Queen,"[19] who sacrificed her youth and life in devotion to her people. To reinforce this persona, she engaged in several visible and deliberate strategies. In addition to having her image painted and reproduced, she engaged in over forty "progresses"— summer trips across the kingdom when, because of poor sanitation conditions, the castles were evacuated for cleaning. Sharpe reports that she spent 1,200 days—almost one-tenth of her time as queen—on progresses, relying on them to reinforce her majesty and her humanity.[20] At each town, the large Royal convoy would encounter the requisite "streets ... decorated with flags and bunting, church bells ... fireworks ... and pageants."[21] The staying power of Gloriana extended well beyond Elizabeth's life. She was almost unquestioningly glorified by historians through the nineteenth century, even though standards of living and religious tolerance had deteriorated badly in England during her reign.

The monarchs who reigned between Elizabeth I and Victoria seemed less interested in managing their images or protecting the reputation of the monarchy than in either defining England as Catholic or Protestant, indulging their own appetites and vices, or fighting with their relatives or members at court. Even Victoria, who understood the importance of positioning herself as the harbinger of a moral, family-centered life, sorely underestimated her subjects' disappointment (and the subsequent boost to republicanism) when she remained in seclusion for ten years after Prince Albert's death. The jubilant crowds present at her Golden and Diamond Jubilees in 1887 and 1897 revealed that the people hungered for a monarch who understood the value of public display.

Fortunately for the Crown, her son and heir to the throne, Edward VII, demonstrated a greater understanding of this concept. From the beginning of his ten-year reign, he realized that survival of the monarchy depended on its "ceremonial, public, and philanthropic roles."[22] He reinstated many of the ancient ceremonies and rites, including the monarch's appearance at the Opening of Parliament. At his first opening in 1901, with Queen Alexandra by his side, he wore a flowing crimson robe and the Imperial State Crown, and read his speech himself (Victoria had abandoned the practice in 1861).

Most notably at the occasion, the libidinous, many-mistressed King's "women friends were seated in the Ladies' Gallery. There was speculation as to whether he would address them."[23] (Some of Edward's mistresses, including Camilla Parker Bowles's great-grandmother, Alice Keppel, sat together in a box at his coronation.) Edward also shaped his subjects' domestic rituals; when he and Queen Alexandra had been married twenty-five years, they followed the German tradition of celebrating their silver wedding anniversary, popularizing the custom within Britain.[24]

Queen Victoria's granddaughter-in-law Queen Mary also understood the potency of pomp in contributing to the monarchy's popularity. Although her husband, George V, was introverted, Mary sought opportunities for the couple to engage in highly visible reminders of Britain as head of a world empire, such as the Delhi Durbar of 1911 in India. A staged ceremony that was as solemn and elaborate as a coronation, it allowed the King to act the part of "mogul emperor, his army passing in immaculate review and [jeweled] elephants kneeling for their Master's salutation."[25]

After Edward VIII abdicated in 1936 and the shy, stammering George VI reluctantly found himself on the throne, his wife, Queen Elizabeth (later the Queen Mother), "wholeheartedly adopted [Queen] Mary's Germanic sense of the sanctity and mystery of the monarchy with all the dedication of a convert."[26] Much of her efforts focused on staging royal events such as her husband's coronation, but astute image management also stressed that the King, the Queen, and their daughters, Elizabeth and Margaret, were members of the "idealized, classless, everyday family their publicity suggested."[27]

After discussion among the Crown, Prime Minister Winston Churchill, and his cabinet, the watershed decision was made to televise Elizabeth II's coronation in June 1953.* The decision to film all of the ceremony except for the anointing and the Communion (at her insistence) had immediate ramifications for the broadcast industry in the United Kingdom. It was predicted that sales of televisions would increase, and in fact, ownership doubled.[28] More significantly for the nation, the BBC quickly installed one hundred military transmitters no longer in use after the war in areas that had previously received no broadcast coverage at all, such as the northeast area of England and the whole of Northern Ireland. The result was that "viewers

---

* The procession of her father George VI's coronation in 1937 was the BBC's first "outside broadcast," aired from a mobile television studio on location; parts of the actual ceremony also were filmed.

outnumbered listeners ... by as much as three to one in some areas."[29] Globally, the ceremony was broadcast to 300 million people in forty-two languages and instantaneously expanded the concept of royal-watching around the world.

Films of the coronation continued to run in movie theaters in England and on the Continent for months. Fervor for the footage was spurred by people's belief that they had witnessed an emotional and almost miraculous transformation, as a reserved and conservative young wife and mother who had grown up in front of them became the quintessential regal and religious embodiment of royalty. For the most part, however, the young Queen was reluctant to consider managing her image beyond allowing coverage of her tours and charitable duties. However, she did rely on some basic marketing strategies that lent her reign an aura of consistency and stability, such as choosing a signature color (Windsor Green) and adopting a royal mascot.*

As heir to the throne, her son Prince Charles's path from awkward teenager to playboy prince in search of a suitable bride coincided perfectly with the growth of many global trends that would fuel interest in his life, including celebrity culture, youth culture, and growing global interest in hypermasculine, athletic activities like skiing and playing polo. Nevertheless, Charles's reluctance to have an image crafted "as if [he] were some kind of washing powder, presumably with a special blue whitener," meant the Palace could not exert much effort to promote an ideal persona for him.[30]

Even if Charles did not understand the power of the press to influence public opinion, his first wife, Diana, certainly did. Her death in 1997 proved to be the turning point for the Palace's attitude toward public relations. The Queen was genuinely surprised at the public outcry over her decision to not fly the Royal Standard at half-mast and to treat the death as a family tragedy rather than as a national matter.† The fallout from this fiasco led her to realize that the monarchy was perceived as out of touch with people's expectations, and that a more human face on the brand was needed. Not surprisingly, many conservative courtiers did not share this opinion: "Some ... loathe the media and would prefer Royal reporting to be confined to the

---

* Saint George slaying the dragon is always attached to the grill of whatever car conveys her.

† The Royal Standard is only flown when the monarch is in residence, and the Queen was at Balmoral when Diana died. It is never flown at half-mast, even when the sovereign dies. In a compromise move, the Queen agreed to allow the Union flag (or Union Jack) to fly at half-mast at Buckingham Palace on the day of Diana's funeral.

daily Court Circular, listing the movements of the [R]oyal [F]amily without any details."[31]

After the Queen's "Annus Horribilus" of 1992, her private secretary, Robin Janvrin, began to work more closely with pollsters and market researchers to better understand where the popularity of the monarchy did or did not lie. He worked closely with the Way Ahead Group, formed in 1994, to tackle issues such as how to keep the monarchy from fading into irrelevance and oblivion. Janvrin's "Marmite theory of monarchy" asserted that changes in the persona of the RFBC should be as slow and imperceptible as those to the packaging of that common British household staple. This approach to unstuff the royal image seemed sensible and reassuring both to the Royal Family and to its stakeholders. Yet even a conservative approach led to some immediate changes, such as relaxing the rules about bowing and curtsying to the Royal Family, in favor of allowing people to shake their hands.[32]

We noted in the previous chapter that by the twenty-first century, media pundits had begun describing the Royal Family as a global brand that needed managing. Soon they were debating whether the Palace's decision to feature pop concerts at the Queen's Golden Jubilee in 2002, or having family members visit the set of the popular soap opera *East Enders,* had taken reform too far. Some recalled the disastrous 1987 TV game show Prince Edward had championed. Titled *It's a Royal Knockout,* it featured the Queen's children (sans Charles, who refused) and Prince Andrew's wife, Sarah Ferguson, in faux-royal costumes, engaging with celebrities in "mortifying stunts such as pelting each other with fake hams.... [T]he show not only managed to trivialize the participants, but the institution of the monarchy itself."[33] Others, such as branding expert Michael Peters, praised the Queen's innovations in the left-leaning *Guardian,* noting he was heartened that she chose to rely on marketing to reconnect with her people.

The early 2000s saw the appearance of press commentary about the creation of the monarchy's official website. Writing for the *Financial Times,* David Bowen compared it to those of other European royal houses. He noted they were all bland except for the Norwegian site, with its "pop-up biographies—and a three-dimensional tour of the main royal palace."[34] He felt www.royal.gov.uk was ambitious but unfocused, but gave kudos to Prince Charles's website (www.princeofwales.gov.uk), because it contains his views on genetically modified food and other issues.

Nevertheless, "royal.gov" offers a wealth of information about the monarchy, special messages to different parts of the realm, and instructions on how to write to the Queen and her family. It even includes a link to job openings; in July 2013, it advertised for a sales and marketing professional to help promote the interests of the Royal Collection Trust at a salary of £30,000 ($50,500).* This post alone demonstrates just how entrenched branding efforts have become in the Royal Household.

In 2005, Charles was heard describing journalists at an arranged photo session as "bloody people." Yet in more recent years, he has bolstered his public relations staff at Clarence House and is more receptive to advice on how to engage more productively with the media. The Queen's former press secretary Dickie Arbiter noted that by 2014, a team of twenty-seven marketing and public relations professionals worked at St. James's Palace, where in the 1980s and early 1990s the staff was one-third that size.[35] In 2013, Charles hired former BBC communications expert Sally Osman to captain the team managing both his image and that of his wife Camilla, Duchess of Cornwall. His former press secretary, who had served as director of public relations for the Manchester United Football Club, also helped mold the public images of Princes William and Harry.

Furthermore, growth within the mass media, and more recently in social media, have fueled the culturally entrenched British tabloids, which use any means necessary to outdo themselves when covering royal-related news, whether celebratory, scandalous, or solemn. Such turf battles mean the monarchy faces greater challenges in maintaining privacy and enjoying a semblance of "normal" family life. Yet the Royal Family seems to have become resigned to the intrusiveness of the paparazzi—only requesting privacy at specific times and places (such as William's years at St. Andrew's University). In relying on tried-and-true branding tactics, the RFBC seems to be gaining increasing control over its public image.

The final category of internal support for the RFBC entails the broad category of highly visible and visual *ritualized cultural practices*. Throughout history, several of these have bolstered the visibility of the monarchy within British and global culture. We have already mentioned the triumphant processions of early monarchs into London after victories on the battlefield. Peacetime-related practices include coronations, weddings or funereal activ-

* "The Firm's" employee salaries are notoriously low compared to what could be commanded in London's commercial sector, but the prestige factor is regarded as unmatched.

FIGURE 6. The Queen at Trooping the Colour, 2012. Photo by Cele Otnes.

ities (e.g., the funerals themselves, as well as several days and nights of lying in state), as well as annual events such as the Queen's birthday parade, known as "Trooping the Colour" (figure 6).

Edward VII's success in achieving the stature of the "people's king" was evident upon his death in 1910. The decision to have a monarch lie in state is not automatic; he was the first monarch afforded the rite since George III. Police estimated that ten thousand people filed past his body each hour, with many waiting in torrential rainstorms. Lines ranging from four to seven miles long "snak[ed] around the streets of Westminster like the black ink that bordered the nation's mourning newspapers."[36] On a happier occasion, the morning of her wedding in November 1947 saw Princess Elizabeth surprised to discover that in the Mall adjacent to Buckingham Palace, "great numbers had slept out, and were having picnic breakfasts, and cooking bacon over little stoves . . . [with] . . . the smell of coffee drifting in."[37]

The mass gatherings for happier occasions typically culminate at the gates of the palace for the traditional balcony wave. One of the most famous occurred on V-E Day, May 8, 1945, when the Royal Family made no less than ten separate appearances, greeted each time by what seemed to be "all of London . . . [with a roar] like thunder." Then, noted acclaimed photographer

Cecil Beaton, "the Royal Family brings forward another figure, clad in black and white. It is none other than Winston Churchill. That he, a commoner, is . . . on the balcony with the reigning family is a break with tradition, but no one denies him this honor since he, perhaps more than anyone else, has brought us to victory."[38]

Often fueling the crowd's enthusiasm is a related cultural practice: parliamentary declaration of a public or "bank" holiday to celebrate a Royal occasion. These have been declared for key events such as the first weddings of Princess Anne and Prince Charles, and Prince William's to Catherine Middleton. Disrupting the everyday routine of the citizenry directs attention (positive or negative) toward that institution. In that regard, not all are grateful for the extra vacation day: critics of the bank holiday for Prince William's wedding claimed it cost British firms £5 billion in lost revenue;[39] others simply groused about the potential logistical nightmare of crowds pouring into central London.

Those unhappy with bank holidays and the events that spur them often simply leave the city, but many others choose to mill around the Mall wearing their Union Jack top hats (which, for all the apathy that the British people claim to accord the symbol, is always on display at these occasions) or waving Union Jack or "happy snap" flags bearing pictures of whoever is being honored. In sections of London, and in fact all over Britain, people sometimes take advantage of a bank holiday to engage in another ritual honoring royal events—the street party. Although labeled an endangered species because of increased costs and regulations, as well as declining community spirit, street parties commemorating such events remain fairly popular, especially in certain parts of the country. Residents on Llanmaes Street in Cardiff, Wales, reminisced about how people had devoted their time, energy, and resources to creating them in the past: "Bunting was strung between the tight Victorian terraces, flags fluttered and trestle tables were laden with home-cooked food. There were egg-and-spoon races, face-painting and fancy dress. A piano would be heaved on the road for a good old sing-song. One time, the men built an open-air bar and called it the Elizabeth Inn to honor the new queen. Another year residents sat guard in their cars all night because of a rumour that their bunting was going to be stolen."[40]

An annual ritual practice that corresponds with the Christmas holiday began in 1932. Sir John Reith, founding father of the BBC, proposed that George V offer a radio broadcast on the holiday to inaugurate the Empire Service (now the World Service), established to serve English-speaking subjects stationed at remote outposts around the world. The king made his first broadcast from Sandringham, his royal residence in Norfolk; a local shepherd introduced the event, and chimes from a nearby church added sound effects. Historically, these broadcasts represent the only time the monarch crafts his or her message without the help of advisers; the themes often revolve around the impact of current events or broader topics such as family and duty. However, the famous author Rudyard Kipling penned the first speech, beginning it with the historic words: "I speak now from my home and from my heart to you all; to men and women so cut off by the snows, the desert, or the sea, that only voices out of the air can reach them."[41] Twenty million people around the world tuned in.

Christmas broadcasts did not become an annual fixture until the Queen took the throne. She has given one every year since 1969; that year, she felt a scheduled holiday rebroadcast of the documentary *Royal Family* would provide the monarchy with enough exposure. In 1957, on the twenty-fifth anniversary of George V's first Christmas address, the Queen's broadcast was televised for the first time (it is now also streamed over the Internet). Given her natural reserve, she understood the challenges she would face in adding a visual component, but also realized that doing so would connect her more intimately with her subjects. Thirty million people around the world watched as she proclaimed, "I cannot lead you into battle. But I can do something else. I can give you my heart, and my devotion to these old islands and to all the peoples of our brotherhood of nations."[42]

One rare religious cultural practice associated with the monarchy is Royal Maundy, which occurs on the Thursday before Easter. The ritual dates from the early 1200s, when King John donated food and other items to the needy. For hundreds of years, the event entailed the monarch washing the feet of the poor; William III ended this practice in 1698. At present, the main features of Royal Maundy are a religious service held at an abbey or cathedral, followed by the Queen's distribution of Maundy coins. Once limited to London, the Queen mandated that the ceremony should occur only every ten years in that city; she now travels around Britain, awarding money to senior citizens and acknowledging their community service. Tradition calls for dispersing a Maundy coin for every year of the monarch's age to each recipient. Although the basic coin design has not changed for many years, a special version was minted for the Queen's Diamond Jubilee.

Some cultural practices, such as the requisite singing of "God Save the Queen" after film and theater performances, have disappeared from the landscape. But by the same token, others have arisen to reflect the times. One of these is the Royal concert. As part of her Golden Jubilee celebration in 2002, the Queen offered two concerts: the classical-themed Prom at the Palace and the pop-focused Party at the Palace. To open that concert, Brian May, guitarist for the rock band Queen, played "God Save the Queen" on the roof of Buckingham Palace—creating what is considered an iconic moment in rock-music history. For the Queen's Diamond Jubilee concert on June 4, 2012, more than one million people applied for the ten thousand free tickets featuring acts including Shirley Bassey, Elton John, Tom Jones, Annie Lennox, and Paul McCartney. At its peak, the concert was watched by 17 million viewers in Britain, and a condensed version airing on ABC in America attracted 6.8 million viewers.[43]

So how do these cultural practices contribute to the relevance of the Royal Family? Professor Mike Robinson describes the power of what he terms the "sense of occasion" that accompanies visible royal activities, attracting even self-professed ardent antiroyalists. He describes the scene when Prince Charles visited his university: "[He arrived] in his big red helicopter, and everybody turned out to see him.... Critical academics, critical Marxists, they're all standing there.... My friend ... was absolutely over-awed, you know you could have carried him out, because he had shaken hands with Prince Charles."[44]

Turning our attention to the five external aspects that we believe have kept the British monarchy salient in consumer culture, we first discuss the *nobility* (or *aristocracy;* the terms often are used interchangeably). This level of society bridges the gap from the more insular world of the Crown to the still highly stratified British class system. The nobility originated when William the Conqueror, himself a duke and count within the Norman feudal system, adopted the model of awarding land to members of his army in exchange for military support. Large tracts dedicated to tenant farming and animal husbandry helped sustain the lavish lifestyles that became the hallmark of the British aristocratic system. C. S. Lewis observed, "The word gentleman originally meant ... one who had a coat of arms and some landed property. When you called someone 'a gentleman' you were not paying him a compliment, but merely stating a fact."[45]

At the heart of the British nobility is a stratified system of peerages. Dukes and duchesses occupy the highest level, accounting for the prevalence of that title among those most closely related to the Queen. Below them are the ranks of marquess, earl, viscount, and baron. In addition, the peer system contains three distinct components: hereditary peerages, life peerages, and honours. Only the monarch can bestow hereditary peerages. The Queen gave Prince William and Catherine Middleton the hereditary titles of Duke and Duchess of Cambridge on their wedding day; William's had previously been held by Queen Victoria's cousin George. Contrary to what the phrase implies, hereditary peerages do not automatically pass to children. In fact, even some of the Queen's grandchildren do not possess them. Furthermore, her female descendants are still ineligible to hold peerages in their own right.

As is true for many class-based systems around the world, the political power of the ruling elite has been greatly reduced in Britain. In 1999, a bill reforming the House of Lords reduced the number of hereditary peers allowed to serve as MPs from six hundred to ninety-two. Life peerages, on the other hand, are appointments to the House of Lords that do not pass to future generations and may or may not be associated with a political party. Although the scandal of "life peerages for purchase" under Prime Minister David Lloyd George in the 1920s tainted the honor for a time, they are still coveted both as political devices and genuine rewards for meritorious service.

Honorary knights and dames are also considered part of the nobility—but this level functions more like a "meritocracy aristocracy." Since 1993, the public has been allowed to nominate people for honours, and nominations are even accepted online.* The prime minister's office selects the honorees, and the Queen (or a member of the Royal Family to whom she delegates the task) presents the awards. Technically, anyone making a significant contribution to British life can be nominated. Most are not celebrities; in 2013 the Queen's Birthday Honours list honored professionals in fields such as medicine, graphic design, plant physiology, and dance. However, Scottish political theorist and republican Tom Nairn notes that the honors system as a whole still clearly favors the elite in British society. He observes that "British Honour-tossing is intrinsically a matter of scalable and multiple tiers and grades: from the supreme, the exalted and the reasonably grand, to the modestly worthy."[46]

For hundreds of years, the monarchy relied upon aristocrats to help keep the peace and defend the realm's interests at home and abroad by contributing the troops that protected their estates. Soldiers were often paid retainers and wore a livery (a uniform in colors associated with a noble house) to signify loyalty. Nobles also were recruited to serve on Royal advisory councils,

* See www.gov.uk/honours.

precursors to the modern-day parliamentary system. Of course, a powerful elite class could also prove troublesome for the Crown. Several times during the history of the British monarchy, factions arose among the aristocracy that often engaged in protracted bids for power. Most notable is the War of the Roses (primarily 1455–1485), a struggle for the Crown between Royal Family members and aristocrats associated with the House of York and the House of Lancaster.

The late nineteenth century saw the peak of economic and political power among the aristocracy; by the 1880s, just ten thousand landowners possessed two-thirds of the total land area in England, Wales, Ireland, and Scotland.[47] But by the end of the First World War, the decline of the noble class was undeniable and irrevocable. Huge chunks of land, on the scale of what Henry VIII had given the nobles when he seized the monasteries in the 1500s, were sold off due to a convergence of calamities. Since the period between the two world wars, most nobles have been forced to pursue a profession (once considered an anathema), rather than relying on income from property holdings.

The monarch's close kin and advisers (many of whom were relatives) came to be known as the "court" because they actually gathered in courtyards at the residences. These days, the term Royal Household is favored, although many in service to the Queen, like her ladies-in-waiting, still stem from the highest levels of society. Even within this select group, "there is a strict pecking order, and various grades are rarely crossed: One can become a 'Woman' even if untitled, but one cannot become a 'Lady' unless one is the wife or daughter of a peer."[48]

If the aristocracy no longer supports the monarchy militarily or even politically, how does it contribute to the robustness of the RFBC? First, and importantly, it contributes social support. Until recently, tradition eschewed the Royal Family's association with commoners, so the aristocracy serves as a source for entertainment. Essentially, the elite serve as a friendship circle for the Royal Family. This fact was in high relief in the summer of 2013, when Princes William and Harry attended the wedding of Thomas van Straubenzee to Lady Melissa Percy, daughter of the Duke of Northumberland, along with their cousins Princesses Beatrice and Eugenie. (In another confluence of royalty and consumer culture, the reception was held at the thousand-year old Alnwick Castle, the setting for Hogwarts School in the *Harry Potter* series.)

As noted above, the aristocracy contributes key staff to the Royal Household, with most of the positions part-time and unsalaried. Yet some household members enjoy other benefits, such as accompanying the Queen on tours. Ladies-in-waiting also may eat lunch at Buckingham Palace whenever they choose.[49]

Finally, many aristocratic families continue to indirectly bolster the heritage component of the RFBC by opening up their estates to paying visitors who wish to experience the aesthetics of British country houses. As portrayed in many novels, television programs, and films, to be a successful member of the British elite meant living a life of pastoral gentility with a bevy of servants and the opportunity to pursue activities such as riding, shooting, hunting, attending balls, and being presented at court. To that point, the Duke and Duchess of Carnarvon, owners of Highclere Castle, where the BBC hit *Downton Abbey* is filmed, prominently display their association with the program on their website. As such, two key contributions of the aristocracy to the RFBC are to act as heritage caretakers and to contextualize the role of the noble class and its connections to the RFBC in the British class system.

The second external bastion of support for the monarchy stems from the *commercial offerings in the marketplace.* Several British citizens whom we interviewed reminisced about receiving souvenir porcelain mugs or coins at their schools to commemorate Royal events. This practice is occasionally resurrected; in 2011, Churchill China in Stoke-on-Trent donated royal wedding souvenir mugs to students at thirty schools.[50] Visits to various cities in England prior to the last two weddings and during the Diamond Jubilee celebration likewise revealed that acquiring event-related royal commemoratives is still a highly popular consumer practice, and not just among tourists (figure 7).

Because of the numerous and important ways the marketplace and the RFBC intersect, chapter 6 covers the subject in depth. But one example demonstrates the compelling nature of the topic. In 2005, the death of Pope John Paul and subsequent scheduling of his funeral forced Prince Charles to move his wedding to Camilla Parker Bowles from April 8 to April 9. Many commemoratives with the old date had already been released, and those bearing the new one had to be hurried into production. Many shoppers embraced the ensuing commercial chaos, snatching up the inaccurate souvenirs both for their narrative value and in the hope that they would mimic other error-laden goods (e.g., postage stamps with images printed upside down) and eventually escalate in price. While one of us was observing this activity at the Buckingham Palace gift shop, a customer approached and advised us to buy and hoard as many of the "wrong-date" souvenirs as possible.

FIGURE 7. Diamond Jubilee merchandise display, Oxford. Courtesy of Kimberly Sugden.

A third entrenched external form of support for the Royals is *Anglophilia,* which becomes especially effervescent around key Royal events. Nowhere is Anglophilia more visible than in America. Perhaps not surprisingly, it was rampant in the pre-Revolutionary colonies, as a sizeable proportion of the white settlers had emigrated from Britain. Through stories and play-acting, the imaginary worlds of colonial children were infused with "English subjects, royals and knights . . . especially of English words and sounds: Humpty Dumpty . . . goosey gander, and Georgie Porgie."[51]

Even after the new country had created its own literature, the pedagogy of American schools remained rooted in works by the English masters. Jane Austen, the Brontës, and the Romantic poets all depicted scenes of a pastoral, elegant England, which contributed to Americans' nostalgia to share what Benedict Anderson describes as an imagined community with the English, leading to the perception that they all shared homogenous experiences, as well as "a common history and a comradeship."[52]

Ambivalence about cutting the royal cord was still evident in the former colonies after the hard-fought War of Independence. Delegates to the Constitutional Convention in 1787 discussed basing the U.S. political system on an elective monarchy. Debates over the first president's title also reveal royal inclinations: *His Excellency, Most Serene Highness, His Elective Majesty,* and *His Mightiness* were considered.[53]

As economic and emotional relations continued to improve between the two nations in the eighteenth century, many Americans drew a clear distinction between "monarchy, which they deplored, and kings and queens, who were seen as ... part of the sentiment and poetry of England."[54] The thriving newspaper industry in the new nation provided its eager citizens with over one thousand articles covering Princess Charlotte's tragic death in 1817, and Americans eagerly sought out the details of her mother Queen Caroline of Brunswick's lurid adultery "trial" before Parliament in 1820.[55] A few years later, much of America was gripped by the throes of Victoriana. Although her coronation in 1838 was described as "muddled and inadequately rehearsed,"[56] it charmed American diplomats, who sent home descriptions of royal activities. Victoria's lavish wedding in 1840 also established the fashions of white wedding gowns and lace veils among more affluent brides, both in Britain and America.[57]

As we noted earlier, royal tours within the Commonwealth and the United Kingdom fanned interest in the British monarchy, and tours to America often gripped the nation. In 1860, Queen Victoria's oldest son and heir apparent, Prince Albert Edward, embarked upon an official visit of Canada, followed by an unofficial visit to the United States. The "idea of sending the heir to the throne on a ceremonial tour of the new world was an innovation" devised by his father.[58] Prince Albert Edward tried to downplay his royal identity by traveling to America under another of his titles, Lord Renfrew, but the thirty thousand people who greeted him in Detroit immediately made "a mockery of the idea that the visit was in any way 'private.'"[59] Teeming crowds greeted the Prince in every major city, and at his final grand ball in New York City the floor collapsed from the weight of five thousand attendees (only three thousand had been invited).[60] In a slightly more tranquil vein, when the Prince visited Trinity Church on Wall Street, the congregation prayed for the Royal Family for the first time since 1776.[61] Newspapers continually drummed home the theme that the world's most eligible bachelor might choose a lucky American girl to be his queen.

Opinions as to why the heir apparent's visit was so popular coalesced around the belief that it smoothed over any residual negativity stemming from the Revolution and the War of 1812. Yet the sizable Irish populations of

Chicago and New York took umbrage at the adoration of the monarch-in-training and the valorization of an institution they perceived as populated by English autocrats. Throughout their visit, their threatened (but unrealized) protests and disruptions needled the security forces guarding the parades and parties for the Prince.

In 1936, the publishing magnate Henry Luce re-released *Life* magazine, which would remain a harbinger of consumer culture through the 1950s. Its inaugural issue on November 23 featured three stories pertaining to the British monarchy. The first reported that the play *Victoria Regina,* with Helen Hayes in the title role, had just made $1 million in its Broadway run. The second featured photographs of Fort Belvedere, King Edward VIII's preferred residence, and his King's Dragon Rapide airplane. A safe twenty-five pages later, the magazine synopsized an interview with Earl Warfield Spencer, Wallis Simpson's first husband, while omitting the fact that she was the King's lover.

Seeking President Roosevelt's assurance of assistance with the looming war in Europe, in 1939 George VI became the first reigning British monarch to visit the United States. The visit lasted six days, included a stay in the White House, and marked the beginning of the "special relationship" between the two nations. Half a million people greeted George VI and Queen Elizabeth in Washington, D.C. She demonstrated the canniness she became known for; visiting the New York World's Fair, she wore "an ensemble of red, white, and blue . . . [leaving] even hard-boiled photographers in awe."[62]

Relatively speaking, Americans' opportunities to view British monarchs on their home turf remain few and far between. The Queen has visited only six times since 1957, although her children and grandchildren have also made tours. However, a steady stream of British cultural products also fueled Anglophilia in the United States. The popularity of the British invasion in the 1960s saw the Beatles, the Animals, the Rolling Stones, the Kinks, and the Yardbirds spawn hysteria not only for rock 'n roll but for other tangible connections to the swinging London lifestyle. These included Twiggy, Mary Quant cosmetics, Carnaby Street boutiques, miniskirts, mod design, and English sports cars.

Since the British invasion, other cultural products have helped fan the flames of Anglophilia across the globe. Sometimes, even savvy pundits are surprised at the popularity of these offerings. Premiering on PBS in 2011, the BBC series *Downton Abbey* was initially derided by critics as a retooling of *Upstairs, Downstairs.* But in 2013, it became the highest-rated PBS series in the United States. The following year, the opening episode for its fourth season (or "series," as they are known in Britain) shattered the viewership level for the season three opener, up from 7.9 to 10.2 million viewers.[63] Season four even featured a royal story line revolving around a racy letter the Prince of Wales (later Edward VIII) had written to his mistress Freda Dudley Ward. *Downton Abbey* also has become a lifestyle brand, licensing memorable images and dialogue for apparel and home products. But perhaps most significantly in terms of propagating Anglophilia, *Downton* has been sold to over 220 broadcasting territories in the world and attracts 120 million viewers worldwide. Nowhere is it more popular than in China, where "there is a voracious appetite for British culture because it is seen as a status symbol of wealth and success."[64]

Although American moviegoers became enamored with early British stars such as Charlie Chaplin, Helen Hayes, John Barrymore, and Stan Laurel, cinema-related Anglophilia peaked in the 1960s, when British films captured six of ten Academy Awards for best picture.* Spurring a new wave of Anglophilia during the 1990s, global box office successes in the British "rom-com" genre bolstered the careers of Hugh Grant, Alan Rickman, Emma Thompson, and Colin Firth (much heralded for portraying George VI in *The King's Speech*). Given Americans' enthusiasm for so many things British, how does their Anglophilia translate into economic support for royal consumer culture?

First, even with the long-term effects of the Great Recession, which first gripped the United States in 2008, Britain still remains the top long-haul destination for American tourists.[65] Every producer of royal experiences we interviewed affirmed the fervor with which Americans embrace England in general and the RFBC in particular. The founding editor of a worldwide royalty magazine told us that he had moved his fulfillment operations to Minnesota to save on mailings, since two-thirds of his subscribers live in the United States.[66] The downside to this situation is that when high-end American collectors curtailed their spending, first after 9/11 and again after the Great Recession, purveyors of royal consumer culture were hit hard.

Also fueling Anglophilia in America are the royalists or monarchists who pursue their passions through various visible means. One such encyclopedic

---

* The James Bond series, the highest grossing film franchise in history, debuted in 1962 with *Dr. No*. Since that time, Bond films have earned $5 billion worldwide when adjusted for inflation.

fan is Theodore Harvey, a Julliard-trained cellist in his mid-thirties who plays in the Dallas Symphony Orchestra. Alluding to the crises that pervaded the Royal Family at the end of the twentieth century, Theodore remarked that now "is a much better time to be a royalist than the 1990s. . . . [T]hey were awful."[67] He first became fascinated with monarchies as a young boy when he read the best-seller *Nicholas and Alexandra,* about the downfall of the Russian royal family. Theodore describes his particular interests as centering on "pre-Beatles Anglophilia," aspects of British heritage that are less popular and commercial and more traditional. He is an enthusiastic participant in events like a recent conference on the modern monarchy at Kensington Palace (where we met him), the Queen's Diamond Jubilee celebration, and tours of famous sites in Tudor history. He has met members of five royal families, primarily at charity or musical events.

Theodore's website* is a fount of information for royalists and monarchists. It includes the genealogies of ten royal families, links to over seventy-five sites (including those devoted to revitalizing deposed monarchies), and a section where he lists and reviews royal-related films that span all monarchies. His Facebook page regularly reminds visitors of important monarchic dates such as birthdays and death days, key initiatives (e.g., the recent Scottish referendum for independence), and attempts to restore fallen monarchies. He notes that his social media endeavors have helped him make many new friends and create a virtual community. As his international connections have grown, he has met and mingled with many of them at Royal events, noting that many are younger than him.

Andrew Lannerd's equally fervent passion for the Royal Family has taken his life in directions he could not have anticipated. After he first skipped college classes to cross the border and see the Queen in Canada in 2002, he began collecting royal-related items. One special category concerns slices of cakes from royal weddings; he owns six.† But Andrew's true passion is interacting with members of the Royal Family: "It's not enough to read about them in books. I want to see them, I want to talk to them. They are living history to me." He has visited Sandringham four times at Christmas to be present when the Royal Family walks to church services and has presented

---

* Theodore Harvey's website can be found at www.royaltymonarchy.com.

† The Queen to the Duke of Edinburgh; Princess Anne to Captain Mark Philips; Prince Charles to Lady Diana Spencer; Prince Andrew to Sarah Ferguson; Prince Charles to Camilla Parker Bowles; Prince William to Catherine Middleton.

flowers to the Queen on ten occasions. He even quit his job to live in London for six months.

As his experience and passion for Britain and the Royal Family have developed, he has evolved into a "royal entrepreneur." So many people were aware of his travels to Britain, they began asking him to act as their guide. As a result, he completed the requirements for a tour operator license and through his company, Transcendent, began taking groups to the "best places" in Britain. Of course, these include many royal sites, as well as Highclere Castle, York, and Chatsworth.* He is planning a tour of Scottish castles in 2016. Still, he admits that he spends more on his passion than he earns from this sideline, noting that "all of my money goes to England."[68]

A fourth external pillar of the RFBC is *British humor*. Most nations likely claim to possess a unique, culturally ingrained sense of humor, but few consider it so central to their national character. That Britain does so is evidenced by the fact that the new UK citizenship test now contains questions about humor. Stand-up comedy and other humorous entertainment is a multimillion-dollar industry within Britain and is one of the few to "experience significant growth in the recent economic downturn."[69]

The English anthropologist Kate Fox points out that "the real 'defining characteristic' is the value we put on ... humour in English culture and social interactions."[70] At first glance, it may seem that the stereotypical British traits of reserve, stoicism, and above all, fear of embarrassment might be antithetical to the myriad elements of the British sense of humor. These include nonsense (think *Alice in Wonderland* or Gilbert and Sullivan), plays on words, parodies, satires, self-deprecation, situational and observational comedy, slapstick, the surreal, whimsy (e.g., Gloucester's annual "World Famous Cheese-Rolling Championship," with five thousand attendees in 2014), and especially irony and understatement. Many cultural observers note that humor offers the British a culturally sanctioned safety valve to escape the tyranny of valorized character traits such as stoicism and reserve.

Of course, of special interest here is how humor intersects with and contributes to the RFBC. The medieval royal courts themselves were great importers of comedy, particularly from France. Joculateurs (mimes), jongleurs (wandering minstrels), goliards (fallen clerics who wrote bawdy satiric poetry and songs), and court jesters were common sources of entertainment.[71] In that sense, William the Conqueror and the invading Normans

* Transcendent Travel can be found at www.transcendent-travel.com.

could be credited with raising the cultural profile of humor in Britain; his predecessors, the Anglo-Saxons, seemed to prefer grimmer forms of entertainment. The epic poem *Beowulf,* likely composed between 700 and 750 C.E., is a prime example.

Royal jesters and storytellers were common in the Tudor courts, and during Elizabeth I's reign, comedic troupes often presented performances in tribute to her. By the seventeenth century, royal caricatures were commonplace, with autocratic, unpopular rulers often vilified in pamphlets and publications. Suzanne Groom, curator of an exhibit of caricatures at Kew Palace, notes that "the ferocity with which they pilloried the royals and the cruel depiction of [George III's spinster daughters] is still startling."[72]

One influential development soon broadened the humorous ways the Royal Family was presented. The term *cartoon* was coined by the influential British humor magazine *Punch,* which debuted in 1841. Its hallmark was its gentle and inoffensive humor, and this stance was reflected in its Royal cartoons. In 1841, after Victoria's second child was born just two years into her marriage, *Punch* ran a prescient cartoon depicting her as the "Royal Lady who lived in a shoe, She had so many children she didn't know what to do." As Victoria's power intensified with the growth of the empire, the tone of *Punch'*s royal material approached that of "sycophantic drivel."[73]

*Punch'*s popularity contributed to the decision by London's burgeoning newspapers to place political cartoonists on their staffs, a practice begun in 1888 by the *Pall Mall Gazette.*[74] As the monarchy's political power ebbed, Parliament became a more popular target, and the *Gazette'*s stance toward the Royal Family remained deferential from the late nineteenth to the late twentieth century.[75] In fact, in the early years of her reign, most portrayals of the Queen did not even show her face; artists would shield her by Prince Philip or other figures, or picture her from behind. Although not above caricaturing the physical features of the family members, cartoonists did not remove their kid gloves until the tumultuous 1990s. With the popularity of the monarchy at an all-time low, the biting commentary was often aimed more at the institution than at individual family members.

Few countries can export such a culturally-laced and class-laden product with success, but since Shakespeare's plays began being produced abroad, many British humor products have proven popular around the world. The comedy show *Monty Python's Flying Circus,* which lampooned Queen Victoria and featured a recurring "Pantomime Princess Margaret," originally ran from 1969 to 1974. Other programs, such as *Fawlty Towers,*

Mr. Bean (better liked outside of Britain than in), *Absolutely Fabulous,* and *The Office* also achieved success in many countries.

Yet the Palace's attitude toward being the target of cultural comedy can occasionally be chilly. Most recently, Clarence House issued a stipulation that broadcasters not use actual footage from the 2011 royal wedding in a satirical manner. As a result, the Australian broadcaster ABC's show *Chaser* had to cancel its planned program. The rarity of this sanction prompted the director of ABC to express disappointment that "any satirical or comedic treatment of the marriage of Australia's future head of state has been banned."[76]

One area where poking fun at the Royal Family flourishes (relatively) liberally is in the commemorative industry. Many items feature a light touch, particularly the T-shirts bearing slogans released before William and Catherine's wedding in 2011. However, the couple limited the use of their image to those commemorative items they deemed "permanent and significant," effectively squelching the ubiquitous celebratory tea towel.[77] Nevertheless, satirical and downright silly items (some of questionable taste) still made their way into the marketplace.

As we noted in chapter 1, the Queen demonstrated her ability to leverage her sense of humor at the opening ceremony of the London Olympics in June 2012. The ceremony's creator, Danny Boyle, had promised to incorporate iconic aspects of England: its agrarian past, its central role in the Industrial Revolution, its love of sport, Shakespeare, and even the National Health Service. What had not been revealed, however, was the famous skit that culminated in the entrance of "007" and "the Queen" by parachute. It was described as "the most unexpected self-deprecating celebrity cameo in the history of modern entertainment."[78] Afterward, the press teasingly referred to the eighty-six-year-old Queen as "the next Bond girl."

The fifth external element supporting the RFBC is one which, because of its dominant role in the international landscape, hardly requires justification. Simply put, the British monarchy is headquartered in *London*—which in 2012 ranked either first or second behind New York on most lists of wealthy, powerful, culture-laden, and competitive global cities. With a city population of 8.4 million (and regional estimates of 12–18 million, depending on which areas are included), London is easily the largest city in the European Union. In 2013, it saw a record 16.8 million international visitors, who spent a record £11.2 billion ($17.3 billion) on shopping and touristic activities.[79]

In terms of understanding London's role in the RFBC, the key fact is that most of the important, aesthetically pleasing, and best-preserved monarchic sites are located in or near the city. Even those structures whose royal roots may have been subsumed by other roles, such as the Houses of Parliament and its venerable tower, clock, and Great Bell, still known by many as "Big Ben,"* are crucial to the RFBC because they serve as locales for the key rituals we mentioned earlier. Venerable British cultural institutions like the National Gallery, the Victoria and Albert Museum, and the National Portrait Gallery all display priceless and often familiar royal artifacts and representations. The Queen alone has been painted by over 140 artists since her coronation. The National Portrait Gallery gathered works by artists such as Lucian Freud, Annie Leibovitz, and Andy Warhol for an exhibition during the 2012 Diamond Jubilee year titled *The Queen: Art & Image.* In 2014, an exhibit at the same museum by Grayson Perry, *Who Are You?,* which explored people's identity from various perspectives, featured a piece titled *Comfort Blanket.* The large tapestry captures core aspects of British identity that range from food to football, as well as iconic cultural contributions, such as Shakespeare, Monty Python, and the Magna Carta. Not only are several members of the Royal Family referenced, but by far the largest image on the entire piece is a caricature of a grinning Queen sporting a tight perm.

Consider the centrality of another venerable London royal venue, Westminster Abbey. Originally the site of a cadre of Benedictine monks in the 700s, Edward the Confessor broke ground on the abbey in 1050, and it was consecrated in 1065. It has been the site of every coronation ceremony since William the Conqueror. It has also been the chosen venue for several royal weddings (including that of Prince William to Catherine Middleton) and funerals. It houses the tombs of seventeen monarchs, including Elizabeth I, Mary Queen of Scots, and Henry VIII's fourth wife, Anne of Cleves.†

Likewise, the Poet's Corner in Westminster Abbey celebrates many of Britain's great authors. Some wrote about royal-related events, created tributes to monarchs, or were named poets laureate by a sovereign.‡ The abbey

---

* The term *Big Ben* originally referred to just the bell. In 2012, the entire structure was renamed the Elizabeth Tower in honor of the Queen's Diamond Jubilee.

† Anne's ability to secure an amicable divorce from Henry, remain accepted at Court, and become a mother figure to Henry's children is one of the more intriguing but less familiar narratives within his "wives" saga.

‡ Although dating from 1591 with the appointment of Edmund Spenser, John Dryden was the first to officially hold the position under this title (1668–1689).

FIGURE 8. *The Queen and Her Abbey* exhibit, 2012. Photo by Cele Otnes.

also features collections of artifacts found at the site during restorations and archaeological digs, and stages special exhibitions. In 2012, it offered *The Queen and Her Abbey,* an exhibition in honor of the Diamond Jubilee (figure 8).

A few Tube stops away, tourists can stake out a place in front of Buckingham Palace to watch the famous Changing of the Guard. Or they can stroll past Clarence House, Prince Charles's official London residence, the former home of the Queen Mother, and the site of many offices for the British monarchy. They can also view St. James's Palace, a Tudor structure that is still considered the official base of the Royal court; it also serves as the London residence for several Royal Family members.

Buckingham Palace is open to visitors only in the summer while the Queen is at Balmoral, but its Royal Mews is open ten months a year. Visitors can view a wide range of royal transportation options, from luxury automobiles to the ornate historical carriages used at official events. These include the new Diamond Jubilee State Coach, which dovetails perfectly with the RFBC's heritage dimension, as it literally incorporates key pieces of Britain's history in its design. These include wood slivers from Sir Isaac

Newton's apple tree, Hut Six at Bletchley Park, beams of many of Britain's famous cathedrals, and many other iconic sites.*

The palace also hosts another iconic Royal event: the Queen's annual garden parties. Originating during Queen Victoria's reign and dating from the 1860s, these were created to replace the presentation of debutantes at the palace but now serve as a way to reward members of the public actively engaged in service. Over thirty thousand guests attend the four garden parties that take place each year (one is held at the Palace of Holyroodhouse in Edinburgh). Buckingham Palace's forty-two-acre garden, with its many species of plants and animals, is not typically open to the public. So for many tourists and Britons, the elaborate, scrupulously maintained grounds at the palace remain one of the monarchy's best-kept secrets. The food and beverage commission for a typical garden party requires 270,000 cups of tea, 20,000 sandwiches, and 20,000 slices of cake.[80]

In west London, bordering Ambassador's Row and the leafy residential area of Kensington, visitors can stroll through Hyde Park and visit the new Diana, Princess of Wales Memorial Fountain, explore Kensington Palace, and take afternoon tea at its Orangery.

A trip twenty miles down the Thames from the Tower of London to Windsor reaffirms the assertion that for centuries, the river symbolized monarchic power. The former Palace of Westminster now serves as the Houses of Parliament. Hampton Court and Kew Palace both serve as active royal tourist sites, and Windsor Castle is one of the Queen's official residences. Vestiges of other royal edifices are still evident. Throughout history, the Thames has played a key role in the staging of royal pageants and events. On June 1, 1533, the procession that preceded Anne Boleyn's coronation made its way down the Thames; it featured over fifty barges, many decorated with gold and silver, as well as a dragon that belched fire.

The pivotal role of the marketplace to the RFBC means that many of London's businesses offer merchandise or experiences that support this commercial aspect. During celebrations of royal occasions, main thoroughfares such as Regent Street, Piccadilly Circus, and Oxford Street are festooned with bunting and banners. Pub owners, restaurants, and shops decorate their windows and interiors with flags, photographs, cutouts of the

---

* Bletchley Park, about fifty miles from London, was the center of British code breaking during World War II. In June 2014, the Duchess of Cambridge attended the official reopening after its restoration; her paternal grandmother had worked in the hut where the German Enigma code was broken.

Queen, and special signage. These activities affirm London's reputation as the world's foremost city in terms of doing up royal spectacles.

If people desire a dose of royal and popular-culture shtick, the famous Madame Tussaud's Wax Museum allows visitors to engage with royal replicas, as well as pop musicians, film stars, and famous historical figures. The successor to the original "Wax Work" on Fleet Street in the 1700s and to the wax effigies of monarchs and statesmen that graced Westminster Abbey for centuries, the museum has long been aware that a photo opportunity with "the Queen" is one of its most popular draws. In fact, Tussaud's has created twenty-three figures of the monarch over her reign. Furthermore, divorce has not diminished Diana's popularity at the museum, although she is safely distant from Prince Charles, his wife Camilla, and Prince Harry. William and Catherine are represented as well, and in 2014, their figures were given a "glamour update."

A third venue where consumers can satisfy their desire for a diversity of royal-related entertainment is the famous theater district in London's West End. The monarchy has long been of interest to playwrights. Theatergoers can choose touristic romps through British history, such as *Barmy Britain* (its poster features Henry VIII flipping a coin, saying, "Heads You Lose"). Or they can engage in offerings of a more contemporary and contemplative nature. In 2013, Dame Helen Mirren reprised her role as the Queen in *The Audience,* which explored the monarch's relationship with each of her twelve prime ministers. One of the West End's most recent offerings, *King Charles III,* challenges the future of the monarchy, raising provocative questions about Prince Charles's transition to the throne.

Returning to the example of the Norwegian royal family that opened this chapter, we believe we can now explain its relative absence (and those of many monarchies) on the global stage of consumer culture. In short, it seems that to remain commercially viable and culturally visible, a monarchy must contribute to the cultural discourses that shape people's consumption habits at different levels of taste, humor, and cost. Furthermore, as we suggest here, it must possess not only engaging narratives but also a rigorous infrastructure and external support system that promotes and protects them. Throughout this book, the mechanisms we have identified in this chapter will reemerge as we unpack the relationship of the RFBC to contemporary consumer culture.

THREE

"A Head Full of Royal"

MARGARET TYLER'S MAJESTIC WORLD

In chapter 2, we discussed how Anglophilia in the United States fuels the popularity of the Royal Family and introduced two avid American collectors of royal consumer culture. Yet we believe it is fair to say that Margaret Tyler, known as "Britain's loyalist royalist," may wear the crown among collectors and consumers of all things relating to the RFBC. In fact, the phrase *head full of royal* in the title of this chapter is one she uses to describe her self-labeled obsession. Even her mode of dress testifies to her fascination with the RFBC (figure 9). On our many visits and overnight stays at Heritage House, where she lives and runs a bed and breakfast establishment in North London, she always greeted us in her "uniform": a red blazer bedecked with a selection of pinned rosettes bearing images of Royal Family members, with a white blouse, navy skirt, and Union Jack belt buckle.

Margaret's décor mirrors the moving tapestry of royal life, continually reflecting the ebb and flow of monarchic events. A divorced pensioner whose four children have long since fled the nest (but have provided four grandchildren), Margaret lives on her own in a four-bedroom "semi-" (short for "semi-detached house," what Americans call a duplex) in an "estate" (planned community) in North London, now a relatively upscale suburban haven for middle-class London commuters. She admits that as her children moved out, "the Royal Family moved in." Margaret's passion is her collection of over ten thousand pieces of memorabilia dating back to Queen Victoria, and her house is quite literally stuffed full of commemorative china, ornaments, paintings, photos, posters, and other diverse souvenirs, which occupy every nook and cranny of her downstairs living space. The exterior facade of Heritage House boldly declares her passion to passers-by, with decorative plaques of Royal Family members covering the brickwork,

FIGURE 9. Margaret Tyler outside Heritage House. Photo by Cele Otnes.

as well as a life-size stained glass Coldstream Guard standing at attention in his box just to the left of her front door. Margaret began collecting royal memorabilia over thirty years ago, when she bought a small glass dish for 25 pence (38 cents) that caught her eye while she was volunteering at a church bazaar. This purchase triggered others, especially at the time of Charles and Diana's wedding in 1981, when her passion really took off. Since then, she has dedicated all her available time and money to amassing royal "stuff."

What was once a hobby has now become a way of life for Margaret. "Once it's in your blood, obviously you're hooked. Once you're hooked—it's all over," she confides, adding, "I would scrub floors if I had to" to finance her passion. She avidly browses shops, markets, and specialist fairs to add to her collection and has become more inventive and resourceful with the passing years. Sometimes she obtains retired display pieces from retail outlets or even official royal exhibitions—often hauling large and bulky items on the Tube (the London underground system) or train, then carrying them the several blocks from the station to her home. At times, she has even rented a lorry ("truck") to haul larger newfound treasures. Her collection contains several (typically life-size) cardboard figures that she acquired from such sources— including Diana (two different ones), the Queen Mother, Charles, William, and Kate—providing a bizarre backdrop for paying guests at her breakfast table. A life-size Prince Edward greets visitors as they enter her cluttered hall. Her most recent acquisition is a huge cardboard poster of Naomi Watts playing the lead role in the film *Diana,* which Margaret persuaded the manager of the Odeon Cinema in Leicester Square, London, to give her.

An important part of her daily routine involves making the rounds of local shops to buy any newspapers or magazines that contain headlines about the Royal Family or information about any forthcoming royal-themed events, films, or television programs. Once she has read her new acquisitions, she adds them to the tall piles of journalistic material that vie for precious space around the walls and under tables, to ostensibly be ironed and added to scrapbooks.

Margaret's collection is ever-increasing, and the media love to feature her during royal events amid her colorful and eclectic objects. This attention has made her a minor celebrity, and many people track her down to give her memorabilia they have found in estate sales. Curators from various institutions, including Historic Royal Palaces, borrow pieces from her collection to use in exhibitions from time to time. Her celebrity status also means that people (tourists, royalists, and journalists) frequently ask for a tour of her home, sometimes staying for several days to absorb her collection and browse the hundreds of books, magazines, newspapers (typically acquired daily), videos, and scrapbooks. She also willingly gives guided tours and prearranged lectures to busloads of tourists who arrive on her doorstep.[1]

Margaret's home is like a museum in many respects, with designated areas for particular Royal Family members. The Queen and Prince Philip, the Queen Mother, Andrew and Fergie, Charles and Diana (as a couple), Edward and Sophie, and so forth all have their own corners. She continually updates these areas, even building a new sunroom extension to mark Diana's life and death. This shrine includes original commissioned works of stained glass that represent Diana's childhood and royal homes (namely, Althorp and Kensington Palace). When Charles remarried in 2005, she added a modest Charles and Camilla corner (somewhat reluctantly at first), a much more humble space than the light-filled splendor of Diana's sunroom. More recently, in 2013, she expanded her William and Catherine section to include Prince George (and, of course, Princess Charlotte in 2015).

Wall-to-wall shelving creaks under the weight of ceramics and other bric-a-brac, while the floor is covered in a dense swath of objects, including fourteen concrete corgis (the Queen's favorite breed of dog), a large wooden replica of the coronation throne, and a chair from the investiture of Charles as Prince of Wales. Even though Margaret hand-placed all these items, sometimes they prove hazardous even to her: in 2000, she fell off the couch while hanging curtains and landed on one of the corgis, breaking its nose and cutting her head badly. She also broke her wrist; though it took three months of intensive physiotherapy to recover from her fall, she is unrepentant over the placement of the corgis.

Not surprisingly, her most treasured possessions are ones that demonstrate her own personal links to the monarchy—particularly a letter from Buckingham Palace acknowledging the good wishes Margaret sent the Queen for her Diamond Jubilee, and a photo of Margaret giving the monarch flowers across the security barriers when the Queen visited Harrow. (Margaret had waited five hours in freezing conditions to hand-deliver them.) Of course, she also has a few stories of her encounters with royalty, including the time she wore a large rosette with Princess Diana's face on it when Diana opened a hospital near Margaret's home. When the Princess saw the rosette, she laughed and said to Margaret, "Oh, you have got it bad."

Collectors would regard several of Margaret's pieces as valuable, but others are much kitschier in nature: Charles and Camilla scarecrows, a Prince William doll in christening apparel, a knitted version of the Royal Family a friend made for her (complete with corgis; see figure 10), and a Fergie weight-loss book, to name but a few. Unlike a museum, however, Margaret's items are not enclosed in display cabinets or behind ropes; she makes them readily accessible to (and touchable by) the many curious visitors who come to inspect her trove of royal memorabilia.

A further difference is that Margaret's displays lack any signage or labeling (figure 11). Instead, she plays a vital role in narrating the origins and significance of each object. Her memory is astonishing; she recalls the details of how she acquired each of her ten thousand plus items and how they relate to the history of the Royal Family. Margaret's amazing sea of objects reflects a feminine style of collecting. Traditionally, male collectors are regarded as more serious and purposeful than their female counterparts, whose

FIGURE 10. Margaret's knitted Royal Family. Photo by Cele Otnes.

FIGURE 11. Items in Margaret's collection. Photo by Pauline Maclaran.

TABLE 1 Margaret's Brand Collector Identities and Their Social Roles

Collector Roles	Business Owner Roles	Media Expert Roles
Historian: educating others about the Royal Family	*Social Facilitator*: providing a space where others can interact around royal objects	*Opinion Leader*: acting as a key source for Royal Family news
Rescuer: giving sanctuary to royal memorabilia	*Individual Facilitator*: personalizing experiences in relation to royal objects	*International Ambassador*: serving as the face of the British public
		Advocate: creating a positive image for the Royal Family

collections of dresses, dolls, perfumes, or china tend to be dismissed as "frivolous" or "tacky," and consequently devalued. In contrast, male collections of cars, guns, or art are likely to be accorded higher status and value, and protected from the curiosity of viewers. Margaret is happy for her many visitors to touch and explore the items in her collection, and she encourages them to take any of the myriad books she owns on the Royal Family (sometimes in multiple copies) to read in her guest rooms, manifesting a relational rather than competitive self through her desire to include others in her passion and to accommodate their wishes.

Likewise, Margaret's social life is rooted in her collection; she can be thought of as a brand collector who enables other consumers to experience the RFBC. During our many stays and visits at Heritage House over an eight-year period, we observed that her persona as a brand collector involved three different identities: Collector, Business Owner, and Media Expert (table 1). The various social roles she expresses in her daily life map onto these three identities, and these roles help shape other consumers' experiences of the RFBC.

First, in relation to her Collector persona, her primary role is as a historian, as she educates others on the past and present Royal Family. She takes her duties for this role very seriously: "I try to get a copy of everything you know, to me, so the people can weigh up whether they like it or whether they don't." History comes to life through her vast array of objects, each representing a particular historical moment that she can elaborate on and discuss. For example, she tells the story of Prince Charles's two marriages while making reference to the many souvenirs of his marriage to Diana, including a Charles and Diana divorce mug and plate (their images divided by a thick zigzag line to represent the fracture of their relationship).

Moving on to Charles and Camilla's wedding tea towels, she laughs at the *Spitting Image** mask of Camilla, recounting her ambivalent feelings in relation to this liaison. Although she has now come to terms with their marriage, there was a time when she could not bring herself to say Camilla's name and could only muster the word "her"—especially when Camilla was Charles's mistress and not yet his wife. Like a magpie specially trained for collecting royal objects, Margaret amasses more and more pieces around her, with little order or categorization. Nevertheless, the breadth of her collection is impressive, as a Kensington Palace curator who has borrowed from Margaret's collection confirmed: "You just say any theme and she had things for it. Like 'kirby grips' [bobby pins] made for girls to decorate their hair for the Silver Jubilee and a makeup compact that was made for Queen Mary's coronation [in 1911]. . . . You just can't find stuff like that anymore."[2]

In her primary role as historian, Margaret helps other people relate to the Royal Family in new ways and with greater understanding. The most iconic brands—Apple, Harley-Davidson, Jeep, Saab, and Mini Cooper—all inspire extreme devotion, and their fervent followers usually possess extensive knowledge about them. In addition, their admirers like to share this knowledge with others, proselytize about the brand, and perpetuate the brand's history.[3] Similarly, Margaret engages in all of these activities through what she describes as her "mini-museum." In fact, hers is literally a living museum, with a "Diana rose" growing in her garden that plays center stage for some tourists. Furthermore, her museum is interactive, fun, and informal, and reflects her own personal tastes. Her understanding of the brand is as a democratic consumption space that can accommodate various points of entry. This is reflected in the way she indiscriminately juxtaposes high-end collector pieces with a healthy accumulation of cheap and cheerful tourist tat. This hybridization is in sharp contrast to traditional institutional collections, which formulate a more serious pedagogical mission and generally lack the foibles or eccentricities that can typify private collections.[4]

On account of the personalized experiences that Margaret offers, visitors to Heritage House are able to feel more connected to the Royal Family both through her narratives and through the objects themselves. It is even possible for her visitors to experience a "contagious magic"[5] as they touch items displayed in a quasi-sacred way or put their hands on pieces that Royal Family members may have actually touched. These include a chair present at

---

* We discuss this satirical television program in detail in chapter 5.

Charles's investiture ceremony, when he became Prince of Wales, and a piece of hotel carpet on which Diana walked. Such sacralization of objects is recognized in consumer culture research as fulfilling the need for "something that is transcendent, numinous or magical."[6] Somewhat paradoxically, even as certain displays can encourage feelings of transcendence, the mundane setting of her standard suburban "semi" and Margaret's friendly chatter humanize the Royal Family, making its members seem more accessible and likeable.

The other social role she performs in conjunction with being a Collector is that of a rescuer of memorabilia that would otherwise be destroyed or put into storage. Some people move and can no longer keep their collection; others acquire pieces that once belonged to a cherished family member. Heritage House provides a safe haven where they know their items will be loved and admired by others, a knowledge that ameliorates any sense of loss or disloyalty they may be feeling. Margaret proudly claims, "I think I'm their conscience ... because if they don't know what to do with something, or Grandma's died—if they're not all that interested—then if they pass it on to me, they know it will be looked after. They know it won't be sold." She relates how one woman, Amy, who had previously visited with her husband, was later obliged to downsize on being widowed. Finding she no longer had room for her collection, and much to Margaret's surprise, Amy arranged for a trailer load of china, glass, and other sundry royal memorabilia to be delivered to Heritage House.

Indeed, it is impossible for Margaret to refuse sanctuary to anything royal. She often cannot keep up with the number of gifts she receives and is still trying to sort sixteen boxes of newspaper cuttings she received several years ago, collating them in a giant scrapbook whenever she has time. A few donors have gone to great lengths to find her. One woman, who gave Margaret thirty scrapbooks that had belonged to her mother, took two years to discover where she lived, finally succeeding with the help of the BBC. An Australian woman who had seen her on television sent her a tin she had inherited from her grandmother with a message explaining, "My Grandma loved this, and I'd like you to have it."

An explanation for this behavior is to be found in the ways material objects often represent extensions of ourselves or others, carrying strong emotional associations that bind us to people and our past.[7] Thus if people discard their mother's scrapbooks or grandmother's treasured commemorative tin, they may feel they are discarding these familial relationships as well, or at least violating them in some way. Margaret assuages the donors' potential guilt by giving the objects a home; the scrapbooks and tin, together with their many memories, live on in Margaret's collection. Some memorabilia donors come to stay at Heritage House especially to revisit the items they have donated. In addition to these personal items, Margaret also rescues many objects from the marketplace that would otherwise have been thrown out—especially from retailers who may have no use for items used in former displays. One of her side rooms is filled with huge museum-quality figures once housed in an exhibit at one of the Windsor train stations.

Aside from Margaret the Collector, there is also Margaret the Business Owner. One of the roles associated with this persona is that of social facilitator, providing a space where people can interact with other royalists and immerse themselves in the RFBC. Apart from larger tourist groups that arrive by bus and stay for a couple of hours, many smaller groups of friends or individuals come to revel in an environment where they can share and reinforce their passion with like-minded others. Recalling how her business developed, Margaret relates how she would spend the evening with paying guests completing quizzes about the monarchy, and notes: "[We would] watch [royal] videos, talk about [Diana] nonstop. Well, talk about *all* the royals nonstop!" Her six-bedroom house allows several guests to stay at one time and to enjoy an extended experience. Most of Margaret's collection is housed on the ground floor, and until recently, the bedrooms (sometimes rented on a contract basis by firms conducting local business) have remained relatively free of commemorative items.

However, since 2012 one of Margaret's rooms, a loft conversion with its own bathroom, has become entirely royally themed. Now called the Sandringham Room, it commands the premium price of £75 ($112.50) per night.[8] This extravagant theming was carried out by Wimdu, a German lettings company* in London, which featured Margaret and her collection in their special promotion for the Diamond Jubilee. A team from Wimdu completely refurbished her room, providing many lavish decorative touches and an array of Jubilee souvenirs. Much to Margaret's delight, the themed decorations included commemorative china by Emma Bridgewater, a contemporary manufacturer located in England's renowned Potteries region.

Margaret also has organized many parties to celebrate events such as the royal wedding in 2011, as well as anniversaries of historical occasions like the

* In American English, a rental agency.

Queen's Golden and Diamond Jubilees in 2002 and 2012, respectively. Her party to celebrate the fiftieth anniversary of the Queen's accession to the throne in 1952 attracted fifty to sixty guests. Her parties to celebrate Charles and Camilla's wedding in 2005 and the Queen's eightieth birthday in 2006 were slightly smaller affairs, with around fifteen to twenty guests. Final numbers are hard to estimate for her events, however, as there are many comings and goings, with curious passers-by often popping in to share in the fun for a few moments. Her guests are always a diverse selection of people drawn from Margaret's various networks of friends, neighbors, paying guests, other royalists (people she may not know but who have heard about the event), and journalists. During her party for the 2011 royal wedding, three Australians (two men in top hats and tails, and a woman in an elegant frock and fascinator) turned up uninvited to join in the celebrations. It was probably no coincidence that an Australian television crew was filming at the time, although no connection was ever acknowledged by the Australian crew or visitors! Indeed, there is usually a television camera crew around to document any festive proceedings Margaret organizes.

Guests are often fervent royalists themselves, but others may be less so, sometimes accompanying a more ardent fan. Margaret is proud of the fact that her parties are inclusive and that she opens them up to "anyone who's interested in the Royal Family." Thus, her bed and breakfast regularly becomes a focal point where royalists can actively participate in the RFBC's narrative as they share a common interest, with the media often documenting their words and actions and beaming them around the world.

It is common for firms to sponsor or facilitate "brandfests,"[9] events to encourage increased brand usage and favorable word-of-mouth (or increasingly, "word-of-mouse") reports. Brandfests help build communities of consumers dedicated to the brand. At the same time, they can enhance brand-consumer relationships. Margaret's celebrations similarly strengthen ties between the monarchy and its people, but they are perceived as more authentic because she is not officially affiliated with the royal brand. This fact gives her greater credibility as a brand ambassador because she is a genuine fan and independent advocate of all things royal, without being tainted by commercial imperatives or the perception of being a hired hand in service to the monarchy.

Margaret's flexibility and willingness to adapt to the needs of her visitors means that in her Business Owner role, she delivers personalized experiences in relation to the RFBC. In this way, she also acts as an individual facilitator, striving to fulfill the diverse expectations of her many visitors. For example, she orchestrates a special tour of her house for German women, a tour designed to tug at their heartstrings because she knows they have strong feelings for Diana. As she discusses a forthcoming party of German tourists, she confides, "I'm just praying for nice weather so I can put them all out here [in the garden with the Diana rose]. When I play 'Candle in the Wind' on my player, they start crying." A French woman who stayed overnight with her two daughters was keen for them to watch Charles and Diana's wedding; Margaret obliged by finding the relevant video and staying up until midnight to watch it with them.

Usually, as we mentioned, Margaret does not have many commemorative items in the bedrooms (apart from the newly refurbished Sandringham room). However, if guests are interested in a specific monarch or time period, she places a display of relevant commemoratives in their rooms, once again customizing her offerings. Perhaps unknowingly, Margaret's behavior mimics the Queen's when the monarch hosts guests at Windsor Castle during "dine-and-sleep" events (see chapter 8). In these ways, she assists in developing personalized relationships between the Royal Family and their fans, work that is unpaid and (largely) unrecognized by the Royal Family. This is not unusual in other brand communities, where community members may perform many duties on behalf of the brand, adding cultural and symbolic value and contributing to the innovativeness of the brand without being paid for their labor.[10] As such, these community members lend a sacred quality to their endeavors, labors of love that transcend commerce.

A third persona Margaret expresses is Media Expert, an identity that involves three separate roles: opinion leader, international ambassador, and advocate. First, as an opinion leader, Margaret's expertise is widely sought after and valued. She has become a key source for the media when there is any Royal Family news. Key characteristics of opinion leaders include expertise, influence, information sharing, and long-lasting involvement with a brand,[11] and they gain their influence through the knowledge they acquire rather than other markers of status. Margaret certainly demonstrates all these characteristics in her deep and enduring knowledge of, and involvement with, the Royal Family. In many ways, she is seen as representing the voice of the common people, the pulse of popular culture in Britain, an image that the media reinforce in seeking her opinion so frequently. On the day Diana died, Fox News was interviewing Margaret by 4:30 that afternoon. She herself had learned about the death when her son woke her at 5:30

that morning, calling her from the United States to tell her the shocking news.

Margaret was featured on the media talking about the birth of Prince George in 2013,[12] proudly showing off a new table built especially to accommodate the many baby items she added to her collection. At the time we discussed these items with her, she had already acquired her usual eclectic assortment of goods: Highgrove baby slippers, a Royal Palace Shops' Coldstream Guards baby suit, Fortnum & Mason royal baby biscuits, and two mugs featuring the message "Keep Calm, It's a Royal Baby."

One key piece on the table was an eye-catching pram piñata, decorated in soft pastels with presents inside, bought from Kate Middleton's parents' business, Party Pieces. This item not only highlights the contemporary intermingling of cultural rituals in global consumer culture (a piñata is a Mexican tradition that often plays a prominent role at U.S. parties and baby showers), but also demonstrates how Margaret is making her own contribution to this cultural mixing. Significantly, by setting the Party Pieces pram piñata beside more traditional British royal baby memorabilia, Margaret validates the Middletons as belonging to the Royal Family and sends a strong signal of her approval. Such sentiments are important, because her opinion often influences the ordinary man (or, more usually, woman) on the street. Many people who recognize Margaret from her television appearances stop to chat with her and seek her opinions on the Royal Family: "Well they see me. . . . Well, I don't know them. They feel they know me. They don't actually know me. But they feel they know me. . . . But I get people stopping me all the time."

Her media expertise also extends to popular culture manifestations of the Royal Family. Margaret is an avid attendee of plays and musicals, films, gallery and museum exhibits, and other performances pertaining to the royal dynasty. In 2008, a local pub produced a play called *Untitled*, about Wallis Simpson and Edward VIII. Margaret attended this event and, true to form, managed to secure many promotional posters for her collection after the play's run had ended. One of her favorite haunts is the Queen's Gallery at Buckingham Palace, which often offers themed exhibits (such as one featuring pieces of art amassed by Victoria and Albert) from the Royal Collection, leaving them on display for several months.

Sometimes Margaret engages in ritualistic visits to exhibits and sites; two of her favorites are Althorp and Kensington Palace—both clearly rooted in the Diana narrative. Her regular visits to Althorp (often to mark Diana's

July 1st birthday) had become so ingrained that Diana's brother Charles, the 9th Earl Spencer, typically greeted her by name when she arrived. Margaret was devastated in 2013 to discover that Althorp was closing its Diana exhibition for good. Under the terms of Diana's will, the possessions she had entrusted to the care of her brother reverted back to her sons when Harry turned thirty, leaving Diana fans like Margaret feeling sad and frustrated. Margaret confessed how much she would miss her "little voyages every year."[13]

Margaret also acts as an international (brand) ambassador because she is so frequently the face of the British public featured on international media. She receives requests for interviews from around the globe: "I've had Australian [reporters], German, and I've been on South African TV ... that's when you know you've gone 'round the world.'" During Charles and Camilla's engagement and wedding, a wide variety of international media sought out her views, including journalists from Japan, Spain, Norway, Denmark, and France. Similarly, at the party for the Queen's eightieth birthday in 2006, there were multiple television crews, including a well-known German "chat" (talk) show host who encouraged Margaret and some of her friends to sing "Candle in the Wind" in the Diana Room, while he accompanied them on guitar.

During media coverage of the royal wedding in 2011, Margaret claims to have appeared in eighty countries (from around thirty media syndicates). During the build-up to the birth of Prince George, she added Russian media to her long list. She is thus something of a "missionary" for the RFBC, another role that is well recognized as one that brand community members perform.[14] Others openly acknowledge this role, as expressed by her long-time friend Dave: "She's an ambassador because she's so available for everybody to come.... It's like an open house." Indeed, following her debut on Russian television, she was then featured in a Russian documentary about the Royal Family, demonstrating not only the global fascination with British monarchy but also her spread of influence as one of their biggest fans.

Margaret has now taken her place alongside the Royal Family and other London sights as a tourist attraction in her own right, and many people come from afar to stay at Heritage House. Her friend Evelyn, who runs the Lady Di Club in Germany and herself has a houseful of Diana memorabilia, often encourages German Diana fans to visit Margaret. Each year, four or five small groups of Diana devotees visit from the country to immerse themselves in Margaret's Diana Room. "Arlette," a Frenchwoman who stayed with Margaret in December one year, said the visit was a Christmas present to herself because she had wanted to see Margaret's collection for a long time. Arlette was so moved by her sojourn at Heritage House that she returned the following year with a collection of five hundred royal-themed postcards for Margaret. Likewise, "Ruth," a fervent Diana collector from Las Vegas whom we met at a conference on the monarchy in 2012, discussed how much she loved visiting Margaret and talking endlessly about the Princess. A Japanese tourist book recommending her bed and breakfast has resulted in various Japanese visitors making a pilgrimage to Heritage House. This testifies to the wider role Margaret plays in attracting tourists to England and encouraging them to embrace Royal Family traditions and heritage.

Nor is it only tourists and media who seek her out; sometimes researchers (like us) do so as well. Margaret received a letter from a Japanese woman who was compiling a book on rosettes around the world and wished to visit to feature Margaret's collection of royal-themed versions. Her letter, addressed to Margaret at "Royal Sleepover," is just one of the many cultural confusions Margaret takes in her stride.

Finally, there is Margaret's role as advocate of the RFBC. Brand advocacy usually occurs when commitment to a brand leads people to actively recommend it to others and defend it from criticism. Such advocacy typically proceeds through word of mouth or, increasingly, through websites such as TripAdvisor where consumers can share opinions. Though she is not computer literate, Margaret's frequent media appearances facilitate her performance as a strong brand advocate for the Royal Family. Her staunch loyalty means she is always trying to create a positive image for them, no matter what the circumstances. Throughout our interviews and many conversations with her, she continually emphasized her admiration for them: "I mean, I think they're the most wonderful family. I never tire of reading about them, I never tire of reading books, or doing my [newspaper] cuttings or whatever—I spend hours on it."

As Margaret has become increasingly well known, she has also gained credibility with Buckingham Palace officials, who sometimes refer media sources to her, a referral she is more than happy to accept on their behalf: "My God, they're sending them around to me now. I don't think it was the Queen or anything *[laughs]*, but just to think that, you know, I was taking the weight off of them." Prince Edward's company featured Margaret in a television special it produced, *Royalty A to Zed;* she was under *F* for *Fan.*

The fact that those associated with the monarchy sometimes refer others to Margaret suggests that these strategists are confident she will always say something in defense of the Royal Family, no matter what misdemeanor or scandal has taken place. Indeed, Margaret takes great care to never say anything that can be interpreted as a criticism. She acts as their avenging angel when their reputation is threatened. She is disdainful when the media treat them unfairly: "I wish people in this country wouldn't actually keep criticizing the Royal Family. I wish they would stand up and say, 'Look, we're very proud of our Royal Family!' You know, but they don't. They keep carping on them; they write reams of material in the newspapers about this or that. . . . Why don't they leave them alone?"

To this end, Margaret uses every opportunity to protect the monarchy's reputation. Recalling being interviewed by one critical reporter, she says: "I wasn't rude to him, but, you know, I really stood up for them." Most people (including members of the House of Windsor) require media training to deal with reporters in a professional manner, but Margaret is self-taught. Despite this potential disadvantage, Margaret has become adept at handling the media and has learned to be on her guard. Although the media may try to encourage her to say something out of place when controversies arise, she is always measured in her answers and careful to maintain a positive outlook.

As a fervent admirer of Princess Diana, it was difficult for Margaret to come to terms with the marriage of Charles and Camilla. In fact, she was initially very distressed at the prospect of their union. However, in true Margaret fashion, she found a way to forgive and justify their love, declaring after their wedding that Charles and Camilla have "got human failings same as the rest of us. . . . Really now, [they] are role models in a way for divorced families who are making second marriages [work]." Thus, like other loyal community members, who give brands plenty of latitude in terms of the mistakes they make,[15] Margaret also forgives members of the Royal Family for their human failings, publicly speaking in their defense and converting others to her point of view. Whereas media interests try to stir up controversy at any opportunity to boost sales and visibility, Margaret works to smooth things over and return public opinion to pride in the monarchy.

So far, our discussions have centered on the roles Margaret plays as an individual in perpetuating interest in the RFBC. Now we delve more deeply into the social aspects of Margaret's collecting passion. Key to Margaret's experiences is the way she and her loosely connected network of royal followers engage with heritage, and how they help shape the consumption experiences of those outside their circle.[16] In particular, we liken Margaret's social network to a "consumer tribe,"[17] a group held together by the strong emotions its members share regarding a brand or product. Consumer tribes are similar to brand communities in that both coalesce around the "linking value"[18] of a product. This term describes the ways brands (or in this case, brand complexes) facilitate connections among people, enabling members to share their passions with like-minded others. Unlike brand communities, however, tribes are typically less stable. Members typically come together for particular events but do not necessarily maintain enduring ties. In short, they are ephemeral, existing midway between more permanent brand communities and one-time-only flash mobs.

Margaret's tribe congregates for particular royal events, usually when she hosts celebrations at her house. Typically, ten to twenty members with differing levels of commitment to the Royal Family appear at any one time. The scholar Robert Kozinets notes that there are four discernible types of members of consumer tribes.[19] Like Margaret, *Insiders* have a passion for the Royal Family and have built social relationships with those who share their interest. As we will see shortly, Margaret, Todd, Victor, and Monica can all be classified as Insiders. Along with Margaret, they are the most highly regarded and influential members of the tribe.

Devotees, on the other hand, do not particularly engage with all social aspects available to tribe members. However, they all share a passion for the Royal Family or for a specific member, such as Diana. Three to five Devotees—like Margaret's German friend Evelyn and her friends—may mingle with Margaret and her coterie at Kensington Palace each year on August 31st to commemorate the anniversary of Diana's death. By contrast, Margaret's friend Dave is a typical *Mingler;* he loves the social aspects but is less committed to consuming and discussing royal memorabilia. He supports Margaret at her events, ensuring everyone is looked after and feels included. Margaret's neighbors and close friends play a similar role, happy to come along for the festivities but expressing less interest in the focal consumption activity, the Royal Family. As its name implies, the fourth group, *Tourists,* is composed of the most ephemeral members. These participants possess neither strong social ties nor a passion for all things royal. Essentially, tourists are curious passers-by who merely stop to see what is happening and join in for a while, or who accompany another member on a one-off visit.

In addition to these four types of brand tribe members, during our many observations and visits with Margaret, we identified a fifth type—that of

Supporter. This category includes people who may provide invaluable assistance to more involved members but who do not themselves participate in consumption-related activities or share any interest in the consumption activity that binds members together. Margaret has many supporters, but key among them are her children. Although they tease her about her collection and suggest ways she should dispose of it, they nevertheless enable its growth and perpetuation through gifts. In fact, an item Margaret considers a crowning glory in the Diana Room is an oil painting of the Princess that her children gave her. After Diana's death, the artist tried to buy it back, but Margaret refused to sell it.

In addition to expensive items that she treasures, her children also delight her with kitschy items, such as a boxed set of windup "Racing Royals" acquired in an ordinary retail store. Furthermore, her grandchildren are now on the lookout for items Margaret might like, providing an activity that helps bind them. One of Margaret's sons, who lives in the United States, brings her magazines and other royal-themed items from across the pond when he visits, and calls to chat about her collection quite often. Other supporters also play key roles—informing her about opportunities to acquire new pieces of memorabilia, bringing gifts to her, or organizing transportation for her larger acquisitions. Although she was unsuccessful in petitioning her estate council to add on to her house (again), her builder helps her accommodate the growing collection, creating shelves and carving out precious additional space in her packed house.

Reflecting their somewhat transitory nature, membership in these five categories can shift over time. For example, "Vincent"—who had played such a key role during the early phases of our research and who was, according to Margaret, "a big personality" within her royal tribe—was no longer participating in group events by 2013. No one in her social circle, including Margaret, could explain where he went or why he disappeared. This lack of knowledge about Vincent's whereabouts is consistent with the loose relational ties formed within a group of this nature.

Tribes are interesting not only in their composition but in the way they support the passion that binds (or at least, marginally interests) participants. One of their key functions is to create rituals and establish traditions. A key attraction of the monarchy for many people is the fact that it is one of the main suppliers of national (and now, global) rituals, perfected over the years to symbolize continuity and majesty. Obviously these events are difficult for anyone living in Britain to ignore. Not surprisingly, Margaret and her associates are all acutely aware of the main national ritual elements, such as cer-emonial music, specific forms of dress and artifacts used (e.g., crowns, orbs, and scepters), processional elements, and regimental participation (e.g., the role of the Household Cavalry in the annual Trooping the Colour cere-mony). Nonetheless, brand tribes often create their own traditions and ritu-als without worrying how these fit with sanctioned brand rituals or how the general public will regard them.

The annual gathering at the gates of Kensington Palace on August 31st to commemorate Diana's death provides an excellent venue from which to observe such unofficial rituals. Each year, fans come from around the world to place tributes to Diana on the gates, often remaining beside them during the day as part of a mourning ritual for Diana (see figure 14 in chapter 4). Apart from Margaret's group, several other tribes participate, including the Diana Circle, the Lady-Di-Club from Germany, and representatives of other regional Diana fan clubs. Each develops and displays its own rituals and tra-ditions. One group of women who come every year bring folding chairs to maintain a vigil near the emotive tributes they place at the gates, drowning their sorrows in champagne throughout the day.

As Margaret and Dave discuss the various roles of their own set, we can see how their activities distinguish them from other Diana clans and mark out their own "trademark" rituals:

MARGARET: "Todd," who dresses in red, white, and blue, he sort of keeps wires and scissors and stuff and helps people put them [flowers and photographs] on the [gates], and people have these pictures plastercized [laminated] and put those up. . . .

DAVE: We know everybody there because Margaret is the star. When Margaret walks up, they say, "There she is," don't they?

MARGARET: They all know me, yes. We're all part of it, we make it for each other. It's almost like a party and yet it's not. . . .

DAVE: [Vincent] is quite the personality, especially down at the gate. . . . He's the man in the white suit. . . . I'm the one that takes photographs.

MARGARET: Yes, but Dave has to take them with my camera, and then with Vincent's, he sort of doubles up [covers both roles].

This conversation reveals how these four people, core to Margaret's social set, take on various tasks during the annual ritual performance at the gates, in roles that are entirely unofficial and spontaneously assumed. For example, Vincent takes up a position of authority by welcoming others who arrive at the gates. His legitimacy in this role stems from his impressive white suit and white jeweled shoes (for which he reports paying £90 [$135]). This attire immediately identifies him as an ardent Diana fan, since white is the color of the Diana rose. Likewise, in her role as minor celebrity, Margaret interacts with those whom, in her own words, she "sees once a year," as opposed to the unknown members of the curious public whom Vincent greets.

Todd, the man with the supplies, acts as an assistant to participants, providing technical help to mount their displays on the railings, while Dave acts as an assistant to both Margaret and Victor. The ways they carry out these duties is not decided on in advance or scripted; instead, their actions emerge as an intuitive response to the interactions that take place among themselves and with others around them—and from an overall desire to belong.

These four people certainly are conscious of the fact that a larger audience beyond core Diana fans often witnesses their behavior. However, they do not enact their roles to gain attention from their audience or to put forward some political point. Rather, they are merely trying to make their own rituals distinct from those of other groups. In that regard, they do not attach any tributes to the railings (apart from Margaret's flowers, which she carries with her most of the day before attaching them). They especially want to distance themselves from "the Diana Circle," a group Margaret regards as extreme and cliquish. Its members refer to February 10, 2005, the day Charles announced his intention to marry Camilla Parker Bowles, as "Black Thursday." Furthermore, the Circle nicknamed her "Cowmilla"—and Margaret and her group would never tolerate such disloyalty or overt criticism of the Royal Family.

In sum, Margaret and her friends create loosely bounded rituals and traditions more for their own personal pleasure and that of their immediate group, in contrast to official pomp and pageantry, which fulfills a more public need. Nonetheless, the tribe's unofficial rituals do reach the public through media sources and those who come to watch their performances. Thus they play their part alongside the official rituals, to ensure the monarchy "survives by being noticed, over and over again."[20] These loosely bound rituals include parties to commemorate Royal Family events, such as the Queen's Diamond Jubilee, William and Kate's wedding, and the christening of Prince George. On these occasions, the tribe carries out the role of socializing and educating others, as well as keeping royal heritage at the forefront of people's minds.

The second function of Margaret and her RFBC tribe that perpetuates consumption and discourse around their common interest is sharing opinions about royal history as it unfolds before them. Although they never air grievances publicly or risk detracting from the Royal Family's public esteem, they feel at ease with each other and able to confide worries or air disapproving opinions from time to time. This enables them to deal with negative emotions and grievances or, indeed, help with grieving, as in the case of Diana's death. Sharing their thoughts and feelings offers Margaret and her tribe an important cathartic outlet, allowing them to collectively come to terms with events that have shocked or upset them.

On the day of Prince Charles and Camilla Parker Bowles's marriage, Margaret held a wedding viewing party. Given the still somewhat controversial nature of the couple, it is not surprising that the event seemed lackluster. In fact, there was a notable absence of the joyous atmosphere that Margaret's celebrations often brought to bear on such a high-profile royal event. Even Dave, while emphasizing his loyalty to the Queen—who he believes contributes to "great stability for Britain on the international stage"—confided later that he had strong reservations about the marriage and believed many others did too. In confirmation of this assertion, we noticed that when a Danish television crew asked the gathering to drink a toast to the newlyweds, there was an air of reluctance. Finally, as bidden, Dave poured the champagne, but no one raised a glass, although someone eventually muttered, "To the day." Such reluctance is in sharp contrast to the customary exuberant toasting and flag-waving that typify Margaret's royal parties.

As well as sharing grievances, the tribe's collective support allows them to share grief, most notably at the aforementioned gates of Kensington Palace every August 31st. Margaret tells us that she is like an "agony aunt"* on that day because "people cry all over the place—it's amazing," and Dave notes that people turn to Margaret to ask, "What do we do?" At other times they seek her out at her home, which becomes like a sanctuary, a refuge in times of trouble. This was very much the case when one member of Margaret's circle, "Hilary," had a dream about Diana that she likened to a visitation. In her dream, Diana was pale and cold, and despite numerous attempts, Hilary was unable to wake her. Highly distressed by her vivid nightmare, Hilary sought solace with Margaret to regain her equilibrium. Using the Diana Room as a type of therapeutic sanctuary, Hilary remained there for several hours,

* A British term for a newspaper columnist who gives advice to people—like "Dear Abby" in American newspapers.

surrounded by the sea of Diana memorabilia, which enabled her to reconnect with Diana in a more positive way and finally restore her composure.

Unlike the raison d'être of the brand community for products like the Apple Newton,* Margaret's brand tribe does not exist to express its discontent with the RFBC. In fact, more often than not, Margaret's tribe engages with royal heritage in a joyous and celebratory manner. As is true of many contexts in contemporary consumer culture, the RFBC contributes to people's enjoyment and experiences of the institution by facilitating aspirational consumption. Thus, a third way Margaret's tribe consumes royal heritage is by enabling its members to share consumption fantasies. For example, Margaret sometimes fantasizes about opening a tea shop in the United States (or closer to home in one of her favorite towns, Windsor) with Dave and Todd. She notes that her son thought this would be the perfect opportunity for her, since she "likes to drink tea and talk about the Royal Family all day." However, she acknowledges that especially the American version of this dream is an impossible fantasy, because neither she nor Dave likes to fly.

On the other hand, she believes some fantasies are more realistic, like one they shared with Vincent (before he left the group) about going to Paris and seeing the tunnel where Diana was mortally injured:

DAVE: You've always wanted to go to Paris.

MARGARET: Yes, I think I will one day, I've got a passport.

DAVE: We could do a B&B.

MARGARET: I don't know whether I'm quite ready for that, to see where she [crashed], I mean Vincent says that he's going to go one day, get a taxi to go through the tunnel and stop where [it happened]. I said, "Vincent, I don't think they'll let you." He said, "Well, I'll tell them to stop," and [Vincent] wants to get out, he'll get killed. . . . But that's what he wants to do.

Of course, fantasies in relation to Diana can also be more positively aspirational, rather than focusing on her death. For example, Margaret has always regretted not buying one of Diana's dresses at the famous Christie's auction in 1997, shortly before her death. She states: "If I'd have known then what I know now, I think I would have remortgaged the house and bought a dress."

* An Apple digital message pad launched in 1987. It acquired a loyal following but was discontinued.

Her friend Jane, knowing of her regrets, found her a substitute of which Margaret remains very proud:

> MARGARET: [Jane] worked at the [hotel]. And she got me the carpet in the Diana room, the green carpet.
>
> DAVE: Which Diana walked on.
>
> MARGARET: Walked on because they [Kensington Palace] used to have their staff parties there, so Diana would have walked on that. . . . When [Jane] got it home she hated it . . . and when she heard I was having the Diana Room built, she said, "I'd like you to have it." So it will always be there.

A piece of carpet may seem like a strange type of memorabilia, but it is a good example of how the tribe's consumption of the Royal Family involves creating their own value around what they perceive to be heritage and how, in turn, they help co-create the meanings around royal heritage. As part of this process, they personalize the RFBC by creating their own rituals and traditions alongside official ones, which they may occasionally even challenge. The fact that this carpet possesses revered properties, having been walked on by Diana, gives authenticity to this quasi-sacred space, an authenticity that draws visitors to it.

The activities of Margaret's group also shape the heritage consumption experience of a wider circle. In particular, Margaret's home is a focus for socializing and educating the Minglers and Tourists, who remain on the fringes of the group, in addition to the Insiders and Devotees, who will certainly be there. On the day of Margaret's party to celebrate the Queen's eightieth birthday, Heritage House takes on a life of its own. As those who are passionate about the RFBC intermingle enthusiastically with reporters, first-time visitors, and peripheral attendees, they draw attention to particular exhibits that appeal to them and recount their own stories. "Monica" (an Insider) has brought along her brother "Anthony" (a Tourist) and proudly displays her knowledge of various items of royal memorabilia as she takes him on a tour of the house. She stops beside a small travel hamper containing an appetizing selection of traditional English foods, educating him on its origins and connection to the Royal Family: "This is what came from the Windsor Exhibition. Look, Anthony, this is what the Queen does when she travels—look at the picnic things. This is what she takes on her travels abroad." In this way, those devoted to the monarchy pass on the personalized history they have learned from Margaret, and stories like these continually circulate and are shared with other sundry visitors. This type of storytelling is a recognized feature of how brand communities maintain and strengthen relational bonds.[21]

Invitations to Margaret's parties are informal, and attendance is often quite haphazard, depending on whom she encounters before the event and whom other guests bring. In fact, guests may include a friend of a friend (of a friend) who knows neither Margaret nor any immediate member of her circle. No matter, they are all used to welcoming strangers and readily accept anyone who seeks to be part of their celebrations, albeit on a temporary basis. This informal, friendly behavior, coupled with the constant buzz of media comings and goings, creates an ambience that draws people in, encouraging them to linger and join in or just spectate from the sidelines. This behavior is consistent with the nature of consumer tribes who are passionate about their favorite brand and like to share their enthusiasm with as many others as possible.[22] The activities Margaret's group undertakes socialize others into appreciating the Royal Family by continually reinforcing positive messages about them and, importantly, making them seem fun.

In addition, the ways hard-core members manage relationships with the media significantly shape their ability to influence the consumption experiences of others. Alongside Margaret, the media often chooses Insiders and Devotees to represent "the British people" and discuss how they engage with the RFBC. As such, they provide a crucial backdrop during Margaret's many media interviews, bringing an authentic touch of English life to the international audiences that watch them. Of course, these members too feed off Margaret's celebrity aura and delight in being in front of the camera, even if only to play a minor supporting role. Yet their presence is important to Margaret. By attending her functions and assisting with the media, they help establish her credibility and demonstrate her sphere of influence.

The importance of group cooperation is revealed when Margaret hosts an eightieth birthday party for the Queen. When a German TV crew arrives to film it, members of the tribe immediately welcome the presenter with a cup of tea, making room for him at the table and including him in their conversation. Once filming begins, they provide the festive background against which Margaret's interviews take place. Undaunted by the numerous retakes required, they throw themselves wholeheartedly into the filming, happily complying with various demands by the television crew. In this way, they not only assist Margaret through a sense of shared moral responsibility common to brand tribes, but also incorporate the media into their own group activities.

In fact, spontaneous group gatherings often lead to the creation of new rituals and traditions, or the adaptation of existing ones. As might be expected, Margaret, ever mindful of what will interest the media and provide a good spectacle, is often a key impetus for this evolution:

> MARGARET: Last time I had a party for the Queen's Jubilee, I had Australian television filming it, and who else? CNN from America filming it. Filming my neighbors munching sandwiches! And I thought, "I've got to get something going here." So I got a Pearly King and Queen to come along because that was visual. Next year [referring to the eightieth party] I think I'm going to try and get . . . what do you call it when they do country dancing with sticks?
>
> INTERVIEWER: Oh, you mean Morris dancers.
>
> MARGARET: Yeah, yeah. Because they're pretty, aren't they? And you need something visual.

Just as she often juxtaposes incongruous items in her collection displays, Margaret follows the same approach in deeming these long-standing English traditions appropriate for her royal event.* Both traditions she mentions are highly aesthetic and performative. Known as London's Cockney royalty, Pearly Kings and Queens (or "Pearlies") symbolize charitable working-class culture. They wear eye-catching black suits and hats covered with as many as thirty thousand mother-of-pearl buttons. As a result, suits can weigh up to twenty-five kilograms (fifty-five pounds). Mother-of-pearl was chosen because only the upper classes could afford real pearls.[23]

The tradition dates from the nineteenth century, when the first Pearly King, Henry Croft, designed a spectacular outfit to draw attention to the charity for which he was collecting. His design was inspired by the Cockney fruit and vegetable "costermongers," or market-traders, who often sewed mother-of-pearl buttons on their clothing. Each London borough boasts a Pearly King and Queen, and these alternative "royal families" avidly raise money for charity. Both their status and titles pass through family lines, although a generous donor to charity can be crowned a Pearly in gratitude.[24]

* Obviously Margaret is not alone in this thinking; on November 11, 2014, Historic Royal Palaces arranged for a large contingent of Pearlies to be present at the Tower of London's Armistice Day ceremony.

Morris dancing in Britain dates back to the fifteenth century, when it is thought the Moors imported it from North Africa. It is rooted in fertility rites and the coming of spring. Although a feature of fifteenth- and six-teenth-century courts, in recent centuries its connections with royalty have been minimal. However, regular displays of Morris dancing typically remain part of localized celebrations, such as those for the Queen's Diamond Jubilee. Grounded in pub culture and working men's clubs, Morris dancing is historically a male activity.[25] Troupes incorporate elements designed to enhance the element of spectacle; they perform in multicolored costumes with bells tied around their calves, waving handkerchiefs or clacking sticks together for particular routines.

That Margaret easily assimilates these traditions into her group's own celebrations without any conflict illustrates the adaptability and fluid nature of the tribe.[26] As we witnessed firsthand during the Queen's eightieth birthday party, this flexibility is often put to good use by members of the media, to stage a more engaging show for their viewers. In response to the German television crew's request for them all to be given Union Jack hats and flags, Dave—himself wearing an enormous red, white, and blue hat—duly doles these out to everyone around the festive table. Its centerpiece is a magnificent cake, a replica of a crown in its purple, bejeweled glory that Margaret ordered specially baked for the occasion. Once they have all secured their hats, the partygoers waved the flags and sing "God Save the Queen," as the German camera rolls.

An impromptu moment occurs, however, when, as the national anthem draws to an end, Vincent calls, "Three cheers for the Queen!" Everyone cheers enthusiastically, but Ruth highlights mistakes they have made in singing the anthem. Two more takes are required before the group give a perfect performance for the camera—and each time, the three cheers are included. Thus, their initial ritual evolves as an iterative process takes place between the group and the media, balancing their own spontaneity with media demands.

The next day, a different television crew orchestrates another event for viewers when they arrange for Margaret, accompanied by Victor, to deliver the magnificent cake to the Queen as she makes her birthday walkabout at Windsor Castle. "It was exhilarating to be so close to Her Majesty," she confessed to us as she proudly discussed her feeling of achievement at having delivered the cake.

In myriad imaginative ways, then, Margaret and the Royal Family brand tribe she assembles around her bring history to life, shaping the heritage consumption experiences of many others near and far. Clearly, the media play a crucial role in these constructions by continually featuring Margaret and her social group on television channels around the world. This dissemination is important because a majority of the Royal Family's fans live outside the United Kingdom; for example, 80 percent of the subscribers to *Royalty* magazine reside in the United States.[27] People are drawn to Margaret's events to watch the pageants she and her circle perform and delve into the royal history that is enacted before them.

Margaret's status as a minor celebrity is important in this respect, drawing in many who wish to have the fifteen minutes of fame Andy Warhol predicted for us all. Celebrity culture is pervasive in contemporary society, disseminated widely by television talk shows and reality TV—and Heritage House provides a perfect venue for the latter. Indeed, Margaret and Vincent participated in the reality television show *Britain's Worst Homes*. It featured four contestants—hoarders whose collections had taken over their houses— who were tasked with redesigning their homes. Obviously, Margaret knew that she was selected because of her overabundance of royal décor. But in the skit on the show where contestants are assigned to buy items to help with their redesign, Margaret chose the only royal-themed item in the entire shop. She then received the dubious honor of winning the title of "Britain's Worst Home" for Heritage House, because she steadfastly refused to change the way she displays her thousands of pieces of memorabilia.

On that note, Margaret has been described in many ways by the media— from "ultra-royalist" to "royal hoarder," and Heritage House was listed in the "World's Craziest Homes Gallery" by the *New York Daily News*. Yet she takes it all in stride, happy to spread the word about her favorite family in whatever way she can and with the help of those around her. Despite her eccentric collection and her numerous roles in that respect, for many she is simply a warm and nurturing mother figure—Dave's nickname for her is "Mum"—who helps them navigate the complexities of royal history in a palatable way. And for Margaret, who like the Queen has four children (and a son named after Prince Andrew), it is first and foremost as a mother that she relates to the Royal Family and empathizes with their trials and tribulations. By allocating a corner to each of the Queen's children, Margaret's collection reinforces the family aspect of the RFBC by emphasizing the monarch's role as a mother. Indeed, one reason Diana appealed to her so much was because Margaret believed she was such a good mother. Once again, Margaret captures the popular sentiment by declaring, "She [Diana] did such a good job on those two boys."

In the following chapters, Margaret's opinions and activities occasionally resurface in our discussions of various key aspects of the RFBC. As a royal collector supreme, Margaret's case reveals that the Royal Family owes much of its continued existence to people like her, who work tirelessly on their behalf, and who offer them unconditional loyalty and support.

FOUR

The Face on the Tea Towels

THE GLOBAL QUEST FOR DIANA

As her collection reflects, Margaret's favorite member of the Royal Family is Princess Diana. Devastated at the news of Diana's death, her deep sorrow moved her to build a commemorative conservatory. This "Diana temple" functions as a quasi-sacred space inside Margaret's house. Although Margaret provides all of the other members of the Royal Family with their own designated corners, she devotes an entire room to Diana. As a material testimony to the power Diana still exerts in the popular imagination, a giant photo of the princess dominates Margaret's collection, acting as a memorial marker to draw the visitor's gaze and step toward the conservatory entrance (figure 12).

Inside the conservatory, a specially commissioned stained-glass depiction of Diana, an angelic portrayal of her in soft pinks, is backlit by the light from Margaret's garden, where a white Diana rose can be seen in bloom during the summer. Two white doves of peace holding a white heart between their beaks adorn each of the adjoining windows. One heart features the words *Halo Trust* inscribed within it, reminding the viewer of Diana's dedicated campaigning for the removal of land mines and other debris of war. These stained-glass panels border a breathtaking array of Diana memorabilia. Colorful cascades of Diana dolls, portraits, pictures, books, magazines, and china evoke the spirit of Diana in the sweep of an eye: her life, her death, her loves, and her hurts all materialize in this dense profusion of objects. Every available space on walls, chairs, tables, and floor is utilized, so visitors' access to the conservatory is limited to little more than a few feet.

Several minishrines are evident in this seemingly random sea of relics, little nooks of order within all the apparent disorder. Each shrine has a small table to itself: on one, tall church candles encircle a portrait of Diana; on

FIGURE 12. Margaret's Diana memorial picture. Photo by Pauline Maclaran.

another, a large biblical-looking tome, a German memorial book to her, is open at an appropriately moving poem and set in front of another large picture. On the ceiling, a giant mural of a smiling Diana—a relatively new addition—beams down from above. As our gaze absorbs this immense profusion of objects, we cannot doubt that Diana lives on in collective memory as one of the most iconic figure of our times.

For many, Princess Diana was the living enactment of childhood fairy tales: a beautiful princess whom some see as victimized at the hands of her cruel, unloving husband and his unfeeling, distant parents (and prior to that, by a real-life cruel stepmother). For others, she was the glamorous star of the Royal Family soap opera that ran through the 1980s and 1990s, as various royal marriages (including her own) crumbled, giving rise to scandals time and time again. For still others, she was a feminist icon who challenged an antiquated patriarchal system incapable of showing emotion or feeling. Her representations, and their interpretations, have been vast and varied, changing with her evolution from innocent, fresh-faced bride to independent humanitarian who harnessed the power of the media to make herself the "Queen of Hearts" (a term Britain's *Sun* tabloid newspaper first used in 1982) in the public imagination. And the public still cannot get enough of her; Amazon.com features well over five hundred books about the princess, each interpreting her life and death in different ways. A film about her love affair with heart surgeon Hasnat Khan was released in 2013 with Naomi Watts as Diana. Stephen Jeffreys, who wrote the screenplay, remarked that "everyone has their own Diana,"[1] meaning people tend to create their own personal image of her.

This chapter tracks the public's fascination with Princess Diana, together with the profound impact she has had on the overall image of the Royal Family. The time between the tragic death of Diana and the birth of her grandson, Prince George, has marked a crucial phase in the history of the British monarchy. In the late eighteenth century, George III and Queen Charlotte attempted to portray the Royal Family as a harmonious family unit,[2] parading their fifteen children about on their constitutionals near Windsor Castle to visibly embody family values for their subjects to emulate. However, their sons' scandals, extramarital affairs, and the many illegitimate children that resulted undermined their efforts. As a result, the concept of the Royal Family really was not successfully engrained in British culture until the reign of Queen Victoria and her consort, Prince Albert.

All succeeding monarchs supported this image, except for Edward VIII, who was unmarried while he reigned. With the marital dissolutions and divorces of Charles and Diana (and a few months prior, of Andrew and Sarah), this image was severely tarnished, and these younger royals contributed to the public's perception of the monarchy as a highly dysfunctional family choked by outdated traditions, restrictions, and limitations. The events leading up to Diana's death in 1997 and the subsequent public reaction represented the biggest threat to the monarchy to date in the reign of Elizabeth II. Thereafter, the monarchy's image was to change significantly, becoming much more professionally managed to ensure that the RFBC incorporated the human and humane qualities Diana had brought to it, qualities now embodied in her sons, William and Harry.

It is fairly extraordinary that a woman from Diana's background could become such a powerful figure in the popular imagination and the beloved heroine of so many marginalized groups. Her aristocratic upbringing is not usually the stuff of contemporary icons, stemming as she did from impeccable English upper-class stock. The Spencers are seen as one of the grandest families in England, one that has been part of the royal court for over two hundred years.³ In fact, Diana's maternal grandmother was a lady-in-waiting to the Queen Mother. Diana was born on July 1, 1961, at Park House, where her parents, Johnny and Frances Spencer, lived on the grounds of the Queen's estate in Sandringham, Norfolk. To Prince Charles, she was literally the girl next door (or more accurately, one of them; she had two older sisters, Sarah and Jane). In fact, Diana became acquainted with Charles during his short-lived courtship of Sarah.

Diana's childhood was far from perfect, and a look into her past reveals parts of her background that resonated with many people and helped them identify with her despite her associated wealth and privilege. As the third daughter, Diana would later confess that she felt unwanted because she was not the long-awaited male heir so important to maintaining the aristocratic family line in Britain.* When Diana was six, her mother left her father for Peter Shand Kydd, whom she married in 1967. A bitter custody battle followed, which Frances lost on account of her adultery. Subsequently, Diana was shuttled between her father in Park House and her mother in London, usually accompanied by a nanny or an au pair. This type of fluid family is one to which people from diverse backgrounds can relate. No doubt it helped imbue Diana with the resilience required to transcend class boundaries, as she would do later in her life. Her father (who became the 8th Earl Spencer when his father died in 1975, thus elevating Diana's title to "Lady") remarried in 1976 to Raine Legge. Daughter of the famed romance novelist Barbara Cartland, she became Countess Spencer. During Diana's formative years, her depiction as a wicked stepmother figure by the Earl's children only reinforced the fairy-tale narrative underlying Diana's life. Raine made many changes to Althorp, the Spencer family seat. Diana and her siblings deeply resented these changes, which included selling valuable artwork from the estate. Perceiving her as the cold and distant controller of their much-loved father, they nicknamed her "Acid Raine."

Diana's education followed the traditional upper-class English emphasis on acquiring the skills and graces to be a proper lady, rather than achieving any strong academic profile. She attended a private girls' boarding school from the age of eleven. Afterward, she went to a finishing school for a few months before moving to London in 1979 to work as a nanny and kinder-

---

* Diana's brother, Charles, now the 9th Earl Spencer, was born in 1964, ensuring continuation of the line.

garten assistant. She lived with three other friends in a three-bedroom flat purchased by her father, where her lifestyle epitomized that of a "Sloane Ranger." This term takes its name from Sloane Square in the wealthy Chelsea area of London, a favorite upper-class haunt. It refers to young upper-class and upper-middle-class females, and sometimes males, identified by their accent (nonregional and very pronounced Oxford English), confidence, traditional upper-class values, anti-intellectualism (intellectuals tend to be too left wing), a public school background,* and a particular style of dress. Ruffle-neck blouses, headbands, pearls, and demure floral skirts worn with ballet pumps defined the Sloane style of the 1980s, as did turned-up shirt collars worn with V-neck jumpers,† set off by a healthy ski tan. This lifestyle group was immortalized in *The Sloane Ranger Handbook* (1982) cowritten by Peter York,[4] style editor for *Harpers & Queen,* the leading high-society magazine of the time.

Even more amazing was the fact that this archetypal Sloane Ranger would become such a cultural icon. Yet Diana's upbringing contained many emotionally turbulent ingredients that would later make her a successful underdog brand in popular culture. Underdog brands develop brand biographies that contain two key narrative elements: a disadvantaged position in relation to a major competitor and an overriding passion to succeed despite the odds.[5] This passion, as well as the overcoming of adversity, lends an authenticity to their ventures that people admire. Their brand narrative is an emotional one with which ordinary people can identify, in a contemporary replay of the David and Goliath story. Apple is the prime example of a hugely successful underdog brand that rose to defeat its behemoth competitor, Microsoft. Compared to other members of the Royal Family, the media frequently emphasized this underdog position in relation to Diana. It was an image she encouraged, especially after her divorce, when she was in direct competition with Charles for the public's attention.

Diana became the most photographed woman in the world and was constantly in the media eye. Significantly, she dramatically transformed the Royal Family into an institution consumed for its celebrity appeal and aesthetic components, as well as for its tradition and majesty. But Diana was not the first family member to inject some controversial luster into the

* In the British system, the term means attendance at a paid, private independent school.
† In American English, sweaters.

portfolio. The Queen's younger sister, the glamorous and vivacious Princess Margaret, was very much the Princess Diana of her day and the first to become a mass-mediated fashion icon.

Britain's endurance of many stark and stoic years of war and postwar rationing meant that when Princesses Elizabeth and Margaret emerged as polished young ladies from their safe haven of Windsor Castle, where they essentially had lived in secret during World War II, they quickly became aspirational models of glamour. Their access to designers such as Norman Hartnell, Christian Dior, and Hardy Amies meant that they served as aspirational fashion role models for British subjects ready to revel in finery, even if only vicariously. Elizabeth's marriage at twenty-one led Margaret to be viewed as the more glamorous; at seventeen, "everybody was talking about her clothes. Every new dress, every hat, every scarf, every pair of shoes she wore made fashion news." With her delicate figure and large blue eyes, Margaret was likened to a "fairy princess."[6]

After the war, the nation became obsessed with the progress of Margaret's love affair with the decorated war hero Captain Peter Townsend, who had served as George VI's equerry at Windsor Castle after his plane was shot down. The sixteen-year age difference between the couple was not nearly as problematic as the fact that at the time, the Royal Marriages Act of 1772 required any member of the Royal Family who wished to marry before age twenty-five to secure the Queen's permission. As the head of the Church of England, the Queen could not permit her sister to marry a divorced man and allow Margaret to retain her title and status within the Royal Family. Foreshadowing the tabloid furor that would surround Charles and Diana, the press hounded Margaret and Townsend for two years, with the *Times* and the *Mirror* competing for readers and encouraging them to take sides in Margaret's choice between love and royal status. Although the family was sympathetic to their romance, ultimately Margaret chose to relinquish Townsend.

In 1960, Margaret married the photographer and commoner Antony Armstrong-Jones. The couple was often photographed in nightclubs, on yachts, or in other luxurious surroundings with celebrities such as Mick and Bianca Jagger, who became known as part of the "Margaret set." She mixed with the glitterati of her era and was at the center of various controversies and scandals that threatened to taint the Royal Family—including her divorce from Armstrong-Jones in 1978. Margaret became a paparazzi favorite, with her celebrity lifestyle and notorious love of parties, particularly on the romantically remote and privately owned island of Mustique, where she had her "home away from home." She was the first member of the Royal Family to be photographed in a two-piece bathing suit. As the Queen's sister, Margaret's patina elevated the appeal of her celebrity friends and kept her and her set on the A-list of journalists' assignments.

In her day, Margaret certainly was the Royal Family's superstar, but she never matched the frenzy with which both the media and public consumed images of Diana. One reason for this contrast is that the popular media were only just beginning to harness their full power in the 1950s and 1960s. Another reason is that Margaret communicated an aloofness that stemmed from her acute awareness of her elite position, a hauteur that prevented her from possessing the common touch like Diana. For these reasons, she would never have competed with Diana for the title "Queen of Hearts."*

From the start, the press and public were captivated by this shy young woman who was to marry Prince Charles. The media began its pursuit of her as soon as it became known that she was his girlfriend. Photographers followed her daily, to and from the kindergarten where she worked. Speculation ran high in the British tabloid press as to whether there would be an engagement, with each newspaper trying to outshine its competitors in terms of coverage and conjecture. At the same time, her boyish cropped-shag hairstyle, known as the "Shy Di," became extremely popular, and a survey of readers of the British website Stylist.com named it the most iconic hairstyle of the last fifty years. Indeed, it has been widely reported that this media attention pushed Charles into marrying her, as the Queen and Prince Philip allegedly told him he would have to make up his mind to stop photographers from chasing Diana. However, the media attention on the nineteen-year-old only intensified after the engagement was announced and would remain feverish throughout her subsequent life, continuing long after her death.

Diana's time in the public eye was demarcated by two of the largest material and cultural spectacles the United Kingdom, and indeed the world, has ever witnessed. These events were her wedding and her funeral—occasions that triggered fanfares of mirth and mourning, respectively. To the media, any story about Diana was (and still is) a gold mine. "A big Diana story could add 150,000 in sales," said Phil Hall, editor of the now-defunct *News of the*

* Margaret's lifestyle took center stage during heated criticism of the Civil List, which specified the allowances Parliament granted to members of the Royal Family. Amid this discussion, Willie Hamilton, the first Labour MP to publicly criticize the monarchy, famously asked, "What is Princess Margaret *for?*"

FIGURE 13. Diana ceiling painting, Heritage House. Photo by Cele Otnes.

World. *Time* magazine's first issue about Diana's death sold a staggering 850,000 copies—650,000 more than a typical issue. A special commemorative edition of *Time* sold around 1.2 million copies.[7] From the moment she became associated with Prince Charles, her life was mediated to such an extent that it has been argued "the image was Diana."[8] Essentially, the phrase means that it is common for magazine articles to tell the story of Diana mainly in pictures, with just the occasional headline.

In a consumer culture dominated by an emphasis on the visual, cultural memory increasingly resides in the visual image, and thus with the power of the media. As the screenwriter Stephen Jeffreys suggested, when we think of Diana, no doubt a particular picture springs to mind for each of us. That image may stem from her wedding, her funeral, or her charity work (such as the famous shot of her in a protective head visor in support of banning land mines). But like the image that dominates Margaret's living room, as well as the one that now dominates the ceiling in her Diana temple (figure 13), whatever picture people conjure up is likely to invoke a special memory and meaning. The multiple ways Diana is represented in the media allow people to weave their own personalized narratives around her, an essential ingredient in her becoming the "People's Princess."[9] In this respect, Diana typifies Guy Debord's notion that in modern society, the authenticity of social life has been superseded by its representation, with images replacing authentic human interaction.[10]

On July 29, 1981, the wedding of Prince Charles to Lady Diana Spencer was the biggest royal spectacle since Queen Elizabeth II's coronation in 1953. It was held at St. Paul's Cathedral, with 3,500 guests attending. A crowd estimated at 600,000 people lined the streets of London to celebrate, and 750 million people around the world watched the wedding on television.[11] Driven to St. Paul's in a golden coach with a mounted military escort, Diana, the archetypal virginal bride, looked resplendent in a dress that was to set bridal trends for the next decade, in addition to reinvigorating the "allure of the lavish wedding."[12] Reinforcing her own underdog image so beloved by the British, Diana chose to have her wedding dress made by British designers Elizabeth and David Emanuel, who were little known at the time. In response to Diana's request for something romantic, they created a spectacular "meringue" gown fashioned in silk taffeta tulle, with trimmings of lace once belonging to Queen Mary. The fitted bodice was decorated with hand embroidery, sequins, and pearls. The media all commented on Diana as the fairy-tale princess. This moniker was hardly an understatement, as she sparkled in a diamond tiara belonging to the Spencer family that held in place an ivory silk tulle veil twinkling with ten thousand mother-of-pearl sequins. A twenty-five-foot train completed the design of what has become one of the most famous gowns in the world.

The splendor and pomp surrounding the wedding, together with her innocent beauty, cemented the construction of Diana in the eyes of the world as the fairy-tale princess come to life. The media and their audiences (mainly women) could not get enough of her image. Most little girls grow up with childhood stories of beautiful princesses, and, as we have observed, global corporations such as Disney have helped spread this phenomenon around the world. The princess myth is a pervasive one that is deeply embedded in our collective consciousness; at its heart is the Cinderella story that one day our handsome princes will come and transform our lives. The media played as much as they could on this sensibility. Immediately after the wedding, two rival American television networks produced their own versions of the romance,[13] depicting a rose-tinted narration of Charles and Diana that culminated in the balcony kiss, a famous high point of the wedding. Such depictions only heightened the fairy-tale aura surrounding the couple, leading to what Marguerite Helmers has described as "a surplus of fantasy" in people's relationships with Diana.[14]

Behind the scenes, however, the reality was rather different. Even before her marriage, Diana had had suspicions about where Charles's real affections lay, suspicions frequently fueled by *Private Eye,* a bitingly satirical current affairs magazine that featured spoof articles about Charles, Diana, and the other woman, Camilla Parker Bowles.[15] Diana's confidence was further shattered when she found a gold bracelet with the intertwined letters *G* and *F* that Charles intended to give to Camilla. She interpreted these letters as "Gladys" and "Fred," Charles and Camilla's pet names for each other. He argued they stood for "Girl Friday" and that the bracelet was a thank-you gift to Camilla for being a trusted helpmate. When Diana confided her fears to her sister Sarah and intimated that she was thinking of canceling the wedding, her sister famously replied, "Bad luck, Duch,* your face is on the tea towels, so you're too late to chicken out."[16]

Just as media attention had put pressure on Charles to commit to marriage, so now a memorabilia market in overdrive ensured that Diana was also cornered. Caught up in the fast flow of contemporary consumer culture, she had become a cultural product. Indeed, the commemorative industry was enjoying a bonanza with official coins and stamps to mark the occasion, as well as myriad commercial products: the inevitable plates, mugs, glasses, thimbles, and other ornaments, as well as placemats, playing cards, bookmarks, and even beach balls.

Almost immediately after the wedding, Diana started appearing on the front covers of magazines as each competed to craft the most glamorous shot of her. In 1983, *Woman* magazine named her the world's number one cover girl. A magazine with Diana on the cover could increase its sales by as much as 40 percent.[17] She left the Sloane Ranger look far behind as she morphed into a fashion icon, becoming the ambassador for many British designers, including Catherine Walker, Bruce Oldfield, Amanda Wakeley, and Arabella Pollen. The idea of a royal figure supporting the British fashion industry is not in itself new; Queen Victoria publicized British fabrics, perceiving this effort as part of her role. As we noted, the famed British designer Norman Hartnell was a favorite of Queen Elizabeth II and Princess Margaret, as well as other members of the Royal Family. Diana, however, took royal fashion influence to new heights. Each dress she wore became a topic for discussion in women's magazines and newspaper columns, with the designs quickly replicated on Britain's High Streets† and in shopping centers and malls around the world.

* The family's pet name for Diana, short for "Duchess."
† Akin to Main Street in U.S. towns and suburbs; many retailers are typically located there in the UK.

Indeed, Diana is regarded by many as the most influential fashion icon of the twentieth century.[18] Her changing sense of style is immortalized in four famous *Vogue* front covers that portray her transformation from shy Sloane to svelte style icon.[19] Her first cover appearance in August 1981 conveys the image of a traditional "English Rose," smiling demurely. Her face is somewhat overshadowed by her heavy diamond earrings and necklace. By the last cover, in October 1997 (a special tribute issue), she is depicted as much more animated—laughing rather than smiling, and sitting cross-legged in a long red halter-neck dress with no jewelry whatsoever. This posture, which Diana adopted in the media as early as 1994, seemed to perfectly encapsulate her newfound freedom, especially after she unshackled herself from the restrictions of the Royal Family. The accompanying *Vogue* editorial read, "Millions rarely heard her speak. Clothes were her vocabulary, a huge factor in her tremendous allure—and from faltering pidgin, she gradually became one of the most fluent fashion speakers of our time."[20]

Alongside this increasing glamorization of Diana lurked the darker side of the tabloid press. Rupert Murdoch, a fierce antimonarchist, was in charge of *News of the World* and the *Sun* newspapers, and did not believe the Royal Family should enjoy any special immunity or respect from the press. The happily-ever-after myth that had accompanied the wedding fever was short lived. Even when Diana was pregnant with Prince William in 1982, the *Sun* was running headlines like "A Public Bust-up!" and "Pregnant Di Falls Down Stairs." It even speculated, "Are Charles and Diana Moving Apart?" These types of headlines continued throughout that year, contributing to an ever-increasing sense of royal fiasco rather than familial harmony. They included, "Loveless Marriage," "Disco Diana Dumps Charles, Old Flame the Prince Won't Forget," and "Fears for Di's Health." Not even the birth of then third-in-line to the throne Prince Harry in 1984 could distract the press for long. By 1987, the tabloids were regularly commenting on the number of days the couple spent apart, and rumors were rife of a rift in their relationship.

Occasionally, Diana was idealized in her archetypal role as mother, particularly in women's magazines or celebrity-focused ones, such as *Hello*. Although this angle praised her devotion to her children and their informal upbringing, neither these images nor those of her charity work were enough to counter the scandalous tabloid depictions. The fairy-tale myth was left far behind; these latter portrayals presented a Diana who was superficial and volatile, a depiction that culminated in the notorious Squidgy Tapes, revealed by the *Sun* in 1992. Referred to as "Squidgygate" (a term evoking the Watergate scandal of the Nixon era in the 1970s), these were recorded telephone conversations between James Gilbey and Diana in 1989 that suggested an intimate relationship. In the course of these conversations, Gilbey used "Squidgy" and "Squidge" as pet names for Diana. Apart from the affection they revealed, the tapes offered many insights into Diana's hostility toward Charles and the Royal Family (she famously describes them on the tapes as "this fucking family").

The tapes were deemed to be of such a sensitive nature that even the anti-monarchist *Sun* waited three years to publish them and did so only when Charles and Diana's marriage was definitely on the rocks. In the meantime, Charles became the central figure of his own scandal, dubbed "Camillagate," later the same year. The *Daily Mirror* printed a telephone conversation with Camilla Parker Bowles during which he famously joked that he might come back as a Tampax, while they bantered about how he might find a way to live inside Camilla's trousers. No doubt, these events (as well as the fire at Windsor Castle) contributed to the Queen noting in her speech on November 24, 1992, that the year had been an "Annus Horribilus."

The year also saw the unfolding of a long list of royal scandals: Princess Anne divorced Captain Mark Phillips, Prince Andrew separated from his wife Sarah (Fergie), who was photographed having her toes sucked by her financial adviser, and Lady Colin Campbell detailed Diana's relationships with four men in *Diana in Private: The Princess Nobody Knows,* serialized in the *Daily Mirror.* Worst of all, Andrew Morton published his bombshell, *Diana: Her True Story,* detailing her attempted suicides, depression, and instability; it was serialized in the *Sunday Times.*[21] The Royal Family had now officially morphed into the royal soap opera, as Prince Charles insightfully quipped to BBC presenter and journalist Jeremy Paxman.[22]

Without a doubt, during the 1990s many aspects of the Royal Family narrative were akin to the soap-opera genre.[23] Diana was the leading lady in this serial, which had the world as its audience, a world that eagerly awaited each new episode. Christine Geraghty has gone so far as to assert that the soap opera is the principal style of narrative through which the Diana phenomenon can be understood and that it can also be used to understand reactions to her death.[24] Soap operas generate "interpretive communities," where members share a common understanding of the codes of the genre and experience similar emotions and fantasies because they interpret the narratives in a common way. Key characteristics of the soap-opera genre suggest immedi-

TABLE 2 Soap Opera Characteristics and Parallels with Diana's life

Soap Opera	Diana's Life
Audience is mainly female	Diana's following was overwhelmingly female[a]
Story lines are continuous; there is no ending as such to the overall drama	The many conspiracy theories around Diana's death mean the drama lives on
Many different stories interweave around a core cluster of characters, while others come and go	Diana's various love affairs
The main characters are often searching for life partners	True for Diana and Charles
Women play major roles and are permitted to be seen as strong characters	Diana epitomizes this perception
Traditional, patriarchal values are challenged by the sanctioning of a feminine sphere where conversation, empathy, and emotions prevail	Diana shook the British establishment by privileging her emotions
The genre permits its heroines not to be perfect; they are allowed to be fallible and change attitudes as they experience crises and conflicts	With her confessed bulimia, as well as her suicide attempts, Diana exposed her vulnerability and endured many crises

[a] William J. Brown, Michael D. Basil, and Mihai C. Bocarnea, "Social Influence of an International Celebrity: Responses to the Death of Princess Diana," *Journal of Communication* 53, no. 4 (Dec. 2003): 587–605.

ate parallels with Diana's life (see table 2). According to Geraghty, these characteristics explain why Diana built such powerful empathy with her audience, an interpretive community of readers composed of women ranging from their thirties to their fifties who could identify with the adversities and setbacks Diana had to cope with and overcome.[25]

In addition, soap operas often contain melodramatic plots, and Diana's life clearly did as well, not the least of which was the fact that her narrative culminated in a tragic youthful death. Ien Ang conducted a study of the soap opera *Dallas* and found that viewers identified on an emotional level with the actions portrayed rather than with the rich lifestyles, which were, after all, inaccessible to most.[26] The royal soap opera and *Dallas* share many narrative tensions between the requirements of love and duty, together with an emphasis on the complexities of sexual relationships.[27] Ang refers to this as "emotional realism" and suggests that soap operas work because they engender "a structure of feeling" where emotions are constantly on a roller-coaster ride that fluctuates between happiness and sadness. He argues that this tension pleases viewers.

Like the alcoholic Sue Ellen in *Dallas* trapped on the Southfork ranch with her oppressive husband, J. R. Ewing, Diana can be seen as the melodramatic, albeit flawed, heroine of the Royal Family soap, trapped and powerless in her circumstances.[28] This emotional identification also explains how even with Diana's privileged background people could still identify with her.

In December 1992, a month after the Queen's "Annus Horribilus" speech, Charles and Diana officially separated; they finally divorced in 1996. The ripples from the Morton book, on which Diana had secretly cooperated, had been far reaching, gaining widespread support for the underdog position she espoused. Morton reinforced this persona by documenting her side of living in a loveless marriage within the restrictive formalities of monarchical traditions. It was a highly emotionally charged book. Resonating with many, it reinforced the soap-opera comparison.

As a result, Charles's image suffered badly, as "the people" tended to side with Diana. In 1993, after their separation, the Royal Family soap opera stepped up the pace in what Morton referred to as the "Battle of the Waleses" in his follow-up book, *Diana: Her True Story in Her Own Words.*[29] Both Charles and Diana attempted to win the hearts and minds of the public. The battleground was space and airtime in the media. Where the prince could rely on a public relations team of around nine official and unofficial professionals, Diana employed only a part-time press officer. As a result, she certainly occupied the disadvantaged underdog position, and her vulnerability in terms of managing the media showed.

More unfavorable press reports surfaced as she moved from one scandal to the next, with rumors of affairs with married men, such as Will Carling (a former English rugby captain) and Oliver Hoare (an English art expert and gallery owner). The year 1993 proved overwhelming for Diana, and she tried to withdraw from the public eye, asking the media for time and space. The press afforded her little sympathy, however, perceiving that she was happy to make use of the institution when it suited her aims. Journalists and paparazzi continued to bombard her at every available photo opportunity.

The royal soap continued in 1994 with Charles's famous documentary, *Prince Charles: The Private Man, the Public Role.* The Prince was interviewed by Jonathan Dimbleby, who had released a sympathetic biography that same year.[30] During the interview, Charles admitted his adultery with Camilla Parker Bowles, although he claimed it occurred only after the marriage had irretrievably broken down. The interview was staged to show his side of the story and to rehabilitate his rather tarnished image in the public eye.

The following year Diana retaliated, causing a much greater media furor in a rival interview on BBC with Martin Bashir. Broadcast to hundreds of millions of people on November 20, 1995, Diana shocked the British establishment by talking on a range of topics that were "intimately personal and sensitive,"[31] an approach not usually adopted by public figures in Britain, least of all members of the Royal Family. Yet it is scarcely surprising that Diana felt she had to tell her side of the story. Earlier that year, her reputation had been further damaged when James Hewitt, a dashing young army captain with whom she had had a five-year affair, gave a tasteless account of their relationship in the book *Princess in Love*.[32] Predictably, he positioned himself as the romantic hero and Diana as a predator who pursued him despite his reservations.

Perceived by her fans as cornered on all sides—by her husband, her ex-lover, the media, and wider institutional forces—Diana appeared to many to be in a powerless position, which resonated with a great many women. The interview was her way of taking back control. Against all professional advice, she went ahead with an interview that was hugely successful in winning over the hearts and minds of the public, as she bared her soul to Bashir.[33] She admitted her affair with Hewitt and freely discussed her bulimia, depression, and self-loathing, endearing herself to many women who, like her, found themselves trapped in similar emotionally debilitating situations. During the hour-long interview, Diana was transformed into their avenging angel, as she constructed herself as the innocent victim of circumstance, overwhelmed by the strength of what she called the "enemy" (Prince Charles and his advisers). Referring to herself in the third and the first person, she famously declared, "She won't go quietly, that's the problem, I'll fight to the end because I believe I still have a role to play and I've got two children to bring up." She struck a further chord, highlighting that "there were three of us in this marriage, so it was a bit crowded," and claimed the emotional high ground in her bid to be "queen of people's hearts." On account of this interview, she was named "Woman of the Year" by *Stern* (a German weekly) as well as *Tagesspiegel* (a German daily). Incongruous as it may seem, this publication even went so far as to rank her interview alongside Winston Churchill's famous "Finest Hour" speech in 1940 as one of the high points in BBC history.[34]

Diana's interview with Bashir marks a pivotal moment not only in the introduction of sexual politics into the Royal Family, but also in taking the monarchy to task and trying to hold it accountable for its actions.

Accordingly, some see Diana as a feminist figure, the strong soap-opera heroine who triumphs over a patriarchal value system (ironically, headed by a woman since 1952) by leveraging the feminine values of emotion and empathy.[35] In contrast, other feminist scholars highlight the unacknowledged underpinning assumptions about whiteness, heterosexuality, and middle-class identity embedded in representations of Diana's femininity.[36] For this latter group, Diana espouses a traditionalist femininity: the caring, nurturing mother image that reinforces essentialist and biologically determined notions of womanhood and women's place.[37]

There can be no doubt, however, that the Queen did not share any feminist interpretation of the interview, favorable or otherwise. Widely rumored to be horrified by Diana's confessional outpourings together with her allegation that Charles was not fit to be king, the Queen instructed the couple to divorce as soon as possible.[38] It is still strongly believed that she has not forgiven the BBC for airing the damaging interview.[39] The divorce took place on August 28, 1996, setting Diana adrift from any formal position in the Royal Family and stripping her of the title "Her Royal Highness" (HRH). Thereafter, she would be known as Diana, Princess of Wales.

In the year leading up to her death, Diana tried hard to reinvent her public image by focusing attention on her charity work, most notably through her role in the efforts against land mines, which made her a quasi-political campaigner. Yet the tabloid press continued to hound her, shaping her life—and more poignantly, her death—with little consideration for the person behind the image or the subject within the object. Five weeks before her death, the *Observer* featured an article entitled "A Trash Icon for Our Times," which critiqued the image of Diana comforting Elton John at the funeral of fashion designer Gianni Versace. The article dubbed the pair "Di and Dwight," referring to the singer's real middle name, and argued that the image encapsulated the hollowness and ephemerality of celebrity culture.[40] Furthermore, the man frequently referred to in media circles as the love of Diana's life, London heart surgeon Dr. Hasnat Khan, could not cope with the media pressure and ended their love affair in early 1997. Reportedly on the rebound from him, she sought solace with Dodi Fayed, the son of Mohamed Al-Fayed, the owner of Harrods who had twice been denied British citizenship. Diana's relationships with Muslim men further heightened her subversive image and her perceived power to challenge tradition.

Almost a year to the day after her final divorce decree was granted, and as they sought to escape the pursuing paparazzi, Diana was fatally injured in a car crash with Dodi Fayed in the Pont d'Alma tunnel in Paris on August 31, 1997. She died a few hours later in the early hours of the morning, and the Sunday newspapers had already gone to press. The papers scrambled to recall headlines that were now too unseemly given the tragic turn of events, but some could not be changed in time. The *News of the World* featured the unfortunate headline "Troubled Prince William Will Today Demand That His Mother Princess Diana Dump Her Playboy Love," and an American weekly, the *National Enquirer,* ran "Di Goes Sex Mad."[41] Overnight, Diana became remythologized, her fall from grace since her fairy-tale wedding rewritten in the public imagination to accord her the status of saint. She became "England's Rose" who cared for those the world had forgotten, the sick and needy, the homeless, AIDS sufferers, and land mine victims. Her image became more akin to that of a global healer,[42] a Mother Teresa goddess as opposed to a sex goddess, an image now reconfigured as a symbol of emotional authenticity rather than shallowness. Like so many before her (Marilyn Monroe, Elvis Presley, James Dean, Jimi Hendrix, John Lennon, John F. Kennedy, and Martin Luther King, Jr., to name but a few), her tragic young death ensured her iconic position and subsequent sacralization in popular culture.

To say the world was shocked is an extreme understatement. Reactions to her death and the huge outpourings of grief that ensued have been extensively documented and analyzed over the years. Elton John's "Candle in the Wind," which he rewrote to commemorate Diana and performed at her funeral, remains one of the world's best-selling singles, with estimated sales of 37 million copies.[43] Like other major tragedies, most people can recall where they were when they heard the news, and the emotions they experienced. Diffusion of the news did not follow the usual pattern of slow-then-rapid dissemination. It was steep from the start, reflecting the high emotional response; the more upset people felt, the more likely they were to pass on the news.[44] It was widely acknowledged that there were unprecedented outpourings of public emotion, epitomized by the ever-growing sea of flowers that encircled the gates of Kensington Palace. Sociologist Frank Furedi argues that what he describes as a therapeutic culture, the "letting-it-all-hang-out" ethos of the United States, has also shaped contemporary British culture and helps to explain the astonishing levels of public mourning.[45] Others refer to it as "a collective moment of madness" when Britain lost its grip and became "like a mawkish, self-pitying, teenage entry in a diary," caught up in an uncharacteristic "outburst of mass hysteria."[46] The media was widely blamed for these seemingly very un-British displays of public emotion.

But was this outpouring of grief for a beautiful young princess really as unique as commentators and commemorators have claimed? In fact, almost two centuries before, the British public had engaged in unprecedented levels of public mourning for another princess, Charlotte Augusta. The granddaughter of George III, Charlotte was heiress presumptive to the throne.* Beautiful, youthful, and intelligent, many considered her to be the potential savior of the monarchy, after her grandfather's long reign and descent into madness and the lifestyle of debauchery and dilettantism favored by her father, the Prince Regent.[47] On November 6, 1817, one day after giving birth to a stillborn son, Charlotte succumbed to complications.[48] In this tragic royal death, public grief served a social function by eroding distinctions among individuals, the collective community, and the object of mourning, much the same way it did when Diana died.[49]

Despite the very different eras in which they lived, there are many fascinating parallels between these two princesses. Charlotte's marriage to Prince Leopold of Saxe-Coburg (uncle of both Queen Victoria and Prince Albert) in 1816 also was imbued with a fairy-tale aura, bringing hope to the British public at a time when the monarchy was unpopular and out of touch with its people. Reinforcing the family values instigated by her grandfather, George III, the couple was seen as a model for the emergent bourgeois family of the time, in sharp contrast to the decadence of her father. Charlotte's death, like Diana's, engendered elaborate displays of public mourning that also accorded her iconic status. Many shops and inns closed for the entire seventeen days between her death and her burial. Openly grieving crowds lined the streets for her funeral, which created its own spectacle throughout the day, culminating at night with a moving torch-lit procession joined by many mourners. Charlotte too was immortalized in the proliferation of commemorative items immediately after her death, including memorial cards, coins, poems, portraits, ceramics, and textiles. Her depiction as "Albion's Rose" (for the oldest known name of the island of Great Britain) foreshadows Diana's appellation as "England's Rose" (the rose is also the symbol of the Princess of Wales) by almost two hundred years.

---

* An heir or heiress presumptive is next in line for the throne after the monarch; accession is assumed unless someone is born with a stronger claim by blood to the throne.

Mythologized through the poetry and prose of the time as a "moral exemplar,"[50] Charlotte's history was rewritten to endow her with many powerful symbolic and allegorical properties, as characterized in the white marble memorial that graces her burial site in St. George's Chapel at Windsor Castle, unveiled seven years after her death. As beloved as she was, the call for public subscriptions to help pay for the memorial engendered criticism; one person wrote that the money was better spent on allowing ordinary children to attend the ballet.[51] Citizens expressed their feelings for Charlotte through their poems, in parallel to the electronic memorials that flourish on the Internet to commemorate Diana.[52] The media may have changed, but the human motivation remains constant: the need to make sense of cruel twists of fate and to find transcendental values in those we admire.

Worldwide, 2.5 billion people watched Diana's funeral in 1997, making it the most widely viewed spectacle in human history.[53] Obviously, with no mass media in existence at the time, Princess Charlotte's event could not have spurred such a global response. Made possible by a sophisticated worldwide telecommunications network, the transmission of Diana's funeral reached two hundred countries in forty-four languages.[54] More than one million mourners lined the three-mile funeral route.[55] A colleague of ours, Kent Drummond, was one of them, and shared his moving memories of the occasion:

By the time Diana's procession actually started, most of us had been standing for eight hours. We were shaking and dehydrated. We knew from the radio that the cortege had left Kensington Palace. Shrieks and wails were coming out of the radio. When the procession began moving up the Mall, the outpouring of grief was like a tidal wave sweeping up from Buckingham Palace. We were all engulfed in it; no one could escape it. As I watched the casket move past, only ten feet away, I started sobbing uncontrollably. Everyone was crying. The women were weeping openly, and the men were crying softly. I looked up and saw the card with "Mummy" on it and I thought my heart would break. Then to see Charles, Philip, the Earl Spencer, and William and Harry walking behind the casket was more than anyone could take. They looked straight ahead and walked with such strength and dignity. And they looked unbearably sad. I thought, here are the most famous people in the world; they can have anything they want, but they still suffer loss, and they still have to go on. My heart went out to them. After they passed by, we cried even harder. That lasted for about twenty minutes.

Overall, it is estimated that two million people made pilgrimages to London to pay their respects to Diana; many contributed to the sea of flowers at Kensington Palace and queued for up to ten hours to sign the books of condolence at St. James's Palace. Of course, Margaret Tyler was one of the mourners. On the day of Diana's death, many maintained all-night vigils outside the gates at Kensington Palace. As night fell, the floral carpet transformed into a forest of flickering flames from myriad tea lights placed among the tributes, arranged as personalized shrines that mourners tended. Some stayed for several consecutive nights.

In total, the public mourning for Diana lasted six days. Newsreels of interviews with mourners at the time give insights into the public's feelings: "Her imperfections were what made her perfect—she shared her imperfections. She wasn't trying to be a saint, she was just a human being." "She was the only woman of prominence on the world stage expressing womanly emotions." "You've got to come, just to be here."[56] These expressions reveal the close identification her followers felt with her, as well as the need to engage in the embodied experience of collective mourning and to share the overwhelming silence of grief that dominated Kensington Palace at that time.

These public displays of emotion were in sharp contrast to the behavior of the Royal Family, who remained at Balmoral to protect William and Harry from the headlines and conduct their mourning in private. The discrepancy between the Queen and her public at this time has been widely analyzed, particularly in Helen Mirren's moving portrayal of her in *The Queen,* which documents her dilemmas at this time. Considered the worst crisis of her reign (as support for the monarchy fell to an all-time low), the Queen was finally persuaded of the need to return to London and speak to her public. It was left to the prime minister, Tony Blair, a master of the politics of emotion, to convey the public's sentiments of the time. He rightly intuited that the phrase "the People's Princess" captured the ethos of what Diana meant to mourners. The title perfectly summed up Diana's accessibility to a wide audience, through the many faces she created and sustained through the media—princess, celebrity, everywoman, confessor, mother, victim, heroine, and manipulator.

All of Diana's different personas allowed people to develop what media scholars describe as "parasocial relationships" with her, related to our earlier discussion of the appeal of human brands. These relationships are one-sided, occurring when fans create bonds of intimacy with celebrities via the media rather than through physical social interaction. Yet, despite their inherent fantasy nature, viewers perceive such bonds as very real,[57] and they become part of a person's "extended self,"[58] like other intimate relationships with family, friends, and lovers.

Reminiscent of our previous discussions of the Royal Family's fairy-tale-turned-soap-opera, we can see how the death of its much beloved heroine and main character brought the narrative to an abrupt end and left its audience feeling bereft and bereaved. Seen from this perspective, mourners were acknowledging that something that had become part of their daily or weekly routine was no longer there; an important piece of their everyday life was now missing. The nature of parasocial relationships is a passionate one. When favorite soap operas conclude, their viewers frequently mourn and campaign to save them, as they do with other favorite cultural products, brands, or stores that change or disappear. In the case of Diana, the narrative was complicated by the fact that many ordinary people wrote themselves into the script, acknowledging their own culpability for her death. This was evidenced on messages accompanying flowers that expressed feelings of guilt that the authors had not sufficiently appreciated Diana while she lived and had contributed to her death by avidly consuming the media whose paparazzi ultimately killed her.

The desire to continue the soap-opera narrative may help explain the many conspiracy theories that have flourished since her death. Although such theories are not particularly new in popular culture,[59] there is no doubt that contemporary social media and Internet technologies have facilitated their circulation to a much wider audience than was previously possible. Conspiracy theories still proliferate around other legendary figures, such as John F. Kennedy and Marilyn Monroe, so it is scarcely surprising that they emerged around the death of Diana. Part of their appeal stems from the fact that it is difficult for people to acknowledge that such an ordinary event (a car crash with a drunken driver) could have killed someone so extraordinary. People want to believe that a more powerful, sinister force was behind the tragedy, because it would make life seem less random and senseless. Conspiracy theories link to the age-old human fascination with the occult and supernatural, while reflecting increasing uncertainties in everyday life that stem from the global economy, paradoxes of technological and scientific progress, and our lack of control over our everyday lives.[60]

Regardless of whether these theories simply reflect an age of anxiety, speculative theories on Diana's death flourish on the Internet (websites, Facebook, blogs, and YouTube videos) and on TV mystery channels, as well as in books and films. Many are fascinating, drawing the reader quickly into webs of supposition and intrigue that satisfy the human mind's fascination with patterns and the need to make sense of the inexplicable. Books range from tough investigative-style journalism, such as *Princess Diana: The Evidence* by Jon King and John Beveridge,[61] who have always maintained they were told of a plot a week before the crash, to the more bizarre meanderings of David Icke. In *The Biggest Secret: The Book That Will Change the World*,[62] he alleges that the Royal Family's bloodline can be traced to a reptilian race from outer space and that Diana's death was a ritual sacrifice.

Mohamed Al-Fayed, father of Diana's boyfriend Dodi, is one of the main perpetrators of conspiracy theories and is said to have spent over £5 million ($7.5 million) on a campaign that accuses the Royal Family of commissioning the British Secret Services to instigate her death.[63] Al-Fayed financed the documentary *Unlawful Killing*, which premiered at the Cannes Film Festival in 2011 and featured his accusations. These included referring to the Royal Family as "gangsters in tiaras," as well as likening the Duke of Edinburgh to the English mass murderer Fred West.[64] The film was subsequently banned in Britain. Some contend that Al-Fayed went to these lengths to cover up his own culpability in the event, as he had authorized his chief of security to drive Diana and Dodi although his employee did not possess the license required to operate that particular model of Mercedes.[65] Yet it is certain that many people believe these theories. Suspicions are further fueled by the fact that ten months before her death, Diana wrote a letter describing a possible plot by Charles to murder her by tampering with the brakes of her car. Indeed, as recently as 2011, around one-third of those polled in a British survey believed Diana was murdered.[66] Even in August 2013, prior to the sixteenth anniversary of her death, reports were circulating of a new investigation into her death by London metropolitan police.

Some of the messages hung on the gates of Kensington Palace on the fifteenth anniversary of Diana's death in 2012 also reflected beliefs in such conspiracies. One read, "It was a well-planned accident," a viewpoint shared by some followers (although by no means all) who make the ritual visit every year. As we have noted, on this day, the gates become a sacred spot once again, decorated with floral tributes, personal messages to Diana, and an array of imaginative collages of her life and work created by individuals or groups (figure 14). Given Margaret Tyler's devotion to the Royal Family, but especially to Diana, it is not surprising that she has marked every anniversary of Diana's death at "the Gates."

FIGURE 14. Diana tributes at Kensington Palace. Photo by Pauline Maclaran.

Another site where Diana is fondly remembered is her burial place. Althorp, in Northamptonshire, has been the stately home of the Spencer family for nearly five hundred years and is the current residence of Charles, the 9th Earl Spencer, Diana's younger brother. He opens his home to the public during August each year and on other specific dates (mainly Sundays). Tens of thousands of tourists and day-trippers have visited the estate, principally to see where Diana was laid to rest on a small, heavily wooded isle in the middle of a lake and to pay their respects at the lakeside summerhouse dedicated to her memory. Referred to as the Diana Memorial Temple (figure 15), it is now interpreted as a site of modern pilgrimage, with up to 2,500 people a day visiting during the summer.[67]

Althorp also hosted the exhibition *Diana—a Celebration,* seen by over one million visitors, until August 2013, when the Earl decided to close that part of the Althorp experience for good. The exhibition regularly toured North America, where Diana has her biggest following, and was a major attraction at locations such as the Mall of America in Minnesota, where it ran for much of 2012. Her wedding dress was a focal point for this exhibition, which filled nine galleries and contained 150 objects. The tour ended in August 2014, when, in accordance with Diana's will, the items were returned to her sons.

We visited the exhibition at Althorp before it closed (as well as when it toured in Toronto in 2005) and saw many of Diana's personal artifacts, clothes (including her famous land mines outfit), school reports, childhood

FIGURE 15. Diana Memorial Temple, Althorp. Photo by Cele Otnes.

photographs, and letters. In a room dedicated to her charity and humanitarian works, three large screens brought her back to life as they replayed
moving moments between Diana and the many sufferers she touched (literally and metaphorically). In contrast, an adjoining darkened room created a
somber atmosphere as visitors stood mesmerized before a large screen that
depicted her funeral cortege silently processing toward Westminster Abbey,
with close-ups of the grieving public. Dominated by an enormous glass book-
case covering one wall that contained condolence books from 125 nations,
the last room reminded visitors of the universal fascination with Diana. In
confirmation of this fact, during our visit a group of Indonesian tourists having their photos taken at the Diana Temple spoke about her popularity in
their country and how it is widely believed that Charles had wronged her.

Tourist websites such as *City Discovery* offer special tour packages around London that incorporate key sites associated with Diana. These include Kensington Palace, St. Paul's Cathedral, and Westminster Abbey, as well as the flat (apartment) where she lived prior to marrying, the kindergarten where she worked, and the Chelsea gym where some of her famous trysts occurred. Another key site on these tours is the Princess Diana Memorial Fountain, set in Hyde Park and made from 545 pieces of Cornish granite, which was opened by the Queen in 2004 (albeit £2 million over budget).

Followers often seek out two memorials to Diana and Dodi at London's most famous department store, Harrods, owned by Mohamed Al-Fayed until 2010. The first of these, dating from 1998, is on the lower ground floor and comprises a candlelit shrine on which portraits of the couple are set above a fountain that flows continuously. In its midst is an acrylic pyramid protecting a wine glass smudged with Diana's lipstick from her last dinner with Dodi at the Ritz Hotel, and a ring Mohamed Al-Fayed alleged to be the engagement ring Dodi intended to give Diana. The second memorial, a much more ambitious one built in 2005, is beside the Egyptian escalator. It features a life-size bronze statue of the couple gazing into each other's eyes as they release a giant albatross, a bird said to symbolize the Holy Spirit, into the sky. Entitled "Innocent Victims," this grandiose tribute mythologizes the couple while evoking and perpetuating the conspiracy theories around their death. In relation to Diana and Dodi's death, the Pont d'Alma Tunnel in Paris has become something of a tourist attraction, associated with morbid tourism and the contemporary urge to visit places where accidents or disasters have occurred, such as Ground Zero in New York City.

Investing in Princess Diana memorabilia remains a thriving business, and indeed, there are fortunes to be made in the sale of her dresses alone. Shortly before her death, Diana initiated the market for her dresses by auctioning seventy-nine of them. These included the famous "Travolta" dress, a stunning blue velvet ball gown she wore to a White House gala dinner in 1985, where she took the floor to dance with John Travolta and won the hearts of Americans. Diana gave her son William credit for suggesting she auction some dresses to raise money for charity. She loved the idea, and the auction, held at Christie's New York, attracted a crowd of 1,100 and raised £5.76 million ($8.4 million) for AIDS and breast cancer charities. The "Travolta" dress fetched the highest bid of £222,500 ($338,250).[68]

Pat Kerr Tigrett, a wedding dress designer married to a multimillionaire, is a high-end collector of Royal Family textiles dating back to the sixteenth century; she purchased four of Diana's gowns at this auction for around £150,000 ($225,000). After Diana's death, she fielded offers from around the world of one million dollars for each.[69] Although perhaps an overestimation of their value (two dresses in this initial collection were resold for £276,000 [$414,000] in 2011),[70] there is no doubt that a Diana dress can fetch a "princessly" sum. The dress she wore for her first official function sold for £192,000 ($288,000) in 2012, around four times the estimated selling price of £50,000 ($75,000).[71] In the same year, designer Elizabeth Emanuel's five-page scrapbook, containing sample fabrics and watercolor sketches of the wedding dress, sold at auction in the UK for £3,194 ($4,791). The year before that, Diana's "back-up" wedding dress and shoes, exact replicas made in case anything should go wrong, sold for £84,000 ($126,000).[72]

Another high-end collector from Las Vegas, "Maria," described herself to us as a "fringe member" of the Diana Circle. She visited the gates of Kensington Palace on the tenth anniversary of Diana's death, and two of her American friends attend annually. Testifying to the quasi-religious significance of these collections, her husband refers to her Diana room as "the shrine." Here, she keeps a treasured collection of Diana dresses in miniature, with each scrupulously replicated in one-fifth scale. Seventy-nine of these are replicas of the Christie's auction dresses; these are supplemented with 120 additional miniature designs. To complete Maria's exhibition, the cornice around the room displays a collection of one hundred Diana commemorative plates. Her collection also now includes memorabilia of William and Kate and a Diamond Jubilee corner.

Pat, Eva, Maria, Margaret, and many collectors like them cherish Diana through the objects they commission, create, or preserve, and the activities they pursue to remember her, such as buying her items at auction or making pilgrimages to Kensington Palace. As such, Diana continues to be an important part of their lives as they create, consume, and re-create a continual flow of memories as personalized narratives, intertwining these with their own life stories and interpretations of what Diana meant to them. On social media sites, many others preserve Diana's memory with pages dedicated to her life and work, as well as annual postings of tributes to mark her death or speculate on its circumstances.

However, Diana's presence is felt not just through memorabilia, tributes, or the continual rehashing of conspiracy theories around her death, but most visibly as the woman who gave birth to two sons, one the heir presumptive to the throne. Many, like Margaret and her friends, see both William and Harry as continuing Diana's story, infusing a much more humane and modern face into the traditions of the Royal Family. Remembered in the public imagination for her powerful mixture of glamour, tragedy, and mystery, Diana may be best remembered for encouraging the monarchy to demonstrate more emotional sensitivity to its public.

FIVE

Pomp and Popcorn

THE BRITISH ROYAL FAMILY ON STAGE AND SCREEN

As we have already made clear, Margaret Tyler loves everything about the Royal Family and avidly consumes media representations of them, whether flattering or otherwise. The richness of royal images in all their many media guises only serves to make her feel closer to what has now become her extended family. Her *Spitting Image* slippers of the Queen and Prince Philip nestle on her floor amid more respectful collector's items (figure 16). They are given equal pride of place despite the fact that this highly popular satirical puppet show relentlessly poked fun at the Royal Family and no doubt contributed much to their soap-opera image during the 1980s and 1990s. Yet Margaret treasures these slippers as a much-loved reference to popular culture, laughing at these images in the gentle way one might tease a friend or family member.

In the last chapter, we explored the power of media images, particularly the press, in relation to Diana. This chapter concentrates on theater, film, and television portrayals of the monarchy more generally, and how these are marketed to and ultimately consumed by the general public. Our media gaze takes us back as far as the time of Shakespeare, as well as exploring contemporary media representations of the Royal Family and their popularization in film and television.

William Shakespeare, regarded by many as "England's cultural figurehead" and the world's greatest playwright, is as crucial as the Royal Family to many people's sense of British heritage.[1] Many English tourist trails list both his birthplace at Stratford-upon-Avon and the Globe Theatre, located on London's South Bank, alongside their descriptions of Buckingham Palace and other key royal sites. But the connections between the two grow stronger when we acknowledge Shakespeare as the first to successfully

FIGURE 16. *Spitting Image* slippers. Photo by Pauline Maclaran.

dramatize the monarchy for a mass audience. Thanks to Elizabeth I's enjoyment of dramatic entertainments, as well as the revenues they generated for her government, London's playhouses and the theater industry they supported were in high demand during the Elizabethan era.[2] The Red Lion Theatre in Whitechapel, built in 1567, was the first structure in the city specifically built for that purpose.[3] It is estimated that between that time and 1642, when the Puritans closed all the theaters, 50 million paying customers (ten times London's population during the period) attended performances in the city.[4]

Historical drama, the main genre to include depictions of royalty, traces its origins to the chronicle-history plays of the 1580s, which portrayed key events during the reign of a particular English monarch. Examples include *The Famous Victories of Henry the Fifth*, *The Troublesome Raigne of John King of England*, and *The True Tragedie of Richard III*. This type of play resulted from renewed pride in England's greatness. The war against Spain, culminating with the victory over the Armada in 1588, awakened a sense of national pride among the English citizenry. As a result, people wanted to know more about the history of their nation. The chronicle-history play itself evolved from morality plays in the Middle Ages and often sought to fulfill a didactic purpose, with allegorical characters designed to teach subjects obedience to their king. These plays typically portrayed the undesirable consequences of rebelling against the monarch and emphasized the nation's welfare by highlighting how the past could inform the present. But because it was initially conceived to convey information rather than to engage the audience with its dramatic effect, the chronicle-history play lacked creative characterization or plot development. Overall, it represented a fairly uninspiring theatrical form—until Shakespeare arrived on the scene.

Like other Elizabethan dramatists, Shakespeare drew his source material from two key chronicles of the time, namely Edward Hall's (1542) *The Union of the Two Noble and Illustre Famelies of Lancastre & Yorke* and the *Chronicles of England, Scotlande, and Irelande* of Raphael Holinshed. It was Shakespeare, however, who turned the chronicle-history play into a more powerful dramatic format. Unlike his fellow playwrights, who conveyed historical fact in disjointed episodic acts, he dared to value artistic integrity over historical literalism. Most significantly, he brought his characters to life by personalizing their struggles and depicting them as individual men and women who experienced emotional conflicts to which his audiences could relate. For example, at the heart of *Henry IV Parts 1 and 2* lies the gripping portrayal of an emotionally turbulent father-son relationship.

Despite Shakespeare's overriding quest for artistic integrity, he was nonetheless mindful of the need to pay homage to Queen Elizabeth I, his patron.[5] Thus, his plays paid tribute to the monarchy to gain her favor and included no open criticism. However, he sometimes did take such a position in covert ways, even falling foul of Elizabethan censorship at times. The box office hit *Shakespeare in Love* highlights this patron-playwright relationship in an otherwise pure fantasy film that speculates on the emotional aspects of Shakespeare's life, about which little is known. In the film, Elizabeth I (played by Dame Judi Dench) is an ardent admirer of the playwright and frequents the theater to see his plays.

Although in total Shakespeare wrote ten plays on English monarchs, his eight plays depicting the Plantagenet kings have made the greatest impact on British culture: *Richard II, Henry IV Parts 1 and 2, Henry V, Henry VI Parts 1, 2, and 3,* and *Richard III.** He also wrote two other royal plays,

---

* We list these here in chronological order of the kings' reigns, rather than in the order in which Shakespeare wrote them.

King John and *Henry VIII*, but these are much less widely known, having failed to capture the popular imagination as the other eight have done.[6] Shakespeare's Plantagenet plays are responsible for the ways most of us think about those periods of history and leaders of the time. Shakespearean scholar Peter Saccio notes, "He has etched upon the common memory the graceful fecklessness of Richard II, the exuberant heroism of Henry V, the dazzling villainy of Richard III."[7]

In general, people expect Shakespeare's plays to offer insights into human nature, and his royal portrayals excel in this respect. Shakespearean kings wrestle with many internal conflicts and passions, as well as with external affairs that affect their rule of the country. This emotional realism, juxtaposed as it is with the mystique of the monarchy, explains why the Plantagenet plays have found eager audiences throughout the last four centuries, and why they are still hugely popular today. Furthermore, the many quotes emanating from these plays that have found their way into our language as everyday expressions testify to Shakespeare's enormous cultural influence on the English-speaking world. Table 3 summarizes the key themes, quotes, film and TV productions, and stars of each Plantagenet play.

Further testifying to the importance and influence of Shakespearean royal portrayals on perceptions of British monarchic heritage is the fact that during World War II, Prime Minister Winston Churchill's government funded the 1944 film production of *Henry V,* starring Laurence Olivier. It was devised as a propaganda device to boost morale during the crucial war years, because it shows a victorious England against all odds at the Battle of Agincourt in 1415. The power of this drama continues to engage audiences. *Henry V*'s latest production featured in the highly publicized 2012 BBC-TV miniseries *The Hollow Crown,* which also offered renditions of *Henry IV Part 1, Henry IV Part 2,* and *Richard II.*

As we will discuss shortly, even if they prove to be blockbusters, contemporary on-screen royal representations often face criticism for their historical inaccuracies and distortions of past events. But this is not a new phenomenon; Shakespeare frequently used poetic license to collapse time, altering historic facts to create or increase dramatic tension. In so doing, he emphasized emotional authenticity and relationship development, key elements that explain his enduring appeal.

Apart from his quest to encapsulate deeper human desires and drives in his characters, Shakespeare also altered historical fact to avoid contradicting the established accounts of the time. History is usually written by the

TABLE 3 Shakespeare's Plantagenet Plays

Key Themes and Quotes

Play Title	Key Themes and Monarchy Portrayals	Famous Quotes	Film and TV Productions/Actor Playing King
Richard II	The nature of kingship. Central theme: whether Richard is deposed by Bolingbroke or is responsible for his own fate. Examines the conflict between legal and divine right to rule, with Richard portrayed as weak and ineffective. Shakespeare's most politically controversial play.	Old John of Gaunt, time-honoured Lancaster. (Act I, Scene I) Teach thy necessity to reason thus; There is no virtue like necessity. (Act I, Scene III)	*An Age of Kings* (UK, TV, Miniseries 1960)—David William *BBC Television Shakespeare: Richard II* (TV, UK, 1978)—Derek Jacobi *The War of the Roses* (English Shakespeare Company): *Richard II* (UK, 1990)—a direct filming from the stage. *Richard II* (UK, TV, 1997)—Fiona Shaw *Richard the Second* (US, film, 2001)—Matte Osian *The Hollow Crown: Richard II* (UK, TV, BBC2, 2012)—Ben Whishaw
Henry IV, Part 1	Approaching the end of his life, Henry experiences guilt over deposing Richard II to become king. Encouraged by the corrupt but charismatic Falstaff, Henry's son and heir, Hal, the Prince of Wales, leads a dissolute life that fractures the father/son relationship	He will give the devil his due. (Act I, Scene II). The better part of valour is discretion. (Act V, Scene IV)	*An Age of Kings* (UK, TV, Miniseries 1960)—Tom Fleming *BBC Television Shakespeare: Henry IV, Part 1* (UK, TV, 1979)—Jon Finch *The War of the Roses: Henry IV, Part 1* (UK, TV, 1990)—a direct filming from the stage *The Hollow Crown: Henry IV, Part 1* (UK, TV, BBC2, 2012)—Jeremy Irons
Henry IV, Part 2	Themes include old age, loss of human life, and old friends and atonement. Henry IV is anxious and worried for the future. On Henry's deathbed, his son Hal is crowned Henry V and promises to atone for his misspent youth.	He hath eaten me out of house and home. (Act I, Scene I) Uneasy lies the head that wears a crown. (Act III, Scene I)	*An Age of Kings* (UK, TV, Miniseries 1960)—Tom Fleming as Henry IV *The War of the Roses* (TV miniseries 1965) *BBC Television Shakespeare, Henry IV, Part 2* (TV, UK, 1979)—Jon Finch *The War of the Roses* (English Shakespeare Company) *Henry IV, Part 2* (UK, 1990)—a direct filming from the stage. *The Hollow Crown: Henry IV, Part 2* (UK, TV, BBC2, 2012)—Jeremy Irons

Henry V	Dramatizes the English invasion of France and Henry V's success at the battle of Agincourt (1415). Explores questions of who has the right to rule and why. In contrast to his portrayal in *Henry IV* (both parts) as well as that of his father, Henry V is a heroic figure with strong resolve, who takes the obligations and duties of his kingly role very seriously.	Once more unto the breach, dear friends, once more (Act III, Scene I) Men of few words are the best men (Act III, Scene II) We few, we happy few, we band of brothers. For he today that sheds his blood with me shall be my brother (Act III, Scene III)	*Henry V* (UK, film, 1944)—Laurence Olivier *An Age of Kings* (UK, TV, Miniseries 1960)—Robert Hardy BBC Television Shakespeare: *Henry V* (TV, UK, 1979) *The War of the Roses* (English Shakespeare Company) *Henry V* (UK, 1990)—a direct filming from the stage The Hollow Crown: *Henry V* (UK, TV, BBC2, 2012)—Tom Hiddleston
Henry VI, Part 1	The loss of French territories and political events leading up to the War of the Roses (House of Lancaster versus House of York). Henry VI is an upright but weak king. Together, the three plays show the repercussions this type of monarch can have on a nation. It justifies the subsequent usurpation of the throne by York, legitimating the Tudor dynasty.	Delays have dangerous ends. (Act III, Scene II) Of all base passions, fear is the most accursed. (Act V, Scene II)	*An Age of Kings* (UK, TV, Miniseries 1960)—Terry Scully *The War of the Roses* (TV miniseries 1965)—David Warner BBC Television Shakespeare: *Henry VI, Part 1* (TV, UK, 1983) *Henry V* (UK, 1989)—Kenneth Branagh *The War of the Roses* (English Shakespeare Company) *Henry VI—House of Lancaster* (UK, 1990)—a direct filming from the stage
Henry VI, Part 2	The struggle for power during the reign of the young king. His inability to control his querulous nobles, together with the inevitability of war.	Small things make base men proud. (Act IV, Scene I) True nobility is exempt from fear. (Act IV, Scene I)	*An Age of Kings* (UK, TV, Miniseries 1960)—Terry Scully *The War of the Roses* (TV miniseries 1965)—David Warner BBC Television Shakespeare: *Henry VI, Part 2* (TV, UK, 1983) *Henry VI—House of Lancaster* (UK, 1990). A direct filming from the stage of Michael Bogdanov and Michael Pennington's seven-play sequence, based on Shakespeare's history plays. This play is formed from *Henry VI, Part 1* and the earlier scenes of *Henry VI, Part 2*. *The War of the Roses* (English Shakespeare Company) *Henry VI—House of York* (UK, 1990)—a direct filming from the stage

(continued)

TABLE 3 *(continued)*

Play Title	Key Themes and Monarchy Portrayals	Famous Quotes	Film and TV Productions/Actor Playing King
Henry VI, Part 3	The horrors of war as Henry VI is deposed by Edward, Duke of York, who becomes Edward IV. Henry VI's wife leads the fighting, while her weak husband watches from the sidelines until his ultimate death.	Having nothing, nothing can he lose. (Act III, Scene III) The smallest worm will turn, being trodden on. (Act II, Scene I)	*An Age of Kings* (UK, TV, Miniseries 1960)—Terry Scully *The War of the Roses* (TV miniseries 1965)—David Warner *BBC Television Shakespeare: Henry VI, Part 3* (TV, UK, 1983) *The War of the Roses* (English Shakespeare Company) *Henry VI—House of York* (UK, 1990)—a direct filming from the stage
Richard III	Richard is depicted as the villainous hunchbacked Duke of Gloucester, who gains the throne through a series of dreadful acts. The War of the Roses culminates in the Battle of Bosworth, with Richard defeated by the Duke of Richmond, who becomes Henry VII.	Now is the winter of our discontent. (Act I, Scene I) A horse! A horse! My kingdom for a horse! (Act V, Scene IV) Off with his head! (Act III, Scene IV)	*Richard III* (US, silent film, 1908)—William Ranous *Richard III* (UK, film, 1955)—Laurence Olivier *An Age of Kings* (UK, TV, Miniseries 1960)—Paul Daneman *The War of the Roses* (UK, TV miniseries, 1965)—Ian Holm *BBC Television Shakespeare: Richard III* (TV, UK, 1982) *The War of the Roses* (English Shakespeare Company): *Richard III* (UK, 1990)—a direct filming from the stage *The Animated Shakespeare: King Richard III* (TV, Russia and UK, 1994)—Antony Sher as the voice of Richard *Richard III* (UK, film, 1995)—Ian McKellen *Richard III* (US, film, 2008)—Scott Anderson

SOURCE: "Shakespeare quotes," *Absolute Shakespeare*, http://absoluteshakespeare.com/trivia/quotes/quotes.htm.

victors, and this was very much the case in Elizabethan England. Elizabeth I's reign was renowned for propagating the "Tudor Myth," which sought to justify her grandfather Henry VII's accession after years of contested claims during the Wars of the Roses. The war culminated with Elizabeth's grandfather, founding patriarch of the House of Tudor who would be crowned Henry VII, killing the malevolent Richard III in battle.* The Tudors painted Henry VII as a saintly hero divinely chosen to save England from more years of civil war. Thus anyone challenging this myth—including England's playwrights—faced punishment not only from the royal court but also ostensibly from God.[8]

The public's abiding fascination with the Elizabethan age has extended into the present; in fact, two of the most successful royal-themed worldwide global box-office (GBO) hits are *Elizabeth* (GBO $82.1 million, 1998)[9] and *Elizabeth: The Golden Age* (GBO: $74.2 million, 2007).† They join other recent blockbusters that focus on a monarch, to wide acclaim. These include *The Queen* (GBO $123.3 million, 2006) and *The King's Speech* (GBO $414.2 million, 2010).[10] Moreover, Shakespeare's *Henry V* (1989) earns its place on an additional list of royal films to gross from $9 to $28 million each, and which are noteworthy because of the star power attached to them. These include *The Madness of King George* (1994), *Her Majesty, Mrs. Brown* (1997),‡ *Young Victoria* (2009), and *Diana* (2013).[11] Each in its own way continues the Shakespearian tradition of depicting archetypal human struggles rather than conveying accurate historical facts and events, a situation that, according to the prominent historian Robert Rosenstone, may "trouble and disturb professional historians."[12]

In personalizing history, however, historical films intensify feelings about events and people, using dramatic effects such as facial close-ups and poignant music to evoke an emotional response from their audiences.[13] As a consequence, films invite us to experience the sorrows, joys, and passions they depict. In contrast, written history can typically only make gestures

* Shakespeare's famous depiction of Richard III as a villain reinforced this myth, probably very deliberately, given Elizabeth I's patronage.

† Two TV miniseries about Elizabeth I were released between these films, both in 2005. One starred Helen Mirren and other Anne-Marie Duff. Theodore Harvey notes that Duff's version was especially careful to portray an aging monarch over the thirty-five-year story arc.

‡ A satiric moniker for Queen Victoria, reflecting the fairly widespread belief that she and John Brown were involved in a romantic relationship. It was also released as *Mrs. Brown*.

toward such depths of feeling. According to Rosenstone, "Film is a postliterate equivalent of the preliterate way of dealing with the past."[14] In other words, the medium behaves more like oral history in the way it passes down stories that may become embellished as they move from generation to generation. Bearing these points in mind, we offer a short overview of a selection of royal films we believe are significant in terms of their emphasis on emotional themes and their influence in shaping perceptions of the RFBC in consumer culture.

The critics typically praise the 1989 film *Henry V* as one of the best-ever adaptations of Shakespeare's work. Kenneth Branagh served as both director and star, portraying the passionate warrior king leading his troops against the French (figure 17). The odds are stacked against the English, with the French far outnumbering them. Although Henry is full of self-doubt, he must remain strong for his similarly skeptical troops, who look to him for leadership and inspiration. The climax depicts a spectacular battle scene that conveys the brutal realities of warfare. It follows Henry's famously moving St. Crispin's Day speech, which contains the line "We few, we happy few, we band of brothers." Although the main theme is leadership, Henry's romance with Catherine (Emma Thompson), daughter of the defeated King Charles VI of France (Paul Scofield), also features in the plot.

Adapted from a play by Alan Bennett, *The Madness of King George* (1994) tells the true story of George III's battle with severe illness and the loyalty of his wife, Charlotte of Mecklenburg-Strelitz (Helen Mirren). George undergoes humiliating and agonizing medical treatments at the hands of his personal physicians. Although George III was never portrayed as a popular king, Nigel Hawthorne brings the king's vulnerability to the fore in his award-winning performance. The film also dramatizes the king's declining relationship with his first son, the Prince of Wales, who schemes to become regent.* At its heart, however, this film revisits an ancient and compelling myth: the vulnerability and fall of the powerful.

Her Majesty, Mrs. Brown (1997) depicts the enigmatic relationship between the bereaved Queen Victoria (Judi Dench) and her Scottish manservant, John Brown (Billy Connolly). The relationship caused much consternation within the Royal Family, not to mention speculation in Victorian England; it was rumored that Victoria had even secretly married him.[15] The

---

* *Regent* is a title for a monarch acting in a temporary capacity; due to his father's illness, George IV was in fact Prince Regent from 1811 to 1820.

FIGURE 17. Kenneth Branagh as Henry V (1989). Courtesy Roland Grant archives.

film opens with Queen Victoria still in mourning for her beloved Prince Albert. Inconsolable after several years, she refuses to return to court and public life. The plain-speaking John Brown, Prince Albert's trusted servant, is sent to coax her out of seclusion. A close bond develops between Victoria and her servant; he becomes her friend and confidant and assumes control of her schedule, much to the dismay of her family and her advisers. The value of common friendship and the loneliness of the monarchical role are the film's overriding themes.

Elizabeth (1998) stars Cate Blanchett in the title role, exploring the early years of her reign, and the many threats she faced. As a female monarch, she is perceived to be in a weak position; her nobles and advisers pressure Elizabeth to marry, arranging a continual parade of potential suitors. Rejecting them all, she embarks on an affair with her childhood sweetheart, Robert Dudley, Earl of Leicester. To her anger and chagrin, she eventually discovers that he is already married. With the demise of this passion as its focal point, the film deals with Elizabeth's transformation from a fun-loving and rather naive girl to a strong, powerful ruler who dominates the men around her. The last scene of the film dramatically captures this transformation; Elizabeth has her hair cut and paints herself with makeup to become the white-faced "Virgin Queen." This becomes her classic image in historical documentation and portraiture.

The sequel, *Elizabeth: The Golden Age* (2007), takes place during the latter part of her reign, which includes the threatened invasion by the Spanish Armada. The theme of sacrifice for one's country continues as Elizabeth once again embarks on an ill-fated romance. This time she falls for Walter Raleigh (played by the darkly handsome and charismatic Clive Owens), but they cannot act on their mutual attraction because of Elizabeth's role, and her responsibilities to her country. Instead, he falls for her lady-in-waiting Bess, with whom he has a child. Raleigh subsequently plays a leading role in defeating the Spanish, affording Clive Owen the opportunity to heroically command a blazing fire-ship into the oncoming armada. Elizabeth walks along a cliff top overlooking the English Channel to watch the devastated Spanish fleet sink in flames, a scene demonstrating Hollywood at its most sensational and melodramatic. Generally considered by critics as a romantic fantasy that took too many wild liberties with historical fact,* *The Golden Age* was still a considerable box office success.

Starring Helen Mirren, *The Queen* (2007) depicts the events immediately following the death of Diana, Princess of Wales on August 31, 1997. Seen from the perspectives both of the Queen and Prime Minister Tony Blair, the drama unfolds around the differing opinions on how to react to the tragedy. In a now-historic moment of tension between the Queen and her public, she conceives of Diana's death as an occasion for private mourning, although her son Prince Charles and Blair recognize the public's desire for an official

---

* For example, in the film, Raleigh replaces Francis Drake as the leading figure in the fight against the armada. However, Raleigh was never actually there!

expression of grief from her. The film offers a very sympathetic portrayal of Elizabeth II, dramatizing the internal tensions she experiences between being a ruler and being a mother and grandmother.

In contrast to *Her Majesty, Mrs. Brown*, *Young Victoria* (2009), starring Emily Blunt, dramatizes Victoria's youth, her ascension to the throne, and the defining romantic relationship of her life, with Prince Albert. After exposing Victoria's early upbringing as isolated and emotionally deprived, with her mother's consort attempting to gain control over her, the film portrays a rebellious and fiery Victoria learning the responsibilities of her monarchical role. Essentially a historical romance, its key focus is on Victoria's courtship with Albert, showing how they eventually developed an enduring love and trust. This film also involved current (or former) Royal Family members in several ways: Sarah Ferguson, the former Duchess of York, was one of its screenwriters, and her daughter Princess Beatrice made a cameo appearance as one of the Queen's ladies-in-waiting. Yet her grandmother the Queen criticized the historical inaccuracies in the film, as well as some of the costumes.[16]

Of all the royal films, *The King's Speech* (2010), starring Colin Firth and Helena Bonham-Carter, is without a doubt the most successful in terms of both its worldwide GBO of $414.2 million and the awards it has accumulated. The plot is simple but captivating. The introverted Prince Albert, who would reluctantly accede as George VI after the abdication of his brother Edward VIII, attempts to cure a childhood stammer that makes him awkward and embarrassed at public events. Aided by his wife, Elizabeth (later Queen Elizabeth, then the Queen Mother), and the unconventional methods of plain-speaking Australian speech therapist Lionel Logue (played by Geoffrey Rush), the King works to overcome his stammer. The drama culminates with the King successfully delivering his first World War II radio broadcast to the nation, as he announces Britain's declaration of war on Germany. The main focus of the film is on the relationship between George VI and Logue, and a key theme is that effective leaders are not born but taught. Moreover, George VI must recognize his own weaknesses and rely on both the help of others and his own determination to overcome major obstacles and ultimately succeed.

Although universally condemned as superficial, we believe *Diana* (2013), the most recent royal film released,* deserves discussion due to its GBO of

* As of December 2014.

$21.7 million. The film was based on Kate Snell's *Diana: Her Last Love,* and depicts the last two years of her life. The central narrative focuses on Diana's love affair with Hasnat Khan and their eventual split, resulting in her turning to Dodi Fayed to make Hasnat jealous. Despite the high-powered casting of Naomi Watts as Princess Diana, critics shared the opinion that she offered a wooden portrayal with little depth or subtlety. In addition, Khan was widely reported to feel angry and betrayed by the film, and allegedly believed it trivialized their romance.

In conjunction with the tenets of successful human and family branding, these contemporary portrayals of royal figures, or of their family members, bring us closer to monarchy by making these people seem "just like us" in a variety of ways. The big screen lays bare the monarchy as composed of human beings with passions, turmoil, and temptations to which everyone can relate, rather than distant, cold, institutional figureheads. Often depicted as having to overcome adversity and face many challenges in life, a monarch shown as vulnerable and flawed helps an audience identify and empathize. Yet significantly and somewhat paradoxically, people also need to know that these figures differ from themselves, to allow the mystery that surrounds the idea of royalty to remain.

In short, members of the RFBC must always be portrayed as existing on a more elevated level than common people, although many films adhere to the narrative that such elevation is not without consequences, often with respect to emotional suffering and loneliness. Thus these films typically emphasize a theme of sacrifice to duty, which puts the welfare of the nation above personal desire (as both Elizabeth films so acutely portray). This sense of sacrifice is what separates "them" from "us," and affords monarchs the authoritarian power we expect them to possess. In his documentary *Monarchy,* David Starkey, the esteemed historian and original director of *The Six Wives of Henry VIII,* identifies a key tension underpinning these portrayals: "On one hand, England required authoritarian might to stand strong against external threats; on the other, it cherished its longstanding tradition of rule by consent of the governed. The dynamic tension between these two impulses enabled the monarchy to survive as the oldest functioning political institution in Europe."[17]

This brings us to a third common theme of these films—namely, the democratization of the monarchy and the idea of rule by consent of the governed. As the world's oldest democracy, since the signing of the Magna Carta in 1215, England (and later Great Britain) has treasured its limitations on absolute monarchy.[18] Thus films that portray the British monarchy continually reinforce the need for a monarch to please the people, particularly in depictions where the people temporarily turn against their ruler (usually their queen, as *Young Victoria, Mrs. Brown,* and *The Queen* reveal). In such situations, the monarchs are shown to be especially vulnerable and to require advice. To this end, a trusted, plain-speaking confidant (usually a commoner) often emerges, who gains the monarchs' respect by virtue of his or her (typically his) knowledge and ability.

Significantly, helper figures hark back to the universal structure of the fairy-tale narrative. Although not all royal films mirror these tales, they often feature people who play vital roles by assisting monarchic heroes or heroines in overcoming obstacles. Elizabeth I has Walter Raleigh to teach her about faraway lands; Queen Victoria has both Lord Melbourne to help her negotiate the ways of government and John Brown to reinvigorate her life after Albert's death; Elizabeth II has Tony Blair to help her respond emotionally to the death of the "People's Princess"; and George VI has Lionel Logue to cure his stammer. Even George III can claim Dr. Willis, the abrasive specialist who treats his dementia and who, although not a confidant, engages George with a directness and authority the King never experiences from others around him.

Accordingly, apart from offering advice in adversity, the plain-speaking commoner counterbalances royal rank and remoteness (with titled Lord Melbourne as the obvious exception). In providing a stark contrast to the rigors of royalty, such characters act as agents provocateurs, calling into question the pomp and ceremony that surrounds royalty and the reasons why we elevate the monarchy to a quasi-mythic status.

John Brown in *Her Majesty, Mrs. Brown* is a prime example of this role. The rugged Scotsman refuses to obey court etiquette and treats Victoria as a fellow human being rather than his queen, calling her "Woman" rather than "Ma'am," and passing her tipples of whisky from his hip flask when they go out riding. At the same time, he brings out Victoria's vulnerability and need for friendship and protection, transforming the somewhat starchy and isolated monarch into a warm, feeling being with whom we can empathize. At times he assumes the superior position; when he introduces her to people living on her estate, Brown, rather than Victoria, is in command as he puts the tenants at ease in the company of Her Majesty.

Of course, a major attraction of all these films is that they teem with pomp and pageantry. As a genre, historical film presents rich opportunities to select aspects of the past that are visually awesome and emotionally stirring. From the battlefields of Agincourt to the ostentatious splendor of the Elizabethan court, royal historical films make the most of their heavily visual narratives. Film as a medium is particularly effective in portraying public ceremonial events and mass conflicts, conceived as the two primary types of human spectacle.[19] Ceremony offers a sense of continuity and stability, where conflicts offer the drama inherent in tumult and change. Both are highly emotive and evoke the power and presence of monarchy, albeit in very different ways.

The historical film is therefore the perfect genre to convey the grandeur of royal ritual, the stateliness of tradition, and the potency of war. Consider the electrifying image of Elizabeth I on horseback, dressed in chain mail, an abundance of red hair flowing down her back, as she addresses the English troops before they go into battle against the armada. Or the magnificent splendor of the delicate teenage Victoria, her bejeweled coronation crown encircling her head, golden orb and scepter in her hands, as she majestically returns the gaze of the crowd that throngs Westminster Abbey. Such momentous media moments reinforce the mystic elements that infuse royalty, while simultaneously asserting pride in national heritage and identity.

Fashion is the other spectacular element of royal historical films—not contemporary fashion, of course, but rather the sartorial splendor that reflects the particular period depicted in each film. Royal historical films thus intersect with another film subgenre, the costume drama, a staple element of British and American cinema since the era of silent films.[20] In this respect, royal films provide the perfect opportunity to represent viewers' indulgences in the (typically historical) luxury aspect of the RFBC, with the characters' opulent ensembles and accessories set against a backdrop of lavish decor and theatrical settings. Consider that in a list of the ten best costume dramas of all time, three of the films we discuss in this chapter rank alongside classics such as *Gone with the Wind* and *Sense and Sensibility.**[21] Further, all eight films that we synopsize received Academy Award or BAFTA nominations or wins for costume design.

From magnificent medieval heraldry emblazoned on the armorial bearings of Henry V and his army, to the somber blackness of Victorian courtly rituals of grief in *Her Majesty, Mrs. Brown,* or the purple splendor of *Young Victoria,* these films all leave their visual marks by contributing to an over-

* Namely, *Elizabeth, Her Majesty, Mrs. Brown,* and *Young Victoria.*

riding sense of royal spectacle. Without a doubt, historical costumes are a major attraction for the (mainly female) audiences of these films. Usually rich and resplendent, they are all arresting in their designs and remarkable for their attention to elaborate detail.*

Nowhere are the excesses of conspicuous consumption more pronounced than in the costumes for the *Elizabeth* films. This excess is highly appropriate; as we have noted, scholars pinpoint the Elizabethan court as a major catalyst in the birth of consumer culture.[22] According to leading anthropologist Grant McCracken, there are two main reasons for this attribution. First, Elizabeth I used lavish consumption to symbolically enhance and reinforce her power as monarch.† Furthermore, she strategically leveraged displays of lavish goods and created opulent consumption events to achieve her political ends. In particular, her noblemen engaged in tremendous competition for status within the royal court and often relied on ostentatious displays of their long-established wealth and lineages when vying for Elizabeth's favor.

Both films about the monarch maximize this infatuation with consumption, particularly with respect to fashion. Although each received acclaim for costume design, critics discussed the wild liberties taken with respect to Elizabeth's dresses. For one critic posting on the *Guardian* blog, it was all too much:

> The film begins in 1585, with Walter Raleigh (Clive Owen) flinging his new cloak over a puddle so Queen Elizabeth (Cate Blanchett) need not step in it. Later, he introduces her to tobacco, a potato and two Native Americans brought back from his transatlantic expedition. All this is more or less true, but it's hard to notice the history because the queen is wearing a giant chrysanthemum on her head. While the first Elizabeth movie faithfully reproduced Elizabeth's outfits from courtly portraits, *The Golden Age* kits her out in iridescent lace collars, foot-high plumes of exotic feathers, electric violet and lime green satin, and marquee-sized gauze cloaks suspended from architectural hoops. She looks fabulous, but it's not so much Nicholas Hilliard‡ as Lady Gaga.[23]

Traveling away from contemporary royal films, we now offer a closer look at the evolution of the royal historical film genre. As we have already shown

---

* Victoria's mourning attire, while not necessary resplendent, was made of expensive crepe fabric and accessorized with specific jewelry.

† Kevin Sharpe, in *Selling the Tudor Monarchy,* supports this point with a plethora of evidence.

‡ An English goldsmith and limner, best known for his portrait miniatures of the court members of Elizabeth I and James I of England/James VI of Scotland.

through our analysis of Shakespearian products, dramas depicting the monarchy are not new. In fact, although the world cinema has seen its share of recent royal blockbusters, the royal film genre is basically as old as the cinema itself. In total, well over sixty royal films exist (see table 4). The first was *The Execution of Mary, Queen of Scots,* produced in 1895 by Thomas Edison.* Silent and lasting less than half a minute, this film relies on clever editing for dramatic effect, replacing the actress playing Mary with a dummy, which is then beheaded. As the first movie to employ special effects, it is regarded as a breakthrough in cinematic technology.[24]

Sixteen years would elapse before another royal film appeared. *Henry VIII,* produced in 1911, lasted twenty-five minutes and featured five scenes from a London performance of Shakespeare's play. Ex-salesman William G. Barker, who had made his name as the newsreel photographer for Queen Victoria's Diamond Jubilee in 1897, conceived of the film as a way for England to enhance its status in the film industry. He achieved this goal by associating film, a medium denigrated and trivialized at that time, with high culture and the arts. *Henry VIII* was quickly followed by *Les amours d'Elisabeth, reine d'Angleterre* (*The Loves of Queen Elizabeth, Queen of England*),† a French silent film starring the legendary Sarah Bernhardt, one of the pioneering actresses of the silent screen. She was already sixty-eight years old when she featured in this forty-four-minute drama focusing on Elizabeth I's love affair with the Earl of Essex.

Bernhardt set the precedent for major stars of their eras to appear in the steady stream of films on the British monarchs that followed. In particular, well-known actors such as Charles Laughton, Merle Oberon, Anna Neagle, Katharine Hepburn, Laurence Olivier, Vivien Leigh, Bette Davis, and Errol Flynn all portrayed royal figures on film in the 1920s and 1930s.

It is often said that history can teach us more about the present than it can about the past, and when we examine royal films across different eras, support for this argument is evident. Against the background of the Great Depression, productions that portrayed the lusty orange seller turned actress turned royal mistress to Charles II, such as *Nell Gwyn* (1935), as well as films like *The Private Lives of Henry VIII* (1933), depicting England's most lascivious monarch, provided some light relief for fun-starved audiences.[25] Later in

---

* The footage depicting Mary's death in this film can be seen at www.youtube.com/watch?v=BIOLsH93U1Q.

† Also known as *La Reine Elisabeth* (*Queen Elizabeth*).

the decade, *Victoria the Great* (1937) and *Sixty Glorious Years* (1938), both starring Anna Neagle as Queen Victoria, reassured the British people of the monarchy's stability during the 1938 abdication crisis.[26]

We mentioned earlier that Olivier's *Henry V* was made for propaganda purposes during World War II, but several other royal-related films were also part of this effort to maintain public morale in the lead-up to war and through the ensuing battle years.[27] Marking George V's Silver Jubilee, *Royal Cavalcade* (1935) depicted the great events of his reign, in both Britain and its empire. It mixed dramatic reenactments with newsreel footage where George V appeared only briefly; most of the time, the director substituted a picture of Buckingham Palace as the King's stand-in.[28] This choice reminded the audience of the institutional longevity and powerful presence of the monarchy rather than dwelling on how the institution is personalized. As we noted earlier, a focus on the individual persona of the monarch is more common in contemporary royal films.

Fire over England (1937) starred Dame Flora Robson in a magisterial portrayal of Elizabeth I as she infused her people with national pride and the courage to defeat the Spanish Armada, celebrating another great English victory. Made at the beginning of the war, *London Can Take It* (1940) also documented British stoicism in the face of adversity and featured the everyday heroism of Londoners during the German Blitz. Significantly, it featured George VI and his wife, Elizabeth, in a bomb-damaged Buckingham Palace, illustrating how they too shared their people's plight. Narrated by a top U.S. journalist of the time, Quentin Reynolds, the film was also a hit in America, gaining much support there for a beleaguered Britain. It ends with a closing shot of the statue of Richard I (the Lionheart) outside of the Houses of Parliament, thus evoking another powerful military leader as further testament to the might of Britain and her monarchs. Overall, this series of wartime films, set within the context of a war-torn Europe, emphasized the nation's power and glory, as well as its many triumphs in adversity. In the process, the films also valorized the role of the monarchy in these victories.

After the end of the war, a more stable period ensued, initiated by Elizabeth II's coronation in 1953, ushering in the depiction of more undependable and wayward monarchs. With an all-star cast including Stewart Granger, Elizabeth Taylor, Peter Ustinov, and Robert Morley, *Beau Brummell* (1954) tells the story of the nineteenth-century upper-class dandy and his volatile relationship with the Prince of Wales (later George IV). Likewise, the 1956 film adaptation of Shakespeare's *Richard III* depicts the

TABLE 4 Royal Film Productions

Film	Date	Country of Production	Stars	Monarch(s)/Characters
The Execution of Mary, Queen of Scots	1895	USA	Robert Thomae	Mary, Queen of Scots
Henry VIII	1911	UK	Arthur Bourchier, Laura Cowie, Edward O'Neill, Herbert Beerbohm Tree	Henry VIII, Anne Boleyn, Duke of Suffolk, Cardinal Wolsey
Queen Elizabeth (Les amours de la Reine d'Angleterre)	1912	France	Sarah Bernhardt, Lou Tellegen, Max Maxudian	Elizabeth I
The Life and Death of King Richard III (Original title: *Richard III*)	1912	France, USA	Robert Gemp, Frederick Warde, Albert Gardner, Carey Lee	Edward IV, Richard, Duke of Gloucester (later Richard III), Prince Edward of Lancaster, Queen Elizabeth I
Sixty Years a Queen	1913	UK	Blanche Forsythe, Mrs. Henry Litton	Victoria, Prince Albert
Anne de Boleyn	1914	France	Laura Cowie, Max Maxudian	Anne Boleyn, Henry VIII
50,000 Miles with the Prince of Wales	1920	UK	Edward, the Prince of Wales	Edward, the Prince of Wales
Anna Boleyn	1921	Germany	Henny Porten, Emil Jannings	Anne Boleyn, Henry VIII
The Virgin Queen	1923	UK	Diana Manners, Carlye Blackwell	Elizabeth I, Lord Robert Dudley
Dorothy Vernon of Haddon Hall	1924	USA	Mary Pickford, Clare Eames, Estelle Taylor, Courtenay Foote	Dorothy Vernon, Elizabeth I, Mary, Queen of Scots, Earl of Leicester
Nell Gwyn	1926	UK	Dorothy Gish, Randle Ayrton	Nell Gwyn, Charles II
The Private Life of Henry VIII	1933	UK	Charles Laughton, Merle Oberon, Wendy Barrie, Elsa Lanchester	Henry VIII, Anne Boleyn, Jane Seymour, Anne of Cleves
Nell Gwyn	1935	UK	Anna Neagle, Cedric Hardwicke	Nell Gwyn, Charles II
Mary of Scotland	1936	USA	Katharine Hepburn, Fredric March, Florence Eldridge	Mary Stuart, Elizabeth Tudor

Title	Year	Country	Cast	Characters
Tudor Rose (U.S. title: *Nine Days a Queen*)	1936	UK/USA	Cedric Hardwicke, Nora Pilbeam, John Mills	Henry VIII, Lady Jane Grey, Lord Guilford Dudley
Fire over England	1937	UK	Laurence Olivier, Flora Robson, Vivien Leigh, Raymond Massey, Leslie Banks	Elizabeth I, Philip II of Spain, Michael Ingolby, Cynthia, Robert Dudley, Earl of Leicester
Victoria the Great	1937	UK	Anna Neagle, Anton Walbrook, Walter Rilla	Victoria, Albert, Prince Ernest, Lord Melbourne
Sixty Glorious Years	1938	UK	Anna Neagle, Anton Walbrook, Walter Rilla	Victoria, Albert, Prince Ernest, Sir Robert Peel
Essex and Elizabeth (*The Private Lives of Elizabeth and Essex*)	1939	USA	Bette Davis, Errol Flynn, Olivia de Havilland, Vincent Price	Elizabeth I, the Earl of Essex, Lady Penelope Gray, Sir Walter Raleigh
The Heart of a Queen	1940	Germany	Zarah Leander, Maria Koppenhofer	Mary Queen of Scots, Elizabeth I
London Can Take It!	1940	UK	Quentin Reynolds (Commentator)	George VI, Elizabeth (later, the Queen Mother)
The Sea Hawk	1940	USA	Errol Flynn, Brenda Marshall, Claude Rains, Flora Robson, Alan Hale	Geoffrey Thorpe, Dona Maria, Queen Elizabeth I
Listen to Britain	1942	UK	Chesney Allen, Leonard Brockingson, Bud Flanagan	Queen Elizabeth (later, the Queen Mother)
Henry V	1946	UK	Laurence Olivier, Robert Newton, Leslie Banks	Henry V
Forever Amber	1947	USA	Linda Darnell, Cornel Wilde, Richard Greene, George Sanders	Amber St. Clair, Bruce Carlton, Lord Harry Almsbury, Charles II
Royal Wedding	1951	USA	Fred Astaire, Jane Powell, Peter Lawford	Tom Bowen, Ellen Bowen, Lord John Brindale
Young Bess	1953	USA	Jean Simmons, Stewart Granger, Deborah Kerr, Charles Laughton	Young Bess (Elizabeth I), Thomas Seymour, Catherine Parr, Henry VIII
A Queen Is Crowned	1953	UK	Laurence Olivier (Narrator)	Elizabeth II, Philip, Charles, the Queen Mother
Beau Brummell	1954	USA	Stewart Granger, Elizabeth Taylor, Peter Ustinov, Robert Morley	Beau Brummell, Lady Patricia, Prince of Wales (later, George IV), George III
The Virgin Queen	1955	USA	Bette Davis, Richard Todd, Joan Collins	Elizabeth I, Sir Walter Raleigh, Beth Throgmorton
Richard III	1956	UK	Laurence Olivier, Cedric Hardwicke, Nicholas Hannen, John Gielgud, Claire Bloom	Richard III, Edward IV, George, Duke of Clarence, the Lady Anne

(continued)

TABLE 4 (continued)

Film	Date	Country of Production	Stars	Monarch/Characters
The Prince and the Showgirl	1957	USA	Laurence Olivier, Marilyn Monroe, Sybil Thorndike	Charles, the Prince Regent of Carpathia, Elsie Marina, the Queen Dowager
Becket	1964	UK/USA	Richard Burton, Peter O'Toole, John Gielgud	Thomas Becket, Henry II, Louis VII of France
A Man for All Seasons	1966	UK	Paul Scofield, Wendy Hiller, Robert Shaw, Orson Welles, John Hurt	Thomas More, Alice More, Henry VIII, Cardinal Wolsey
The Lion in Winter	1968	UK	Peter O'Toole, Katharine Hepburn, Anthony Hopkins, Timothy Dalton, John Castle	Henry II, his wife Eleanor, Richard I, Philip II of Spain
Anne of the Thousand Days	1969	UK	Richard Burton, Geneviève Bujold, Irene Papas	Henry VIII, Catherine of Aragon, Anne Boleyn
Cromwell	1970	UK	Richard Harris, Alec Guinness, Robert Morley, Dorothy Tutin, Timothy Dalton	Oliver Cromwell, Charles I, the Earl of Manchester, Queen Henrietta Maria, Prince Rupert
Mary, Queen of Scots	1971	UK	Vanessa Redgrave, Glenda Jackson, Ian Holm, Timothy Dalton	Mary Queen of Scots, Elizabeth I, David Riccio, Henry - Lord Darnley
Lady Caroline Lamb	1973	UK/Italy	Sarah Miles, Jon Finch, Richard Chamberlain, John Mills, Laurence Olivier, Ralph Richardson	Lady Caroline Lamb, William Lamb, Lord Byron, George IV, Duke of Wellington
Henry VIII	1979	UK/USA	John Stride, Claire Bloom, Barbara Kellerman, Julian Glover	Henry VIII, Catherine of Aragon, Duke of Buckingham
Lady Jane	1986	UK	Helena Bonham Carter, Cary Elwes, John Wood, Patrick Stewart	Lady Jane Grey, Guilford Dudley, John Dudley, Duke of Northumberland, Henry Grey, Duke of Suffolk
Henry V	1989	UK	Kenneth Branagh, Derek Jacobi, Simon Shepherd, Ian Holm	Henry V
Orlando	1993	UK/Russia/ France/Italy/ Netherlands	Tilda Swinton, Billy Zane, Quentin Crisp	Orlando, Shelmerdine, Elizabeth I

The Madness of King George	1994	UK	Nigel Hawthorne, Helen Mirren, Ian Holm, Rupert Graves, Rupert Everett	George III, Queen Charlotte, the Prince of Whales
Restoration	1995	USA/UK	Robert Downey Jr., Sam Neill, David Thewlis, Ian McKellen, Hugh Grant, Ian McDiarmid, Meg Ryan	Robert Merivel, Charles II
Richard III	1995	UK/USA	Ian McKellen, Annette Bening, Jim Broadbent, Robert Downey Jr., Nigel Hawthorne, Kristin Scott Thomas, Maggie Smith	Richard III, Elizabeth I, Henry Stafford, Duke of Buckingham, Lord Rivers, Edward IV
Her Majesty, Mrs. Brown	1997	UK/Ireland/ USA	Judi Dench, Billy Connolly, Geoffrey Palmer, Antony Sher, Gerard Butler	Victoria, John Brown
Elizabeth	1998	UK	Cate Blanchett, Geoffrey Rush, Joseph Fiennes, Richard Attenborough	Elizabeth I, Sir Francis Walsingham, Robert Dudley, William Cecil (1st Baron Burghley), Thomas Howard (4th Duke of Norfolk), Phillip II of Spain
Shakespeare in Love	1999	USA/UK	Gwyneth Paltrow, Joseph Fiennes, Geoffrey Rush, Judi Dench	Shakespeare, Elizabeth I
The Last King (Original title: *Charles II: The Power and the Passion*)	2003	UK/USA	Rufus Sewell, Rupert Graves, Shirley Henderson, Martin Freeman, Ian McDiarmid, Helen McCroy	Charles II, George Villiers (Duke of Buckingham), Catharine of Braganza, Lord Shaftesbury, Sir Edward Hyde, Barbara Villiers (Countess of Castlemaine)
To Kill a King	2003	UK/Germany	Tim Roth, Dougray Scott, Olivia Williams, Colin Redgrave, Rupert Everett	Oliver Cromwell, Sir Thomas Fairfax, Lady Anne Fairfax, Charles I
The Libertine	2006	UK/Australia	Johnny Depp, Samantha Morton, John Malkovich, Rosamund Pike	John Wilmot (2nd Earl of Rochester), Charles II
The Queen	2006	UK/France/ Italy	Helen Mirren, James Cromwell, Michael Sheen	Elizabeth II, Prime Minister Tony Blair
Elizabeth: The Golden Age	2007	UK/France/ Germany	Cate Blanchett, Geoffrey Rush, Clive Owen, Rhys Ifans, Samantha Morton	Elizabeth I, Sir Francis Walsingham, Sir Walter Raleigh, Mary, Queen of Scots, Philip II of Spain

(*continued*)

TABLE 4 *(continued)*

Film	Date	Country of Production	Stars	Monarch/Characters
The Other Boleyn Girl	2008	UK/USA	Natalie Portman, Scarlett Johansson, Eric Bana, Jim Sturgess, Kristin Scott Thomas	Anne Boleyn, Mary Boleyn, Henry VIII, George Boleyn, Catherine of Aragon, Jane Seymour
The Young Victoria	2009	UK/USA	Emily Blunt, Rupert Friend, Paul Bettany, Miranda Richardson, Jim Broadbent, Mark Strong, Thomas Kretschmann	Victoria, Albert, Lord Melbourne, Duchess of Kent, William IV, King Leopold
The King's Speech	2010	UK	Colin Firth, Helena Bonham Carter, Derek Jacobi, Geoffrey Rush	George VI, Queen Elizabeth, Edward VIII, George V, Winston Churchill, Wallis Simpson, Princess Elizabeth, Princess Margaret, Queen Mary, Duke of Gloucester
Anonymous	2011	UK/Germany	Rhys Ifans, Vanessa Redgrave, Rafe Spall, David Thewlis, Joely Richardson	Edward de Vere (17th Earl of Oxford), Elizabeth I, William Shakespeare, William Cecil, Robert Cecil
W.E.	2011	UK	Abbie Cornish, Andrea Riseborough, James D'Arcy, Oscar Isaac, Richard Coyle, Geoffrey Palmer	Wally Winthrop, Wallis Simpson, Edward, George V, Queen Mary
Hyde Park on Hudson	2012	USA	Bill Murray, Olivia Williams, Samuel West, Olivia Colman	Franklin Roosevelt, Eleanor Roosevelt, George VI, Queen Elizabeth (later, the Queen Mother)
Diana	2013	UK/USA	Naomi Watts	Diana, Princess of Wales
A Royal Night Out	2015	UK	Sarah Gordon, Bel Powley, Emma Watson, Rupert Everett	Elizabeth I, Princess Margaret, King George VI, Queen Elizabeth (later, the Queen Mother)

evil machinations of the King (whom Olivier imbued with much-acclaimed charisma) as he conspires to steal the throne from his brother, Edward IV.

The 1960s were characterized by political and social upheaval, and films like *Becket* (1964) and *A Man for All Seasons* (1966) reflected the turbulent times. These interpretations portrayed righteous characters in opposition to monarchical authority, reflecting the rebellious zeitgeist of the decade.[29] Feminism was also emerging on the sociological and political agenda, so audiences saw more feisty female characters as well.

Geneviève Bujold's performance as Henry VIII's ill-fated second wife, Anne Boleyn, in *Anne of the Thousand Days* (1969), epitomizes such interpretations. In her recent cultural analysis of changing historical representations, feminist philosopher Susan Bordo describes Bujold's performance as depicting a "sixties rebel girl" and "the first truly iconic Anne."[30] She delivers a magnificent final speech to Henry—albeit one without any historical foundation. Nevertheless, it reinforces Anne's firebrand image and resonates with newly emergent feminist values: "And remember this: Elizabeth shall be a greater queen than any king of yours! She shall rule a greater England than you could ever have built! Yes—MY Elizabeth SHALL BE QUEEN! And my blood will have been well spent!" Similarly, Vanessa Redgrave and Glenda Jackson give passionate performances as the two feuding sisters, Mary and Elizabeth, in *Mary, Queen of Scots* (1971). In this version, both characters are much more strong-willed and independent than in prior portrayals.

The scandals that beset the Royal Family throughout the 1990s provided a very different context against which productions like *The Madness of King George* (1994), *Her Majesty, Mrs. Brown* (1997), and *Elizabeth* (1998) could expose the more salacious and personal aspects of royal lives. Films like these appealed to audiences who no longer regarded figures of royalty as role models and who were much more aware of the discrepancies between the monarchy's public and private personas.[31] Each juxtaposed speculation with historical fact to indulge in imaginative, personalized accounts that can be neither proven nor disproven, including the reasons for George III's madness, Victoria's true relationship with John Brown, and Elizabeth I's relationship with the Earl of Leicester. Together, they eschew the importance of adhering to historical fact in favor of recreating visual accuracy and aesthetically powerful images.

Television has also played its part in changing representations of royalty. The BBC has enjoyed a long-standing reputation for its fastidiously researched, world-class historical dramas, many of which revolve around the lives (and frequently the loves) of monarchs. Some of its programs have provided the impetus for major film productions, as was the case with *Her Majesty, Mrs. Brown*. BBC miniseries such as *The Six Wives of Henry VIII* (1971) and *Elizabeth R* (1971) were successfully exported to U.S. television channels.

Although subsequently serialized on BBC2, the most widely popularized royal series in the last decade did not originate with the BBC. Produced in Ardmore Studios, County Wicklow, Ireland, for the American television channel Showtime, *The Tudors* (2007–2010) was a highly successful historical drama (or fiction, depending on one's point of view). It was widely panned by historians and television critics alike for taking many liberties with key historical elements, including character names, event timelines, depictions of relationships, costume design, and physical appearances. The *New York Times* critic Ginia Bellafante accused it of playing "a game of historical hopscotch,"[32] and David Starkey panned it as "gratuitously awful," accusing it of bringing shame on the BBC. He complained bitterly about the twists of history that saw Henry VIII's sister "Margaret" (whose real name, Mary, was changed by producers so audiences would not confuse her with Henry's daughter), being sent away to marry the King of Portugal instead of the King of Scotland. He opined, "There's only one reason for that: so that she can have a bonkorama in a supposed ship's cabin with the hunk who plays the Duke of Suffolk."[33] Other production choices support Starkey's suspicion. With ample supplies of sex, passion, scandal, and intrigue, *The Tudors* is much more about popular entertainment than historical education. As Michel Hirst, the show's creator and writer, explained, "Showtime commissioned me to write an entertainment, a soap opera, and not history."[34]

Casting the big-screen heartthrob Jonathan Rhys Meyers (*Bend It Like Beckham, Mission Impossible 3*) as Henry VIII certainly enhanced *The Tudors*' soap-opera appeal. Without a doubt, however, this choice represents one of the most striking examples of historical misrepresentation in the series. Rhys Meyers's Henry scarcely ages in the series, apart from the fact that his hair turns gray. More egregiously, he remains slim—in stark contrast to the real Henry, whose looks, mobility, and health were increasingly affected by his weight. In fact, his portrayal is a far cry from that in the 1970 BBC miniseries *The Six Wives of Henry VIII*. Australian actor Keith Mitchell's portrayal of the King in that program is widely considered to be historically accurate, as he captures his transition from an athletic young prince to an aging and ailing tyrant.

Despite the casting of Rhys Meyers and many other distortions, audiences loved *The Tudors*. In Britain, the first two series averaged 2.2 million viewers,* although viewership declined considerably for the third.[35] The program also exerted a wider impact, restimulating interest in the Tudor period,[36] including increased visitors to Hampton Court Palace[37] and a rash of new books on such characters as Catherine of Aragon and Anne Boleyn.

Indeed, since the advent of *The Tudors,* Anne's image has flourished on websites, Facebook pages, and blogs turned into self-published books; T-shirts and mugs also support this renewed interest.[38] In her recent cultural timeline, Susan Bordo updated the queen's image for the Internet era, naming her "viral Anne." For these reasons, the historian and writer Tracy Borman applauded the series; she believes it brought Henry VIII and his court to life for contemporary audiences, encouraging them to dig further into history and explore the stories for themselves.

Apart from historical drama in all its many rich and imaginative guises, another important contribution of television has been to highlight the more humorous aspects of royalty. As we discussed in Chapter 2, humor and comedy in general play an important role in British culture, dating back to early music hall days and beyond.[39] A particularly influential program format within British comedy, popular from the 1960s on, draws heavily on the tradition of group revues at British universities that rely on clever satire and piercing wit.[40] The now-iconic *Monty Python's Flying Circus* (1969–1974) and the sharply satirical *Spitting Image* (1984–1996) are both good examples of this comic style. They regularly poked fun at all aspects of the establishment, and members of the Royal Family were frequently targets.

Spitting Image mercilessly parodied the Royal Family (see figure 16). The Queen Mother always was seen with a bottle of gin (known as her tipple of choice), and Prince Philip, Duke of Edinburgh carried a blunderbuss.† In Britain, this object is understood as symbolizing its owner's lack of subtlety and precision—reflecting Prince Philip's renown for making misstatements during royal occasions. *Spitting Image* portrayed Princess Margaret as always inebriated and Fergie, the Duchess of York, whose battles with her weight were well documented by the tabloid press, as spending her time rooting for

* In American English, "season."
† A short-barreled firearm.

truffles. Diana was portrayed as the archetypal Sloane Ranger, who never passed up an opportunity for self-promotion.

Another hugely popular British comedy that featured royalty was *Blackadder,* an infamous series that gained a cult following during (and after) its run on BBC between 1983 and 1989. In the initial series, Rowan Atkinson starred as Edmund Blackadder, son of "Richard IV," one of the young "Princes in the Tower" imprisoned in 1483. In contrast to what occurred in real life, in the series Richard IV survives his imprisonment. Each of the subsequent three series took place in a different era, with Atkinson playing descendants of the original Blackadder. Three series revolved around his relationship with well-known royal figures: Richard IV, Elizabeth I, and the Prince Regent, Prince George (later George IV, played by Hugh Laurie). The hilarious comic sketches depicted the obsequious Blackadder trying to curry royal favor, assisted by his dense and dirty man-servant, Baldrick. The royal characters usually were portrayed as even stupider than Baldrick, and even shallower and more and egocentric than Blackadder. In 2004, the series was voted the second-best British sitcom of all time.[41]

The antiestablishment ethos of British comedy means there is no escape for royal figures, who have been regarded as appropriate targets since *Punch* published its satirical "Court Circular," which reported on John Brown's supposed lack of official duties at Balmoral.[42] Similar to the Bakhtinian notion of carnival as a topsy-turvy space where everyday norms are suspended and the usual order of things reversed, the comic aspects of royalty serve to suspend the deference and respect normally accorded the monarchy (as was true in the portrayals of the monarchs' commoner confidants in the films described above). But as is also true with carnivals, this situation represents only a temporary suspension of norms. Because this inversion is temporally and spatially contained, and limited to special occasions, it ultimately may help reinforce the status quo. Describing the Royal Family as a great "source of comedy," Rowan Atkinson, a friend of Prince Charles and a guest at William and Catherine's wedding, justified his regular mockery of royal figures as "undoubtedly born out of love and respect and wanting them to carry on."[43] He added, "The last thing I would wish is to discredit the British establishment or the monarchy because I need it there—a) as a source of inspiration and b) as a source of comedy." In fact, Atkinson returned to television as Edmund Blackadder's descendant during a one-time promo-

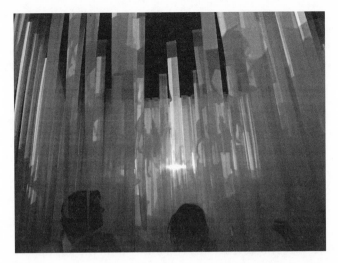

FIGURE 18. Watching Queen Victoria's Diamond Jubilee. Photo by Cele Otnes.

tion for a series of BBC live-music concerts to commemorate the Queen's Golden Jubilee.

The three most popular monarchs portrayed on film and television are women: Elizabeth I, Victoria, and Elizabeth II.[44] They have been portrayed 106, 85, and 82 times, respectively. The popular male monarchs have been portrayed less often: Henry VIII (79 times), Charles II (55), Richard I (46), Richard III (40), George III (36), and Edward VII (34). Yet even depictions of Henry VIII and Charles II largely focus on their relationships with women. This decision makes sense when we remember that the audience for historical and costume drama is mainly female, coupled with the fact that many of these monarchs' wives and consorts were strong women in a man's world.

In terms of film appearances made by the monarchs themselves, Queen Victoria is credited with the largest number of screen appearances and also was the first to appear, starring as herself in the 1897 Diamond Jubilee procession, which reached eager audiences on screens around Britain. Compared to those times when others have portrayed her, however, many of her own appearances were fleeting, often intended to symbolize the solemnity of a moralistic Victorian era and endorse bygone British imperial might. In 2012, an exhibit at Kensington Palace featured film clips of her Diamond Jubilee parade projected onto long white reflective strips, providing visitors with a 360-degree immersion in the broadcast (figure 18).

Rose Tapley was the first to portray the monarch, in *The Victoria Cross* (1912), a silent film about Florence Nightingale and the Crimean War. In 1913, two actresses, Blanche Forsythe and Mrs. Henry Lytton, portrayed Victoria over her lifetime in the now-lost seven-reel film *Sixty Years a Queen,* which was also released in America. Four years later, Mrs. Lytton depicted her in *Disraeli* (1916). Both were minor parts, and in a 1929 film by the same name, Victoria appears only at the end, as a remote figure sitting in regal splendor on her throne.[45] She has also featured in comedy, with Peter Sellers famously playing her in *The Great McGonagall* (1974), the story of unemployed Scotsman William McGonagall's ambition to become poet laureate. McGonagall (played by Spike Milligan) gives a hilarious performance reading his dreadful poetry before a cross-dressing Peter Sellers as Queen Victoria (Prince Albert is dressed like Hitler from the waist up). Testifying to the cultural ubiquity of her image, Victoria even appears in the television series *Doctor Who,* when the Doctor and his assistant time-travel to nineteenth-century Scotland and defend the monarch from both an attacking werewolf and avenging warrior-monks.

Despite her many superficial appearances, comic or otherwise, cinemagoers have had their choice of many biographical portrayals of Victoria. The first of note was *Victoria the Great* (1937), by British film producer Herbert Wilcox, who also produced *Sixty Glorious Years* (1938). Both starred Wilcox's wife, Anna Neagle, as Victoria, and both were hugely popular, especially with working-class audiences. For the first time, viewers were afforded depictions of the monarch's private as well as public persona, and were shown some of the tensions that could arise between these two contexts. Yet the thematic emphasis still rested more on politics, especially encouraging patriotism in a prewar audience. It was only in more recent films, such as *Her Majesty, Mrs. Brown* (1997), *Victoria and Albert* (a 2001 BBC miniseries), and *The Young Victoria* (2009), that the Queen would be portrayed with any real emotional depth.

This last film was geared toward a post-Diana audience. In the same way Diana became an icon, Victoria is shown to be a victim of tradition, as she utters lines like "Even a palace can be a prison."[46] The film asserts that her rebellious image and freethinking spirit enabled her to transcend this confinement, to become the humane if formidable queen who is well documented. Emily Blunt's passionate portrayal of the younger queen repositioned the steely monarch's image for a new generation and spurred a resurgence of interest in Victoria and Albert as a royal couple, in terms of both their romance and their visions for society.

Elizabeth I, the second most portrayed monarch in film, featured in over a dozen full-length films about her life. She has been portrayed by more celebrities than any other monarch, including Sarah Bernhardt, Bette Davis, Flora Robson, Jean Simmons, Glenda Jackson, Helen Mirren, and Cate Blanchett. With her brilliantly bejeweled red hair, white makeup, and unique Elizabethan style of power dressing, her image is as distinctive as the elderly Victoria's sternly plump profile. Both queens are human brands in their own right, inspiring instant recognition and evoking multiple associations.

Like Victoria, Elizabeth conjures up the age named after her, but there can be no doubt that the Elizabethan Golden Age conjures up richer romantic and mythic connections than does the sobriety associated with the Victorian era. Moreover, Elizabeth's identity as the Virgin Queen allows for infinitely more sexual speculation than does that of Victoria, the archetypal mother figure to both her family and her people. The many political intrigues and threats to Elizabeth's life, coupled with one of England's greatest victories in its defeat of the Spanish Armada, explain why her story continues to appeal to new generations.

Sarah Bernhardt offered the first portrayal of Elizabeth in *Les amours de la Reine d'Angleterre* (1912). On the whole, Bernhardt portrays a rather bland Elizabeth, lacking any real passion either in romance or in anger, an Elizabeth subsumed by Bernhardt's own personality rather than the reverse.[47] Elizabeth's portrayal in another silent movie, *The Virgin Queen* (1923), was by the multinamed and titled socialite and actress Lady Diana Olivia Winifred Maud Manners Duff Cooper.* Allegedly close to the Royal Family of the time, it was rumored that she had captured the eye of the Prince of Wales (later Edward VIII).[48] Her performance was generally panned by critics of the time. Somewhat arrogantly, she wrote in her autobiography: "I was cast for Queen Elizabeth and in spite of a red wig and shaved eyebrows my full young face could not give a suggestion of her fleshless aquilinity.... I had little hope or faith or charity for the Virgin Queen with all its gross anachronism, but I delighted in it as an inartistic lark."[49]

It was not until Flora Robson's interpretation of Elizabeth in *Fire over England* (1937) that any actress succeeded in imbuing convincing depth in the character. Robson read Elizabeth's history meticulously and often changed her lines in accordance with her research. Never known for her

---

* She received all of these names at birth, except her surname, Duff Cooper, which she acquired upon marriage.

beauty, Robson's powerful portrayal focuses on the queen's compassion, ambition, and wisdom, rather than on sexual attractiveness or romantic interests. In this respect Robson's portrayal, often thought to be the most historically realistic,[50] is very different from the preceding ones or, indeed, those that followed. Most later portrayals, in fact, constructed their narratives around Elizabeth as a queen in love. This is especially true in *Essex and Elizabeth* with Bette Davis, and *Young Bess* with Jean Simmons.

The same criticism can also be levied against contemporary Cate Blanchett depictions of Elizabeth. Blanchett may offer the "sexiest" portrayal of the monarch—a revamp consistent with contemporary third-wave feminism and empowerment through sexual expression—but critics regard her representations as lacking the realism of Robson's. Similarly, Glenda Jackson's *Elizabeth R* (BBC miniseries, 1971) was pathbreaking in its time. It depicted a highly confident, independent Elizabeth who was adept at politics but overly harsh in personality. This interpretation communicated as much about the discourse of sexual politics that was pervasive in the 1970s as it did about Elizabeth's own character.

Of all the portrayals of Elizabeth Tudor in the history of film and TV, however, Helen Mirren's performance in *Elizabeth I* (BBC miniseries, 2005) is considered the most empathetic in terms of her ability to convey the person rather than the icon, the woman beneath the crown.[51] A multiple award-winning actress, Mirren has played three British queens to date.* But it is her recent portrayal of Elizabeth II that is most widely known and admired. In that role, she leverages her unique ability to get under the skin of the persona she is playing and absorb herself body and soul into the part. Her poignant performance of the Queen's painful ordeal during the seven days after Diana's death reawakened its audience to the monarch's humanity and vulnerability at a time when she faced the greatest criticism of her reign.

More recently, in 2013, Mirren played the Queen again in a stage play, *The Audience,* in London's West End (the production and its star subsequently moved to New York City in 2015, garnering rave reviews). This work charts the Queen's life through her weekly audiences with most of her prime ministers during her (then) sixty-year reign. Although the Palace reportedly disapproved of this theatrical production (but supposedly not of *The Queen*), Mirren received much critical acclaim and was credited with bringing "an air

---

* Queen Charlotte in *The Madness of King George* (1994), *Elizabeth I* (2005), and Elizabeth II in *The Queen* (2006).

of dignified solitude"[52] to the role, as well as "compassion, grace, affection, and humour."[53] Mirren's performances as the current monarch also seem to have sparked new interest in the unofficial persona. In 2014, the West End featured another stage play, this time focusing on the Queen's relationship with Margaret Thatcher. Aptly titled *Handbagged* to reflect both women's penchant for carrying their purses on their arms, the comedy speculates on the two powerful women's often-conflicting ideas of Britain's role in the world. Two different actresses each play the Queen and Thatcher, with much of the comic effect stemming from their older selves conversing with their younger ones. Other portrayals of the present Queen are few and far between, probably because writers perceive that there is less room for speculation about her private life while she is still alive. Thus, she herself has made most of her screen appearances, mainly in documentaries to commemorate various milestones, such as her coronation. These include the 1953 *A Queen Is Crowned,* narrated by Laurence Olivier, and a recent film that commemorates her jubilee year, *The Diamond Queen* (2012), presented by Andrew Marr. This film highlights personal aspects of her life, as well as numerous state visits and other official events. One exception to her lack of characterization is *The Queen* (2009), a British television docudrama that comprises five episodes, each focusing on a key event or crisis of her reign. Each features a different actress playing the Queen, none particularly well known.*

Nor should we forget *Royal Family* (1969), a two-hour film commissioned by the Queen and Prince Philip that documents a year in the life of the Queen, her husband, and their children. The film portrays her "orchestrating a family barbecue at Loch Muick with Philip, Charles, Anne, Andrew, Edward and the corgis; laughing with her children at an American sitcom . . . trading stories around the table at lunch [and] decorating a Christmas tree."[54] Watched by three-quarters of the British public across its five airings—and an estimated 400 million in 130 countries—it gave its audiences a chance to view the informal side of royal life in tandem with the Queen's busy schedule.[55] However, many viewers said it just made the Royal Family seem too ordinary and risked diluting the monarchy's mystique.[56] Even the BBC's David Attenborough, one of its producers, noted that the monarchy "depends on mystique and the tribal chief in his hut. If any member of the tribe ever sees inside the hut, then the whole system . . . is damaged and the tribe eventually disintegrates."[57] Since the initial airings, it has not been

---

* Emilia Fox, Samantha Bond, Susan Jameson, Barbara Flynn, and Diana Quick.

rebroadcast until recently, when the National Portrait Gallery included a small segment in its Diamond Jubilee exhibit, *The Queen: Art & Image*. It is generally believed that she now regrets doing this film.[58]

Apart from Mirren, the actress most associated with playing Elizabeth II is Jeannette Charles, the Queen's lookalike, who has been cast in numerous television comedy programs and shows. Her career reflects the fact that portrayals of the present monarch, heavily influenced by the irreverent spirit of the 1960s, are often humorous. The Queen's doppelgänger has made regular appearances in Spike Milligan's *Q*, a BBC series of quirky comedy sketches (1969–1982), and even surprised one contestant on Channel 4's *Big Brother*, who thought he was meeting the real Queen! She also played the monarch during an assassination attempt in 1988's raucously comic *The Naked Gun: From the Files of the Police Squad!*

As contemporary celebrity culture becomes ever more pervasive, media representations of royal figures exert concomitantly more influence on our perceptions of royalty. Just as Emily Blunt offered us a more sensual, softer Victoria, and Cate Blanchett a more winsome and intriguing Elizabeth I, so too Helen Mirren contributed new understandings of the current queen, revealing her humorous and affectionate sides. Celebrity endorsers' potential impact on a brand image is well known, as their own personal attributes and history can act as an endorsement of sorts. The same could be said for the celebrities who are cast in iconic roles; their own heritage within the industry and popular culture and the quality of their performances become ingrained within the larger narratives of the RFBC. Furthermore, any special attributes a celebrity may possess likewise imbue the brand with new meanings it may have lacked.[59] In the case of these three formidable queens, each a powerful brand in her own right, association with such celebrated actresses lends a touch of glamour, together with an accessibility that makes them much more "real" for present-day audiences.

Even with so many new forms of entertainment, the film industry still relies on new or little-known narratives about the Royal Family to help achieve success at the box office. *A Royal Night Out*, for example, was released on May 8, 2015—the seventieth anniversary of Victory Day in Europe (VE Day). It depicts the young Princesses Elizabeth and Margaret on that evening in 1945, escaping from the confines of Buckingham Palace to mix with the celebrating crowds and find adventure. Likewise, 2015 also saw the anticipated release of the first original series for the E! Network—a one-hour weekly drama titled *The Royals*, about a contemporary British royal family. Following the plot formula that proved so successful for *The Tudors,* the program offers what its star, Elizabeth Hurley, describes as an "extreme, sexy adventure into royalty."[60] Finally, for those who wish to focus on Hilary Mantel's recent literary interpretations of Henry VIII's court, both *Wolf Hall* and *Bring Up the Bodies* have already been adapted for the theater and are being filmed to air on BBC Two in 2015. Award-winning actor Damian Lewis, acclaimed for his recent role in the drama *Homeland,* portrays Henry VIII.

As this chapter shows, media such as film, television, and theater make important contributions to constructing the RFBC in the popular imagination, and they are unlikely to diminish in influence in the foreseeable future. Most certainly, many other actresses, actors, directors, and producers will take their turn at interpreting members of the past, present, and future Royal Family, as the media once again revitalize images of royalty for new audiences in new times.

SIX

Marketing the Monarchy

In chapter 3, we discussed how much Margaret Tyler loves shopping for royal merchandise and how the collection that has taken over her house runs the gamut from cheap, tourist-targeted souvenirs to high-end bone china made by revered British potteries to a chair from Charles's investiture as Prince of Wales in 1969. In this chapter, we focus on how the RFBC consistently intersects with the marketplace in ways in and out of their control. From visiting traditional manufacturers and merchants who bear Royal Warrants to snapping up endless varieties of commemoratives in souvenir shops that target royal tourists, people can experience the intersection of marketing and the monarchy in myriad ways. The RFBC's interface with commerce through granting Royal Warrants dates back many centuries. Yet the Royal Family's strategic decision to develop their own consumer brands is a much newer phenomenon and in part reflects the growing pressure on the monarchy to contribute in some meaningful way to Britain's economy. To that end, the Royal Collection Trust, Duchy Originals, Highgrove, and the Windsor Farm Shop—all brands the RFBC itself has established within the last thirty years—reflect the increasing interweaving of royal interests with consumer culture.

Before examining the practices of royal branding more closely, however, we begin by explaining the long-standing practice of granting Royal Warrants. Essentially, these signify the bestowal of approval by Royal Family members upon purveyors of products and services in specific categories.* The practice of granting Royal Warrants is not limited to the British monarchy; it also occurs in Europe and Asia.

---

* Party-planning businesses have historically been excluded; this means the firm owned by Prince William's in-laws likely is ineligible for the designation.

In Britain, warrants are always issued to a specific individual within a commercial firm. Those companies that have supplied goods or services to one or more Royal Family member for at least five years can apply to the Royal Household for consideration. At present, the Queen, Prince Philip, and Prince Charles have awarded over eight hundred warrants.* The practice peaked with Queen Victoria; in an effort to boost British commerce, she granted over one thousand such recognitions. Each grantor bestows his or her honor separately, so firms can receive warrants from more than one family member; a few even hold the designation from all three. As head of the Royal Household, the Lord Chamberlain informs recipients of the designation and reviews renewal applications.

The main benefit for grantees is the right to visibly display a heraldic symbol and a statement of being granted the honor, which begins, "By Appointment to . . ." with the grantor's name following. Nevertheless, strict guidelines regulate the display of these elements. For example, Charles's warrant features the traditional symbol for the Prince of Wales—three white ostrich feathers encircled by a gold coronet (figure 19). As is true for all warrants, it may be displayed only in the window and once inside the establishment. The symbol may also appear discreetly on company stationery.

Although clearly intended as a sign of prestige, some argue that the warrant can deceive consumers who seek vicarious enjoyment by imitating authentic royal purchase patterns. This criticism is rooted in the fact that warrants may be granted to firms that regularly supply members of the Royal Household and not necessarily the Royal Family itself. Such gray-area endorsements are akin to instances where celebrities tout products but then reveal that they do not actually use them. Hugh Faulkner, secretary of the Royal Warrant Holders Association, defended the inclusion of Royal Household purchases, noting, "The fact that she [the Queen] does not [use a particular good] is irrelevant. . . . [It] goes into Buckingham Palace."[1]

On one level, it may seem that when the Queen, Prince Philip, or Prince Charles grants a Royal Warrant, they engage in celebrity endorsement, a marketing practice that leverages the fame of well-known figures by paying them to promote a product or service. In so doing, marketers seek to transfer a celebrity's symbolic and aesthetic assets to the promoted brand—a phenomenon called the "halo effect." The Royal Family has been aware of this concept since the late nineteenth century, the nascent stage of the advertising

* The Queen Mother also bestowed them during her lifetime.

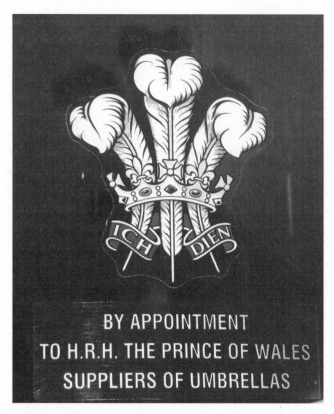

FIGURE 19. Prince of Wales Royal Warrant. Photo by Cele Otnes.

industry. In 1882 the actress Lillie Langtry, the high-profile mistress of Queen Victoria's son Albert Edward,* was hired as one of the earliest celebrity endorsers on record when she became the face in ads for Pears Soap, the world's first registered brand.[2] Renowned for her beautiful skin and sexual magnetism, she testified, "Since using Pears Soap I have discarded all others." Lillie brought a new, glamorous allure to this famous British brand (also a warrant-designee), and was the first woman to earn money from product endorsement.

With increasingly rigorous standards of beauty, fame, and youth pervading global consumer culture, celebrity endorsement continues to be commonplace, with almost one-fourth of all ads in Britain and the United States relying on the tactic.[3] Just as George Clooney's smooth smile on billboards

---

* Upon Victoria's death in 1901, Prince Albert Edward acceded the throne as Edward VII.

around the world recently encouraged people to buy Nespresso coffee makers, so too the Royal Warrant bestows on its holders a major competitive advantage in the global marketplace. Simply put, it symbolizes the pinnacle of authentic British craftsmanship and quality.*

In fact, reinforcing the global appeal of the RFBC, the Royal Warrant is likely to carry more clout with consumers outside of Britain, especially in Asian countries and the United States, where many consumers hold the Royal Family in high esteem and the designation is seen as the ultimate marker of luxury.[4] In Britain, where cynicism often surrounds the Royal Family, some key British brands actually downplay their royal connections.[5] Two very popular brands—After Eight chocolates and Jacob cream crackers—actually removed the warrant from their packaging, even though they chose to retain the honor.

The most controversial instance of warrant removal involves Harrods, London's high-end department store. In 2000, its owner, Mohamed Al-Fayed, accused Prince Philip of masterminding the fatal car accident involving his son and Diana, Princess of Wales. Shortly afterward, Al-Fayed received word that the Duke would not renew his Royal Warrant and Al-Fayed would have one year to remove the Duke's symbols from the store's packaging and stationery. Ten years after the press broke the story, Al-Fayed revealed that he had taken down all four of Harrods's warrants (one from each living grantor, as well as the Queen Mother's) and burned them, saying they were a "curse" on the store.[6]

Yet the Royal Warrant differs from a standard celebrity endorsement in one vitally important way: grantors within the Royal Family receive no compensation for permitting their personal insignias to appear in shop windows or in e-commerce communications. In addition, designees continue to charge the monarchy for purchases. It is safe to assume, however, that the Royal Household enjoys the same volume discounts their suppliers offer other customers; imagine how much Twining's Tea over 1,200 members of the Royal Household must drink in one year alone! Given the lack of financial remuneration for the warrant, it is fair to say that the honor is somewhat above the sphere of the marketplace and all its commercial (and thus potentially crass) connotations.

Royal Warrants date from 1155, when Henry II provided the Weaver's Company with a Royal Charter, the initial name for a monarch's reward for

* Only a few foreign firms hold the warrant, but foreign subsidiaries operating in Britain are eligible.

loyal service. By the fifteenth century, the Royal Warrant of Appointment superseded the Charter and was typically granted to royal tradesmen. Many occupy important roles in British history—such as William Caxton, Britain's first printer, who received a warrant in 1476. Lists of the enterprises that have held warrants over time offer an interesting glimpse into how the Royal Household's needs have both evolved and remained the same. In 1684, the list included a haberdasher, a button maker, and a locksmith—as well as more puzzling appellations, such as a Watchmaker in Reversion, an Operator for the Teeth, and a Corn Cutter. In 1775, a dispute broke out between two parties as to which deserved the title "Bug Destroyer to Her Majesty." (Apparently, the titles of Royal Rat-Catcher and Royal Mole-Taker were undisputed).

The current list of grantees, arranged by category on the Royal Warrant Association website,* reflects both mundane and privileged aspects of the monarchy. For example, one firm holds the warrant for portable toilets. Probably the most eclectic category is "Sports, Hobbies, Pursuits and Pastimes." It contains several gun makers, manufacturers of sporting equipment, the world's leading dealer in philately (reflecting the long-standing royal interest in stamp collecting), taxidermists, and even the Hebridean Island Cruise line.

Historically, many grantees conducted business on Jermyn Street, just a short walk from St. James's Palace. As a result of changes in the retail mix of the street and the understated ways awards are displayed, we initially found it difficult to spot warrant holders there. However, we eventually identified a cluster of stores displaying the honor, which also led to the discovery that Jermyn Street's retail mix is overwhelmingly masculine. The street is lined with purveyors of men's apparel, shoes, leather goods, cigars, umbrellas, ties, shaving accessories, and military collectibles. One grantee offering men's apparel displayed two posters of classic fashion trendsetters: the American crooner Bing Crosby and the Duke of Windsor (formerly Edward VIII; see chapter 8 for more on his sartorial style).

One of the most interesting grantees, located between Jermyn Street and St. James's Palace, is John Lobb, Ltd. Bootmaker, which bills itself as the best shoemaker in Britain. The store boasts two warrants, from the Queen and Prince Charles. Lobb is famous not only for taking four months to a year to handcraft each pair of footwear, but also for its over twenty thousand

* www.royalwarrant.org.

wooden lasts, "life-size replicas of top people's feet ... essential for making the perfect boot or shoe, contoured to every last corn and bunion."[7] It displays warrants from many countries—and even a satirical one, in line with the British tendency to poke fun at achievements with a dose of humility. Just down the street is D.R. Harris, the Royal Family's favorite chemist's,* also bearing the warrant. A walk up to Piccadilly Street reveals that the back of the famous gourmet food store Fortnum & Mason—which renamed its fifth-floor tearoom the Diamond Jubilee Tea Salon in 2012—features a large, full-color Royal Warrant on its second-floor exterior.

Another interesting royal connection prominently displayed on Jermyn Street is a statue of Beau Brummell, the impetus behind the dandy movement, which was a notable fad among the British nobility and aristocracy in the nineteenth century. The Regency era of 1811–1820 was so named because George III's son and namesake (later George IV) assumed the role of Prince Regent, acting as the monarch by proxy after his father was deemed unfit to rule. The era signified a broader cultural shift toward appreciating aesthetic excess, especially among the aristocracy, and the Prince Regent enthusiastically embraced this trend. A prominent hallmark among these men was their dedication to impeccable fashion sense and meticulous attention to detail in their appearance.†

Complementing the Prince Regent's ideals and interests, dandies "shunned all social conventions of work, association [and] family responsibility to devote themselves fully to ... a superficial idleness and the leisure life."[8] Like Brummell, most did not emanate from the aristocracy but sought acceptance into London's most elite social circles. Brummell clearly succeeded; the Prince Regent apparently devoted hours to watching his protégé prepare for the day, as dandies encouraged daily bathing and teeth cleaning even before these became culturally-engrained practices.

Brummell's commemorative statue on Jermyn Street is appropriate, given how dandyism boosted demand for fine apparel and for the tailoring required to meet the exacting standards of fit and finish. Credited with creating the suit-and-necktie combination that replaced long pants over knee-length breeches, he therefore helped tailors increase fabric sales. Furthermore, one review of the BBC biography *Beau Brummell* notes that he could lay claim to being the world's first "metrosexual."[9]

---

* In the United States, a drugstore.
† No female cultural equivalent to the dandy existed.

Most grantees participate in the Royal Warrant Holders Association, described as "a peerage for trade."[10] This analogy is almost oxymoronic, given that aristocrats historically shunned trade as a livelihood, and earning money through commercial ventures especially was considered beneath them. The association was founded in 1840 for the purpose of holding a sumptuous annual dinner where its members celebrated Queen Victoria's birthday. The event was strictly gentlemen-only, but female warrant holders could offer a man to attend in their place. As the association evolved, it began to police the misuse of warrants and warn businesses to refrain from discussing the Royal Family's shopping patterns. Given the cultural mores against tooting one's own horn that pervade Britain, the dinner represents members' only collective opportunity to celebrate their status. To discuss being a grantee too enthusiastically (or heaven forbid, to talk about the Queen's favorite brand of tea or how much soap the Royal Household was buying per month) was to risk "being caught showing off or 'swanking.'"[11]

The RFBC's reach into the commercial sphere now extends beyond merely bestowing the warrant. Increasingly, it creates brands that even compete with some of these firms. The importance the monarchy places on its own commercial enterprises, and the potential to extend its visibility and reach through these activities, were brought into relief in 2014. That year, it was revealed that in 2012, William and Catherine had secretly established companies to protect their brand and intellectual property rights.[12] Catherine's is called CE Strathearn—combining the initials of her two names Catherine Elizabeth and another of her titles, Countess of Strathearn. William's is titled APL Anglesey, after his middle names, Arthur Philip Louis, and the town where the couple lived in Wales until they married. When the British popular press compared the couple to celebrities like David and Victoria Beckham for making this move, royal aides stressed that it was merely intended as a preventive measure and a paper exercise, not an indication that the companies would actively engage in trade.

For the moment, the couple's companies remain dormant. However, their aides would not deny that this status could change. As a result, the news has fueled much speculation about the types of business ventures they could develop. This discourse was amplified when news broke that Prince Harry also had established a company, named Tsessebe after an African antelope. But royal trademarks are only enforceable within the United Kingdom and the European Union, and the RFBC has almost no recourse when companies outside of these boundaries try to capitalize on the monarchic halo.

Several Chinese firms have already done so; one introduced a Prince Harry line of underwear, jewelry, and watches, and a company that manufactures wood pulp and chemicals now uses the moniker "Prince George."

Though the main royal brands are the Royal Collection Trust, Duchy Originals, Highgrove, and the Windsor Farm Shop, only one arm of the Royal Collection Trust is responsible for producing commercial goods for sale. Comprising a priceless collection of artworks and other historically significant items housed across eight royal residences, the Royal Collection dates back to Henry VIII and is formed from the private collections of monarchs since that time. It is one of the largest collections of artworks in the world and contains 7,000 paintings, 500,000 prints, and 30,000 watercolors and drawings, many by great masters such as Rembrandt, da Vinci, Van Dyck, and Gainsborough, to name but a few. The Queen does not own this collection but instead holds it in trust for the nation and her successors. Media pundits (especially those on the staff of left-leaning publications) often criticize the monarchy and the Royal Collection Trust (as it has been known since 1993), noting that the public's access to the full scope of the collection is limited, and no official inventory is available.[13]

The Royal Collection Trust (hereafter, "the Trust") is the department of the Royal Household responsible not only for the Royal Collection but also for managing public openings of the Queen's official residences. These include three separate areas of Buckingham Palace—the State Rooms, the Royal Mews, and the Queen's Gallery. In addition, it manages the current and former residences of Clarence House, Windsor Castle, Frogmore House, and the Palace of Holyroodhouse in Edinburgh (including its Queen's Gallery). Likewise, the Queen's Gallery adjacent to Buckingham Palace is a key commercial venue for the Trust. Visitors can admire temporary themed exhibits that feature items from the Royal Collection, and view some of the thousands of objects of art and other historic items the Queen guards for the nation and her successors.

In recent years, the Trust has focused on achieving two major goals: making the Royal Collection more accessible to the public and deflecting criticism of the way it handles these treasures. Because perceptions of mismanagement could reflect badly on the Queen and the monarchy as a whole, the Trust has increasingly promoted exhibitions, talks, e-learning resources, and online shopping. These are designed to enhance public perceptions of the Trust's brand, to encourage people to engage with the history of the Royal Collection, and to foster appreciation for its cultural significance.

One of the main ways the Trust engages the public is by staging exhibitions at the residences it oversees. A 2014 exhibition in Windsor Castle, titled *Royal Paintbox: Royal Artists Past and Present,* displayed paintings, drawings, and sculptures created for the Royal Family over the last 350 years. In another exhibition, *Poetry for the Palace: Poets Laureate from Dryden to Duffy,* visitors learned about the close relationship between monarchs and these honored literary figures.*

In its 2012 annual report, the Trust reported that it had successfully increased the number of British visitors to its exhibitions by 100,000 from the previous year.[14] Touring exhibitions around Britain, now a regular activity, are seen as a key way to engage the domestic audience. Furthermore, the Trust launched its first online resource, the e-Gallery, in 2002. It now contains details of more than 227,000 works of art, with more pieces continually being added. It also offers a range of innovative resources designed to encourage visitors to linger and learn more about the collection's history.

Browsing the site, we found a particularly apt section entitled "Royal Portraits: Building the Brand." Like Kevin Sharpe's meticulous *Selling the Tudor Monarchy,* it reminds us that the concept of branding royal figures is not new, and that the symbolic aspects of a monarch's image have long played a highly significant role in the monarchy's survival. Designed for art students, this section offers a fascinating overview of how key Royal Family members in the sixteenth and seventeenth centuries used portraiture to strategically promote themselves. Consider, for example, a portrait of nine-year-old Edward VI, Henry VIII's invalid son who succeeded him in 1547, which conveys Edward's authority and suitability as heir to the throne through the use of several clever visual techniques. To suggest power and potency, his stance imitates that in his father's famous portrait by Hans Holbein. The recognizable gold coronet and white feathers of the Prince of Wales on Edward's sleeve further assert his regal status. The deer park in the background, symbolizing hunting, suggests a further parallel with the prowess of his once-athletic father. At the same time, it significantly masks Edward's frail constitution and history of ill health (he died in 1553 at age fifteen). Such a representation might have caused insecurity among his subjects or, worse still, spurred an inclination to rebel against the monarchy.

* An implicit expectation of poets laureate is that they will create poems that resonate with key historical moments. The current poet laureate, Carol Ann Duffy, wrote "Rings" at the time of William and Catherine's wedding in 2011.

Similarly, a portrait of James I of England (simultaneously James VI of Scotland) by Paul van Somer conveys the monarch's divine right to rule through the symbolic codes included by the painter. As James stands resplendent in his state robes and crown, the window behind him reveals the words "Dieu et mon droit" ("My divine right"), to reinforce royal tradition. The newly built Banqueting House in the background, the first to introduce the classical Italianate style into English architecture, testifies to the King's contemporary sense of style and capacity to envisage the future. The insights into these artworks demonstrate how the Trust offers intriguing pedagogical material to help make the monarchy more accessible to a broader audience, while demonstrating to the British public that the Royal Collection is in safe hands. Proactive management of such publicly available content helps counter republican arguments that the nation, rather than the monarchy, should oversee the collection.[15]

Relatedly, one of the Trust's most important sources of income comes from the usage fees publishers and broadcasters pay to reproduce the works of art in its care. The registrar maintains a supply of over 2,500 images dedicated for this express purpose. As is the case with any stock photography service, the Trust charges its clients based on color, size, usage, and the types of rights requested.[16] This revenue source not only provides financial support for the monarchy but also supports the goals of disseminating items in the collection and improving the image of the Trust in Britain and the world.

The Trust produces merchandise in conjunction with specific displays at the royal residences, as well as operating the retail shops and ticket offices located on-site. It also supplies merchandise to classic high-end British department stores such as Harrods and John Lewis. Buckingham Palace alone boasts four shops (although the Garden Shop is only open during the summer months when tourists can tour the palace), and there are three at Windsor Castle. The Trust is a registered charity, and it retains all profits from its retail sales to maintain and conserve the Royal Collection. Its 2013–14 annual report cited total retail sales of just over £17.5 million ($29.2 million). The Trust's increasing (and increasingly sophisticated) commercial ventures are vital to enhancing the brand's public accessibility, both in Britain and abroad.

The Trust's online shop, which began operations in 2011, is also a key revenue resource. Complementing the retail shops, this click-and-mortar outlet ensures that Royal Collection replicas, chinaware, and other souvenir-type items are instantly accessible all over the world. This is especially important when customers seek high-quality souvenirs of major royal events, such as William and Catherine's wedding. One outcome of that happy occasion was a 46 percent increase in sales through the Trust's offline shops. A whopping 75 percent of 2011 online sales consisted of wedding-related merchandise, testifying to its facilitation of virtual participation in royal events. In addition, the website allows access to all merchandise contained in shops of the Royal Collection Trust.

Sales of Royal Collection commemorative china constitute the heart of retail activity. For every royal occasion of note, the Trust commissions a line of fine-grade porcelain items, all made in England. Recent lines have included a pattern celebrating the Queen's Diamond Jubilee and the births of Prince George and Princess Charlotte. In January 2014, it launched a Victoria and Albert line, inspired by a pattern originally produced in 1840 and on display at Windsor Castle. Featuring the intertwined letters V and A, it includes a cake stand (£250/$417), cup and saucer (£95/$158), and coffee mug (£35/$58).

In that vein, we would be remiss if we did not acknowledge the historical and cultural importance of ceramics as a unique and noteworthy royal commemorative category. Historically, such pieces have enhanced other cherished British rituals, such as teatime, garden parties, and holiday dinners. But English pottery manufacturers not only created special commemorative pieces for royal events; they also distributed free pieces to schoolchildren, encouraging the cultural practice of ceramic collection and display. As chapter 9 describes, some still follow this tradition.

Given their exceptional lifestyle and access to centuries of well-preserved and often one-of-a-kind porcelain patterns, the Royal Family historically has had the means to indulge a ritualistic use of ceramics that is beyond the reach of ordinary households. In fact, the Queen can choose from forty-seven porcelain services for dessert from the sets in the China Corridor (or China Museum) at Windsor Castle,* although not all feature enough pieces for the 160 guests the dining table can accommodate. Famous sets include Queen Victoria's turquoise-rimmed pattern with her monogram on each plate, two sets that George IV acquired from the Sèvres factory in France, and one by the English company Worcester. Decorated with badges of the Order of the Garter, it is featured at the Order's annual luncheon in June.[17]

---

* At Windsor Castle dinners, the main course is always served on silver-edged plates.

Not surprisingly, the Royal Family's china sets are made of much finer bone china than the English (and increasingly, Chinese) potteries use for middle-market commemorative items. The growth of the ceramics industry in Britain stemmed from an abundance of two natural resources—clay and coal. Although most of the clay is in southwest England, the central area around Stoke-on-Trent (known as "the Potteries") is rich in the coal required to heat kilns. Coal is heavier and more expensive to move than clay, so the factories were located near the carbon deposits. These abundant resources soon enabled England to become "potters to the world."[18] Most major British manufacturers that are still successful on a global scale (e.g., Crown Derby, Minton, Spode) established their factories there. Perhaps most famous of all is Wedgwood; its ubiquitous (typically light blue) Jasperware line achieved renown in Britain and beyond, and has featured several royal commemoratives.

Italian craftsmen working in the fifteenth century were the first to mark historical events on commemorative ceramics. In Britain, the earliest pieces date from Charles's I reign in the late seventeenth century, but very few items were produced, and even fewer of these crudely rendered pieces survive. Commemoratives have been fired for each succeeding monarch. Many have increased significantly in value; in 1999, a Charles II charger fired in 1673 sold for $152,000.[19]

Because of a lack of mass-production technology and an inability to render human forms in a clear, sophisticated manner,* English potteries, like most industries, did not truly flourish until they benefited from Industrial Revolution innovations.[20] Certain cultural events, such as George III's Golden Jubilee and Princess Charlotte's tragic death in 1817, still spurred production. But by Queen Victoria's accession, technological advances allowed lithographed images to be transferred onto ceramics, diminishing the need to hand-paint commemoratives.

An extensive range of memorabilia was released during Victoria's reign around events like the Great Exhibition of 1851, Prince Albert's death, and three prolonged military interventions. Furthermore, the potteries expanded their commemorative lines to mark other key British people and events, including military victories, boxing matches, performing artists, sports figures, and even murderers whose crimes gripped the nation. Propagating the

* For instance, George I and George II are often indistinguishable on commemorative ware.

practice of commemorating cultural events likewise encouraged consumer practices of bequeathing, collecting, gift giving, and preserving ceramics.[21]

Of course, as this book (and many collectors' homes) attest, commemoratives are hardly confined to ceramics, and other types of manufacturers also created items designed to fuel the desire to accumulate royal memorabilia. Many British monarchs were heavy smokers. Consistent with the inclusion of collector cards in cigarette packages during the 1930s, the Imperial Tobacco Company commemorated George V's Silver Jubilee in 1935 by including fifty cards, entitled "The Kings and Queens of England 1036–1935," in packages of its John Player's brand.[22]

We discussed the practice of collecting ceramics with both retailers and people who had amassed numerous pieces of (often quite expensive) royal commemoratives, and whose passion led them to antique fairs, websites, and retailers in search of even more pristine pieces. One retail manager noted that the former co-owner of his store used to gleefully tell customers that buying commemoratives was like enjoying a "history lesson in ceramics!"[23] Of course, the potteries also were at the mercy of the fiascos that beset human and family aspects of the RFBC, and they often suffered as a result. When Edward VII's coronation was postponed due to appendicitis, most firms could not respond quickly enough to change the date on their designs. As a result, commemoratives with the correct date have become more valuable than the errant pieces.

Edward VIII's planned coronation, which spurred a large production of advance commemoratives, never even came about—meaning many firms were stuck with large caches of irrelevant inventory and financial losses. Other potteries simply painted over the coronation details, converting pieces into abdication memorabilia. One mug seems to best capture this confusing state of affairs. Its caption reads "The Uncrowned King" and provides the dates for both his accession and his abdication. Yet its design still features a beribboned banner, clearly retained from the coronation version, which reads, "Long May He Reign."[24] (In fact, abdication pieces are worth much more than those created for the coronation).

Although the market is awash with commemorative porcelain created over hundreds of years, in the twentieth century, innovative manufacturers renewed their efforts to commission top designers to create pieces, which has led to a diversification in designs from the standard formal portraits or photographs of Royal Family members. For example, one mug commissioned for Charles's Investiture as Prince of Wales in 1969 did not feature him at all; offered in a range of neon colors, it sported a dragon and scripted letters. One seller of the item on Etsy described it as "oh-so-flower power styling."[25] Given the proliferation of porcelain over the centuries, it is not surprising that specialist dealers exist, and numerous catalogs and books have been published in the category,

Returning to the current landscape of marketing and the monarchy, one recent dramatic change is the way members of "the Firm" often are now directly involved in oversight of royal brands. Prince Charles is well known for offering pronouncements and interventions in his attempts to push environmental concerns and sustainability issues to the forefront of public discourse. His brand, Duchy Originals, is probably the most recognized within the monarchic stable. The ethos of this food brand reaffirms and reflects Charles's passionate commitment to reversing the destructive elements of modern farming methods, as well as to preserving agrarian skills threatened with extinction. Pursuing his lifelong passion for protecting heritage and tradition, in 1990 he created an organic food line named after his estate, the Duchy of Cornwall.*[26] All of its products are made from crops grown on the property. Charles donates the profits to the Prince of Wales Charitable Foundation, which he established in 1979. This charitable umbrella includes organizations that reflect his interest in social enterprise, the built environment, opportunities for young people, and harmony with one's natural or man-made environment.

Duchy of Cornwall oat biscuits, the most familiar product in the line, was also its first, made from oats grown on Charles's Highgrove Estate. A staple on the cheeseboards at upper-class dinner parties throughout Britain, more than 70 million packages have been sold to date. Duchy Originals now boasts 230 products and is sold in 30 countries. Its product line includes free-range meats, dairy and egg products, jams and marmalades, biscuits and bakery items, and beers and cider. Sales have contributed more than £11 million ($18 million) to Charles's charities since its inception. To maintain the brand's royal aura and lend authenticity to its spectrum of offerings, he approves the recipes and ingredients for each product. He supposedly sampled over one hundred versions of oat biscuits to ensure they reflected the most desirable combination of savory and sweet ingredients.

---

* Edward III established the duchy in 1337; by charter, it passes to the monarch's oldest son and heir to the throne. It spans 130,000 acres and 23 counties in southwest England, and contains urban and rural commercial enterprises, forests, and other natural resources.

When Charles initially began to oversee an organic line in the early 1990s, he faced much derision. Of course, the organic food movement was not nearly as widely accepted across the world as it is today. Recently, however, he has been heralded as something of a visionary. These days, people expect to encounter a wide range of organic products in major supermarkets, and the global demand for this food category is predicted to rise to $8.8 billion by 2015.[27] Waitrose, Britain's most upscale supermarket chain, has long supported Duchy Originals. Perhaps this is unsurprising, given that it holds a Royal Warrant to supply groceries to the Queen and Prince Charles, and previously had received one from the Queen Mother.

In 2009, Waitrose took a significantly larger step in its support when it formed a partnership with Duchy Originals after the brand's first financial losses since 1996, to the tune of over £3 million ($4.9 million). As was the case for many premium brands, especially organic products, consumer demand dropped following the severe 2008 economic recession. Under the terms of the licensing agreement, and bolstered by its multimillion-pound investment in the brand, Waitrose became the exclusive manufacturer, distributor, and seller of Duchy Originals in Britain. It also planned to more than double the number of products in the line.[28] Waitrose's marketing efforts have boosted Duchy's flagging sales, and its promotion of the brand has helped increase consumers' understanding of the values on which it is based.

Waitrose's initial advertising campaign to celebrate its royal acquisition features British celebrity chef Heston Blumenthal describing the organic and sustainable principles that underlie Duchy Originals. Walking through the fertile fields of the Duchy of Cornwall Home Farm in Gloucestershire, Heston tells viewers about the "seed of an idea" planted twenty years before, to encourage a way of farming that respects both nature and animals and preserves traditional farming methods. He emphasizes the commitment to food excellence that pervades both Waitrose and Duchy Originals, and the brand values they share.

Not inconsequently, these values are synonymous with a British upper-class lifestyle; indeed, Waitrose boasts the most affluent customer base in the British grocery market. In fact, it is often the butt of class-based humor, and in 2012, a social-media effort backfired badly for just this reason. A Twitter campaign encouraging shoppers to finish the sentence "I shop at Waitrose because . . . " resulted in a barrage of mocking completions, including " . . . their colour scheme matches my Range Rover" and " . . . the toilet paper is made from 24-c[ara]t gold thread." In spite of the satirical comments, the partnership between Waitrose and Duchy Originals seems to be a success. According to a release on Waitrose's website, in 2012 the brand earned a profit of £3.23 million, with Charles's charities receiving almost £2.9 million.

Following this success story, the Prince recently extended his branding expertise to encompass Highgrove, the residence in Gloucestershire where he lives with the Duchess of Cornwall. The wooded parklands that surround Highgrove House, together with the nine-hundred-acre Home Farm where pedigreed cattle and sheep graze, form Highgrove Estates. Here in the gardens and surrounding land, Charles has put into practice the organic and sustainable principles he has espoused over the last twenty-five years. One result is an abundance of wildflower meadows that welcome diverse varieties of bees, butterflies, and other threatened insects. Willow beds provide a filtration process for the sewage that empties onto them, affording Highgrove's visitors (about 23,000 each year) an opportunity to engage in a bit of royal toilet humor in the gardens.[29]

Since its inception as an on-site shop featuring produce items, the Highgrove brand initially expanded to two other locations, one in Bath and the other in nearby Tetbury. In addition, Fortnum & Mason and the Windsor Farm Shops now stock Highgrove products. As with the Duchy brand, all profits revert to the Prince's charities. The Highgrove brand also maintains an impressive online presence.* Despite supporting an exclusive image based on quality British craftsmanship, the website offers some home and garden products in its ever-expanding range at surprisingly accessible price points. Shoppers on a modest budget can find low-priced terracotta pots for £5 ($7.50), jute garden waste sacks for £3.75 ($5.60), or in a less functional vein, a decorative mug bearing the Prince of Wales's insignia for £11 ($16.50). The more affluent can splurge on a Highgrove Hen House for £3,750 ($5,625) or a willow sculpture of Clarence the cow for £2,750 ($4,125).

Apart from offering home and garden products, the website promotes the Highgrove brand by touting events at the estate that reinforce its brand values. Seasonal workshops teach traditional skills in danger of extinction, from compost making to willow weaving. Garden tours promote the success of the sustainable methods used to create and maintain the gardens. The more hedonistic visitor can purchase an afternoon Champagne Garden Tea Tour (£145/$217.50

---

* www.highgroveshop.com.

for two) or an elegant St. David's Day Black Tie Dinner, both in the Orchard Restaurant, where chefs prepare tasty dishes using organic local produce.

The publicity surrounding Charles's recent establishment of two off-site Highgrove Shops helped him expand the brand and garner public attention. It has also added to his long list of titles; the *Guardian* named Charles "Britain's poshest greengrocer."[30] The first shop—and the only one that remains open outside Highgrove's grounds—opened in 2008 in Tetbury, a quaint English market town in the Cotswolds with a 1,300-year history. Steeped in royal connections, its claim to fame is its proximity both to Highgrove and to Gatcombe Park, Princess Anne's home.

Following the success of the Tetbury launch, a second shop opened in 2011 in Bath, a historic Roman spa city about twenty-five miles from Highgrove. A World Heritage Site and major tourist destination, this location was perceived as a promising expansion opportunity for the royal retail chain. Located in a Georgian townhouse in the heart of Bath, it featured a traditional stone façade and pale-blue paintwork, like its Tetbury twin. Unfortunately, even the heir to the throne could not deter the building owner's plans for redeveloping the site, and although it was attractive to locals and tourists, the Bath location closed in June 2014.

The final royal-branded retail site (at present) is the Windsor Farm Shop. Leveraging the working farmland that borders Home Park, the Crown's 655-acre spread adjacent to the castle, it opened in October 2011. Recognizing that too overt a royal connection might not appeal to (and might even discourage) possible customers, the shop played "down its royal connections with a low-key name and only a hint of 'royalty' in the logo."[31]

Located inside two renovated Victorian-era potting sheds, Windsor Farm Shop specializes in meat grown on the farms or offered by local businesses, as well as local fruits and vegetables. The interior of one shed is akin to a "Royal Whole Foods," with its many organic and locally grown products bearing logos of the different royal farms. Customers can also buy high-end picnic hampers laden with royal-branded goods. The Balmoral hamper, for example, includes Windsor Farm Shop items such as beer, tea, cookies, preserves, cake, and biscuits, as well as Buckingham Palace Port (figure 20); in 2013, the hamper retailed for £200 ($330).

The merchandise assortment in the adjacent shop focuses on gift items such as local condiments, teas and coffees, gift baskets containing quintessentially British foodstuffs, kitchen gadgets, and souvenir items branded with the Royal Farms logo. A restaurant that caters to tourists and residents of the

FIGURE 20. Windsor Farm Shop "Balmoral" hamper. Photo by Cele Otnes.

nearby towns, such as Ascot, Runnymede,* and Datchet, offers healthy lunch options and traditional English desserts. In a nod to its increasing popularity, the Farm Shop recently was added to the itinerary of the Windsor City Sightseeing Bus tour.

Although it will remain unavailable for a few years, a new royal brand in Windsor is in the offing. In 2011, the RFBC entered into a partnership with the renowned Laithwaites Wine Company. The firm planted 16,700 champagne-variety grapevines on land managed by the Royal Farms, the Duke of Edinburgh's private enterprise. News about the potential production of royal bubbly has already boosted consumer demand for sparkling variants and was hailed by one vineyard owner as "simply the biggest boost the English wine industry ever had."[32]

So far, we have discussed the retailing and branding efforts the RFBC controls—or, in the case of Duchy Originals, previously controlled. But

---

* Site of the signing of the Magna Carta on June 15, 1215; it was the first of many documents of that name, and the first to limit the absolute power of the monarchy.

obviously, many marketing efforts that leverage the Royal Family exist, and often thrive, out of their sphere of influence. Furthermore, the impact of these endeavors on the image of the RFBC is not always positive. One marketing channel that often receives a great deal of publicity, and which the Royal Family cannot theoretically control, is the auction. Compared to bartering and paying fixed prices for goods, auctions are relatively rare forms of retail exchange. But with the development of the Internet, electronic auctions have proliferated, making it easier for buyers to participate in both online auctions and traditional ones. eBay, one of the most successful auction sites, is awash with commemorative items that represent past and present monarchs from across the globe.

Of more concern to the managers of the RFBC's image, however, are auctions by those whose goals are clearly more financial than reverential. Often houses that are considered highly prestigious organize royal-themed sales. The largest firm in the world, Christie's, opened in London in 1766; one of its main competitors, Sotheby's, had opened there in 1744. Christie's held its first "royal sale" in 1773, when it auctioned off items that belonged to the Princess of Wales.[33] As we discuss in chapter 8, Sotheby's handled both the jewelry and household sales of the Duchess of Windsor, both containing many valuable royal relics. In chapter 4, we described the first auction of Diana's dresses that she herself organized; many of those pieces have reappeared several times on the market in auctions and private sales. The Royal Collection Trust often bids on artistic and literary treasures, but it does so through an intermediary, so attendees are not aware of the Trust's interest.[34]

In June 2006, Princess Margaret's children, Viscount Linley and Lady Sarah Chatto, justified auctioning their mother's possessions to help pay an inheritance tax of £3 million. Their father, Margaret's ex-husband, the Earl of Snowdon, was seemingly as horrified as many members of the public. The event represented the first time the private possessions of a reigning monarch's sibling had been offered for public sale.[35] Certain media sources warned that the auction risked evolving into another royal fiasco. One friend of the Princess was quoted as saying it had "all the dignity of a royal car boot sale."[36] Purportedly, the Queen hurriedly intervened, suggesting that her niece and nephew donate to charity the proceeds of the items Princess Margaret had received as official gifts.[37]

Testifying to the enduring appeal of royalty, Princess Margaret's collection, sold in 788 lots, netted Christie's an impressive £9.6 million ($14.4 million)—nearly twice the value of the presale estimate.[38] Many pieces fetched much more than twice their predicted value. At £5,760 ($8,654), for example, a tiny gold hedgehog brooch sold for more than one hundred times its original estimate. Hundreds of bidders crowded into the event or bid by phone. Many items of historical importance went under the hammer, including the Princess's wedding tiara (£926,400/$1,389,600), a necklace worn by her grandmother Queen Mary for her 1937 coronation (£993,600/$1,490,400), and a Fabergé clock, also a gift from Queen Mary (£1,240,000/$1,860,000).

In 2013, Viscount Linley authorized another auction of Princess Margaret's jewels, known as "the Princess Margaret Collection," to be sold at auction in Birmingham. It featured a secondhand Cartier watch the thrifty Queen Mother had bought her daughter for £100 in 1940; its presale value was estimated at £150,000 ($248,000). As was the case with the 2006 auction, Linley was criticized for holding the sale.

Once again, the auction demonstrated the Queen's inability to control fiascos stemming from the "minor royals." A 1930s cast-iron balustrade from the Princess's rose garden in Kensington Palace had to be withdrawn from the auction, because it emerged that its sale would have infringed strict heritage laws forbidding the removal of fixtures and fittings from royal residences. Had the item been sold, Margaret's children could have faced a seven-year prison sentence.[39]

In 2009, Christie's oversaw an auction of former possessions of Prince George, Duke of Kent, and his wife, Princess Marina. Prince George was the fourth son of the Queen's grandparents, George V and Queen Mary. Shot down during World War II, he was the first member of the English branch of the Royal Family in five hundred years to die while serving in the military. Many items were antiques collected by former monarchs; some dated from the 1700s. A pair of George II Soho tapestry panels from 1725 sold for over $77,000, and two George III mahogany hall benches from 1760 fetched over $310,000. Overall, the sale netted the couple's descendants over £2 million.

Often, longtime servants or others with access to the Royal Family offer items for inclusion in royal-themed sales. Most of these (e.g., signed Christmas cards, correspondence about daily activities) do not hold much potential to embarrass the Royal Family; however, two recent auctions contained items that did. In 2012, executors of the estate of a Miami playboy placed on eBay a pair of the Queen's underwear that she had left on a private plane during a 1968 visit to Chile. There was no question of authenticity; the item bore the Queen's *EIIR* monogram and other symbols. The underwear fetched twice the estimate of $18,000—once again demonstrating the persistent but somewhat perplexing proclivity for items at royal auctions to be underestimated in presale.

While that auction no doubt proved annoying within Palace circles, its irritation factor was probably fleeting compared to the sale of 20,000 photo transparencies in 2013. Their source was the collection of former royal photographer Ray Bellisario, known as "London's first paparazzo" and a relentless pursuer of the Royal Family during the 1960s and 1970s. Bellisario pioneered the "off-guard, up-close shots beloved of today's celebrity magazines."[40] The transparencies included such unflattering images as Prince Charles riding his bicycle in the rain, Princess Anne falling off her horse, and a young Prince Andrew stepping in horse manure. He had also captured the Queen and her uncle, the frail and exiled Duke of Windsor, walking on the grounds of Buckingham Palace when he secretly visited London for medical treatment. Both denied that the meeting occurred, but Bellisario caught it with his telephoto lens from three blocks away, saying he knew "inevitably [the Queen] was going to come out with her dogs."[41]

We have already observed that the RFBC's marketing efforts for its merchandise now rely on online shopping sites. Not surprisingly, the Internet has increased the reach of royal memorabilia dealers. From eBay to more personalized websites, many people offer royal merchandise through computer-mediated sources. Again, these sources often remain outside the RFBC's control. Furthermore, over the last fifteen years, websites supported by avid royal memorabilia collectors have mushroomed. Content usually includes both items for sale and information or discussion about the Royal Family. Although much (still) centers on Diana, other topics—from current royal tours to historical vignettes of past royal figures—also are favorites.

The owner of Everything Royal, Los-Angeles based Alicia Carroll, is one such dealer specializing in the British Royal Family.* She claims to own one of the world's largest private collections of memorabilia. Apart from selling a large range of items, Carroll keeps her readers up to date on many royal happenings, such as tourism opportunities, news, auctions, and bits of gossip. A former actress, Carroll became interested in the Royal Family during the 1980s, when, like many others in the United States, she was glued to media stories of Charles and Diana's fairy-tale wedding. This inspired her passion for royal collecting and trading in souvenirs and memorabilia.

* www.everythingroyal.com.

For her first visit to England, Carroll reportedly took several thousand dollars of her savings and invested in royal commemoratives bearing the Queen's image. When she discovered that she could sell them for a profit, her business began.[42] Her merchandise categories include signed royal correspondence, posters and photographs, plates and figurines, commemoratives, books, newspapers and magazines, royal dolls, and videos, among others. However, much of the material she displays is not for sale, which means sections of Carroll's website are devoted less to her business and more to her passion as a fan. Accordingly, sites like Carroll's often act as cultural intermediaries, spreading informal information about the members of the RFBC, sometimes even on topics that St. James's Palace may be trying to suppress. Like Margaret Tyler, Carroll acts as a brand ambassador, appearing all the more authentic because of her voluntary role in promoting the RFBC, her occasional criticism of "the Firm," and her assumed role as expert.

Carroll's homepage reflects her enduring admiration for Diana, Princess of Wales, with a photo of her face superimposed on one of Kensington Palace and hyperlinks to descriptions and prices of the seventy-nine dresses auctioned in 1997. After entering the site, visitors encounter an official Jubilee photo of the Queen resplendent in her diamond tiara and regal attire (although, throughout the site, she clearly plays second fiddle to Diana). Below this image are the words "A wonderful tribute to Her Majesty Queen Elizabeth II," hyperlinked to a YouTube video where viewers can watch an unofficial Jubilee tribute.

For all her glowing tributes, Carroll is not shy about criticizing the Royal Family for the shoddy way she believes Diana was treated. In an Everythingroyal.com catalog released in 2003, Carroll included a pointed diatribe against Prince Charles, his then-mistress Camilla Parker Bowles, the Queen, and even Britain as a whole. She wrote, "It is shameful for the Queen to be so accepting of Camilla Parker Bowles.... [S]he has moved into the late Queen Mother's residence, Clarence House, with not so much as a tsk tsk from the British people whose taxes partially paid for the renovation."[43] The website now contains more toned-down rhetoric, but Carroll still notes the absence of any substantial memorial to Diana in London.

The growth of websites like Carroll's encourages behavior we alluded to earlier—namely, Royal Household staff selling gifts the Royal Family gave them, or items they have acquired through surreptitious, ethnically questionable, or perhaps even illegal means. These include salvaging items from trash bins—even, purportedly, Diana's nail clippings. Carroll herself was implicated in a larger scandal in 2002, when she confirmed to the media that she had obtained royal mementos from palace staff who approached her frequently, eager to profit from their associations with the Royal Family.

In particular, Prince Charles's trusted valet Michael Fawcett allegedly sold items Charles and Diana had received as gifts, keeping 10–20 percent of the proceeds for himself. Diana's ex-butler Paul Burrell was deeply embroiled in a similar dispute about many of her possessions. In 2002, he was brought to trial on charges of stealing over three hundred items from Diana's estate, including some belonging to Princes William and Harry. Burrell previously had told the Queen he had removed some items for safekeeping after Diana's death, and the Queen had reported the conversation to others. When these facts became known during the trial, the charges against Burrell were dismissed.

Although these controversies shed light on Royal Household staff cashing in on their associations, this practice is not surprising, given the money potentially at stake. Royal and Regal memorabilia dealer Peter Smith notes, "It's not until [the staff] get elderly that they realize that the cards . . . tucked away in the back of a drawer could be worth $70,000 or $80,000."[44]

The final unofficial merchandising source we discuss focuses less on sales of royal merchandise and more on documenting the history of these objects. The Museum of Brands, Packaging and Advertising, tucked away in a mews street* in London's fashionable Notting Hill, is a trove of historic links between royalty and commerce. Briton Robert Opie founded it in 1984. Opie is a consumer historian with a passion for collecting packages and promotional wrappings, and the museum's 12,000 original items document the rise of branded packaging from the Victorian era to the present day. Its display cases teem with colorful boxes, wrappings, tins, and bottles and jars of every size and shape. Some displays document the changing logos for particular brands over more than a century.

Offering a chronological tour of the simultaneous rise of branded packaging and consumer culture, the museum shows how including the Royal Family in promotions and products was common practice from Victoria's reign onward. Its development went hand-in-hand with the Industrial Revolution and intensifying competition among manufacturers to attract customers. During this era, transportation forms and interconnections also became more sophisticated. This situation allowed foreign goods, especially

---

* One formerly containing stables.

those from the British colonies, to flood the marketplaces of Britain. Victorian department stores like Harrods and Selfridges eagerly welcomed these exotic goods, as customers increasingly relied on retailers to fulfill their consumption-laden aspirations.

Incorporating iconic British images helped manufacturers evoke patriotism not only in their homeland but throughout the empire.[45] The marketing term *country-of-origin effect* recognizes that a product's geographic origin can directly shape consumers' attitudes and perceptions toward that offering. The principle dates from 1887, when the British government made country-of-origin labeling compulsory for all products manufactured outside the country. The requirement marked Parliament's attempt to stem the flood of imported goods and enable consumers to easily discriminate among options. Nationalistic symbols on packaging became regular fixtures that denoted British manufacturing origin and helped cash in on national pride. These included John Bull, a patriotic figure invented in 1712 by a Scottish mathematician, akin to the American Uncle Sam. Also popular were "Britannia" (a woman in a toga and Roman helmet, bearing a shield and trident) and various lions used in British heraldry.[46]

By the late 1860s, images of the Royal Family had become commonplace on packaging and promotional material. Queen Victoria, Prince Albert, and the Princess of Wales (later Queen Alexandra) were the favorites, as manufacturers attempted to differentiate their products from many others bearing the royal coat of arms.[47] A magazine ad in 1884 for Cadbury's cocoa depicts a train carriage with the product's Royal Warrant vaguely discernible on its side. The ad draws the viewer's eye to the carriage window, where a seated and characteristically stern Queen Victoria savors a cup of cocoa with a female companion. In an 1871 ad for Glenfield starch, the Princess of Wales is featured in an extravagantly flounced ball gown. The obvious implication is that its magnificence is clearly attributable to the starch—rather than the bevy of Royal Household staff who doubtless contributed to the gown's effect.[48]

Toward the end of the nineteenth century, several royal events in quick succession afforded commemorative opportunities aplenty. These included Victoria's Jubilees of 1887 and 1897, and Edward VII's coronation in 1902. During these decades, manufacturers produced a huge range of commemoratives, particularly tins and boxes of biscuits,* sweets, tea, and tobacco—all

---

* The British term for cookies.

FIGURE 21. Cadbury's Chocolate Empire Box. Photo by Cele Otnes.

bearing royal figures typically encased in decorative motifs and royal insignia.

The category of royal-commemorative candy boxes deserves special mention, because it reinforces the cultural significance of another important traditional English industry—namely, confectionery. Toffee manufacturers had already established footholds in Britain by the end of the nineteenth century, and by the 1920s, makers like Cadbury and Rowntree's began offering assortments of chocolates in tin boxes, so people could include them in new leisure activities such as picnicking and "motoring." Tins containing assorted biscuits and other sweets also became popular and remain standard fare in many royal retail displays. Royal commemorative boxes remained reverential (see figure 21), and any liberties taken with images of the Royal Family typically involved removing potentially unappealing elements. In the 1920s, for example, a famous Rowntree's chocolate tin reproduced a photo of a smiling and debonair Prince of Wales in his Royal Navy uniform—minus the cigarette he had been smoking.[49]

As Opie's museum demonstrates, during this period Victoria's face lent allure to a variety of items: a Diamond Jubilee pocket knife, Victorian bouquet perfume, and even a Diamond Jubilee chair. A Golfer Oats advertisement proclaimed, "The latest development of Jubilee Year," featuring an official portrait of Victoria framed in oats beside the tag line "Ask for Golfer

Oats" and a packet of the product. A wry pun along the bottom reads, "The two safeguards of the constitution."

The museum display is arranged so visitors can trace the history of the RFBC in advertising and packaging from the 1851 Great Exhibition* to the wedding of William and Catherine. The exhibit reveals that as the decades progress, commemorative packages become more ephemeral. These include, for example, paper candy boxes for Basset's Liquorice Allsorts that feature a Charles and Diana engagement photo, a roll of kitchen paper towels celebrating the Queen's Golden Jubilee, and varieties of "crisp" packages, featuring flavors such as Coronation Chicken.†

The exhibit shows that earlier images of the Royal Family on packages and promotions are reverential and tend to replicate exact likenesses by copying official photographs or portraits. This is in sharp contrast to the ways the Queen and her family often appear nowadays, however, with irreverent imagery, particularly caricatures and cartoons, appearing in royal retail assortments alongside more respectful ones. As we have discussed, the antiestablishment British comic strain, popular since the late 1960s, fuels the demand for less respectful images. But another likely reason is that caricatures and satirical images are not regulated by the tight legal controls that dictate the use of official royal images.

In fact, during the Victorian and Edwardian eras, the monarchy had much less control over its image. While Royal Warrant designees were allowed to associate themselves with the monarchy, many unsanctioned firms also alluded to associations. Some product names unabashedly drew links to the monarchy: Alexandra oil, Empress Brand condensed milk, Regina Queen of Soaps, King and Queen safety matches, and Victoria window blind cord. Others featured emblems and royal images liberally in their promotional materials.[50] A formal portrait of Edward VII in his regalia dominated an ad for Horniman's Pure Tea, bearing the tag line "A right royal drink." Indeed, royal word plays were rife on packaging during these unregu-

---

* The Great Exhibition, codirected by Prince Albert, was held in the Crystal Palace, built for the exhibit in London's Hyde Park. It was the first international display of manufactured goods and technologies. Exhibitors stemmed from twenty-eight countries; during its five-month run, six million paying visitors attended.

† Crisps is the British term for chips; Coronation Chicken, a cold dish featuring curry, herbs, and spices, was created at London's Cordon Bleu school. It was first prepared for Elizabeth II's coronation celebrations in 1953.

lated times; an ad for Boisselier's Chocolates featured a portrait of Queen Alexandra holding a chocolate box with the tag line "Fit for the Queen."

Current regulations, however, stipulate that including royal images or even royal associations in ads is strictly forbidden without prior permission from St. James's Palace. The only exception is for images that promote a book, newspaper, or magazine article about a Royal Family member. The Lord Chamberlain's Examiners are responsible for regulating image usage. Even if it grants approval, the office enforces strict guidelines regarding usage of the royal crown, flags, and photographic or color representations. It also advises firms whether their intended use of motifs, words, or images contravenes the law. Any implied associations that could lead people to believe that products have acquired royal patronage are forbidden, and company names can no longer include the words *king, queen, prince, princess,* or *royal.* Similarly, using royal names on products is illegal if the usage suggests connections to a Royal Family member. Even photographs of a royal visit to a company's premises or exhibition stand, or any use of products or services by members of the monarchy, is prohibited in ads.[51] (That being said, we saw several clearly doctored posters in pubs, depicting Royal Family members enjoying beverages underneath a usually cheeky headline).

Of course, firms can try to skirt these regulations by relying on "celebrity product placement." This concept represents a hybrid between product placement (embedding a brand as it might "naturally" occur in a scene where audiences would see it, as in a person's home in a film) and celebrity endorsement, where a well-known figure is paid to use a product and testify to its merits. Although the Royal Family decidedly is not paid, and the Queen frowns upon any suggestion that they exploit their position for capital gain,* many firms offer gifts to Royal Family members, hoping the media will depict them putting these goods and services to use. Chapter 9 explores two recent manifestations: the "Kate effect" and the "Prince George" effect.

Furthermore, some firms believe that if this strategy is unsuccessful with the Royal Family itself, they can try their luck with the newest royal in-laws, the Middletons. From time to time, the Middletons have stirred up contro-

---

* In 2010, a scandal erupted when the former Duchess of York was taped offering access to her ex-husband Prince Andrew for £500,000. It echoed a similar incident a decade prior with Sophie, Countess of Wessex, Prince Edward's wife. Oddly, in both cases journalists posed as fake Arab sheiks to entice the women to be indiscreet in their discussion of the Royal Family and business interests.

versy by accepting gifts and special deals. In 2011, Catherine's sister Pippa was photographed carrying one of four personally embossed Modalu handbags the manufacturer had given her. Sales rocketed for the British-designed, Indian-made luxury brand,[52] with turnover soaring that year from £1 million ($1.5 million) to over ten times that amount. Modalu has extended its "Pippa range" to include shoulder bags, wristlets, and wallets. Likewise, in 2013, reports circulated that Land Rover had provided both Kate's mother and her siblings with high-end models at huge discounts, in return for their roles as unofficial brand ambassadors. For those few lucky firms, such successful product placement is akin to winning the lottery.

Although we tend to think of such endorsement as a recent practice, in fact it dates back to Victorian times, when manufacturers commonly tried to obtain royal patronage by pressing their wares upon the Royal Family, especially at trade exhibitions. Victoria's son Prince Albert Edward was renowned for his susceptibility to such overtures. In 1889, accompanied by the shah, he attended the Paris Exhibition, where he received a bottle of Bushmills whiskey.[53] Later the distiller maximized this endorsement opportunity in a campaign depicting the prince pouring a drink of Bushmills for the shah. Similarly, in 1894, Terrabona Tea & Coffee depicted Albert Edward in an ad, accepting a box of products at an exhibition in Olympia, London.

Given that the British monarchy often serves as an object of satire, it is probably unsurprising that several ad campaigns (some of them short lived) have taken liberties with the proclivities of the Royal Family. In 2005—a full thirteen years after Charles and Camilla's famous "Tampax" telephone conversation (see chapter 4) and the year the couple married—the global advertising agency Young & Rubicam created a campaign for its Australian tampon brand, Cottons. It featured the headline "Well done, Charles, you're finally in!" In 2011, Victoria appeared in an ad in the London Underground for the American brand Jack Daniels whiskey (figure 22). The copy spun a tale about the firm sending the Queen a bottle and never hearing whether she had enjoyed it or not (apparently, the creative team had not researched the fact that she only drank Balmoral whiskey). Three years later, in 2014, the walls along the long escalators in the Underground featured posters for the new play *King Charles III*. No posters could be hung, however, until Charles's face had been pixelated.

Royal impersonators also have figured in ads and other promotional efforts. Resembling a living or deceased member of the RFBC can prove

FIGURE 22. Jack Daniel's Queen Victoria ad, London Tube station. Photo by Cele Otnes.

lucrative, as former waitress and single mother of two Heidi Agan discovered when she found she could earn up to $1,000 a day for impersonating Catherine, the Duchess of Cambridge.[54] We discuss one of the most recent commercials to go viral after successfully featuring impersonators, in conjunction with William and Catherine's wedding, in chapter 9. But Pizza Hut's commercial for its "Crown Crust," released around the Queen's Diamond Jubilee, provides a fitting end for our chapter. It features a flirty Harry, a besotted William and Catherine, a sulky Charles who complains about still waiting to reign, a curmudgeonly Philip, and the Queen—the only one who maintains a regal air. While the others muck about with the menu, she proclaims, "One will order for everyone," and then proceeds to eat her pizza with a knife and fork.[55]

In summary, the Royal Family of the second Elizabethan age is the first to enter the commercial sphere with brands of its own, although it did not pioneer the notion of leveraging existing products and services to enhance the monarchy's cultural and economic cachet. With four active brands in its stable, and royal grapes under the watchful eyes of caretakers in Windsor, it seems likely the RFBC will continue to pursue its own strategic commercial opportunities, and to keep a watchful eye on those over which it has no control.

SEVEN

Storying the Monarchy

ROYAL TOURISM AND HISTORIC ROYAL PALACES

In chapter 3, we described how media outlets across the globe now seek out Margaret Tyler for her expertise as a Royal Family collector and commentator. Yet we note her influence does not stop there; organizations that create and promote royal-related events also borrow items to embellish their displays and discussions and to enrich visitors' experiences. In this chapter, we briefly discuss key developments within the domain of royal tourism, a subset of tourism research that remains overlooked. Later, we turn our attention to exploring how one organization, Historic Royal Palaces, plays a key role in preserving, managing, and orchestrating visitor experiences.

Academics and practitioners whose work intersects tourism are faced with a panoply of issues to address, such as access, conservation, preservation, and representation at tourist sites. As a result, the term *royal tourism*—and the related broader phrase *heritage tourism*—often go undefined. Even the recent book *Royal Tourism* does not define the concept. We believe it is important that an understanding of royal tourism reflect the interests of both consumers and producers. As such, we define royal tourism broadly as the subset of heritage tourism that encompasses creating, exploring, or questioning people's connections to the past, present, and future of specific monarchies, or to the institution of monarchy as a whole. Furthermore, we concur with an observation by Mike Robinson,* who notes that the "meta-message of world heritage [is] that . . . tangible reminders of the past . . . remind us of the success and failure of humanity." In our case, these reminders pertain to the RFBC and its cultural, geographic, political, and social associations.[1]

* Director of the Ironbridge International Institute for Cultural Heritage, University of Birmingham.

Defenders of the British monarchy often argue that it is a vital tourist draw. Supporters of the institution like to break down how much it costs British citizens to maintain the monarchy per year. Buckingham Palace recently claimed the cost for 2012–13 to be about £33.3 million ($51.1 million), or 53 pence (81 cents) per person. Of course, critics immediately point out that this figure does not reflect the money required for security detail, extras such as private hospital suites for Royal births, or Royal tours.[2] In truth, except for the specific records of how many people visit a particular site, or data recorded by specific organizations, it is very difficult to accurately assess the economic impact of royal tourism. The industry traverses at least two dozen sectors (e.g., accommodation, entertainment, retail, transportation), which all clearly serve nontourists as well.

The BBC's former economics correspondent Evan Davies asserts that 10 percent of all tourists visit the United Kingdom because of their interest in the Royal Family but notes that many more "are attracted [to] Britain . . . as a unique and glorious heritage center, to which the monarchy makes an inestimable contribution."[3] But doing away with the monarchy while retaining its trappings would likely not be as alluring for tourists, since the Royal Family "acts as a sort of charismatic megafauna for the entire royalty-tourism ecosystem."[4] In short, deriving or predicting an accurate, comprehensive tally of the impact of royal tourism on the British (and in fact, the global) economy would require large-scale coordination across organizations ranging from the Royal Collection Trust to retailers around the world who shill souvenirs from sidewalk kiosks.

As is true for most tourists, those who consume royal events, exhibits, and experiences often do so to satisfy their desires for aesthetic pleasure, edification, elitism, and/or entertainment. They also may make explicit connections to their citizenship, ethnicity, genealogy, or gender. Yet we also know many people who would never visit even the most impeccably preserved royal sites on political or moral grounds, even if taking this stand denies them access to unparalleled artistic works and architectural wonders. On the other hand, of course, each year millions of interested people visit castles, exhibitions, gift shops, memorials, museums, palaces, parks, private homes, ruins, ships, statues, and other sites associated with the ten-century-plus royal narrative.* In addition, people intersect with the Royal Family at

---

* Castles differ from palaces; as fortified structures, castles served a military function as well as meeting the monarchy's residential and bureaucratic needs.

other venues they may not even consider touristic, including "theatres, festivals, theme[d] pubs and clubs, cafés, and restaurants ... sporting facilities, specialty retail, and events of every kind."[5]

Between 2012 and 2014, the Diamond Jubilee, Prince George's birth, William and Catherine's Royal tour of Australia and New Zealand, and their subsequent whirlwind visit to New York City helped sustain global interest in visits to royal sites. Table 5 summarizes the historically significant and (mostly) well-trodden royal venues in Britain. Many are entwined in the narratives of William the Conqueror and his descendants, but the Scottish monarchs also attract the tourist gaze. If people wish to focus solely on sites and experiences that pertain to the Queen, many in this table would qualify. But they could also attend one of four annual racing events, each on a different continent, that bear her name.[6] Or they could visit "Queen Elizabeth Land" in Antarctica, the Queen Elizabeth II September 11th Garden in Lower Manhattan, or the only statue of her posing with her ubiquitous handbag, in Brisbane, Australia. One highly anticipated and highly visible global link between the Queen and global tourism (royal and otherwise) is Heathrow Airport's Terminal 2, renovated in 2014. Renamed "the Queen's Terminal," it cost £2.5 billion ($4.3 billion) and is projected to serve 20 million passengers a year.[7]

Outside of Britain, popular commemorative sites dot the globe. One now-iconic landmark is the Place d'Alma, near the Paris tunnel where Princess Diana suffered her fatal injuries in 1997. Mourners converted a nearby replica of the Statue of Liberty's torch already on display into a memorial to the princess.* Many visitors did not even realize the replica originally commemorated France's gift of the statue to America and thought "it was built in [Diana's] honor."[8]

In addition to permanent installations, each year dozens of temporary touristic offerings that pertain to the RFBC appear around the world. They reflect the fact that as representations of the Royal Family have become increasingly intertwined with popular culture, they have mirrored the nature of global touristic experiences in general, becoming "fragmented ... and more idiosyncratic."[9] In 2013, New York's Metropolitan Museum of Art mounted an exhibit on royal silver, Boston's Museum of Fine Arts hosted two separate exhibits (one on royal letters, the other on British royal portraits), and even the Kremlin, associated with the regime that brought the

---

* Chapter 4 discusses other aspects of dark tourism related to her death.

Russian monarchy to a violent end, offered *The Golden Age of the English Court: From Henry VIII to Charles I.*

Reflecting the consistently high levels of Anglophilia in America, the United States offers its own touristic homages to the monarchy. One of the most prominent is the former Cunard ocean liner the *Queen Mary,* docked in Long Beach, California, and now a museum and hotel. Since 2013, it has housed the temporary but long-running exhibit *Diana: Legacy of a Princess,* which features over two thousand royal-themed items, including nine of her famous dresses. The ship offers a variety of talks and teas, including a "Little Royal Tea" for children. Elsewhere, idiosyncratic homages to the RFBC crop up: on June 21, 2014, visitors to the train station in Hyde Park, New York, could enjoy free hot dogs and lemonade in honor of the seventy-fifth anniversary of a visit to the area by George V and Queen Elizabeth, celebrating the informal picnic of American food they shared with President and Mrs. Franklin Roosevelt.[10]

Many European countries increasingly tout their connections to the RFBC. In 1714, George Louis of the German electorate of Hanover became George I of Great Britain. During his dual reign, he and his family returned to his native region almost every summer, and his son George II continued the tradition. To mark the three-hundredth anniversary of the beginning of Britain's House of Hanover, in 2014 the German National Tourist Office launched an elaborate touristic initiative. Its offerings included an interactive Royal Heritage Route on its website, as well as organized tours of many German cities. Highlights included visits to "the beautiful and fairy-tale like Marienburg Castle, owned by Prince Ernst August of Hanover, a new exhibition of [Hanoverian] Crown Jewels . . . the birthplace of Prince Albert, and the recently restored . . . summer residence of the British Crown.[11]

The significance of visiting sites that have honored, horrified, hosted, and housed the Royal Family is highlighted by the fact that half of the *Illustrated Encyclopedia of Royal Britain* contains descriptions of over 120 castles, palaces, and stately homes.[12] Yet the dynamic nature of royal tourism means that sites not typically considered tourist draws can become temporary, but vital, focal points in the royal narrative. Consider how London's St. Mary's Hospital was overrun both by day-trippers and overnighters who joined global media crews on royal baby-watch when Prince George was born in July 2013. Naturally, once the Duchess and Prince George were discharged, interest in the hospital receded. But as the birthplace of three princes and a princess in a little over three decades, the hospital's Lindo Wing is entrenched in the royal saga.

As the staff at St. James's Palace has turned to more sophisticated marketing techniques to promote the Royal Family, its understanding of the importance of touting touristic experiences to promote the brand has grown. On occasion, the Queen and her relatives have contributed visible gestures to spur these efforts. Foremost among these was the Queen's decision in 1993 to open Buckingham Palace to the public, despite her natural reticence and desire to keep her public and private lives distinct. But the decision not only provided the funds to restore Windsor Castle after a devastating fire; it also provided visitors with cherished access to the Royal Family's most-used residence. During its two-month summer season in 2012, 558,000 people toured Buckingham Palace,[13] and in 2013, foreign tourists ranked the tour as the top "Only in Britain" activity. (The third-ranked attraction, Edinburgh Castle, was the only other royal activity listed.)[14]

Likewise, in 2003 the Royal Family engaged in a coordinated series of visits to tourist attractions across Britain. At Legoland Windsor, the Queen viewed "a miniature plastic version of herself, Buckingham Palace and the [T]rooping of the [C]olour ... while Prince Edward ... visited a caravan [RV] park in Mid-Wales." Meanwhile, Prince Charles ventured northward to take in the Royal Mile in Edinburgh, so named because it links Edinburgh Castle and the Palace of Holyroodhouse. In the aftermath of the 9/11 terrorist attacks, Americans had severely curtailed their overseas trips. To offset the ensuing economic losses in the United Kingdom, Charles and Princess Anne stepped in as touristic ambassadors. Charles wrote a foreword for Visit Britain's "Map of Royal Britain," while the Princess Royal worked with the National Tourist Board to encourage Americans to resume their visits.[15]

The profit potential of royal tourism attracts a gamut of businesses from small-scale entrepreneurs (e.g., those offering activities such as the "Middleton Country Tours" and "the Royal Walking Tour") to companies such as Thomas Cook, originator in 1841 of the all-inclusive organized group tour. Cook offered a range of itineraries in its "royal globetrotting guide" during the Queen's Diamond Jubilee Year. A press release touting its Canadian itinerary offered a non sequitur that alluded to the Queen and Prince Philip's courtship and the newlyweds' subsequent visit to Canada: "Like the Mounties, Princess Elizabeth got her man and The Queen and Prince Philip made their first appearance ... in Newfoundland."[16]

Royal spectacles, including triumphant returns from war, coronations, weddings, and funerals, have long proved compelling to both domestic and foreign tourists. Until the twentieth century, most royal ceremonies took place behind closed doors at key religious sites or monarchic residences. Nevertheless, through royal proclamations posted in key locations—and later, through pamphlets and newspapers—subjects typically received advance notice of such events. Often they lined the streets to cheer (or jeer) the celebrants, to witness the elaborate symbolic and sycophantic pageants,* and to glimpse the processions of participants. Sometimes these events revolved more around gore than glory; observing beheadings and executions was a popular pastime, especially during the bloodier years of the House of Tudor.

Some scholars argue that the first true royal tourists were those undertaking religious pilgrimages in the Middle Ages to honor sainted or martyred monarchs and worship at sacred sites honoring them. Key among these was St. George's Chapel in Windsor, where the pious and pitiable Henry VI was reburied in 1485 after his murder and first burial at Chertsey Abbey in 1471. By 1534, the same year the Act of Supremacy established Henry VIII as head of the Church of England, a movement to bestow sainthood on Henry VI was in full force. Pilgrims journeying to Windsor marveled and prayed over the King's relics, which supposedly contained miraculous powers. Until the Enlightenment, when the cult surrounding Henry VI dissipated, migraine-prone pilgrims sought a cure by traveling to his tomb to try on his hat.[17]

By the mid-1500s, travel in Britain and Europe had broadened beyond pilgrimages or commercial ventures. Unprecedented developments in architecture, art, philosophy, and science during the Renaissance had sparked a thirst for knowledge—and even to learn simply for learning's sake. Education became a form of capital the wealthy and ambitious aspired to accrue. Traveling and its poorer cousin, "tourism,"† were valorized as activities designed to broaden the mind and enhance cultural understanding.[18]

From approximately 1600 to 1830, the "Grand Tour" became engrained as a requisite activity for young men of the highest noble families, with their tutors in tow.[19] Those occupying the highest social strata in Britain and on the Continent held the belief that true appreciation for and understanding

* These pageants were elaborate theatrical street displays, usually depicting the monarchs as mythical figures or gods.

† Compared to travel, tourism typically implies shorter, less intellectually engaging expeditions.

of human creative endeavors required a substantial time commitment. Grand Tour itineraries in the earlier centuries often lasted up to three years and reflected the relentless pursuit of architecture, art, culture, nature—and no doubt, the sowing of wild oats—in Germany, France, and especially Italy.

The Grand Tour's impact on royal tourism, although indirect, was most evident after sojourners returned home to Britain. In addition to tangible objets d'art, many aristocratic sons returned with the desire to renovate their homes to emulate the fashionably elegant Baroque and Italianate styles dominating the Continent. After three Grand Tours in 1714–1719, the Right Honorable Richard Boyle, 3rd Earl of Burlington, became a pronounced advocate of the Italian Palladian architectural style, rooted in the symmetrical designs of classical Roman temples. The "architect Earl," as he was known, helped ensure that the style became the preferred choice for country houses and public buildings in England during the early to mid-1700s.

In addition, these returning dilettanti often tried to replicate the elaborate gardens and outdoor structures characteristic of European palaces and homes, sometimes with the explicit goal of creating a "country house grand enough to receive a monarch."[20] These efforts spurred local residents and curiosity seekers to visit these country houses, especially since the Grand Tour remained out of reach to the lower social strata. But by the eighteenth century, the middle class had begun to mimic these Continental travel patterns, albeit more modestly.

To accommodate the increase in visitors, by the 1800s a few of the larger country estates had begun to rely on ticketing systems and guides. But even into the twentieth century, most tours were "very informal with housekeepers showing visitors around,"[21] much like Elizabeth Bennet's visit to Mr. Darcy's estate in *Pride and Prejudice*. As early as the fifteenth century, travelers to the Tower of London knew that for a "tip" (bribe), a groundskeeper or household staff member would take them on a personal tour. Even residents of the "grace and favour apartments"* in the palaces sometimes showed guests around and invited them for tea.[22] Considering the sophisticated marketing and logistics systems currently in place at most royal sites, such informality is now almost inconceivable.

Of course, nothing thrilled visitors more than an actual royal sighting. In 1802, one visitor reported that while George III and his family enjoyed their

---

* The term for accommodations at royal residences the monarch typically offered rent-free to relatives, courtiers, or others valued by the court and the nation.

evening stroll on the Windsor Castle grounds, they bowed to spectators. Fifteen years later, a staff member informed another visitor that the now-blind, gravely ill King sat in the room directly below, his beard extended to his breast, wanting only to play the piano and be left alone.[23]

As interest in the Grand Tour waned in the nineteenth century, other types of touristic activities emerged, with many owing much of their growth to the fact that both members of the Royal Family and the aristocrats who orbited them initially found these activities appealing. In the centuries before drugs and healthful habits helped stave off disease, people often followed physicians' recommendations for natural cures. Belief in the therapeutic benefits of heated, mineral-laden water had existed for centuries, even as regular bathing habits were shunned. However, since "thermae" were developed in Roman times, spas had remained off limits to all but the upper crust of society. In the seventeenth century, entrepreneurs began to develop public facilities for the bourgeoisie, which would burgeon with the spread of the Industrial Revolution. By the first half of the nineteenth century, successful spa-based towns had developed in Britain, chief among them the fashionable, historic Bath. With its original spa built by the Romans in the first century A.D., the city—as well as Cheltenham, Leamington, and others—boomed as it accommodated people's desire to "take the waters."

The historian Gilbert Sigaux argues that the spa industry marks the beginning of real royal tourism, as it spurred monarchs in both Continental Europe and Britain (especially George III and the Prince Regent, later George IV) to visit these sites for their health, and to engage in the social nexus of requisite balls, promenades, assemblies, and other scripted activities. Spa resorts became sites where royalty, aristocracy, and the bourgeoisie devised grandiose plans to colonize the world.[24] Royal Family members from Britain and the Continent—as well as their courts—flocked to the spas, where prominent physicians in residence and scholars wrote treatises for the medical community touting their specific waters, and both medical and social interventions were tightly regulated.[25]

The appeal of the spa towns soon trickled down to the lower levels of the social strata. Towns began catering to the middle class, which created its own lower-orbit mélange of competitive social events. Members of the working and lower classes witnessed the growth of these parallel social infrastructures, from their vantage points as the servants and laborers hired to maintain the infrastructures of the spa towns. Still, time off allowed them to absorb the available attractions, albeit from the social margins. Importantly, they wrote to family and friends about the towns, disseminating information even before railroad travel, well established by the 1840s, spurred real growth in British tourism.

Royal influence on the spa industry even extended to the far-reaching corners of the British Empire. By the 1880s, New Zealand had achieved international fame for its natural beauty and thermal wonders. Thirty years after the Treaty of Waitangi made it an official British colony, Queen Victoria's son Prince Alfred visited Rotorua in 1870, "establishing it in the wealthy social circles of Europe."[26] Thomas Cook included New Zealand in some of his colonial itineraries, helping Rotorua's spa on the North Island to solidify its reputation as the premiere attraction in the country. Yet by the early twentieth century, calamities such as volcanic eruptions, arduous travel conditions, and difficulty maintaining the quality of the springs took their toll, and Rotorua receded as an attraction.

England's spa towns had also begun to decline in popularity. By the 1850s, Britons were engaging in more foreign travel, and they shifted their choice of spa destinations to the Continent. At the same time, improved transportation had opened up many previously inaccessible leisure options within the British Isles. One type in particular, the seaside resort, began to flourish. As had been true for the spa industry, initial interest in visiting the seaside stemmed from physicians' recommendations that their patients bathe in and drink salt water. By the 1750s, Dr. Richard Russell had established a thriving practice in Brighton ("Brighthelmston" until the late 1700s), prescribing sun, sand, and sea to his ailing patients.

In 1765, George III's brother the Duke of Gloucester made the first royal visit to Brighton. But it was the arrival of the Prince of Wales (later George IV) in September 1783 that brought the town its most ardent royal fan. Establishing a semipermanent residence, he invested in property and visited regularly for the next forty-four years. The historian E. W. Gilbert asserts that "fame as a health resort and the building of the Royal Pavilion as a seaside residence ... were the main causes of Brighton's extraordinary expansion between 1760 and 1830."[27]

The phrase *seaside residence* hardly does justice to the exotic and ornate Royal Pavilion, George IV's home (figure 23). Built by the famous architect John Nash and requiring eight years to complete, its construction along the shore of an English seaside town was incongruous, to say the least. The architectural style, known as "Hindoo," reflected "Islamic temple architecture and a taste for the exotic that flowered in the Regency period."[28] The

FIGURE 23. Royal Pavilion, Brighton. Courtesy of Paul Kapp.

exterior boasted enormous onion-shaped domes, minarets, and cupolas, in homage to both Turkish- and Indian-style mosques. The interior reflected George IV's eclectic tastes and passion for collecting Chinese art. In the high-domed Banqueting Room and Music Hall, the King enjoyed entertaining his guests with an orchestra that "dressed in Turkish costumes [with] sometimes himself singing . . . baritone."[29]

Some scholars disagree about George IV's true influence in ingraining the seaside holiday into British culture, where it remained the most popular vacation choice until the 1970s. For instance, Brighton historian Sue Berry argues that the city was already growing rapidly prior to the Prince Regent's first visit. She asserts that by 1800, just seventeen years after his first visit, it was already "Britain's largest and most fashionable seaside watering place."[30] Be that as it may, Brighton's residents initially trumpeted his infatuation with their city. Local merchants decorated their storefronts with the Prince of Wales's personal badge to signify his patronage. Even as residents became immune to, and even disenchanted with, his presence, tourists flocked to the Pavilion both when George IV lived there and after he abandoned Brighton in 1827.

Although his brother and successor, William IV, shared George IV's enthusiasm for the town, Victoria despised the thought that so many residents and tourists were eager to invade her family's privacy. Declaring the Pavilion gaudy, in 1850 she sold the building and its grounds to the city for £50,000 ($85,000)—one-seventh of what it cost George IV to build it. Victoria had many of the furnishings transported to Buckingham Palace, although when the Pavilion was opened to the public, she returned many original paintings and fittings. (It was not until George V's reign, however, that some of the more ornate pieces of the Chinese collection from the Pavilion were retrieved from storage to form the basis of Buckingham Palace's renowned Chinese Dining Room.)[31]

Once the city of Brighton purchased the Pavilion, it positioned the building as an idiosyncratic treasure and a bold testament to George IV's aesthetic vision. Critics of the overly indulgent king, however, viewed it as a glaring reminder of his life as a dilettante. After two restorations in the first half of the twentieth century, in the early 1980s the city embarked on a meticulous overhaul to recreate the Pavilion as it had existed during its heyday. Beyond repairing exterior leaks and cracks, many intricate interior fixtures were restored. Regilding the 26,000 cockleshells on the Music Room ceiling took a team of artists four months; restoring the entire room required eleven years.[32] Displays at the renovated Pavilion now include artifacts from more controversial aspects of George IV's life, including the wedding ring he presented to his Catholic commoner bride, Maria Fitzherbert, during their secret (and illegal) marriage ceremony in 1785. In 2014, the Pavilion Foundation announced it would begin work on the Saloon, "the last of the three great staterooms ... to be restored since the Palace came into public ownership."[33]

Victoria's aversion to Brighton did not extend to seaside destinations as a whole. In 1845, she moved the official royal seaside residence to the Isle of Wight, about eighty miles from London. There, Prince Albert designed and oversaw the building of Osborne House. Modeled after an Italianate villa, its minimalist elegance provided a stark, deliberate contrast to the Pavilion. Albert outfitted it with large windows, laid out elaborate gardens, and commissioned a miniature Swiss cottage playhouse, complete with garden plots and a working kitchen, to amuse the nine royal children.

Osborne House, currently open to tourists year-round, recently added Victoria's private beach, as well as her bathing machine, to its list of publicly available attractions. In the late nineteenth and early twentieth centuries, it was considered scandalous for women to be seen in bathing suits, so they were wheeled into the water in horse-drawn, enclosed carriages. After changing, they would climb out from behind curtains into the water, protecting their modesty at all costs. As table 5 shows, Osborne House remains a popular tourist destination, no doubt because Victoria died there in 1901.

Victoria and Albert were responsible for spurring touristic interest in another relatively remote area of Britain as well. The couple's first official visit to the Scottish Highland region occurred in 1842.*[34] It was laced with diplomatic activities, but Victoria also engaged in royal tourism in the most literal sense, visiting sites focal to her family history: "We saw the [Scottish coronation] Regalia, which are very old and curious ... also the room in which James VI of Scotland and the First of England was born, such a very, very small room with an old prayer written on the wall. . . . We walked out and saw the mound on which the ancient Scottish kings were always crowned."[35]

The couple first visited the large Scottish country estate known as Balmoral in 1848, where they participated in a range of regional activities from salmon-spearing to deer-stalking to attending torch-lit balls. After purchasing the over-17,000-acre estate in 1852, Albert immediately began overseeing a complete reconstruction of the home. Furnishings featured liberal use of the Royal Stuart tartan, as well as newly commissioned Balmoral and Victoria patterns. Although not the Royal Family's official Scottish residence,† Victoria, Albert, and their brood typically spent many weeks at Balmoral every year. As had been true of George IV's passion for Brighton, the family's regular visits drew residents and tourists who hoped to incorporate a Royal sighting—or at least, the patina of Royal proximity—into their holiday narratives. Tourists who had been drawn initially to the Scottish landscapes immortalized by the poets Sir Walter Scott and Robert Burns now had an additional reason to visit. As the Scottish railway system expanded, the "Royal Deeside," as the picturesque countryside surrounding the River Dee was known, became popular among the elite; they could

* George IV's visit twenty years earlier spurred such a craze for tartan and kilts that Scottish mills could not keep up with the consumer demand.
† This is the Palace of Holyroodhouse in Edinburgh.

TABLE 5 Key Royal Tourist Sites in Britain

Name	Type of Site	Location	No. of Tourists (est.)	Main Royal Associations	Begun (approx.)
Althorp	Private home	Northamptonshire, England	80,000	Princess Diana	1688
Balmoral	Occupied royal residence	Aberdeenshire, Scotland	80,000	Victoria onward	1856
Banqueting House, Whitehall	Overseen by Historic Royal Palaces	London, England	31,000	Charles I	1606; rebuilt 1622
Buckingham Palace (state rooms)	Occupied royal residence	London, England	522,000	Victoria onward	1703
Canterbury Cathedral	Cathedral	Canterbury, England	969,088	Henry IV interred	597; rebuilt 1077; 1174
Castles of King Edward (Beaumaris, Caernarfon, Conwy, Harlech)	Castles	Gwynedd, Wales	499,802	Edward I	1295; 1283; 1289; 1289.
Castle of Mey	Unoccupied royal residence	Caithness, Scotland	25,000	Queen Elizabeth, the Queen Mother	1572
Claremont Landscape Garden	Former royal residence	Esher, Surrey, England	170,007	Princess, Charlotte, Queen Victoria	1715
Edinburgh Castle	Castle	Edinburgh, Scotland	1,400,000	David II of Scotland, James V of Scotland, Mary, Queen of Scots	12th century
Hampton Court Palace	Overseen by Historic Royal Palaces	Middlesex, Greater London, England	524,000	The Tudors, William and Mary, Queen Anne	1514
Hillsborough Castle	The Queen's official home in Northern Ireland; now overseen by Historic Royal Palaces	Hillsborough, Northern Ireland	8,000	The Queen and her family	1770s; royal use began 1922

Name	Description	Location	Number	Associated royalty	Date
HMY *Britannia*	Former royal yacht	Edinburgh, Scotland	295,090	Elizabeth II	1954
Palace of Holyroodhouse	The Queen's official home in Scotland; overseen by the Royal Collection Trust	Edinburgh, Scotland	255,309	Mary, Queen of Scots (mother of King James I)	1671
Kenilworth Castle	Castle ruins	Warwickshire, England	136,000	John I	1120s
Kensington Palace	Overseen by Historic Royal Palaces	London, England	405,000	Georgians, Princess Margaret, Princess Diana, Prince William and family	1605
Kew Palace	Overseen by Historic Royal Palaces	London, England	31,000	George II, George III	1631
Leeds Castle	Castle	Kent, England	497,779	Edward I, Catherine of Aragon	1119
Osborne House	Former royal residence	Isle of Wight, England	248,544	Victoria and Albert	1845
Royal Pavilion	Former royal residence	Brighton, England	313,360	George IV, William IV	1787
Sandringham	Occupied royal residence	Norfolk, England	>250,000	Edward VII onward	1771
St. Paul's Cathedral	Cathedral/abbey	London, England	1,789,974	Royal services of Thanksgiving	1708
Stirling Castle	Castle	Stirling, Scotland	401,843	Coronations (Scottish)	Early 12th century
Tower of London	Overseen by Historic Royal Palaces	London, England	2,507,000	William I, Tudors, Edward IV, Henry VI, Crown Jewels	1078
Westminster Abbey	Cathedral/abbey	London, England	1,776,369	Coronations	960s–970s

afford the expensive and still relatively remote journey and the accommodations near the estate.

Victoria herself boosted the area's popularity by publishing two volumes of diary excerpts. At first, she offered *Leaves from the Journal of Our Life in the Highlands,* published in 1867, only to the Royal Family and her circle of friends. When she agreed to an expanded printing, the first edition of twenty thousand copies sold out quickly, and after multiple printings, the book became "out and away the best seller of the year."[36] Its success spurred Victoria to produce a second volume, published in 1883. Plans for a third volume were abandoned, because the family felt it provided too many details about her close relationship with her Scottish ghillie (personal servant), John Brown.

Although access to Balmoral Castle remains relatively restricted, the estate contains a restaurant, rental cabins, and on-site as well as online gift shops. These carry goods produced on the estate in addition to iconic Scottish brands, such as Harris Tweed. Visitors can engage in ranger-led tours, pony trekking, off-road riding, and RunBalmoral, "a half marathon race, all at times when no member of the royal family is in residence."[37] About 85,000 people visit each year, and several hundred thousand enjoy the liberal walking rights* to tramp over its extensive grounds.[38]

Throughout the nineteenth century (and even during the Civil War), Americans visited England in increasing numbers. As they shared accounts of their travels among their social circles, visitors began to agree on the importance of visiting London's three touristic "lions": Westminster Abbey, the Tower of London, and St. Paul's Cathedral, each steeped in royal history. Even as their numbers increased, in the early nineteenth century tourists were afforded almost unfettered access within the sites. Ultimately, however, unruly and damaging behavior led the preservation-minded to create tighter security measures. Especially urgent was the need to quash tourists' (especially Americans') desire to collect pieces from each site, or to carve their initials into priceless artifacts. By the 1820s, reckless relic hunting had become so rampant in Westminster Abbey that souvenir-seekers had chipped virtually all of Mary Queen of Scot's nose off her tomb. Rather than offering enlightening commentary about the sites, docents spent their time tailing tourists and begging them to stop damaging Royal memorials.

* Many privately-owned tracts of land in Britain feature public rights of way, often in the form of faint tracks that run through the property.

Two world wars and a devastating global economic depression in the first half of the twentieth century led to the stagnation of British and European tourism. Many promising sites had endured damage, and after World War II, potential visitors on both sides of the Atlantic stayed home to rebuild their lives and communities. Domestic tourism, however, received a boost with the spread of paved highways and railroads, and through laws such as the Holidays with Pay Act of 1938. Furthermore, foreign travel remained time consuming. Even elegant ocean liners, such as Cunard's RMS *Queen Mary* (active from 1936 to 1967) and RMS *Queen Elizabeth* (1938–1969), required ten days to complete the round-trip voyage from New York to Southampton.

In 1958, Pan American Airlines pioneered the first transatlantic jet service, and by the 1970s, the global airline industry was firmly established. At the same time, the British government began increasing its financial commitments to bolster the industry. In 1974, Parliament passed the first official policy guidelines pertaining to British tourism, and the following decade saw it establish many tourist governing boards and organizations. As the government increasingly outsourced and decentralized heritage management, more organizations were formed or restructured as charities, answering to Parliament and a board of trustees. In the rest of this chapter, we explore the workings of one such charity—Historic Royal Palaces (HRP).

Originally rooted in a government organization, HRP was reconstituted as a charity in 1998 and receives no funding from Parliament. Its contract emanates from the Department for Culture, Media, and Sport, which oversees activities related to tourism, leisure, and "creative" industries in Britain. HRP's Royal Charter defines its two primary charitable purposes. First, it is charged with conservation of five now-unoccupied Royal residences in and around London: the Tower of London, Hampton Court, the Banqueting House at Whitehall Palace, Kensington Palace, and Kew Palace. These are designated as unoccupied to distinguish them from those the Royal Family currently uses—although the monarchy retains part of Kensington Palace for its own use. In 2014, HRP also became responsible for overseeing Hillsborough Castle. Located approximately twelve miles from Belfast, it still serves as the Royal Family's official residence in Northern Ireland, and features 98 acres of gardens.

HRP's second purpose is to provide access for public education and enjoyment at its palaces. To do so, it relied on eight hundred employees in 2014, with plans to increase its staff by 10 percent the following year. In 2013, HRP reported gross sales of £80 million ($134 million). We chose to explore

HRP's role within the panoply of royal touristic organizations for several reasons. First, much of its operations center on attracting visitors, through managing ticket sales, retail, catering, functions and events, memberships, and donations. Second, HRP seeks to make these sites meaningful to contemporary visitors by measuring each initiative against its goal to "help everyone explore the story of how monarchs and people have shaped society, in some of the greatest palaces ever built."

In line with this objective, HRP has recently entered into brand relationships with key global partners that are highly visible within consumer culture and that reinforce the luxury-brand dimension of the RFBC. In 2012, it formed an alliance with De Beers to create a re-presentation of the Jewel House at the Tower of London; the exhibition now explains the role of each piece of regalia in the coronation ceremony, as well as how the Tower's design protects the jewels. Both brand partners clearly hope to benefit from the "halo effect" emanating from an association with the world's most treasured gemstone on one hand, and some of the most unique and valuable bejeweled artifacts in human history on the other.

When we first spoke with HRP's chief executive, Michael Day, in 2005, he stated that the three issues his organization found most challenging were change, money, and relevance. Change primarily referred to the challenges of steering an organization rooted in the traditionally conservative civil service system into the twenty-first century. Money and relevance speak directly to the second reason HRP represents an excellent case in royal touristic management. In 2013–14, it collected £51.9 million ($88.2 million) in ticket sales—up 15 percent from the year before—from 4,032,000 visitors. These sales account for slightly over 60 percent of its revenue, so HRP must continually focus on its visitors' experiences, balancing long-range conservation and education goals at each property with a well-planned itinerary of short-term events and exhibitions. Of course, much of what repeat visitors encounter at each property will be similar, but HRP seeks ways to foster continuous innovation at its sites and to maintain contemporary relevance. As such, it sustains a sense of vitality and change both at the Royal residences and within the organization.

Another reason HRP serves as an excellent case in royal touristic management is that information on its activities is so accessible. Accountable both to its board of trustees (four of whom are appointed by the Queen) and to Parliament, it produces detailed reports, annual and otherwise.[39] HRP's diligence in collecting and reporting data means it can assess both aggregate visitor numbers at each Royal residence and the popularity of specific exhibits and events.

HRP now strives to make its brand visible to visitors. Souvenir gift bags emblazoned with four-color photographs at each palace now feature the words *Historic Royal Palaces* in large type. Yet it knows that many if not most visitors, especially nondomestic ones, remain unaware of the organization. Increasingly, it is finding ways to place itself and the properties front and center during valued cultural moments in British history. For instance, HRP worked closely with the London Organising Committee of the Olympic and Paralympic Games (LOCOG) in 2012 to host the cycling time trials at Hampton Court Palace. Furthermore, the Tower of London housed the medals for the Olympic events. The carefully preserved state of the properties and their picturesque settings spur many requests for use in films and television programs, and as backdrops for fashion photography shoots, product launches, and key public events.

To provide a relatively holistic picture of HRP's activities, we offer a brief history of how each residence is situated within the dynastic narrative (with the exception of Hillsborough Castle, acquired as we began this chapter). We describe how HRP strategically integrates the events, exhibits, and experiences it offers at each residence into its overall goals of conservation, education, and preservation.

We begin with the Tower of London, which, along with Windsor Castle, is one of the oldest royal structures still in use today. In 1988, the Tower was designated a UNESCO World Heritage Site. According to Mike Robinson, who sits on the United Kingdom's UNESCO site-selection committee, this is the ultimate endorsement a historical entity can achieve. It signifies that the site is worthy of "global ownership," meaning its uniqueness and fragility are significant to people around the world, not just those in its own proximity.[40]

After his coronation in London in 1066, William I ordered a series of fortifications built around the city. Among these was the White Tower, an imposing edifice made of stone imported from his native Normandy that dominated the London skyline and asserted "the physical power and prowess of the new Norman monarch."[41] Distinctive features within the Tower's complex include barracks, a moat, and fortifications that ring the compound. Its strategic location along the Thames made it crucial to London's defense system and convenient to other Royal residences on the river. In the ensuing centuries, as future monarchs evaluated the Tower's strategic location and roles, they ordered it expanded and reinforced.

Although never a favored residence, the Tower has proven (and still proves) useful in myriad ways. Much of its historical and narrative significance stems from its use as a fortress and prison. Significantly, some inmates included monarchs who had been captured by relatives who coveted the crown. Most notably, in 1483 twelve-year-old King Edward V, who had acceded upon his father's death, was imprisoned prior to his coronation. He was soon joined by his younger brother, Richard, Duke of York. Over the next few months, Tower staff saw the two boys less and less frequently and eventually assumed that their uncle had ordered them murdered. He also declared their parents' marriage illegal, making the boys ineligible to reign, and had himself crowned as Richard III.

During the Tudor period, as the monarchs' religious preferences swung from Protestant to Catholic and back again, imprisonment in the Tower often was the first step in an agonizing religious persecution for those who were labeled heretics. The Tudors also used the facility to punish their own kin: when Henry VIII's oldest daughter, Mary, was crowned, she locked her half-sister, Elizabeth, in the Tower for two months. Most famously, Henry VIII's wives Anne Boleyn and Catherine Howard were imprisoned there and subsequently beheaded. (In 2006, a contemporary sculpture was installed in memory of the ten people executed on Tower Green.)

Over the centuries, the Tower has served a variety of more benign functions, and was the site of both the Royal Mint and the Office of Ordnance, responsible for supplying the British Army and Navy until 1830. More unusually, it housed the Royal Menagerie for six hundred years. It contained exotic animals (e.g., lions, elephants, ostriches, and kangaroos) given to the monarchs. In the early 1830s, the animals were moved from the Tower to form the basis of the London Zoo.

By the nineteenth century, the Tower had become one of London's must-see attractions, but its legacy as a visitor attraction predates that era by centuries. Around 1644, some of Charles I's gilt armor was moved to the site, and visitors in the 1650s reported viewing additional suits of armor on display. In the late 1680s, in the wake of the Civil War, an exhibit to promote monarchic rule, known as the Line of Kings, was commissioned. It featured certain English rulers on lifelike, life-size wooden horses, complete with actual battle armor for both the monarch and his mount. Not only was it designed to valorize kingly rule in general, but it singled out the warrior kings who had brought glory to England. Those rulers regarded as dastardly, such as Richard III, were excluded. Over the centuries, the Line of Kings acquired new figures—but never included a female monarch, although Elizabeth I's head was carved for the display.*

By around 1750, the Line of Kings was described in guidebooks. *An Historical Description of the Tower of London and Its Curiosities,* published in 1784, offers facts and frank opinions about the featured monarchs. It describes Henry VIII as "in his own proper armour, being of polished steel, the foliages whereof are gilt, or inlaid with gold. In his right hand he bears a sword, but whether of cruelty or mercy will hardly, I think, admit a doubt. His reign is marked with the divorce and murder of his wives, the destruction of religious houses and monasteries, and by a defiance of all laws divine and human."[42]

Originally designed to be aesthetic rather than accurate, in the 1820s sweeping changes (such as removing a seventeenth-century musket from William the Conqueror) improved the authenticity of representation. After several configurations over its five-hundred-year run, the exhibit, billed by HRP and the Royal Armouries† as the "world's longest-running visitor attraction," now includes eighteen monarchs, one Prince of Wales who never ruled, and eight noblemen. Many restored wooden horses dating from the 1600s also are on display.

By the mid-1800s, the Tower was selling tickets and concessions, and by 1901, the year Victoria died, annual visitors had reached half a million.[43] For those who enjoyed the darker aspects of its history, features such as Traitor's Gate and the Bloody Tower contributed to the impression that "almost the very stones [at the site] had developed a taste for murder."[44] Given the renown of the Tower's gruesome history, HRP can hardly shy away from this aspect; nor does it choose to do so. Tower guidebooks feature prominent descriptions of the grislier aspects of the residence. HRP also embellishes the dark-tourism element by staging ghost-story retellings, "spooky tours," and the nightly Ceremony of the Keys. During this event, the famous Yeomen Warders (or Beefeaters) lock up the Tower to keep it safe from intruders. But at the same time, HRP promotes the Tower's more aesthetic, benign, and whimsical aspects. These range from propagating the legend of the ravens

* The Line of Kings video produced by HRP is available on YouTube: www.youtube .com/watch?v = xukUBr1AiX8.

† The Royal Armouries (with three locations) originated with Elizabeth I's decision to place military items on display. It contains 75,000 items from the National Collection of Arms and Armour, National Artillery Collection, and National Firearms Collection.

who continue to live on site* to touting the discovery of the fragile but elaborate fourteenth-century wall paintings in the Byward Tower.

By the end of World War II, the Tower had ceased to serve as a prison, and its touristic narrative increasingly emphasized another type of safekeeping role: protecting priceless objects. Since 1303, it has housed one of the most famous assets of the monarchy, the Crown Jewels. The term refers to the coronation regalia that remain the property of the Crown rather than any individual monarch. The regalia include jewel-encrusted orbs, scepters, and crowns that play prominent, meaningful roles in the ceremony, as well as less ornate but still symbolically potent artifacts. (The plate, or formal tableware coated with gold or silver that is used during coronation banquets, is also on display.) Some gems are breathtaking in their singularity and size. They include the 105.6-carat Koh-I-Noor diamond (once the largest in the world) that the British Empire acquired when overtaking India's Punjab region in 1849.

Following Charles I's defeat and execution in 1649, Oliver Cromwell ordered the Crown Jewels destroyed, melted, and sold, thinking this action would signal the monarchy's irrevocable destruction. As a result, by the time the monarchy was restored in 1660, almost all the original Crown Jewels had been irretrievably lost. Only two pieces that featured during the most sacred part of the ceremony—when the monarch is anointed with holy oil—survived. Fortunately for the Royal Collection Trust, a yeoman of the guard loyal to Charles had purchased the twelfth-century coronation spoon for sixteen shillings (about £105/$180 today) and returned it to the Crown when the monarchy was restored.

Although the Crown managed to recover a few gemstones, Charles II essentially required a new set of regalia for his coronation. Because the cost to replace them was staggering, he and future monarchs often rented genuine stones to use at ceremonies, replacing these with paste copies for display. Even after a botched robbery attempt in the 1600s, visitors were still permitted to touch the Crown Jewels. That changed in 1815 after one woman reached through the theft-deterrent bars, damaging a crown.

The Tower's major exhibit in 2014 clearly resonated with a crucial cultural event: the hundredth anniversary of Britain's entry into World

---

* According to legend, Charles II ordered the Tower's six resident ravens protected, believing their departure would portend the fall of the kingdom and the Tower. Ravens (their flight feathers trimmed) still live on the grounds.

War I.[45] To commemorate the staggering number of casualties, HRP secured several corporate partners and commissioned ceramic artist Paul Cummins to work with stage designer Tom Piper to create 888,246 ceramic poppies—one for each life lost across the British Empire—to spill into and fill the Tower's moat (figure 24). Titled *Blood Swept Lands and Seas of Red,* the first poppy was planted on July 17, 2014, by the Tower's longest-serving Yeoman Warder, and the installation was declared officially open on August 5, 2014. Relying on over 18,000 volunteers, who planted 70,000 poppies each week,[46] the public became increasingly captivated as it watched the installation spread. Visitors reported their feelings of sadness and awe both day and night (HRP had lit the Tower's grounds). A major philanthropic aspect of the event was the announcement that HRP would sell the poppies on its website and donate the proceeds to six military-related charities.

As the exhibit stretched into its final weeks, "the poppies," as it became known throughout the world, became a focus of contention. This was not because of any ideological intent, but because as its scheduled removal grew closer, an outcry arose to keep it in place. The *London Evening Standard* launched a "Save Our Poppies" campaign, and the exhibit's fate became the lead story on the nation's news programs.[47] The argument became one of entitlement: the public, media, and political figures argued that although over four million people had already visited it, anyone who so desired should be able to view such a moving, important exhibit. But frost had already begun to damage the fragile ceramic flowers; furthermore, HRP had promised delivery to those who had paid £25 (plus postage) per poppy,* so retaining the installation was not viable.

The night before the Armistice Day ceremony on November 11, which would see the final poppy planted,† London's Mayor Boris Johnson penned an article where he revealed that the "authorities at the Tower . . . have listened and they have taken action."[48] Ultimately, HRP decided to retain two parts of the installation at the Tower until the end of November and to take part of the exhibit on tour around Britain. The traveling poppies would then become part of the permanent display at London's Imperial War Museum. The exhibit's success was unparalleled in HRP's history; ultimately, more people visited the Tower during the exhibit than in the whole of 2013.

* To prevent profiteers from capitalizing on the demand for poppies featured in the exhibit, and because each signified a loss of life, eBay banned the resale of poppies on its site—but not before people tried to list them for double and triple HRP's original price.

† On that day in 1918, a cease-fire in Europe effectively ended World War I.

FIGURE 24. *Blood Swept Lands and Seas of Red.* Courtesy Thomson Reuters.

Hampton Court Palace, located about twelve miles from London, was originally built by the powerful Cardinal Wolsey, who for many years was Henry VIII's closest advisor. Some historians note that Wolsey claimed he gave Henry the palace in recognition that his lifestyle was even grander than the King's. But it is more commonly believed that Henry seized Hampton Court after Wolsey failed to persuade the pope to secure Henry's divorce from his first wife, Catherine of Aragon.*

The Tudor monarchs Henry VIII and Elizabeth I strained the royal treasury by indulging their ultralavish tastes in fashion and court entertainment, and through conspicuous, competitive consumption. These tendencies were especially pronounced when they entertained foreign monarchs or other dignitaries. Henry's reign has been described as "one endless sequence of tourneys, disguisings, entertainments, and pageants."[49] The court's rationale for such indulgences was that these opulent offerings helped England appear equal in global standing to the other powerful nations of Europe—but espe-

* G. J. Meyer makes the first argument in *The Tudors.*

cially in comparison to France, whose court was an object of envy and emulation throughout Europe.

In that vein, banquets were some of the more expensive (or, to Henry's critics, egregious) indulgences at Hampton Court. HRP's recent restoration efforts reflect the importance of royal gastronomy. In addition to presenting the kitchens as they existed during Henry's reign, HRP has recently restored the Chocolate Kitchen, reflecting the popularity of chocolate as a drink in the late seventeenth and early eighteenth centuries. While the upper class often gathered at commercial chocolate houses, the truly elite commissioned kitchens for their homes to be staffed by chocolate millers and preparers. In February 2014, the Chocolate Kitchen reopened at Hampton Court, and it now features chocolate-making demonstrations. The café and gift shops in the palace also sell related chocolate items.

Although HRP has devoted much attention to Hampton Court's massive interior, it also understands the touristic allure of more than sixty acres of diverse grounds. They contain a rose garden, a privy garden with symmetric designs and sculptures, the Great Vine (dating from 1768 and still producing an annual crop of black grapes), and a maze built at the end of the seventeenth century for William III and Mary II. Drawing on both the British appreciation of gardens and tourists' love of elegant exterior spaces, HRP has restored the appearance and functionality of much of the grounds. In 2014, it replanted one of the six original kitchen gardens to its eighteenth-century working state.[50] Relying on old paintings, letters, a plan from 1736, and the 1706 magnum opus *The Retired Gardener,* which discussed crops suitable for gentlemen, HRP planted a cornucopia of fruit trees, as well as several thousand vegetables and flower varieties. Highlighting royal food heritage and the increased cultural (and international) obsession with the "foodie" lifestyle, Hampton Court also hosted the BBC's Good Food Festival in August 2014.

An equally ambitious project, albeit aimed at a completely different visitor segment, is the Magic Garden, scheduled to open in summer 2015—coincidentally, the year the palace celebrates its five-hundredth anniversary. Designed to foster creative and interactive play, it features a climbable crown, a fire-breathing dragon that sprays water, an entrance area with a "strange topiary" of oddly carved trees and shrubs, and a large tournament ground for "royal jousting" and other events. One of the truly new additions to Hampton Court, with "every feature ... designed to be climbed upon, swung from, and hidden in,"[51] it offers children and families a way to create new links from the past to the present.

In 1520, Henry VIII seized another of Cardinal Wolsey's elaborate palaces—York Place in central London. Prior to his marriage to Anne Boleyn, it was their primary city home. Succeeding monarchs also favored Whitehall Palace—Henry's name for the structure—and commissioned additions. One of the most esteemed was the second Banqueting House for the palace (the first was destroyed by fire), built by the famous architect Inigo Jones for James I in 1622. The first example of Italian-inspired classical architecture in England, it featured over four hundred tons of pillars and a fifty-five-foot ceiling. Not only the site of elegant banquets and dances, it also was a favored venue for the staging of the masque, a form of entertainment traceable to Henry VIII's court in 1527. Masques combine pageantry, theater, opera, and dance with stories that focus on the "contest between love and riches."[52] The Banqueting House was the only part of Whitehall Palace that remained after the palace burned to the ground in 1698.

The hallmark of the Banqueting House is the set of highly ornate paintings on the ceiling that Charles I commissioned from the artist Peter Paul Rubens, probably during a visit to England in 1629–30. The completed paintings were shipped to England and installed on the ceiling in 1636. Charles I paid Rubens £3,000 (equivalent to £250,000/$429,000 today) and a gold chain. The ornate series of painted panels depicts the union of England and Scotland that resulted from his father James I's coronation. Portraying the monarch as a godlike figure surrounded by heavenly creatures, it reinforced the fundamental assertion of the divine right of kings. This dogma asserts that monarchs' power stems only from God; thus, no mortals can wield authority over monarchs. This belief would contribute to Charles I's downfall, and in 1649 he walked under the famous ceiling to step onto the scaffold and face death by execution—the only monarch in the royal lineage to meet such a fate. The Banqueting House bore witness to the full circle of destruction and rebirth for Charles's family, however. In 1660, a procession celebrating the monarchy's restoration made its way back to the building, where Parliament swore loyalty to his son Charles II.

Although small compared to HRP's other London properties, the Banqueting House is in high demand, sometimes for quite prominent civic and cultural events. Such notables as Nelson Mandela and George W. Bush have attended functions there. HRP also rents out the Undercroft, James I's drinking den on the lower level of the building, for parties and special occasions. It plans to restore and re-present the structure in the next few years.

In 1699, William I and Mary II sought a retreat from London's foul air and bought Nottingham House, the forerunner of Kensington Palace, then outside the city limits. The high points of Kensington Palace's role in the dynastic narrative occurred during the reigns of the Hanoverian kings George I and II. Continuing Henry VIII's legacy, these kings generously bestowed royal patronage on musicians such as Georg Frideric Handel (who taught harpsichord to George II), and to myriad artists, sculptors, architects, and landscape designers who oversaw and executed palace improvements. Chief curator of HRP and cultural commentator Lucy Worsley describes the intrigue that occurred not only within the Royal Family but also among the palace's artisans and staff during the tenure of the Georgian court.[53]

However, George III's predilection for the more pastoral Windsor Castle and Kew Palace relegated Kensington to a home for "minor royals," a role it retained for almost a century. In 1837, however, the palace's visibility in the royal saga made a dramatic rebound. Two of these so-called minor members were the Duke of Kent's widow, Princess Victoria, and her only daughter and namesake. When the young Victoria's uncle William IV failed to produce a legitimate heir, it became clear she would succeed him. On June 20, 1837, the eighteen-year-old princess awoke in Kensington Palace to learn she had become queen. Just three weeks after her accession, she relocated the Royal Household to the recently remodeled and expanded Buckingham Palace, the first monarch to take up residence there.

From Victoria's exodus until around 1960, Kensington once again occupied a minor role as a royal residence. That year, however, the Queen's sister, Princess Margaret, and her new husband, Antony Armstrong-Jones, moved into apartment 1A—which actually consisted of twenty rooms. Margaret's jet-set lifestyle did not strictly align with her sister's tenets of duty, family, and morality. At the same time, however, the Queen's younger sister injected glamour into the royal narrative during a period when the image of the RFBC was perceived as a bit staid.

The public could visit parts of Kensington Palace after Victoria opened it to the public on her eightieth birthday. In 2008, HRP began a £12 million ($18 million) refurbishment and restoration. Strategically, the effort was designed to counter the perception of the palace as hard to locate and harder still to understand and enjoy. Michael Day noted in 2012 that the standard walk-through tour with headphones was "dreadful ... all the significant moments in history were lost."[54] In addition to creating a new canopied entrance to commemorate the Queen's Diamond Jubilee, HRP restored the

FIGURE 25. The Orangery, Kensington Palace. Photo by Cele Otnes.

gardens and added a courtyard terrace and café. One feature of Kensington Palace that taps into the luxury-laden aspect of the RFBC is its Orangery, built for Queen Anne as a site for court entertainment in 1704 (figure 25). The only royal palace in London where visitors can enjoy traditional afternoon tea, it also serves breakfast, lunch, and special meals, such as holiday brunches.

New permanent exhibits in the palace focus on Victoria's life as a princess, while explaining the experiences of earlier monarchs who lived there. Other displays are devoted to Princess Margaret and Princess Diana. In March 2012, the Queen and Prince Philip officially reopened the palace. HRP had hoped the renovation would boost yearly visitors from 250,000 to 350,000; in fact, 400,000 toured it in 2013.

As it does for each residence under its care, HRP seeks to enhance visitors' emotional engagement by animating the narratives contained within the palaces' walls. To prepare visitors for the dramatic changes a remodeled Kensington Palace would offer and ensure it would still attract tourists during its construction phase, HRP offered a transitional exhibit in 2010 and 2011. Titled *Enchanted Palace,* it was staged in the rooms that could remain open and focused on stories pertaining to each of the seven princesses who had lived there. Contemporary artworks, key texts such as poems (with some painted on the walls), atmospheric lighting, textiles, and sound effects conveyed the narratives pertaining to each royal figure. HRP enhanced the theatrics of the exhibit by relying on actors and its employees to play the respective roles of Detectors and Explainers. Detectors impersonated palace servants from different eras; their job was to engage visitors by communicating the daily goings-on of palace life. As experts on the rooms and exhibits, Explainers offered historical details and perspectives regarding the way each princess was represented.[55]

Enchanted Palace reinforced its linkages to contemporary life by commissioning famous British fashion designers to create innovative, highly aesthetic gowns to represent each princess. For example, Dame Vivienne Westwood created "A Dress for Rebellion" to represent Princess Charlotte. Each dress was staged without a mannequin, and Westwood's kinetic design conveyed Charlotte's charge down the Grand Staircase in an attempt to escape her dysfunctional family. Another creation, "A Dress for Dreaming of Freedom," was composed entirely of origami cranes and hung from the ceiling in Princess Victoria's bedroom, symbolizing the lonely princess's desire to experience life beyond the palace grounds.

The edgy contemporary installations garnered media attention beyond HRP's imaginings: *Vogue* wrote a blurb about the exhibit, and a story ran in the Arts section of the *New York Times.* Even though HRP was aware that *Enchanted Palace* might be perceived as controversial and cutting-edge, the attention surprised Day, who noted, "We'd never been in the *New York Times* for anything before."[56]

Kew Palace is the last royal residence in England to be acquired by HRP. It is located within the three-hundred-acre Kew Gardens, founded in 1759. From its inception, the Gardens were supported by the monarchy and nobility as a center for botanical research, reflecting widespread cultural interest in botany in the eighteenth century. Victoria donated Kew Gardens to the nation when she became queen. Still an active research center, it currently houses the widest variety of plant species in Britain. Like the Tower, it has been designated as a UNESCO World Heritage Site.

The relatively modest Kew Palace, originally known as "Dutch House," is all that remains of a much larger complex of palatial buildings. One edifice on the grounds that has survived is a nearly fifty-meter-tall (163-foot) pagoda built in 1761 that HRP is currently restoring. It is one of the five remaining "follies" (or structures created purely for decoration and enjoyment) out of sixteen that were designed for George III and his family. A visitor map in process by HRP will mark the location of each.

George III bought Kew Palace in 1781 to satisfy his penchant for rural life. It was the site of three Royal weddings, including the double ceremony of William, Duke of Clarence (who became William IV), and Edward, Duke of Kent (Queen Victoria's father). Kew was the site of George III's severe bouts of what may have been the hereditary disease porphyria, and where he endured his horrific treatment regimens to combat it. HRP has incorporated the saga of his illness into a tour of Kew's Royal Kitchen, preserved circa 1789. It was during this period that the King was again allowed access to his knife and fork, after his first bout of "madness" had subsided.

Compared to the more regal, glamorous palaces in its stable, HRP faces special challenges in drawing visitors to Kew's modest country-home status. Nevertheless, it still finds ways to leverage the (sometimes quirky) narratives associated with the structure. For example, Queen Charlotte's rustic cottage, located in the gardens and under HRP's care, was a favorite afternoon tea spot for the Royal Family and once home to exotic animals (including kangaroos). It now contains an exhibition of 150 satirical engravings in its Print Room, as well as an upstairs "Picnic Room" that offers panoramic views of the grounds.

Clearly, with its Salacious Gossip Tours, exhibits of portraits of Charles II's mistresses, and discussions of tragedies such as miscarriages and murders, HRP does not (and in the Internet age, cannot) take totally to heart historian Walter Bagehot's warning that the British monarchy's "mystery is its life. We must not let daylight in upon magic."[57] Yet while it does pull back the curtain on many aspects of past royal life, HRP also strives to maintain the magic of these residences and offer touristic experiences that are unavailable in less extraordinary settings.

In so doing, HRP calls into play several key strategies. First, it relies on the technique we reference in the title of this chapter, namely "storying the monarchy." HRP emphasizes how the narratives embedded within each edifice remain real and relevant to current visitors and, in so doing, help these visitors co-create and co-own these stories. In short, the royal residences—and their conferences, concerts, cultural events, exhibits, festivals, gift shops, publications, and rituals—become repositories not only for stories about past monarchs and others who lived there, but also for the global events and day-to-day discoveries of contemporary visitors.

In 2005, for example, HRP staged an exhibit at Kensington Palace titled *The Queen's Working Wardrobe*, featuring iconic outfits she had worn while engaged in duties around the world. (The accessories displayed included some from Margaret Tyler's collection.) The outfits ranged from the Queen's uniform from her Auxiliary Territorial Service (ATS)* days, to the modest but still glamorous black gown and veil she wore when she met the pope. It featured a "Memory Wall" where visitors could post their own recollections about the ensembles and events on small pieces of paper, supplementing the displays the curators had crafted. Many wrote of seeing the Queen in person while she performed her duties, and some even described their roles at different occasions. A curator of the Royal Ceremonial Dress Collection at HRP observed, "We had quite a lot of ladies who wrote things like 'I remember being in the ATS. And I remember when Princess Elizabeth came... .' [Another wrote] 'How fantastic. . . . I worked at Norman Hartnell between 1945 and 1967, and two of the dresses that I made with my own hands were on display.'"[58]

Second, HRP works diligently to leverage links between events in the past and the present. Day describes how a Tower of London exhibit on Guy Fawkes that had been planned for months coincided with the London terrorist bombings in July 2005. He noted that Fawkes committed "arguably one of the first acts of major terrorism. . . . [O]ther people wanted to bring down the King, and they planned to blow up [Parliament]. . . . That's terrorism."[59] The ability to juxtapose the old with the new through exhibits, artifacts, or practices enables HRP to demonstrate the relevance of the Royal narrative to today's world—assuming, of course, that one believes it is relevant in the first place.

Third, HRP focuses on creating a distinct persona for each residence, by leveraging each building's strengths and unique features. Creating a unique sense of place reinforces the legacy of the monarchy, in terms of both its narrative breadth and its material treasures. Day describes how he and his staff engaged in an exercise to discern the personality of each palace, incorporating

* Princess Elizabeth served as an auto mechanic for the Auxiliary Territorial Service; she joined at age nineteen, and reached the rank of junior commander.

the findings from market research on visitors' perceptions: "So we said [to ourselves] ... how would you characterize each of the palaces? ... And we came up with three words for each: Tower of London: powerful, intriguing, and ancient. Hampton Court: majestic, romantic, and flamboyant. Banqueting House: dramatic, exuberant, and revolutionary."[60] By constantly considering how to reinforce the personalities of the palaces, HRP strives to create narratives that are fresher and more engaging than if it merely positions and promotes the residences as repositories of monarchic material culture.

Finally, although it relies liberally on traditional print media such as brochures, posters, signs, and mailings, HRP also communicates its strategic initiatives through an active, visible social media presence. Recently, it began featuring favorite photos of each palace from visitors' postings on Instagram. It also maintains a Twitter feed, where it offers information on palace activities (including job openings) and retweets visitor pictures and content. By May 2015, HRP's Facebook page boasted over 226,000 "likes." It also launched a members' blog in 2013, where it discusses the special events staged for contributors, such as lecture tours in the United Kingdom and the United States that feature HRP's curators and historians.[61]

In short, HRP must maintain and enhance the iconic status of its royal properties in the face of competition from London's many now-free museums and other popular attractions, such as the London Eye and Legoland. In so doing, it strives to connect royal narratives to visitors' contemporary lives and experiences. We now turn our attention from these properties, dispersed around a relatively wide geographic area, to a town where royal tourism permeates almost every aspect of daily life.

EIGHT

Weekends in Windsor

CASTLES, CHINA, AND CORGIS

Over the years, as we became more familiar with Margaret's routines, we came to realize that she and the Queen share a fondness for Windsor, a town that looms large in the Royal narrative and houses the largest and oldest inhabited castle in the world.* Known as the Queen's second home, Windsor Castle's pastoral location offers her the perfect antidote to London's urban congestion. Its proximity to London allows the Royal Family to enjoy leisurely weekends after duty-packed workweeks and to devote themselves to their passions—although Windsor does play key roles during official functions. The Queen's fondness for Windsor is well documented. She leaves Buckingham Palace "on the dot at three on Friday afternoon" to spend many of her weekends (as well as the entire month of April and much of June) at Windsor Castle.[1] Her personal flag, the Royal Standard, flutters on top of the iconic Round Tower from the time she arrives until she exits the castle walls.

Although Windsor has appealed to many monarchs throughout the ages, the Queen has specific reasons for favoring it. First, it is only about a forty-minute drive west of London, in the county of Berkshire, now known as part of the city's suburban "stockholder belt." Some might find its position in the flight path to Heathrow Airport antithetical to claims that it is a rural retreat. But the Windsor estate contains over 15,000 acres and includes the castle, its grounds, Windsor Great Park (open to the public), Home Park (for the Royal Family's private use), the Royal Landscape (public gardens, lakes, and fields), Windsor and Swinley forests (comprising over half of the estate), commercial property, two golf clubs, and Royal Ascot Racecourse.

---

* At approximately 44,593 square meters (480,000 square feet).

FIGURE 26. The Long Walk, Windsor Great Park. Photo by Cele Otnes.

The Great Park consists of 7.7 square miles (12.4 kilometers) of public space, sees almost 2.5 million visitors a year, and contains important sites and mementos of royal history. Bill Bryson, the popular American author, self-professed Anglophile, and former president of the Campaign to Protect Rural England, observes that the park "incorporates into its ancient fabric every manner of sylvan charm: deep primeval woodlands, bosky dells, wandering footpaths and bridleways, formal and informal gardens and a long, deeply fetching lake. Scattered picturesquely about are farms, woodland images, for-gotten statues, a whole village occupied by estate workers and things . . . [from the Queen's] trips abroad . . . obelisks and totem poles and other curious expressions of gratitude from distant [Commonwealth] outposts."[2]

One of the park's highlights is the Long Walk, a 2.65-mile (4.26-kilom-eter) multiuse path that extends from the castle to the Copper Horse on Snow Hill, a famous statue of George III commissioned by his son and namesake and completed in 1831 (figure 26). The town's website notes that this highest point in Windsor is one of Britain's most photographed spots, and names it as one of the top places to "get down on one knee." It mentions other picturesque sites in the park, including the Savill Garden, the Royal Landscape, and the two-thousand-year-old Roman ruins installed at Virginia Water, a man-made lake.

In terms of future activities, plans are in the works to provide a permanent walkway around Windsor, to be endorsed by the Queen. It will commemorate the date she becomes the longest-reigning monarch in history: September 9, 2015. The newly formed Outdoor Trust, which supervised the creation of London's Jubilee Walkway and Jubilee Greenway, is overseeing the 6.32-kilometer (3.97-mile) walk, with 63 markers of interest mirroring the 63 years and 211 days she will have reigned by that date. Designed as a ninety-minute circuit, it represents an attempt to broaden Windsor's tourist appeal beyond the castle.[3]

But Windsor holds especially poignant memories for the Queen because it is where she spent much of her youth. In 1940, as the London Blitz increased in intensity, she and Princess Margaret were secretly sequestered at the Windsor estate, where they remained until the war ended. Edward VIII's abdication four years earlier meant that while she lived at Windsor, "Lilibet" (as she was known to her family) knew that she would one day become queen, and it was there that she received much of the training for that role. She and Margaret were tutored at home (by such notables as the vice-provost at Eton and the archbishop of Canterbury), and their governesses taught them French.

Unlike Princess Victoria, who had been forbidden to play with nonroyalty, the young princesses interacted with local children. Like their mother, they joined the Girl Guides, the venerable British institution founded in 1910. At the suggestion of their governess, Marion Crawford, the 1st Buckingham Palace Unit was formed in 1937. It was restarted at Windsor. To earn her Sea Ranger rank, Princess Elizabeth gained her boating permit and took her mother out on a dinghy. Elizabeth chose to become a patron of the Girl Guides when she became queen in 1952. Since that time, the organization has often made use of Windsor Great Park. In 2014, the fifth WINGS International Girl Guides Jamboree took place there, attended by six thousand people from over forty countries.

One popular tradition the princesses and the local children enjoyed at the castle was staging the traditional Christmas "panto," or pantomime, a uniquely family-oriented English form of theater.* Fearful that Elizabeth and Margaret's sheltered existence was beginning to resemble that of "princesses in a tower," their governess lobbied the headmaster at the Royal School

---

* Typically based on fairy tales, pantos combine musical numbers, slapstick comedy, dance, and humor.

in Windsor, whose pupils were children of the castle staff, to write a panto-mime with parts for the princesses. These were staged during the holiday seasons from 1941 to 1944. Attendees were charged seven shillings, and the proceeds went to the Wool Fund to purchase material for soldiers' blankets.[4]

It was also during her years at Windsor that Princess Elizabeth began corresponding with her third cousin Philip Mountbatten; they had first met when she was thirteen and he was eighteen. A member of the exiled and financially strapped Greek Royal Family, Philip's British and German rela-tives supported him through his school years. After taking a commission in the Royal Navy during the war, he often spent holidays with the Royal Family at Windsor. In 1943, seventeen-year old Elizabeth was thrilled when Philip joined the family for Christmas and attended all five performances of the pantomime *Aladdin,* even helping backstage with the props.[5]

Yet as is true of any family home, Windsor Castle also holds its share of less happy memories for the Queen, her family, and her ancestors. More dis-tantly, it was the site of Catherine of Aragon's last encounter with Henry VIII in 1532 before he banished her to pursue Anne Boleyn, Charles I's burial in 1649 (after becoming the only reigning monarch to be executed), the deaths of George III, George IV, William IV, and Prince Albert, Edward VIII's abdication speech in 1936, and the Queen Mother's death at the Royal Lodge in Windsor Great Park in 2002. Furthermore, the friendship between Princess Margaret and King George VI's equerry Peter Townsend, which began at Windsor and grew into love, would later prove to be devastatingly disappointing for the couple.

Windsor has seen one form or another of Norman-styled structures since the late eleventh century, when the Conqueror commissioned it as part of the western ring of fortifications to be placed within a twenty-mile radius of London.[6] Records reveal that the monarchs' first use of the castle as a Royal residence dates from Henry I's court in 1110; it was also the site of the first Royal wedding in 1121, when he married his second wife. The manpower and material required for the castle's expansions and renovations during the Middle Ages helped the town enjoy economic viability even when other areas suffered from the consequences of near-constant wars. Yet as is true for all Royal residences, the care and attention Windsor received waxed and waned over the centuries, depending on each monarch's level of interest.

The first significant period of construction at the castle began in the 1300s. Edward III—born within its walls and known as "Edward of

Windsor" in his youth—chose to make it the setting for a new chivalric order. He based the concept on the Knights of the Round Table of Arthurian legend, which enjoyed a resurgence in cult status in the Middle Ages.[7] In the 1340s, Edward invited skilled jousters from all over Europe to demonstrate their skills in tournaments at Windsor. Archaeological evidence discovered in 2006 indicates that Edward had actually created a round building for the table (not to be confused with the castle's iconic Round Tower).[8] Edward III later simplified his plans regarding his chivalric order, modifying them into what became the Order of the Garter. He installed the first knights in 1348, and it remains "the highest personal honor . . . a monarch can confer."[9]

Establishing the Garter at Windsor cemented the castle's position as the monarchy's main symbol of chivalry. Membership in the Order is limited to the reigning monarch and twenty-four Knights and Ladies of the Garter, as well as three special categories. These are the Prince of Wales, Royal Knights and Ladies (members of the Royal Family), and Stranger Knights and Ladies (royalty from other countries). The Order's roster is populated primarily by politicians, military officers, and aristocrats; one notable exception is New Zealander Sir Edmund Hillary, the first to scale Mount Everest. Nonroyal women could not become Lady Companions until 1987; to date, only three have received the honor.

The Garter ceremony at Windsor Castle remains a popular draw for tourists and the media alike. The investiture of new members and celebratory luncheon is held on Garter Day, coincidentally the Monday of Royal Ascot Week. (In a nod to the timing, the prayers include one for the Queen's horse to win at the racecourse.) These events are held out of public sight in the castle's Throne Room, which otherwise is included on the standard castle tour. After these events, the group processes to St. George's Chapel in signature long blue velvet robes, plumed black velvet hats, and large Garter insignia supported by heavy gold chains. The public can apply for tickets to watch the procession in the castle's Lower Ward; in 2013, over seven thousand viewers chose to do so.

The Order's aesthetic appeal is indelibly ingrained in the Windsor touristic experience, because St. George's Chapel is laden with the symbols of heraldry associated with each knight and lady. These include coats of arms, crests, and gilt stall plates—enameled, engraved metal insignia affixed to the chapel stalls. They "date from the 14th century to the present [and form] an assemblage of original heraldic work without parallel."[10] As such, among its other appeals, the chapel serves as a mini-museum of chivalry. But because it serves a local active congregation, it is always closed to tourists on Sundays, much to the chagrin of day-trippers.*

Windsor's roots as a tourist destination stem from its appeal to religious pilgrims. In 1471 the pious Henry VI was murdered in the Tower of London. A few years later, Richard III had his body moved to St. George's Chapel. Soon after, Henry VI developed a cult following, and pilgrims began to make their way to Windsor to visit his resting place.[11] From approximately 1350 to 1550, St. George's also was thought to house a fragment of the True Cross—the one upon which Jesus was crucified. Until pilgrimages fell out of fashion during the Reformation, religious tourists were economically important to the town. In contrast to modern trekkers to Windsor, pilgrims often stayed overnight and filled the coffers of innkeepers and restaurateurs.

The chapel became (and remains) an important sacred site for the Royal Family and for those who wish to pay homage to dead kings and queens. Eleven monarchs and their relatives rest there, including the Queen Mother and Princess Margaret. Henry VIII is buried under its floor, next to his third and favorite wife, Jane Seymour. The prominent tombs of George V and Queen Mary are located at the rear of the chapel. As we will discuss, Windsor Castle and its environs were important in the lives of both their sons who would become king, Edward VIII and George VI.

From the 1500s to the 1700s, the castle was used by the monarchs mostly as a hunting retreat and a place to escape the epidemics of contagious disease that periodically gripped London. Although primarily a champion of Hampton Court, Henry VIII was interested enough in Windsor to make it the home for his priceless treasures, which ultimately formed the basis of the Royal Collection. This trove began with a series of drawings of life at court by the favored court painter Hans Holbein—who by 1536 was referred to as the "King's Painter."

Charles II brought many important pieces of artwork and furniture to Windsor, including volumes of drawings by Leonardo da Vinci and a "splendid set of silver furniture presented to him by the City of London in about 1670."[12] He spent much of his time trying to reacquire some of the Royal Collection's treasures that Cromwell had sold overseas to pay his armies' expenses. Charles also created the Long Walk, hoping to evoke comparisons between Windsor Castle's grounds and those of Versailles in Paris.

---

* Members of the general public can attend Sunday services at the chapel, except during special royal events.

The castle saw its heyday as a royal residence during the reigns of George III and IV. Both kings added substantially to the Royal Collection, with George IV especially determined to recover lost treasures. But his major contribution was the extensive re-envisioning of the castle's exterior and interior reconstruction—which remains virtually intact today. Prior piecemeal additions and restorations at Windsor not only had resulted in a residence that was confusing and uncomfortable, but also had left it devoid of architectural unity. The King hired the architect Jeffry Wyatt* to direct the Gothic reconstruction.

The castle redesign, completed in 1828, featured "generous windows for comfort, and fanciful towers and battlements for romance."[13] Wyatt also raised the height of the Round Tower† by thirty feet, bolstering the castle's most iconic aspect. The result reinforced Windsor's reputation as the world's most romantic castle. This was exactly George IV's goal, as it now served a key role "in the inflation of monarchial splendor and ceremony, which began as a deliberate response to the French Revolution . . . and to any inclined to support it."[14]

The arrival of two train lines in 1849 spurred Windsor's growth as a royal tourist town. Each vied to serve Queen Victoria's Royal Train; as a result, an area of about six thousand people found itself with two train stations serving two different railways, not even half a mile apart on the same street.[15] The stations' similar names, Windsor & Eton Central and Windsor & Eton Riverside, prompt travel books and websites to remind readers to pay close attention to the station where they arrive and depart. To further confuse matters, the larger Windsor & Eton Central station now bears a sign with the name Windsor Royal Station—a name not included in any ticket-booking systems. Reflecting the increasing affluence of the Windsor-Berkshire area and its desire to serve tourists, this station was recently reconfigured for high-end shopping.

The importance of Windsor Castle in the RFBC's history certainly has not been lost on the monarchy itself. Successful branding strategy requires selecting a memorable and palatable name—one that crystallizes its essence and conjures up pleasant associations for its consumers. Depicting probably the most blatant monarchic understanding of this truism, in 1917 George V believed being at war with the Kaiser, his first cousin, necessitated a change

* Upon receiving a knighthood, Sir Jeffry changed his last name to Wyatville, believing it more suitable for a peer.

† It was first built by Henry II in 1170.

from the Royal Family's all-too-German moniker House of Saxe-Coburg and Gotha to something quintessentially English. For weeks, his advisers dug through the annals of British history for a name that would remind British subjects that although their King and Queen might stem from German ancestry, they were really and truly English after all. In the end, the King's private secretary, Arthur Bigge, suggested the name House of Windsor. With connotations stretching back to William the Conqueror, it was felt that "the name was enough to redeem a tarnished crown."[16]

The castle remains open to visitors even when the Queen is on site, offering tourists added hope that they might see her or her family on its grounds. Yet it is much more likely that such encounters will be limited to the likenesses for sale at Windsor's many souvenir stores or at the high-end gift shops the Royal Collection oversees on the castle grounds. But if visitors are disinterested in souvenir shopping, they can always pose by renderings of the Queen, Prince William, Catherine (complete with pram), or Prince Harry, each appearing on a different side of a replica K6 English red telephone box across the street from the castle (figure 27). The installation was part of the British Telecommunications Artbox project launched in and around London in 2012 to mark the Diamond Jubilee and the Olympics.[17] In yet another confluence of royalty and popular culture, the iconic phone boxes were introduced in 1936 to commemorate George V's Silver Jubilee.

Windsor Castle also proves compelling to younger tourists. As is true at Buckingham Palace, a Changing of the Guard ceremony is held almost daily, and crowds typically can get a closer view of the soldiers' uniforms and armaments than is possible at the Queen's London residence. Furthermore, one of the castle's more popular rooms contains Queen Mary's large and meticulously outfitted dollhouse, as well as dolls and accessories that Princess Elizabeth and Princess Margaret received from the King and Queen of France. For children and adults whose tastes run toward militaria, the Grand Staircase features Henry VIII's original suit of armor and displays of gifts received during the glory days of the British empire. The panoply of priceless paintings, furnishings, tapestries, and voluminous amounts of Royal china on display in the castle can overwhelm those trying to take it all in during one visit. No doubt, many visitors take advantage of the fact that their admission tickets are valid for one year.

On November 20, 1992—the Queen and Prince Philip's forty-fifth wedding anniversary—fire broke out in the castle's Private Chapel. Unfortunately, the smoke detectors and sprinklers had been dismantled for upgrading. The

FIGURE 27. Royal telephone box, Windsor. Photo by Cele Otnes.

castle brigade arrived quickly but was only onsite for eight minutes before extreme heat forced its withdrawal.[18] Prince Andrew, the only family member present, joined the human chain working frantically to save artwork, armor, furniture, tapestries, and other valuables from the Royal Collection. The Royal Library, located near the State Apartments, also had to be evacuated of its priceless books, manuscripts, and collection of Old Master drawings, including over seven hundred by Leonardo da Vinci alone.[19]

After fifteen hours, 250 firefighters pumping 1.5 million gallons of water brought the blaze under control,[20] although it smoldered in pockets for some six weeks. The impact was severe: "105 rooms, including nine of the finest ... in the State Apartments, or nearly one-fifth of [the c]astle was damaged or destroyed ... [totaling] approximately 9000 square meters [97,000 square feet]."[21] Naturally, the Queen was devastated.

Miraculously, only two items from the Royal Collection were damaged beyond repair. The damage to the structure, however, was initially estimated at £42 million ($70 million)—and like most royal residences at the time, it was uninsured. Two days after the fire, an article in the *New York Times* stated that officials "assumed that the cost of repairs would be borne by tax-payers"[22]—but both the officials and the *Times* were sorely mistaken. The declaration caused an uproar in the tabloid press, elicited scathing comments from Labour members of Parliament, and prompted suggestions that the Queen's tax-exempt status be immediately examined. Clearly, the suggestion that the public bear the cost to renovate the castle during a severe economic downturn did not amuse MPs or British citizens. After all, 1992 was a year during which three out of four of the Queen's children faced failed marriages, and the Royal Family's status as a beacon of morality and stability dimmed considerably. Deferring to the outcry fueled by liberal-leaning newspapers, the Queen succumbed and agreed not only to seek funds elsewhere, but to limit the Civil List and pay income tax (previous monarchs had done so, but her father, George VI, had secured a Royal Exemption).

Ultimately it was agreed that about 70 percent of the funding for the restoration would be derived from two sources: increasing admission fees at Windsor Castle and—more significantly to eager RFBC fans and tourists—opening Buckingham Palace to paid visitors. On November 17, 1997, just under five years after the fire, £5 million under budget and with a spate of exciting architectural and archaeological finds to celebrate, the Queen hosted a dinner for those who had worked on the restoration. When the castle subsequently reopened to the public, they were allowed more access to the interior than was the case before the fire.

Given Windsor's importance to the RFBC, we sought to gain a deeper understanding of the seasonal rhythms of the town. In addition to visiting several times during the touristic high season, we also braved the chill on April 9, 2005. That day, we stood with Margaret Tyler and a sparse crowd (including many foreign reporters) to watch Prince Charles and his new bride, Camilla, speed away in a Rolls-Royce after their wedding at Windsor's Guildhall and a blessing ceremony at St. George's Chapel. Although the British media had covered the festivities nonstop since early morning, the relative quiet that pervaded Windsor contrasted starkly with the huge, ecstatic crowds at Charles's first wedding to Lady Diana Spencer. Nevertheless, those in attendance seemed to be more pro-Charles than con, with some shouting, "God Bless You, Sir!" as the couple sped past.

We also wanted to see what Windsor was like in a decidedly nontouristic time of year—namely, the winter holiday season. Would the royal focus that typically dominated the town during the tourist season compete with the locals' desire to celebrate? In other words, would the shops still be stuffed with royal-themed holiday merchandise and gifts, anticipating demand from tourists and locals for such items? In fact, we discovered that at least during the week before Christmas in 2012, Jesus (and Santa) clearly trumped the Royal Family. One merchant told us that except for members of bands from around the world who participate in London's New Year's Day parade, Windsor tourists are basically nonexistent during the winter months. This comment notwithstanding, reflecting the global status of the RFBC and the increasing levels of discretionary income in their country, we did see a few busloads of mostly Chinese tourists pull up in front of the castle. Of course, one advantage for winter visitors is that they are afforded easy access to royal ceremonials, even those performed in a chilly mist (figure 28).

In short, Windsor's residents clearly co-opt the trappings of monarchy and enfold them into their holiday celebrations. Shoppers could hardly miss seeing the large lit evergreen placed behind the imposing statue of Queen Victoria at the castle gates. The renowned choir of Saint George's School at Windsor Castle offered a performance of Handel's *Messiah* at its name-sake chapel. Even the gift shops within the castle grounds offered few royal-themed holiday souvenirs, except for the velvet Christmas ornaments of monarchs and other iconic figures that it offers all year.

Also eschewing its typical royal-themed offerings, the Theatre Royal Windsor advertised a Christmas pantomime of *Jack and the Beanstalk,* starring the 1975 "Bond girl" Britt Ekland.* Instead of serving tourists, pubs and restaurants hosted locals enjoying holiday parties. One evening, we saw the castle staff queuing up in their evening clothes and boarding buses to Buckingham Palace for the Royal Household's annual holiday party. In short, the winter Windsor is quite different in density and design than its manifestation in the tourist season.

---

* Commercial pantos often feature former models and actresses; in 2014, Mick Jagger's ex-wife Jerry Hall starred in a panto in Richmond, a London suburb, where she has a home.

FIGURE 28. Wintry Changing of the Guard, Windsor. Photo by Cele Otnes.

Windsor is also an important locale because many residences in the Great Park have played important roles within RFBC narratives, with two sites especially exerting an indirect impact on the Royal Family's visibility within consumer culture. Prince Albert's death in 1861 propelled Queen Victoria into a state of "epic mourning."[23] He died in the Blue Room in Windsor Castle at age forty-two, in the same bed where George IV and William IV had breathed their last. The Queen's decision to wear widow's weeds (an all-black ensemble of wool crepe dress, veil, and bonnet) beyond the culturally sanctioned two-year First Mourning period, dressing in black for the rest of her life, led to her nickname the "Widow of Windsor." Thirty-six years later, she was commemorated in the Diamond Jubilee edition of *Baby's A.B.C.* as the rhyme for *Q:* "Q is for Queen/and a widow, poor thing/Whose Baby will/one of these days be a King."[24]

Fashion pundits bemoaned Victoria's extended mourning as detrimental to their industry, especially since court ladies also were mandated to wear black for two years (and following the Queen's lead, her ladies-in-waiting wore black for their entire time in service). Yet the cult of death inspired by the Queen did enhance the bottom lines of other commercial enterprises.

Upper-class women imitated her by accessorizing their fashionably cut mourning attire with elaborately designed jet jewelry and hair ornaments.* Considering Victoria's imperious nature, it is ironic that her mourning practices helped democratize death-related consumption practices. Sonia Bedikian notes that manufacturing processes developed in the Industrial Revolution helped make formal mourning wear more affordable. Middle-class women could then copy aristocratic styles of dress, enhancing their perceived status in society. Lower-class women who found even cheaper goods out of reach could participate in Burial and Friendly Societies, which loaned appropriate clothing to mourners in need.[25]

Victoria's persistent mourning also affected Windsor Castle and its environs. She insisted that her household staff dust Albert's room daily, and lay out his gloves and hat. The queen was fascinated with a fad of the times: postmortem photographs, taken of people in their hour of death. She incorporated these into her travel routines[26]: "A photograph of [Albert's] corpse . . . lying on his deathbed surrounded by an evergreen wreath was hung a foot above the pillow on the unoccupied side of every bed . . . the Queen ever slept [in]. . . . Photographs from all angles of the Prince's room in the castles . . . were taken and hung everywhere. . . . Servants were supplied with photographs so when they dusted objects . . . they could replace them exactly as before."[27]

Victoria's stature allowed her to take the notion of permanently commemorating Albert's life and achievements to conspicuous and civic extremes. She hired craftsmen to create statues, memorials, and a large mausoleum for Albert (and for her as well, when the time came) to be located at Frogmore, her private home on the periphery of Windsor Great Park. It remains one of the few relatively private Royal residences. Although open to the public since 1990, in fact it is accessible only a few days out of the year. Such exclusivity imbues it with greater royal mystique than more frequently visited (and often congested) sites. The likenesses on the couple's tombs date from the time of Albert's death because "it would not do for a young Albert to be paired with an aged Victoria."[28]

A second key residence close to Windsor Great Park rooted in the human, family, and luxury-brand aspects of the RFBC is Fort Belvedere, home of the Prince of Wales, who later acceded the throne as King Edward VIII but

* *Jet* is a term for "brown coal," although it is a rich black color. Hair ornaments featured locks from lovers or from the deceased, and were popular in Victorian times prior to the spread of commercial photography.

whose coronation never occurred. In 1930, the Prince began to renovate the turreted home—described as a "gothic folly designed... for the profligate George IV."[29] The Prince viewed it as a "peaceful enchanted anchorage" where he could entertain his friends and lovers (typically married women). His perception was a far cry from the way his punitive, stern father, George V, described it—as a site for his son's "damn weekends."[30]

The story of Edward VIII and Wallis Simpson, the woman he would eventually marry, is a vivid example of how the RFBC is reinterpreted as cultural values and aspirations change. In the 1930s, as Europe endured a prolonged and dispiriting economic depression, Hitler and Mussolini began to stoke the fires of discontent, resulting in the twentieth century's second massive war. Amid such unrest, Edward VIII's decision to abdicate to marry Mrs. Simpson, a twice-divorced American, was regarded as foolish and immature by his family, most MPs, and even some British subjects (although Edward was extremely popular in his home country and throughout the empire).

Bessiewallis Warfield was born into a prominent Baltimore family that had fallen on hard times. When her genteel widowed mother resorted to running a café from her rented rooms, she offered such elaborate dinners that her guests literally ate the profits.[31] Family insecurity about money was "implanted so deeply in Wallis's psyche that she never entirely shed her worry ... of what might lie around the corner."[32] Her second marriage, to the British-American businessman and former Coldstream guard Henry Simpson, provided her with an entrée into London's high society, and eventually into the royal circle. The couple first met the Prince of Wales when they were last-minute substitutes for an aristocratic weekend house party in 1931. Subsequent encounters spurred Wallis and her husband to spend beyond their means in their attempt to keep up with the fashion and travel demands of the elite.

By 1933, the Simpsons had become part of the Prince's regular weekend entourage at Fort Belvedere. Just one year later, Wallis had supplanted all his other mistresses. After a weekend at Fort Belvedere in 1935, Lady Diana Cooper noted, "Mrs. Simpson was glittering, and dripped in new jewels and clothes."[33] Some of her jewelry would achieve iconic status as their romance unfolded. One in particular, a bracelet by Cartier, featured nine crosses that ran the gamut of precious stones. Each represented an ordeal the couple had borne together, and per royal tradition, each was inscribed in the Prince's (and later, the King's) handwriting. One cross marked an unsuccessful assassination attempt in July 1936; he inscribed it with "God Save the King for Wallis."[34]

The couple's affair had been common knowledge in British aristocratic circles for two years when George V died in January 1936, and the Prince acceded. But in stark contrast to media coverage in the 1970s, when Princess Margaret's marriage began to falter, in the 1930s the Royal Family could still rely on the British press to be discreet. That summer, the King and Wallis sailed on the yacht *Nahlin* on a long Mediterranean holiday. American newspapers ran photos of the couple, but "amazingly, the story was still ignored in the self-censoring and obedient British press."[35] Headlines about the couple only began to appear in Britain one week before the King gave up the throne. Yet once the story made the papers, the media realized that royal stories were too valuable to keep under wraps, and public demand was insatiable. Simply put, the skyrocketing sales resulting from coverage of the affair spelled the end of the Royal Family's privacy.

Objections to Wallis stemmed not so much from the fact that she was an American and a commoner but rather that she was a divorcee with two ex-husbands still living (although even one would have proved problematic). Many MPs believed the marriage could irretrievably damage the monarchy, and the prime minister threatened to resign and dissolve the government if the King insisted on marrying her. Only Winston Churchill was a staunch supporter, calling Edward's devotion to Wallis "one of the great loves of history."[36]

In a speech that Churchill polished, the King abdicated on December 11, 1936, after reigning just ten months and twenty-two days. Manufacturers quickly remade the molds for his coronation souvenirs to feature his brother and his wife, who would become King George VI and Queen Elizabeth on the same day Edward's ceremony had been scheduled. For her role in nearly causing a constitutional crisis and being the most "headlined and interest-compelling person in the world,"[37] *Time* named Wallis its first Woman of the Year in 1936. Reflecting his fondness for Windsor Castle and Fort Belvedere, Edward asked to be styled as the Duke of Windsor. The couple married in Paris in 1937; she wore a gown by the American designer Mainbocher, in a shade that became known as "Wallis blue."

As the European crisis deepened, it became clear that the Duke advocated appeasement of Germany and Italy. In October 1937, Hitler hosted the couple for a ten-day tour of Nazi Germany. He structured it as an official state visit, and Wallis's place card at the state dinner even featured the title

"Her Royal Highness," even though George VI had denied her the title. Much to the shock of both the Royal Family and Parliament, a widely released photograph showed "the Duchess smiling broadly and enjoying the pomp and pageantry as the Führer leans over to kiss her hand."[38]

British intelligence was aware of a Nazi plot to kidnap the couple and install the Duke as Britain's puppet king after Germany won the war. To foil the endeavor, George VI dispatched his brother to serve as governor of the Bahamas. The couple continued to fuel Anglophilia among the American upper crust, socializing in Palm Beach and New York City as often as the King permitted them to travel. Yet for most of their marriage, they lived in a "grace and favour" home located in Paris's Bois de Boulogne that the French government provided for £25 a year. Wallis filled her days with shopping, daily hair appointments at home, devising meticulous rules for her staff, and hosting elaborately planned parties. On the days of these events, sous-chefs would sort the salad leaves to be the same size; the Duchess also insisted that meat and fish portions for her guests be as identical as possible.[39]

The décor of the Windsor Villa, as it was known, reaffirmed the couple's perception that although Edward no longer reigned, his place in the illustrious lineage would not be forgotten. To the Royal Family's dismay, he had managed to take many priceless historic heirlooms into what became essentially a permanent exile from Britain, and he and the Duchess prominently displayed these items. They included Edward VII's red and gold Royal Standard from St. George's Chapel, which bore the arms of the Prince of Wales, the desk from Windsor Castle where the Duke had signed his letter of abdication, and valuable portraits of family members.

Wallis preferred to accumulate rare or one-of-a-kind pieces that only the richest people could afford. Her collection of Louis XVI furniture was so exquisite that the French government requested she leave it to the Palace of Versailles in exchange for the couple's years of virtually rent-free living. She reveled in the jewels the Duke designed for her, and when his interest in doing so flagged, she began to have her pieces reset in contemporary styles. Wallis spent much of her time being fitted for gowns and suits by Balenciaga, Mainbocher, Dior, or other couturiers. Her passion paid off in the form of inclusion on international lists of best-dressed women for forty years.

The Duchess attributed her penchant for fashion to her belief that "I'm nothing to look at, so the only thing I can do is dress better than anyone else."[40] She leveraged her slim figure and chiseled, somewhat severe features as a scaffold for her "pared-down, sleek minimalism."[41] Typically, she chose highly tailored, sometimes austere gowns and suits of the choicest fabrics that would draw admirers' eyes to her signature jewels. She was the living embodiment of her famous mantra, "You can never be too rich or too thin." She also used couture to demonstrate her renowned wit. When Cecil Beaton (a favorite among the Royal Family) photographed Wallis for *Vogue* in 1937, she wore a white organza gown designed in collaboration by Schiaparelli and the surrealist Salvador Dalí. It featured a "giant lobster and matching flame midriff panel."[42]

Fashion was not just Wallis's interest; the Duke also enjoyed making sartorial statements. He was known for his eclectic pattern-mixing and for sporting flamboyant socks, a vibrant golf wardrobe, and a double-breasted lounge suit (one more casually cut than traditional ones). He also favored kilts, especially when playing his bagpipes, and loud variants of checked tweed fabric. Diana Vreeland once observed that the Duke "had style in every buckle on his kilt, every check of his country suits, in the way he put together sports clothes."[43]

Global fascination with the couple was brought to light upon Wallis's death in 1986. When the Duke had died fourteen years earlier, the Royal Family sent Lord Louis Mountbatten, his cousin, to persuade Wallis to return the historically important possessions. She reported that Mountbatten would "sweep through the villa, picking up this and that, and exclaiming 'Ah, this belongs to the Royal Collection.'"[44] Wallis parted with relatively few items, choosing to bequeath most of her estate to the Institut Pasteur in support of medical research.

At this point, the fate of the couple's estate became entwined with that of a wealthy Egyptian Anglophile, whose life would later intersect the Royal Family's in unforeseen ways. After Wallis's death, Mohamed Al-Fayed, a wealthy businessman and co-owner of Harrods, took out a fifty-year lease on the Windsor Villa and bought all of its contents except for the Duchess's jewels. He then spent $2 million on renovations, converting it into a private museum open only to historians, friends, members of the Royal Family, and important guests of the Ritz Hotel in Paris, which he also owned.[45] Apparently, he believed this acquisition would help him acquire his long-sought British citizenship. After his application was denied, he decided to sell the contents of the home.*

---

* He applied a second time a few years later and was denied again.

In all, two significant auctions of the Windsors' possessions took place. The first, in 1987 by Sotheby's Geneva, featured only Wallis's jewelry. The presale estimate was $7 million; in fact, it brought in seven times that figure, set the record for a jewelry auction,[46] and attracted buyers such as Elizabeth Taylor and the Cartier archives. The Cartier crosses-to-bear bracelet we described earlier sold for $450,000 In 2010, in a smaller sale, it would sell again for over $970,000.[47]

In 1997, Al-Fayed commissioned Sotheby's New York to auction the entire contents of the Windsor Villa. With over 40,000 objects in 3,200 lots to be sold over nine days, it was the firm's longest sale in history. Sotheby's relied on over fifty specialists in such areas as Asian art,* coins and medals, militaria, and photographs. During the villa's restoration, the Duke's staff had hidden thousands of family photos from poachers in the mahogany-lidded bathtub; these were also included.

One week before the auction date in September 1997, Al-Fayed's son Dodi was killed with Princess Diana in Paris; ironically, they had visited the Windsor Villa on the day they died. Sotheby's delayed the auction until February 1998. Mirroring the undervaluing for the earlier jewelry sale, the original presale estimate of $7 million garnered three times that amount. It was thought that the Royal Collection bid anonymously on several histori-cally important items. One of the more bizarre bidders was psychic spoon bender Uri Geller, who paid over £1,110 ($1,800) for a "small silver medicine spoon . . . [for] his collection of spoons with a history."[48]

The success of these auctions signaled that at least some people were ready to forgive the Windsors their lifestyle of listless luxury and to release any resentment regarding their relationship with Nazi Germany. Instead, Sotheby's auction catalog painted the Windsors as the "most romantic cou-ple of their age" and dwelled upon the sacrifices they (but especially he) had made to remain together: "The lives of the Duke and Duchess of Windsor have passed into legend. The story of the King who gave up an Empire for love still retains its fascination . . . sixty years after Edward VIII signed away his inheritance to marry Wallis Simpson."[49]

Although their romance no doubt contributed to their appeal, another factor is that although the Duke was a lapsed king, he was still authentic royalty. Yet unlike the Royal Family, the Duke and Duchess were accessible

* The couple owned eleven pugs during their marriage, and had acquired a large collec-tion of ceramic ones from China.

to everyday people—or at least to celebrities and those in European high society. In short, they represented a curious hybrid of titled royalty and celebrity, which afforded them the perfect combination of mystique and accessibility.

The couple's appeal has not been lost on entrepreneurs or commercial entities. Most notably, several portrayals of their love story have appeared on stage and on the small and large screen. These have ranged from a musical titled *Always* (which closed in London after a short run) to the more recent play *The Last of the Duchess.* This rendition was unusual because it focused on attempts to protect Wallis from journalists at the end of her life. In so doing, it provided commentary both about the paparazzi's intrusiveness and exploitation of the aged.[50] Although it was critically acclaimed, most interpretations—including the feature film *W.E.,* which Madonna directed in 2011, have been panned.

Reflecting the global aspect of the RFBC, a burgeoning aspirational middle class means that consumers around the world are increasingly infatuated with haute couture, designer purses, and luxury labels. Perhaps now more than ever, people empathize with Wallis and Edward's appreciation of the finer things in life and their desire to indulge their eccentric and (for some) exquisite tastes. To that end, the marketplace still tries to leverage the Windsors' appeal. As we noted in chapter 6, our visit to London's fashionable Jermyn Street in 2013 brought us face-to-face with a nattily dressed Duke of Windsor on a poster in a store window. That same year, Sotheby's announced more auctions of the Windsors' former property, including their 1941 custom-built Cadillac limousine, nicknamed "the Duchess." Another lot of Wallis's jewels, some making their third appearance at auction, came up for sale in 2013.

In addition to the narrative-laden homes in Windsor's Great Park, the town itself offers attractions to royal-watchers. It is bordered by the River Thames and the prestigious, all-male Eton College—itself a bona fide royal site, as the studious Henry VI founded it in 1440.* Alumni, or "Old Etonians," include Prince William, Prince Harry, a host of minor English royalty, several future kings of foreign countries, and former prime ministers. In Britain, *public school* actually refers to a fee-paying, independent institution that serves to educate the upper classes, including nobility and

---

* The term *college* may confuse American readers; Eton offers the equivalent of grades 9–12 in the U.S. system.

royalty. A public school education is a crucial marker of social capital and a predictor of future success comparable to admission into "Oxbridge" (Oxford or Cambridge). Since the nineteenth century, with increases in the standard of living, public schools have become more accessible to the middle classes. Many offer partial and full scholarships to deserving applicants, but most students pay full tuition. At Eton, tuition and fees for the 2014–15 school year came to over £36,000 ($60,000).

Bordered by the Thames and Eton, Windsor is able to battle London's ever-encroaching suburban sprawl and retain its bucolic setting. But even its remoteness from the site of Prince George's birth in London on July 22, 2013, did not dampen enthusiasm for the event in Windsor. The last week of July saw tourists queuing up for tours of the castle and boat rides on the Thames. River levels permitting, July is the typical month for "Swan Upping," an annual five-day swan census and ceremony on the Thames that dates from the twelfth century. Orchestrated by the Queen's swan marker David Barber and the Queen's swan warden (currently Oxford ornithology professor Christopher Perrins), the census assesses the health and population of swans in the river.[51]

The Crown co-owns the birds along with two London livery companies, the Worshipful Company of Vintners and the Worshipful Company of Dyers.* The Queen has attended the highly scripted and elaborate ritual only once. Skiffs are festooned with swan-bedecked flags and EIIR pennants, scarlet-uniformed swan counters shout "All Up!" when they spot birds, and the crew stands at attention and toasts the Queen as they glide past Windsor Castle. Although sometimes "lampooned as an absurdity of the modern monarchy," the census has helped diagnose and address environmental causes for declines in the swan population.[52]

Like "Farmer" George III and Victoria, the Queen loves Windsor's pastoral setting, primarily because she can immerse herself in two of her passions—dogs and horses. (In contrast, at Balmoral, she and her family enjoy grouse hunting, deer stalking, shooting, and fishing). Dog ownership is a passion the Royal Family shares with many of its subjects, with Victoria owning the widest variety of dog breeds among the monarchs. She owned one of the first Pekingese in Britain, as well as collies, Pomeranians, and Borzois, a gift from the Tsar.

---

* The monarchy claims only "unmarked mute" swans, as quieter birds are perceived as more regal.

Diana dubbed the Queen's trademark squadron of low-lying corgis and dorgis a "moving carpet." (Dorgis, a breed the Queen claims to have originated, apparently stem from a romantic encounter between a corgi owned by the Queen and a dachshund owned by Princess Margaret). She received her first Pembroke Welsh corgi, which she named Susan, for her eighteenth birthday. Since then, she has owned over thirty of the breed; most are descended from her first. On her various estates, she owns Labradors, gundogs, and cocker spaniels. She names them all herself, recently endowing a litter of Labs with monikers from the Harry Potter series.[53]

Becoming a favored royal dog vividly demonstrates how monarchic association with a brand (in this case, a breed) can affect popularity. Prior to 1933, when George VI acquired his first corgi, it typically was found on farms as a herding dog. Almost immediately after the breed became part of the Royal Family, its popularity soared in Britain and America. In the United States, it was the twenty-second most popular breed in 2014, above the Boston terrier and the Chihuahua.[54] In the twenty-first century, the corgi's popularity began declining in Britain, and the breed was placed on a watch list as potentially endangered. But during 2012—the Queen's Diamond Jubilee year—there was a notable uptick in the registration of Pembroke corgi puppies, attributable to people's deference to the Queen.

More significantly, the corgi has morphed from more than just a dog breed into an element of consumer-culture kitsch that symbolizes the British monarchy, through quirky web-based humor across the globe. In 2012, *Time.com* ranked corgis as the eighth most popular Internet meme to appear in blogs, on YouTube, and on Tumblr. Along with diamonds and a crowned silhouette, the artists at Google selected the corgi as an iconic item in their "Google Doodle"* to honor the Queen's Diamond Jubilee.[55] One journalist observed that corgis now compete with cats as the most anthropomorphized and satirized animal on the Internet. Searches for "Pop Corgture"[56] yielded websites laden with dogs dressed in costumes, as superheroes, and in graphic fan-fiction stories. These uses reveal that their associations have spread beyond just that of royalty. Blogs like *corgiaddict.com* and *countrycorgis.blogspot.com* also exist. At the end of December 2014, there were over 184 Facebook groups and 23 Facebook fan pages devoted to corgis or corgi-related topics.

* Temporary renditions of the Google logo on its homepage; they typically honor achievements or people, or mark holidays and cultural events.

Although the Queen's dogs feature at all her homes, at Windsor she indulges in what is universally understood to be her passion, her love of horses. She began riding lessons as a very young girl and received her first Shetland pony at age four. Her childhood bedtime ritual involved unsaddling all of her thirty miniature horses, and she enjoyed leading her nurse Marion Crawford ("Crawfie") by a harness around the garden.[57] She spent many happy hours riding with her father in Windsor Great Park; when war duties detained him, Elizabeth would ride with her groom.

This lifelong passion has served the Queen both therapeutically and ceremonially. Beautiful, strong, well-bred, and impeccably trained horses have always been focal to Royal fanfare; they have pulled ornate, historic carriages during Royal weddings, funerals, and coronation processions, and infused Royal parades with power and elegance. Indeed, for forty years, the Queen rode her own mount in the annual Trooping the Colour parade, and other Royal Family members often ride in public parades as well.

The Queen is an equestrian entrepreneur and has raised and trained horses since the Aga Khan gave her the filly Astrakhan as a wedding gift in 1947.[58] Her horses have won four of the five classic flat-course races in Britain; only the top prize at the Epsom Derby eludes her. She often visits her breeding and foaling locations, with one of them, Polhampton Lodge Stud Farm, less than an hour's drive from Windsor. She often incorporates visits to horse farms into the itineraries of her royal tours, and has sent mares to Kentucky for breeding.

One equestrian-related decision leading to a cascade of positive outcomes was the Queen's association with the American trainer Monty Roberts, who had gained a following in the American West for developing gentler techniques for breaking horses. After inviting Roberts to give a demonstration at Windsor Castle's indoor riding school, the Queen saw merit in his methods and arranged for him to conduct workshops around Britain. She also encouraged him to write his autobiography. It subsequently sold two million copies and was the basis for the 1998 film *The Horse Whisperer,* starring Robert Redford and Kristin Scott Thomas.

Each May, the castle grounds are the site of the famous Royal Windsor Horse Show, which began in 1943 as a fundraiser for the war effort. The five-day event features competitions and displays that highlight carriage driving, jumping, and breed showing from around the world. It also spotlights one of Prince Philip's favorite activities. In 1971, after retiring from playing polo, he helped standardize the rules for the sport of combined driving. This rubric includes any event that features a horse, a driver of whatever vehicle is being pulled, and a groom or a navigator. Until recently Prince Philip drove a "four in hand," where he controlled four horses with one hand. As recently as May 2014, at age ninety-three, he was seen driving a carriage in Windsor Park.

The Queen chose Windsor as the site to kick off her Diamond Jubilee celebration in May 2012, a month before the London festivities. Demonstrating yet again the global appeal of the RFBC, the Diamond Jubilee Pageant featured over 550 horses and their handlers from around the world, including Canadian Mounties, Russian Cossacks, and real American "cowboys and Indians." In a nod to popular culture that attendees surely recognized, the celebrities who entertained included Dame Helen Mirren, who had won both an Oscar and a BAFTA for *The Queen* in 2005. Reinforcing her daughter's reputation as a respected equestrian,* the Queen appointed Princess Anne Master of Ceremonies.

As much as the Queen enjoys riding and engaging in the business aspect of horses, she is an equally keen spectator at "an indelible date in her calendar,"[59] the Royal Ascot races held every June. The racecourse is located about seven miles from the castle, and the four-day event attracts approximately 300,000 visitors. Ascot owes its existence to royalty; Queen Anne first saw a stretch of flatland she thought would be excellent for racing in 1711, and the first official races began that year. By 1813, the site was protected by a parliamentary decree that made Ascot Heath a racecourse location in perpetuity. A century later, it received further protection when Parliament established the Ascot Authority, creating an executive board to guide its future. In 2006, the racecourse became part of the Crown Estate holdings. As overseer of the property, the Queen now presents the trophies for several key races.

Given its royal roots, it is not surprising that luxury consumption pervades at Royal Ascot. In 2012, one hundred bars and food outlets at the racecourse sold over 50,000 glasses of champagne, 173,000 pints of beer, 50,000 pistachio and raspberry macaroons, 35,000 locally grown spears of asparagus, and 2,500 fresh lobsters.[60] As is often the case when elite society is involved, the race serves as the nucleus for a host of luxury-laden activities. The Queen sets the tone by hosting an elaborate lunch at the castle for her racing set prior to the first races. The pageantry of the Royal Procession at Ascot, which follows

---

* Princess Anne and her daughter Zara participated on the British Olympic equestrian team—Anne in the 1976 games and Zara in 2012. That year, Great Britain's team won a silver medal.

the lunch, has been a fixture of the event since George IV originated it in the 1820s. At Ascot Gate, members of the Royal Family take their traditional positions in "landaus, each drawn by a team of four horses ridden by two scarlet-coated postillions [or "post-boys"], with footmen in red livery and black hats seated at the back," riding into the racecourse grounds.[61]

For many who attend, Royal Ascot's appeal rests as much in people-watching as in watching the races themselves. Ascot's fashions often represent a bizarre amalgam of aristocratic norms, fashion trends, British eccentricity, and humor. Since its early days, ladies in the Royal Enclosure have typically worn elegant dresses with unique (sometimes outlandish) hats, with men attired in safer options (e.g., morning coats and top hats). Cecil Beaton, the same photographer who shot Wallis Simpson for *Vogue,* designed the black-and-white costume palette for the Royal Ascot scene in the 1956 stage production of *My Fair Lady.* Contrary to what that scene implied, Royal Ascot does not restrict its attendees' color choices; in fact, it only did so in 1910. That year, requisite all-black attire reflected a nation in mourning for Edward VII.[62] In an interesting example of how popular portrayals can cycle back to shape consumption choices, after the play's success in 1958, women in the Royal Enclosure collaborated to limit their ensembles to black and white the next year; "to complete the illusion, *My Fair Lady* music was piped across course and paddock."[63]

In these liberal sartorial times, when high-fashion displays include minimal hemlines, thigh-high slits, and cleavage, Ascot's organizers have felt compelled to codify norms pertaining to attendees' attire. In 2012, organizers created a brochure and video explaining the more exacting requirements for the various seating areas. Violators quickly found that one of Ascot's twenty "dress-code assistants" would offer items to help them achieve compliance—but those receiving assistance also received a bill to cover rental costs for the apparel.[64]

The dress code is more relaxed within the less tony Grandstand area, although women are still restricted in terms of how much skin they may show (e.g., no strapless dresses, no bare midriffs; skirts must be a modest length). Interestingly, given their popularity among aristocrats and royalty at events such as high-society weddings, fascinators are now banned from the Royal Enclosure. Ladies must wear hats featuring circumferences of four inches or more. But as longtime Ascot-watchers and attendees know, hats are not restricted in terms of verticality, overall dimensions, or subject matter. As a result, these items often convey their owners' personalities, proclivi-

FIGURE 29. Royal Ascot hat. Courtesy Thomson Reuters.

ties, or loyalties (figure 29). In 2012, many hats were British-themed, reflecting the "Summer of London" events of the Jubilee and the Olympics. The dress code is not without its critics. Sarah Ditum, writing for the left-leaning *Guardian,* believes that such specifications reflect the aristocratic ideal of "keeping the wrong people out, not coaching them how to fit in. . . . [T]he rich . . . prefer not to be confronted with the sight of other people trying to articulate the signs of privilege, or worse [worry] . . . that their own commonness might start to show."[65]

For the Queen, watching the races from the Royal Box allows her to do more than observe the fruits of her equine investments. Photos at Ascot often capture her as much more relaxed than her typical regal public demeanor reflects. Behind firmly fixed binoculars, she follows the races with keen attention, provides encyclopedic commentary about the competitors, and urges on her chosen champions with vigor. Her ecstatic clapping on Ladies' Day in 2013 alerted spectators that her horse Estimate, favored at 7–2 odds, had won the coveted Gold Cup. It was the first time in Ascot's 207-year history that a monarch's horse had won. Since the Queen does not gamble, she did not reap any of the £1.5 million payout by British bookmaker William Hill. As the owner, however, she did earn over £155,000 ($250,000) in prize money. Estimate's performance created a stir with respect to protocol, as the Queen typically presents the Gold Cup to the winner. This time, Prince Andrew did the honors, bestowing the trophy on his mother.

Reflecting yet another interesting intersection of royalty and consumer culture, the Queen's first racing manager, Henry Porchester ("Porchie"), became the 7th Earl of Carnarvon upon his father's death in 1987. The family home, Highclere Castle, is where *Downton Abbey* is filmed. In the 1970s, the Queen named one of her race horses after the locale, and in 1974, Highclere gave the Queen the first victory ever for a British monarch in France's prestigious Prix de Diane race.

Besides accommodating the flurry of activities during June, Windsor Castle is also used for other types of entertainment, ranging from intimate weekend parties to larger affairs of state. In the first case, the Queen often invites a small group (typically eight to ten people) to enjoy a "dine-and-sleep" at the castle. Her parents revived this Victorian tradition after World War II. Guests literally receive royal treatment; each is assigned a valet or lady's maid who unpacks suitcases, lays out toiletries, prepares baths to desired temperatures, and "before departure time repack[s] everything with tissue paper."[66] Besides enjoying drinks and a meal in the State Dining Room, the highlight of the visit for many is the visit to the Royal Library. Upon arrival, each guest finds a particular display of items from the Royal Archives, created to reflect his or her interests. For instance, the director of the Victoria & Albert Museum was shown a letter to Queen Victoria from the 8th Duke of Devonshire, in which he suggested the name for the institution.[67]

With a Print Room containing over 30,000 drawings and watercolors from the Royal Collection, the Royal Library contains unsurpassed portfolios of drawings by artists like Michelangelo, Leonardo da Vinci, and Raphael. Among its more unusual items are natural history drawings that depict native flora and fauna. *The Florilegeum of Alexander Marshall* contains 159 folios of such drawings and is the only surviving "flower book" by an English botanical artist from the seventeenth century, the peak period for the art form.[68] The Royal Library also contains thousands of maps and coins.*

The Queen also relies on the castle's elegant atmosphere for diplomatic occasions. At her May 2012 Diamond Jubilee lunch, sovereigns from twenty-six countries joined twelve members of the Royal Family for a meal of all-British cuisine that included Windsor lamb, Kent strawberries, and English asparagus. Yet the Queen's guest list stirred up some controversy, because two invitees (King Hamad of Bahrain and King Mswati III of Swaziland) had been accused of human rights violations. While the monarchs ate and socialized, over one thousand protestors gathered at Buckingham Palace.

Since the days of religious pilgrimages, Windsor and its environs have attributed much of its economic health to its role as a royal-imbued town—one whose star has risen when the monarch favored the castle, as has been the case through the Queen's reign. As such, the town's royal patina extends beyond the castle's abundant display of rare and beautiful goods, its carefully landscaped grounds, and the whispers of history emanating from the homes, statues, and edifices within the Great Park. Windsor also allows visitors to see a residence integral to the life of the current Royal Family and to observe events like the Garter Ceremony, the Royal Windsor Horse Show, and Royal Ascot. As a result, and because Windsor helps offset the typically more congested royal sites in London, it is likely to remain important in the constellation of royal consumption, and to the RFBC, even as the central figures of the monarchy change.

---

* Upon approval of an application, the Royal Library allows scholars and authors access to the facility.

—————

NINE

William and Catherine

REMAKING THE MONARCHY

Like so many others in Britain and around the world, Margaret had relished the thought of a royal wedding for a long time, an anticipation that made Prince William's marriage to Catherine Middleton all the more appreciated when it did eventually come to pass in 2011 after their ten-year courtship. The spatial alterations that took place in Margaret's living room to accommodate this happy event reflect the significance she accords it. Now her breakfast table, the focal point of the room, is decorated exclusively with an assortment of William and Catherine memorabilia, ranging from McVitie biscuit tins to royal mugs and wedding dolls. As usual, Margaret pays little attention to elitist cultural distinctions between the objects in her collection, playfully juxtaposing Royal Collection Trust edition plates alongside two William and Catherine garden gnomes (voted one of the most ridiculous royal wedding memorabilia items by one website).[1]

Tellingly, however, Margaret also has dispersed this new memorabilia around the room and woven it into other displays, as if symbolically reinforcing the new lease on life that this popular union has provided the monarchy as a whole. Confirming this notion, William and Catherine's smiling faces beam down from dangling wedding bunting that bedecks Margaret's ceiling. Beside the breakfast table, an enormous photo of Diana that had once dominated the room is now joined by life-sized cardboard cut-outs of William and Catherine as they looked on the day they announced their engagement, as well as a larger-than-life mannequin of Catherine, dressed in a replica of the now-famous royal blue Issa wrap dress she wore that day. On the cluttered breakfast table in front of the photo, a miniature Catherine bridal doll, watched over by Diana, rises up to take her turn in the limelight, reminding us that another English Rose is blossoming (figure 30). At the

FIGURE 30. Margaret's William and Catherine table. Photo by Pauline Maclaran.

time we visited in June 2012, William and Catherine were the most important members of Margaret's adopted (royal) family, and she was already
anticipating the extra space needed for the royal baby memorabilia that
would surely follow.

Of course, excitement over royal weddings is nothing new; people have
long enjoyed their accompanying celebrations and festivities. To fully understand the cultural frenzy over the 2011 royal wedding, we need to delve into
the historical aspects of these rituals. When Henry VIII married his first
wife, Catherine of Aragon, the wedding celebrations lasted two weeks and
included daily jousting competitions, banquets, pageants, and masked balls.
It is really only within the last hundred years that the wedding itself, rather
than the processions or celebrations attached to it, became such a central
public spectacle. Prior to that time, the actual ceremonies were private
affairs, accommodating small retinues of spectators. No doubt this was just
as well in the case of the flirtatious and philandering Prince of Wales (later
to become George IV), who was forced into an arranged marriage in 1795 to
Caroline of Brunswick. Finding her repellent, the prince, who was noticea-
bly drunk and sulking during the wedding ceremony, spent his wedding
night lying in a drunken stupor on the bedroom floor.

Even Victoria's marriage on February 10, 1840, the first to attract a global
media audience, was conducted in a private ceremony in the Chapel Royal of

St. James's Palace. This event, however, marked an important moment in the evolution of royal weddings into national celebrations. In the lead-up to Victoria's wedding, the newly emergent print media, especially national newspapers and magazines in both Britain and the United States, fueled a frenzy of interest not all that dissimilar to the public's preoccupation with William and Catherine's marriage 171 years later. On Victoria's wedding day, crowds flocked into St. James's Park in the early hours, lining the streets from Buckingham Palace to the Chapel Royal to catch a glimpse of their monarch with her handsome consort in his dashing red field marshal outfit. The crowds cheered continuously as the bridal procession made its way through the streets towards St. James's Park. It was an arranged marriage, insofar as Albert's uncle King Leopold (of Belgium) had helped promote it.* Nevertheless, the public regarded Victoria and Albert's union as romantic, and the Queen's love for her husband-to-be was widely discussed and sanctioned.

Victoria's wedding set the precedent for many traditions of the lavish or "white" wedding, such as wearing a white dress and veil and carrying a bouquet. Until that time, it had been more usual for royal brides to marry in color. Instead, Victoria wore a magnificent white silk satin dress and flowing veil, both trimmed with Honiton lace, one of the most famous and valuable varieties available in England. Rather than signifying purity as is often assumed, Victoria's choice of white had more to do with her strategic decision to support the traditional handmade lace industry in Britain and Ireland, which was severely threatened by the Industrial Revolution and the invention of machine-made laces. The white dress displayed the Honiton lace to its fullest advantage, and in wearing it, Victoria ensured that sales would skyrocket, with lace placemats and handkerchiefs becoming much-desired items populating the trousseaux of Victorian brides.

Victoria's veil was held in place by a fetching garland of orange blossoms (symbolizing purity) interlaced with sprigs of myrtle (symbolizing love and domestic happiness). Henceforth, it became a royal tradition to tuck a piece of myrtle in the bridal bouquet, a tradition Catherine Middleton also followed. Myths still circulate about this tradition—such as the one claiming that Catherine's sprig stems from the original myrtle in Victoria's bouquet. Author and gardener Charlotte Germane dispels this myth, however, explain-

* In the same way, Lord Mountbatten played matchmaker for his nephew Philip and the then-Princess Elizabeth, prior to their marriage in 1947.

ing that the myrtle bush in the gardens of Osborne House originated from a posy given to Victoria by Prince Albert's grandmother. Regardless of its origins, there is no doubt that Victoria gave her daughter, also named Victoria, a cutting from this myrtle for her marriage bouquet in 1858, spurring the ongoing tradition that both Queen Elizabeth II and Princess Diana also followed.

Victoria instigated another well-known tradition at her daughter's wedding: waving to the crowds from the balcony at Buckingham Palace. Apparently, the queen felt sorry for the assembled crowd and ordered her family to go out onto the balcony to smile and wave as a reward for her people's loyal and patient wait.

Despite the pomp and pageantry surrounding Victoria's wedding, it was only with the marriage of her great-grandson Prince Albert (later George VI) to Lady Elizabeth Bowes-Lyon (later the Queen Mother) on April 26, 1923, that the whole ceremony became a public affair. The first royal wedding to be filmed (and then shown on newsreels in movie theaters), the couple was married in Westminster Abbey instead of the Chapel Royal, in a deliberate attempt to lift public spirits after the ravages of World War I. Like Victoria, the bride supported local industry; this time, her train was made of machine-made lace, rather than the handmade lace Victoria had sponsored, reflecting changed times and attitudes toward industrialization. Making her own unique contribution to royal bridal tradition, Elizabeth Bowes-Lyon unexpectedly left her bouquet of white heather and white roses at the tomb of the Unknown Warrior on her way into Westminster Abbey in memory of her brother Fergus, who had been killed in World War I. Subsequent royal brides have all had their bouquets laid on the tomb the day after their weddings, once the official photographs have been completed.

Since Victorian and Edwardian times, royal weddings have become increasingly spectacular as media innovations incrementally enabled a more sophisticated reach in real time to audiences around the world. Elizabeth's marriage to Lieutenant Philip Mountbatten (whose new father-in-law, George VI, styled the groom as Duke of Edinburgh after the wedding)* on November 20, 1947, was the first to simultaneously reach a mass audience. Broadcast by BBC Radio, it reached 200 million people around the world. Once again, a royal wedding served as a happy event to lift the nation's spirits, this time after the destruction and deprivation caused by World War II. In fact, one of

* He became Prince Philip of the United Kingdom in 1957.

Princess Elizabeth's most treasured wedding gifts was enough ration coupons to help her secure a proper trousseau, as many goods were still rationed into the early 1950s.

By 1960, when the wedding of the Queen's sister, Princess Margaret, to Antony Armstrong-Jones (created Earl of Snowdon) took place, television had become the norm in households across Britain and the United States. The first royal wedding to be televised, the couple took their vows before an audience of some 20 million viewers. Margaret Tyler remembers the excitement when a bank holiday in honor of the celebration allowed everyone to stay home and watch the wedding.

By contrast, some thirteen years later, in 1973, the fast pace of technological development allowed Princess Anne's marriage to Captain Mark Phillips to be watched by 500 million people around the world. And in 1981, by the time the "wedding of the twentieth century" (as it is deemed by many culture-watchers) took place, Charles and Diana's ceremony reached an audience of 750 million. Egged on by the adoring crowds that had come to cheer them as they appeared on the balcony of Buckingham Palace, they introduced the balcony kiss, albeit a rather tentative one on Charles's part. In 1986, Prince Andrew and Sarah Ferguson followed suit with a more enthusiastic smooch—and with two royal weddings in a row following the practice, a new tradition was established. As they took their turn on the balcony, William and Catherine brought their own touch to this new ritual by responding to the crowd with a lingering second kiss.

The romance surrounding William and Catherine is part of their huge appeal. Most people took it for granted that they married for love, given that Catherine's social status as a commoner clearly flew in the face of the typical monarchic strategy of securing spouses from within royal circles, or at least within aristocratic ones, to protect the lineage of future heirs to the throne. Furthermore, many interpreted Charles's clear break with tradition—with his second bride, Camilla Parker Bowles—as at attempt to right a wrong from early adulthood. He had first fallen in love with Camilla in his early twenties, but pressure from his family and from court circles led him to succumb to the expectation that he would select a bride with a more lustrous pedigree.

Thus, until recently, love matches within the RFBC clearly were the exception rather than the rule. The Act of Settlement dictates that neither monarchs nor their heirs are permitted to marry Roman Catholics because, since Henry VIII's break with Rome in 1534, the monarch has served as head of the Church of England.* The marriage of Charles and Camilla in 2005 set a major precedent in allowing an heir apparent to the monarchy to marry a divorcee. Half a century before, Princess Margaret, then third in line to the throne, essentially was forced to forgo the love of her life, Group Captain Peter Townsend, in 1955. The former equerry to George VI was divorced with two sons. In following protocol, the Royal Family experienced angst over the situation, with many noting that George VI treated Townsend like the son he never had.

Prior to the House of Windsor's accession, marriages of monarchs or heirs apparent (heirs presumptive have had slightly more freedom of choice) usually were arranged for political reasons.† Apart from Prince Charles and Queen Elizabeth II, only two monarchs, Edward IV and Henry VIII, and one heir apparent, Edward the Black Prince, have followed their hearts rather than political expediency when marrying.[2] In addition, when he married Lady Elizabeth Bowes-Lyon, Edward VIII's brother the Duke of York (later George VI) did not anticipate that he would accede.

Furthermore, royal weddings can have far-reaching effects on the nation and beyond, effects that may be unanticipated at the time. For example, the marriage of King James IV of Scotland in 1503 to Margaret Tudor, daughter of Henry VII, eventually led to the creation of the United Kingdom. As we discuss in chapter 8, it was widely believed Edward VIII's insistence on marrying the twice-divorced Wallis Simpson would have caused a constitutional crisis. As nominal head of the Church of England, Edward would have violated the Church's prohibition against marrying divorced people whose ex-spouses were alive. Given the long-standing political pressures attached to royal marriages, it becomes easier to understand why Prince Charles felt it was his duty to find a suitable bride and why he believed that marriage to Diana should not prevent or dissuade him from having a mistress.

Throughout history, kings and heirs apparently have seen romantic liaisons outside of marriage as the perfect way to balance their desires with those of the state. Such royal liaisons are now incorporated into touristic narratives, especially in the Salacious Gossip Tours and exhibit of portraits

---

* The 1701 Act of Settlement prohibiting English monarchs from marrying Catholics is being repealed, but this reform has yet to be approved by all sixteen Commonwealth Realms.

† An heir apparent is one whose succession appears certain; an heir presumptive is one whose right to the throne may be superseded by the birth of someone more closely related to the monarch.

of Charles II's mistresses at Hampton Court in 2012. Despite the controversy surrounding the marriage of Prince Charles to Camilla Parker Bowles in 2005, marriage to a former mistress still represents an important milestone in the history of royal weddings. The fact that Charles retains his claim to the throne despite marrying a divorcee marks a major reform in the monarchy, one that reflects the realities of contemporary British family life.

Bearing in mind this historical background on royal weddings, it becomes apparent how the marriage of William and Catherine reinforces certain traditional rituals while introducing modern elements. One key difference is the now-accepted lack of political pressure in the choice of a future royal consort. No longer is it a prerequisite that a royal bride or groom forge or shore up international alliances or top up the royal coffers with personal wealth. However, political motivations have given way to commercial and media-driven imperatives. In her role as the future queen of the United Kingdom, Catherine will still be expected to serve as a diplomatic asset, embracing the ambassadorial roles she and William will occupy, which promote Brand Britain on the international stage.

In this respect, the Royal Family has learned from past mistakes and, in particular, from Princess Diana's naïveté when thrown into a media morass that swiftly engulfed her. Importantly, palace officials provided Catherine with plenty of training on handling the media. In addition, there are crucial differences between the two women—differences which ensure that Catherine will be better able to cope with her future role. When Catherine married William, she was ten years older than Diana and had already had nine years as his romantic partner to prepare for the media attention that would follow. In addition, she and William had cohabited and established a solid foundation for their relationship (their temporary breakup in 2007 notwithstanding). By contrast, Diana had met Charles a mere thirteen times before they were married.[3] This lack of quality time, together with her youth and the almost thirteen-year age difference, left her ill-prepared to cope with the many challenges of her new, intimate relationship with the Prince, or the numerous pressures from royal duties that quickly beset her.

Another key difference is that Catherine is not from an aristocratic family. Moreover, Catherine's ancestry includes English working-class stock on her mother's side. Whereas William's maternal great-great-great-great-grandmother was Queen Victoria (born 1819), Catherine's was Jane Harrison (born 1795), the wife of a miner who toiled in brutal conditions at the coalface in Durham, Northern England. Even Catherine's maternal grandmother, Dorothy Harrison (1935–2006), started her married life in a council flat, although she left it well behind her as she pursued a more aspirant middle-class lifestyle (her family had nicknamed her "Lady Dorothy").

Though Dorothy encouraged her husband, Ron Goldsmith (1931–2003), to set up a construction company, the couple never completely transcended their working-class roots. It was Dorothy's daughter and Catherine's mother, Carole (born 1955), who would achieve this feat in a major way, defying current statistics showing that England's level of social mobility is one of the lowest in the developed world.[4] While Carole was employed as a British Airways air hostess, she met her future husband, Michael Middleton, who worked for the airline as a flight dispatcher. Unlike Carole's, his lineage was solidly middle class and included several generations of solicitors; it also contained aristocratic connections. Catherine's paternal great-grandmother, Olive Lupton (born 1881), who married Noel Middleton, was a society beauty educated at Roedean School, one of the top British independent girls' schools. A descendant of Sir Thomas Fairfax (1612–1671), a leading parliamentarian general in the English Civil War, she was related by marriage to Beatrix Potter. Allegedly, the Fairfax connection makes Catherine and William distant cousins (twelfth, fourteenth, fifteenth, or seventeenth, depending on the source consulted).

Together, Catherine's parents carved out a typically British upper-middle-class lifestyle for themselves and their children, Catherine, Philippa ("Pippa"), and James, born in 1982, 1983, and 1987, respectively. Carole was inspired to create her own business when the children were young, and she had difficulty finding appropriate treats to include in their birthday party bags. Showing an entrepreneurial flair that would prove to be the making of her family, Carole began creating bags to sell to other mothers. She founded a mail-order party company in 1987, beginning operations from her garden shed. Estimated to be worth more than £30 million ($75 million), both Middleton parents now run the highly successful Party Pieces online, offering a huge range of innovative party products, including themed tableware, decorations, party bags, games, and other activities. Catherine often helped her parents with the business, and her sister works for the company full-time. In many ways, as the RFBC becomes more adept at executing the marketing tactics recommended by St. James's Palace, Catherine's commercial background may benefit "the Firm" more than any aristocratic lineage could have.

Described in the media as "a welcome breath of non-aristocratic fresh air for the royal family,"[5] the Middletons have helped considerably in modernizing the image of the monarchy, lending it a more authentic resonance with the lives of ordinary people. As such, they fuel a powerful new brand narrative, that of British upward social mobility—into which the RFBC, and in turn, Brand Britain, can tap. The Middletons reaffirm the mythic notion of the self-made man—or, in this case, self-made women—if one counts both Carole and Catherine Middleton. This meme pervades current British culture and reinforces a belief that meritocracy can coexist with aristocracy and blend with an even newer source of agency—namely, powerful matriarchy. Of course, members of the Royal Family themselves have demonstrated this concept on a fairly consistent basis since Victoria took the throne.

But the Middletons contribute more to the RFBC than merely a blurring of class distinctions; they have also glamorized a monarchy bereft of female sexual allure since Diana's death. The Middleton family, especially the women (and even more selectively, as the royal wedding demonstrated, Pippa Middleton's bottom), are all highly photogenic, supplying an endless stream of decorative material for the tabloid press and gossip magazines. Such glamour ensures that not only Catherine but the rest of her family as well have become fixtures who slot easily into contemporary celebrity culture.

The Middletons' charms—and what some regard as Carole Middleton's highly ambitious infiltration into the Royal Family—have not proved pleasing to everyone, however. Indeed, rhetoric that seemed to border on the vicious was circulated that Carole Middleton had insisted Catherine attend St. Andrew's University in Scotland specifically to "land" Prince William. Even within the Royal Family, the snobbery inherent in true aristocratic practices means that the Queen may never invite the Middletons to celebrate Christmas at Sandringham.* Even if that unlikely event occurs, they might expect to spend most of their time having to curtsy to all the other Royal Family members, including their own daughter. Even the Queen's children exhibit such snobbery; Princess Anne reportedly threw a fit over the possibility that she might have to curtsy to both Camilla and Catherine even though she, after all, is the only one of the three women born into royalty. To avoid this situation, the Queen drew up the Order of Precedence in 2005 at the time of Charles and Camilla's marriage; it dictates that the blood princesses (Anne, Eugenie, and Beatrice) must be curtsied to by newer arrivals such as Camilla and Catherine.

* The Queen is the private owner of Sandringham Estate. Located in Norfolk, it opened to the public in 1977 and includes her country retreat, a restaurant, a royal museum, shops, and a six-hundred-acre park.

Furthermore, the Middletons' livelihood is based in trade, a concept that does not sit comfortably with the English upper classes. Such a livelihood flies in the face of the ideal of old money passing down through generations and the high social, cultural, and economic capital that such transfers imply. This snobbery remains entrenched in the British class system, even as some members of the gentry sit shivering in stately homes they can no longer afford to heat. Indeed, elitism remains rife in England, where over one-third of MPs—including nearly 50 percent of the ruling coalition in 2013— were educated in public schools like Eton and then attended private, fee-paying universities.

As noted above, traditional British high-society circles are more likely to portray Carole Middleton as a social climber who used her daughter to reach the pinnacle of the social ladder, rather than hailing her as an outstanding example of entrepreneurship, a woman who multitasked between raising her three children and building a business empire. It is even rumored that certain old-moneyed folk whisper, "Doors to manual," when she enters the room, mocking her previous role as an air hostess. Nor is Catherine immune from this kind of mockery; allegedly, she and her sister were once nicknamed the "Wisteria Sisters," because they were "highly decorative, terribly fragrant and with a ferocious ability to climb."[6]

Most significantly, however, as successful self-made entrepreneurs, Catherine's parents could afford to send their children to independent schools, ensuring their entry into high society and the type of social circles where Catherine would eventually meet her prince. She attended Marlborough College in Wiltshire, a well-known boarding school with annual fees of around $50,000. After graduating, she entered the University of St. Andrews, Scotland's first university (founded in 1413) and one of the United Kingdom's highest-ranked educational institutions. Long associated with what one journalist describes as "sloaney types,"[7] St. Andrews appeals to the English upper and upper-middle classes. Initial impressions of Catherine may lead to the perception that, like Diana before her, she fits the Sloane image perfectly. Yet in an update of their iconic book *Cooler, Faster, More Expensive: The Return of the Sloane Ranger,* Peter York and Olivia Stewart-Liberty rule out Catherine as a proper Sloane because she lacks one crucial prerequisite. Simply put, the wealth of Sloane Rangers must run at least three generations deep.

Myriad media representations tell the story of how William and Catherine met at the university and how their friendship turned into romance. Again tapping into the fairy-tale element of the RFBC, an eager public has consumed this (relatively, at least) rags-to-riches tale of a present-day Cinderella who finds her prince. In a very modern take on Cinderella catching her prince's eye at the ball, Catherine's parallel moment occurred when she sashayed down the catwalk at a student fashion event in a see-through black slip, mesmerizing William, who had paid £200 ($300) to sit in the front row. It cost just £30 ($45) to make, and its creator, Charlotte Todd (who launched her first line as a fashion designer the night before William and Catherine's wedding), sold it at auction in 2011 for £78,000 ($117,000).[8]

William and Catherine's courtship set another major precedent, not only because they were the first royal couple to live together before marriage, but also because it was so lengthy. In 1795, George IV only met Caroline of Brunswick on the day of his marriage, a not-uncommon arrangement for royal marriages at the time. Contrast this situation to William and Catherine's ten-year courtship, during which the press gave her the moniker "Waity Katie." Of course, the media never ceased to speculate on when the couple would marry. During those years, other interested parties made erroneous, and costly, claims about the couple's impending nuptials. In 2006, the now-defunct retail chain Woolworth's commissioned a line of engagement souvenirs—including kitchenware, mouse pads, dolls, and slippers—because they were sure an engagement would be announced. They planned to place 100,000 products on the shelves within forty-eight hours of an announcement, to gobble up their share of what the company's marketing director estimated would be a £14.3 million ($21.5 million) commemorative market. (This estimate proved later to be a gross understatement.) When the couple split temporarily in 2007, the company had to shelve the designs. Unfortunately, Woolworth's closed its last stores in 2009, one year before the actual engagement was announced, so they could never resurrect the designs for profit.

"Good things come to those who wait" is an old English saying that was certainly true for those involved in the royal memorabilia market, which finally got its long-awaited boost when William and Catherine announced their engagement on November 16, 2010. Manufacturers, designers, and department stores alike rushed to maximize the lucrative opportunity they had patiently anticipated. William had proposed to Catherine a month before the official announcement, when they were holidaying together in Kenya. Speaking animatedly in a televised interview to mark the joyful occasion, William related the trials and tribulations of carrying his mother Diana's precious sapphire and diamond ring in his rucksack for three weeks.

As they confided the high points of their romantic trip to viewers, they seemed to resemble any other young couple of their generation in love. Just as their cohabitation had reinforced their image as a thoroughly modern, down-to-earth pair, so too their engagement story, involving surprise, romance, and an exotic location, underlined how elaborate engagement rituals that afford the couple a narrative worth sharing have become a crucial part of the contemporary wedding.[9]

Committing to marriage meant William and Catherine also ensured royal-watchers around the world of their increased influence on consumer culture. Within hours of the announcement, H. Samuel, a well-known jewelry chain, was offering two versions of the engagement ring—one at £179 ($269) and a more upmarket version at £750 ($1,125). The firm's timeliness was rewarded with a 30 percent increase in sales.[10] Not surprisingly, given its new role in the global economy, China's manufacturers rushed to cash in on the news. Factories in Yiwu quickly produced tens of thousands of cheap replica rings to meet rising demand from the United States and Europe.

Catherine had influenced fashion styles ever since being linked to William, but now her impact would intensify considerably. Her famous blue wrap engagement dress cemented the fame and fortune of the Issa brand as women rushed to buy it; the dress sold out within twenty-four hours. In fact, Issa's chairwoman noted in a *Vogue* interview that this rush nearly caused the company to go out of business, as it could not produce the dress quickly enough. Since this corporate near-death experience, Issa has capitalized on its associations with Catherine and was quick to add maternity sizes to the line in response to her first pregnancy.[11] Similarly, new stock of the white Reiss dress she wore in engagement photos was swiftly commissioned to satisfy eager shoppers.

Catherine's love of mixing designer labels with High Street brands means her choices often are available to the masses; as a result, people perceive her as being "just like us."[12] She is already credited with boosting the British economy by £1 billion ($1.5 billion),[13] as demand for her favorite brands has soared. J. Brand jeans, dresses from Reiss, Whistles, Zara, Topshop, and LK Bennett shoes are just some of the instantly recognizable brands she supports. Regarded in many quarters as a trendsetter, fashion designers around the world avidly study her choices. As soon as she appears in an outfit, they take out their sketchpads, and consumers rush to wherever the fashionable brands are available.

Catherine also boosted the fortunes of British designer labels such as Temperely, Mulberry, and Burberry. Once a brand that had once lost its luster due to overlicensing and overexposure, Burberry now is considered one of the top ten luxury brands in the world. Top handbag designer Lulu Guinness admits to styling her bags in smaller sizes, reflecting Catherine's preference for carrying clutch purses on official occasions.[14] Furthermore, Catherine's stylish choice of hats and fascinators has given a much-needed boost to the millinery sector, just as Queen Victoria in her time revitalized the British lace industry.[15]

In a small town in the American West, Susan Kelly runs a website called *What Kate Wore,* which has had over 12 million hits since its inception. Women visit to swap information about what outfit Catherine is wearing and where she bought it. This site has also been responsible for influencing many American women to buy the British brands Catherine favors. Yet in addition to the snobbishness stemming from aristocratic circles, Catherine also has her detractors within the fashion world. Mary Portas, the retail guru of British television (her latest show is titled *Mary, Queen of Frocks*), claims that Catherine does not possess a sufficiently unique sense of style to warrant the commonly-held perception that she is a style icon. In addition, English fashion designer Dame Vivienne Westwood, known for her eccentric ways and love of all things punk, has berated Catherine for buying too many clothes and not making a sufficient effort to "shop green."*

Recently, author Hilary Mantel offered a cutting critique of the cultural notion of reducing royal women to their fashion choices. As we note in our preface, she recently won the Booker Prize twice (for books about the Tudor monarchy, no less). Furthermore, she is the first female author to be a repeat winner. In a now infamous lecture at the British Museum in 2013 titled "Royal Bodies," she described Catherine's portrayal in the media as "a jointed doll on which certain rags are hung," a "shop-window mannequin, with no personality of her own ... designed by a committee and built by craftsmen, with a perfect plastic smile and the spindles of her limbs hand-turned and glass-varnished."[16] Her seeming attack on Catherine caused an outpouring of sensational journalism in Britain when her words were taken completely out of context. Mantel was set up as a hate figure by the tabloid

---

* Dame Westwood's punk sensibilities did not stop her from accepting honors from both the Queen and Prince Charles; as we note earlier, she also happily accepted a commission to create a gown for a recent exhibit at Kensington Palace.

press, her words misrepresented to the extent that even Prime Minister David Cameron felt obliged to comment. He leaped to Catherine's defense, and in the process illuminated the fact that he had not read the entire speech either.

In truth, Mantel was offering less of a personal onslaught on Catherine and more of a commentary on what she perceives to be the fate of royal women in general. This fate revolves around serving as bodies reserved for breeding and looking good rather than being allowed any deeper substance. As such, her commentary is actually highly supportive of royal women and represents a plea for them to be treated as human beings.

However, Mantel's incisive comments may have overlooked the commercial interests that drive this fascination with "royal bodies"—not just to spur sales of newspapers and magazines, but also to oil the wheels of the fashion industry, and ultimately the broader market system. Contemporary consumer culture finds a way to commodify most things, and as we repeatedly observe in this book, clearly the Royal Family is no exception. The Centre for Retail Research estimates that the royal wedding generated £527.1 million ($790.6 million) for retailers, with souvenirs and memorabilia accounting for around £199.1 million ($298.6 million) of this total.[17]

Of course, there were traditional commemorative items, such as coins, stamps, and porcelain souvenirs. This last category provided a welcome boost to British potteries, as sales had been flagging in the face of stiff competition from Chinese manufacturers. Likewise, the United States–based Franklin Mint launched a two-doll Catherine collection (pre- and postwedding) to complement its Diana collection, estimated to have appealed to its largest-ever customer base. Each Catherine doll retailed for $195 (£130), with an easy payment option of $65 (£43) over three months.

Then there was the Royal Collection Trust's official line of souvenirs, including a tankard, a plate, and a pillbox—all made of English fine bone china gilded in 22-carat gold and crafted by Stoke-on-Trent's potteries. After many rumors to the contrary, the Trust also added a much anticipated tea towel to its range. But consistent with the couple's desire be featured only on more permanent commemoratives, the design broke with tradition and featured only their interwined initials instead of their images, as was customary.[18] The Trust's retail director reported huge demand for all items, with 60 percent of orders stemming from overseas. Not surprisingly, demand was the highest from U.S. consumers—as nothing stokes the financial flames of Anglophilia like a royal wedding.

Apart from traditional commemoratives companies, huge numbers of British and international brands also got caught up in the engagement excitement. Some made allusions to the couple in promotional campaigns and advertising messages, but others launched special products in anticipation of the forthcoming marriage. In the United States, Dunkin' Donuts created a limited-edition heart-shaped donut, and *Time* produced a special commemorative issue featuring the royal wedding kiss on its cover. In Britain, most brands tried to get in on the act. There were souvenir Oyster card holders,* a special royal wedding mobile phone by Alcatel, and as we noted earlier, a Knit Your Own Royal Wedding pattern kit for patriotic needle enthusiasts (see figure 10). It featured ten members of the wedding party, including the archbishop of Canterbury. Although it featured many signature details, such as the Queen's monochrome outfit and pearl necklace, its creators had to improvise for Catherine's wedding gown, which remained secret until she arrived at the ceremony.

Even British Airways did not let the opportunity pass, commisioning a special series of royal portraits of William, Catherine, the Queen, Charles, Prince Philip, and Prince Harry to be painted on the exteriors of six of their aircraft. From everyday items such as Schweppes mixers in royal wedding bottles or Proctor & Gamble's commemorative Fairy Liquid bottle, to the more humorous, eclectic, and resistant "Royal Wedding Sick Bags," the imaginative powers of the marketplace seemed unlimited.

Although beer is excluded from the official royal wedding breakfast (the Royal Family prefers wine and champagne), British breweries have long adhered to a tradition of producing special beers to mark royal occasions. With sales in excess of £18 billion ($27 billion) per year, beer is by far Britain's most popular alcoholic drink. In particular, it is heavily associated with the construction of masculinity; British males are fiercely proud of their beer heritage. Beer drinking is a daily ritual for many men, who pop into their local pub after work; it is also widely consumed during sporting events, particularly football.† As a red-blooded male who likes sports (albeit aristocratic ones like polo), Prince William himself has been known to lift a pint or two on many occasions. In fact, the British consume an average of 20 million pints of beer per day, and nine of every ten pints consumed come from local breweries. Most royal wedding paraphernalia is designed

* Oyster cards are travel passes used in London's underground and bus systems.
† In American English, "soccer."

TABLE 6 Special Beers to Commemorate the Royal Wedding

Name of Brewer	Name of Beer
Blackfriars	HRH His Royal Honeymoon
Blue Anchor	WnK Royal Ale
Brewdog	Royal Virility Performance
Castle Rock	Kiss Me Kate
Chiltern	I Will
DevilFish	WnK
Durham	Something Blue
Elgood's	Windsor Knot
Flipside	English Crown
Harvey's	Royal Nuptial Ale
Leek	Gotcha Will
Lees	Middleton's
Marston's	Perfect Union
Moodley's	Royal Match
Shepherd Neame	Middleton to Windsor
Truman's	Consummation Ale
Two Roses	RoyALE Wedding
Ulverston	Seal of Approval WK
Woods	Right Royal Ale

to appeal more to women, but the wide range of celebratory beers in pubs and liquor stores across Britain enabled men to engage with the event, albeit in a somewhat more irreverent, unromantic manner than female celebrants.

The royal wedding inspired a wide range of celebratory beers, some more cheekily named than others.[19] Most listed in table 6 were crafted at one of approxiately seven hundred microbreweries that preserve traditional brewing methods, eschewing the new technologies espoused by multinational brewers, which dominate the beer market. Growth of microbreweries in the last thirty years is attributed to the Campaign for Real Ale (CAMRA), an effort that resonates strongly with British masculinity. This masculinity is encapsulated in the microbrewery Brewdog's Royal Virility Performance, said to contain aphrodisiac ingredients; three bottles of beer supposedly equal the strength of one Viagra tablet! In addition, the most popular sites for beer drinking—traditional pubs and their new variants, gastropubs— also climbed on the royal wedding bandwagon. In 2011, a Windsor establishment restyled itself the Duchess of Cambridge pub. Later, as news of

Catherine's labor spread around the world, it offered a beer specially introduced to mark the occasion—Heir Raiser.

Aside from creating commemorative products, many companies devised special promotions and advertising campaigns that drew on the royal wedding theme. The most popular promotional tie-in is T-Mobile's spoof wedding video, created by the Saatchi & Saatchi ad agency, which quickly went viral around the world. Landing atop YouTube's list of Britain's most popular video ads in December 2011, as of December 2014 it had clocked more than 27.9 million views, 8.5 million of which occurred during the first week.[20] It featured look-alikes for all the major Royal Family members, as well as the archbishop of Canterbury, bumping and grinding down the aisle to the strains of "House of Love" by the English pop band East 17.

The creative inspiration for this media sensation was the "JK Wedding Entrance Dance," which has received over 85 million hits on YouTube since its posting in 2009. At the beginning, it seems to portray a conventional wedding procession, but then it quickly turns into an unconventional celebration down the aisle. Through this juxtaposition of very diverse associations that erode distinctions between high and low culture, the Royal Family once again was embedded and re-presented in the popular imagination of Britain and the world. Such connections serve to make the RFBC more popular and more widely liked and appreciated by a new generation.

As the royal wedding beers and T-Mobile video illustrate, the British sense of humor once again played a major cultural role in the public's enjoyment of this royal ritual. In the weeks before the wedding, T-shirts, tea towels, aprons, badges, and other paraphernalia displayed in shop windows and draped around market stalls blazed out an irreverent array of catchy slogans: "Never mind the Wedding: Let's go to the Pub," "Ta [Thanks] for the Bank Holiday," "Royal Male" (a spoof on the Royal Mail, the national postal service), "I-am-not-a-royal-wedding-mug," "I was invited to William and Catherine's jolly posh Royal Wedding," "Game Over," and "Catherine loves Willy."

Slogans such as "It Should Have Been Me" alluded to the humorous delusion that many women assumed they too could have had a shot at William, since he chose a bride outside of aristocratic circles. Most of the humor was lighthearted, although some was inevitably more cutting. Perhaps the tackiest example was the satirical *Private Eye*'s "Royal Wedding Mart," which included the "Princess Diana Hologram Projector." This device projected the image of William's dead mother on the wall so Diana could look down on the royal wedding from "heaven."

Many years of media anticipation culminated in a few weeks of incredibly intense merchandising that no one in Britain could avoid if they tried—and of course, some did, to no avail. April 29, 2011, was a day of elation in London and predictably caused much excitement in the rest of Britain and around the globe. One million people packed the streets of central London, all hoping for a glimpse of the procession. The day drew the attention of all those except the most hardened of antiroyal skeptics. It is generally agreed that one thing the British (and the RFBC in particular) do well is pomp and pageantry, and in this regard, the royal wedding was a triumph. As we note in chapter 2, the aesthetic and sophisticated backdrop of London looking its spectacular best contributed greatly to the anticipatory ambiance. The elaborate staging of this very public royal ritual made it a huge broadcasting event, attracting over two billion viewers in 180 countries around the world, and over 24 million (or over one-third of the population) in Britain alone.[21]*

With the wedding day declared an offical bank holiday, there was a relaxed, happy atmosphere in London, with less frenetic rushing around and work-weary commuters. The capital was festooned in red, white, and blue, with bunting strewn across every available railing, tree, and building. Eager vendors—from street traders to retail giants—added to the ambience by selling themed products. Some small vendors draped themselves in Union Jack flags or painted their faces to create a more festive impression as they mingled with the crowds, touting their wares. Burger King issued free gold crowns, knowing that many wearers would appear on television around the world and act as unwitting (and more importantly, uncompensated) brand ambassadors. The venerable London department store Selfridges handed out free wedding cake baked by the official royal wedding cake maker, Fiona Cairns. Colorful royal wedding cupcakes abounded at London bakeries, and Krispy Kreme sold gold-ring donuts.

The event also revitalized the cultural practice of street parties, as over 5,500 official applications for road closures were filed across Britain. Marks & Spencer claimed to have sold over two million sausages and one million chicken drumsticks during the week leading up to the wedding; Tesco, another leading UK grocery chain, sold 120 miles of bunting. Overall, just

* Pauline watched the royal wedding on television in France with a group of French friends equally fascinated by the event, despite that fact that France's monarchy was abolished in 1792. Cele spent most of the day watching the television coverage and monitoring her friends' Facebook posts. Some reported waking at 4 A.M. to watch it live, posting photos of themselves in tiaras enjoying tea and scones.

the wedding day was estimated to have generated £1–2 billion for the British economy, including £500 million in merchandising and commemoratives.[22]

In London, jubilant crowds feverishly waved flags as they shouted, "We want Catherine"; some excited fans even jumped into the fountain outside Buckingham Palace to secure a better vantage point. As had been true for Princess Elizabeth's wedding over sixty years before, many people had camped for several days in tents and gazebos outside Westminister Abbey to secure optimal vantage points. Across London in Hyde Park, Trafalgar Square, and many other public spaces, thousands gathered in front of the giant screens that would relay the wedding ceremony. Revelers picnicking in Hyde Park dressed for the occasion; a group of girls wore elaborate white wedding dresses, while some young men sported top hats and tails. Many others wore masks or were inspired to design flamboyant outfits, supplying an endless stream of extraordinary sights amid widespread merriment. Champagne fizzed and strangers swopped stories of their escapades.

Those who told us about being in London that day described an atmosphere that was extraordinary, with an overriding sense of shared community. As the click-clacking of horses announced the arrival of carriages bearing the newlyweds from Westminister Abbey back to Buckingham Palace, the throngs lining the Mall became a sea of outstretched arms waving cameras and mobile phones in attempts to capture shots of the passing splendor that thousands craned their necks to glimpse.

One of our informants described children, their faces often painted red, white, and blue, talking to whomever they chose, enjoying a new freedom in this unusually trusting environment. For many, it was a family day out that will never be forgotten. More than fifty members of the Royal Family attended the wedding, as well as over forty guests from the dwindling monarchies around the world. They included Scandinavian monarchs King Harald V and Queen Sonja of Norway, as well as Queen Margrethe II of Denmark, the autocratic King Mswati III of Swaziland (who left his thirteen wives at home)—a reminder of the diverse forms monarchy can assume. Out of 1,900 guests, the Middletons invited 100 and William and Catherine invited 250. The rest were relatives, foreign royals, official dignitaries, or celebrities.

In relation to the RFBC, however, the public sense was one of renewal, with the wedding seen as heralding a new image for the family, an image that is more informal and in touch with the people even while it maintains its majestic roots. Tabloid headlines spoke of a new beginning, "not only in the love affair between the newlyweds, but also the affair between the nation and its first family."[23] Tellingly, Diana's spirit was also there. William had made sure this would be the case; Westminster Abbey's last great event had been her funeral in 1997, and the first hymn sung at the wedding, *Guide Me, O Thou Great Redeemer,* had been included both at that event and at the tenth anniversary memorial service.

Thus the wedding was a celebration as much of the past as of the present, and a manifestation and reinforcement of royal lineage. Of course, the most tangible symbol of its longevity was eighty-five-year-old Queen Elizabeth, who appeared serene and secure in the knowledge that this day was ensuring the future of the British monarchy. Beside her, the eighty-nine-year-old Duke of Edinburgh maintained the regal aplomb befitting a royal consort, despite his advanced years. Resplendent in a medal-bedecked red military uniform with a long sheathed sword at his side, commentators observed that his eyes still had their customary glint as he chatted with Pippa Middleton on the balcony.

In short, inasmuch as the wedding rituals reinforced the majesty of the monarchy, they also symbolized the royal phoenix rising from the ashes of bygone scandals, marking new beginnings and indeed, new additions to the Royal Family—most obviously, the Middletons. Catherine's story perpetuates a powerful myth that anyone in Britain can move up the economic and social ladder.[24] Her fairytale transformation is perhaps best symbolized by her understated arrival at Westminster Abbey. She arrived as an ordinary citizen in the Queen's black Rolls-Royce (figure 31) and departed the ceremony as William's wife, the Duchess of Cambridge, in all the splendor of the 1902 State Landau, the same horse-drawn carriage that had transported Prince Charles and his new bride, Diana, from their wedding.

Fashion was everywhere at the wedding itself, from Victoria Beckham's Christian Laboutin shoes and David Beckham's Ralph Lauren suit, to the solemn nun in black Reebok sneakers who sat beside other official church dignatories in the front pew of Westminster Cathedral, just a few seats from the couple. There were fashion faux pas in evidence as well, with perhaps the most visible residing on the heads of William's cousins Princesses Eugenie and Beatrice—dubbed the "mad hatters" by one online publication. Eugenie's dramatic Philip Treacy hat design was generally considered overkill with her vivid Vivienne Westwood outfit. Beatrice's gigantic ring-and-bow hat was widely considered by fashion commentators to have ruined the elegance of her taupe Valentino Haute Couture dress and coat, and was swiftly dubbed the "toilet

FIGURE 31. Catherine Middleton in the Queen's Rolls-Royce. Courtesy of Kimberly Sugden.

seat." Members of a Facebook group titled "Princess Beatrice's Ridiculous Royal Wedding Hat" posted mocking pictures of William's cousin with monsters on her head. The princess had the last laugh, however, when the hat sold for £81,100 ($121,650) at a charity auction, after forty bidders vied for it.

Apart from such minor distractions as the royal sisters' millinery missteps and the brash head-to-toe cobalt outfit worn by socialite Tara Palmer-Tomkinson, most eyes were reserved for Catherine. As she stepped out of the Queen's classic 1977 Rolls-Royce Phantom at the doors of Westminister Abbey, months of speculation over the design of her wedding dress came to an end. Sarah Burton, creative director for the legendary designer Alexander McQueen, had designed the ivory satin bridal gown with its handmade lace bodice and long sleeves, an elegant but not ostentatious design that resonated with the wider context of a country in economic crisis. Sarah Burton also designed the cowl-neck white silk bridesmaid's dress for Catherine's sister, Pippa. Its elegant but simple design was swiftly replicated and offered for sale at the British department store Debenhams for £1,995 ($2,992).

A royal wedding is very much akin to other big media events, such as the Olympic Games or state funerals, which interrupt normal television programming; all of these are touted and transmitted as historical moments that should not be missed.[25] People crowd together to watch them no matter where they are—at work, in pubs and airports, on community screens—in short, wherever they can find a television. Such events become an important part of the collective memory, an "I remember when" scenario that parents and grandparents pass on to their young. They unite diverse communities and sundry groups of people, albeit on a temporary basis, through unifying messages such as "The world watches."[26] Papers were peppered with headlines that encouraged readers to share a collective royal wedding moment: "Celebrate Our Happiest Day" (*Daily Express*); "Will and Catherine: The People's Wedding" (*Express & Star*); "One Beautiful Bride: One Great Day to Be British" (*Daily Star*); "The New Romantics" (*London Times*); "Love Reigns" (*People*).

The most frequent phrase was, of course, "fairy tale," a theme emphasized again and again in headlines around the world. Many were directly reminiscent of Charles and Diana's wedding some years before. In fact, some of the headlines describing William and Catherine's big day could easily have applied to that 1981 event as well: "Royal Wedding: A Fairy Tale," "The Real Appeal of the Royal Wedding: Women Still Want a Fairy Tale," "Royal Wedding: Is This a Fairy Tale? No It Is the Real Thing," "It Really Was a Disney Fairy Tale."

Once the wedding and the couple's ten-day honeymoon in the Seychelles Islands were over, William and Catherine quickly adapted to their role as the "young royals." They became the Royal Family's most glamorous and likeable face, completing a hugely popular nine-day royal tour of Canada in June 2011. After this success and a three-day visit to California shortly afterward, where they attended a UK Trade and Investment (UKTI) event, the couple was flagged as the new ambassadors for British business. Reports circulated that they would undertake future tours with the express purpose of promoting British brands and highlighting British trading opportunities.

Leveraging the Royal Family as representatives for "Brand Britain"—a promotional campaign designed to boost the image of Britain's commercial and touristic endeavors around the globe—is an important initiative for the British monarchy, defining its purpose for the twenty-first century. In this regard, William and Catherine have been heralded as replacements for Prince Andrew, the Duke of York, whose role as trade ambassador has been somewhat discredited in recent times after a series of scandals.

In 2012, William and Catherine again played prominent roles, representing Team GB and Paralympics GB before and during the Olympic Games, together with Prince Harry, to heighten public support for sportsmen and women. The leading young members of the Royal Family were gathering force, becoming ever more popular as the new friendly face of what had been regarded (until recently anyway) as a rather stuffy, unglamorous monarchy. That year, the British Olympic Games and the most-watched-ever Paralympics, together with the Queen's Jubilee Celebrations, provided a succession of historic media events that kept British spirits high.

As 2012 drew to an end, the perfect excuse to continue the celebration arrived on December 3, when William and Catherine announced that they were expecting a baby the following summer. The world waited impatiently for this next big event, with Catherine's bump closely scrutinized by the global media throughout her pregnancy. During this time she continued to influence fashion, and her clothes, maternity or other, were as quickly sought after and copied as ever. As she had done in the past, Catherine stuck to her customary clever choices of mixing High Street chic with designer brands. Indeed, she stayed so slim for the first part of her pregnancy that even when she was six months pregnant, she could still fit into a £38 ($57) Topshop polka dot dress. It sold out within hours, to many buyers who were not pregnant.

As the birth drew closer (although palace officials had never provided a precise due date), the commercial pace started to quicken, as products and promotions tied to the royal birth began to appear. British designers Emma Bridgewater and Sophie Allport added royal baby mugs to their collections, and British babywear brand Huddle and Bliss introduced its Royal Baby Collection with the slogan "Fit for Your Prince or Princess," with Royal Crown babygrows,* layettes, and other baby accessories. Two book titles that included "Royal Baby" in the title and another titled *The Royal Nappy*† rapidly appeared on Amazon.

As might be expected, each choice Catherine was spotted making hit the press (or the papers' online sites) in a flash, immediately influencing retail sales. When she was pictured leaving Blue Almonds, a luxury baby boutique in Kensington, London, with a white Moses basket, the low-cost British supermarket chain Asda immediately reported a 57 percent increase in online sales of similarly-styled baby baskets. But at £35/$55, they were a fraction of the cost of those at its high-end rival.

Once again, the British sense of humor was often in full view, with baby bibs bearing slogans such as "I love my Auntie Pippa" or "I love my Uncle Harry" and toy manufacturer Fisher-Price launching a royal throne musical training potty. Lots of permutations of the ubiquitous "Keep Calm" meme abounded

---

* In American English, "onesies."
† In American English, "diaper."

FIGURE 32. "Keep Calm: It's Only a Royal Baby" display. Courtesy of Ashleigh Logan.

on merchandise (figure 32). For fun-loving mothers-to-be, Mothercare introduced a white maternity T-shirt with a gold crown emblazoned across the front and "Future Princess" in pink italics.

The most irreverent promotion tying into the royal baby theme must certainly have been one by the Irish bookmaker Paddy Power, which runs a prominent chain of betting shops in Ireland and Britain. It had acquired a reputation for sponsoring risqué advertising stunts that challenge the codes of political correctness. True to form, the chain was giving odds on the forthcoming baby's weight, hair color, sex, and name. As a publicity stunt to promote the odds, they organized four adult-sized "babies" (complete with beer guts) to pose in nappies and crowns outside Buckingham Palace, St. Mary's Hospital (where Catherine was to give birth), Boujis (Prince Harry's favorite nightclub), and even on the London Underground (clearly to the amazement of travelers).

Following the commemorative trend for the royal wedding, the royal baby commercial pot did not bubble over merely with lower-end merchandise; upmarket retailers also tried to boost flagging sales in a nation still

FIGURE 33. Fortnum & Mason's royal baby display. Courtesy of Kimberly Sugden.

feeling the effects of a prolonged, severe economic recession. Even as they waited for news of the royal arrival, many retailers themed their displays in celebratory ways, as a display of royal baby items at London's leading culinary department store, Fortnum & Mason, illustrates (figure 33).

One of the most elaborate and expensive promotions to reference the royal baby involved the five-star hotel Park Lane Grosvenor House in London. It commissioned custom children's furniture designers Dragons of Walton Street, which had created nurseries for William and Harry, to create a "Suite of Dreams." It came complete with a lavish crib, handcrafted baby furniture, a themed Beatrix Potter baby-changing area, and a Balmoral Silver Cross stroller. Starting at £2,230 ($3,580) per night, the hotel offered its guests three different packages: Clarence (one night), Windsor (two nights), or Buckingham (three nights).

In contrast, the Royal Collection Trust exhibited characteristically royal reserve, announcing it would wait until after the baby was born to produce its official commemorative range. Nevertheless, its Grenadier Guard baby suits on sale at Kensington Palace and Buckingham Palace gift shops were widely thought by media sources to be a subtle attempt to generate extra sales. Most traditional British potteries also refrained from producing commemorative porcelain pieces until after the birth, so they could complete their ready and waiting designs by adding the name and sex of the new heir to the throne. Upmarket British designer Milly Green, however, showed a more entrepreneurial spirit, launching a royal baby commemorative place setting in Crown Trent fine bone china. The ingeniously gender-neutral range of cups, bowls, and plates depicted "royal" storks, rocking horses, and prams, bordered with red, white, and blue bunting.

As the birth date neared, hundreds of journalists vied for space outside the private Lindo Wing of St. Mary's Hospital in London, where the royal birth was to take place, following a tradition established for the Queen and Princess Diana. Many members of the media, and even some royal fans, spent over three weeks in front of the hospital, anxious not to miss the moment. The *Daily Telegraph* and the *Sun,* both right-wing papers, streamed live feeds from the hospital to keep readers and audiences continuously updated. Free mobile apps provided updates; others, such as "Name the Royal Baby," tied into the theme. Of course, because the media were ensconced for so long with nothing to report, reporters looked for every opportunity to create stories. In the process, they ensured that the royal birth carried more public momentum than ever before.

Once it was apparent that Catherine had finally gone into labor, the thousands who gathered outside Buckingham Palace served as a reminder that royal births have always been very public affairs. But as the renowned monarchy historian David Starkey highlighted on CBC News, at least now the crowds were outside. In the past, people often crowded into the royal bedchamber as a queen gave birth. In fact, the home secretary traditionally stood outside the delivery room to verify that the baby was not swapped. This protocol was last followed for the birth of the Queen's cousin Princess Alexandra in 1936, and was abandoned prior to Prince Charles's birth in 1948. Nor has royal baby-watching ever been solely a British occupation; many in the crowd were tourists, who had been arriving daily outside the Lindo Wing in the lead-up to the birth. Testifying to its global fascination, one Japanese visitor was reported as saying that the royal baby had been in the news every day in Tokyo, so she wanted to see the occasion for herself.[27]

On July 23, 2013, the official announcement was displayed on the historic easel reserved for that purpose, just inside the Buckingham Palace gates: "Her Royal Highness The Duchess of Cambridge was safely delivered of a son at 4:24 P.M. The baby weighs 8 lbs. 6 oz." His Royal Highness Prince

George of Cambridge, third in line to the throne and the Queen's third great-grandchild, had arrived. In a world of Disneyfication and themed shopping malls, it is not always easy to discern which rituals are "official" and which are not. A bell-ringing town crier, turned out in full traditional costume of red, blue, and gold greatcoat and plumed trilby hat, proclaimed the birth from the steps of the Lindo Wing, reading details from an authentic-looking "royal" scroll. Many mistakenly thought seventy-six-year-old enthusiast Tony Appleton was an official part of the royal ritual. Albeit impromptu, his appearance set an appropriately colorful and historic tone, providing another interesting example of the spontaneous creation of unofficial ritual and pageantry that we described in chapter 3.

London began to celebrate; the crowds reacted excitedly and champagne corks flew through the air, as people buzzed with the good news. The city's landmarks joined in: Trafalgar Square's fountain lit up blue for a boy, as did the Golden Jubilee bridges across the Thames; the BT Tower proclaimed, "It's a Boy," and the London Eye's curve, rising high across the London skyline, gleamed in red, white, and blue lights. Across the Atlantic, many Canadian landmarks, including the Peace Tower and Parliament buildings in Ottawa, as well as the CN Tower in Toronto, also lit up blue. The most spectacular landmark was without a doubt Niagara Falls, with its blue waters tumbling magnificently against a darkening evening sky.

In London, traditional gun salutes were fired the following day from Green Park and the Tower of London, and the bells of Westminster Abbey chimed across the city for three hours nonstop. Crowds gathered once again to see the Duke and Duchess of Cambridge leaving the hospital with their newborn. Margaret Tyler was there, waiting patiently for many hours and determined not to miss this once-in-a-lifetime opportunity. Her friend Terry, an equally committed royalist, had slept on a bench for six nights so as not to miss the occasion! Reflecting the fact that people often engage in "ritual longing,"[28] Margaret spoke for many when she told the *Washington Post,* "I'm not going to miss this.... When they walk out that door, that will be our history." (True to form, Terry, Margaret, and her friend Dave were also present for the vigil outside of St. Mary's that occurred prior to the birth of Princess Charlotte in May 2015. A photo of Margaret in the *Daily Mail* displayed her in a vivid Union Jack blazer and a T-shirt bearing a photograph of Prince George with the caption "I was here first.")

As William and Catherine, their baby son in her arms, came out to greet the awaiting photographers and royalists, every minute detail was carefully scrutinized. These included Catherine's custom-made powder blue polka dot dress by British designer Jenny Packham; the royal shawl from British knitwear company G. H. Hurt and Son, made of soft merino wool; the baby blanket made by Brooklyn-based Aden + Anais; and the Britax baby car seat where Prince George nestled snugly as William proudly drove his family off in a black Range Rover.

In testimony to "the Kate effect," G. H. Hurt's website was soon warning customers that delivery of the shawl might be slower because "demand for this item has increased." Likewise, Aden + Anais reported that its website traffic had doubled, and it saw its highest number of visits ever in one day. Many other companies lost no time jumping on the royal baby bandwagon. VisitBritain showed off its new poster campaign, which promoted Britain as a family-friendly tourist destination. The campaign leveraged the by-then iconic photo of William and Catherine with their newborn on the steps of the Lindo Wing. With its large message written in bold, "Welcome to Great Britain" (with *Great* emphasized in red shading), we are reminded that although it is difficult to provide an overall figure, one source estimates the RFBC to be worth £500 million ($750 million) in tourism every year[29] and an overall £1.5 billion ($2.25 billion) to the UK economy as a whole. The Centre for Retailing Research predicted that the royal baby alone would contribute £247 million ($370.5 million) to the British economy in the nine weeks before and after the birth. Of that figure, large expenditure categories include spending on festivities, £80 million ($120.5 million); souvenirs and toys, £78 million ($117 million); books, DVDs, and media connected to the event, £89 million ($33.5 million).[30]

Even the initially reticent Royal Collection Trust lost no time launching its official commemorative china, which appeared in Kensington Palace's gift shop just two days after the birth. The upmarket range included a limited edition loving cup, teddy bears, pillboxes, tea towels, velvet cushions, silver tankards, and even Christmas tree decorations (leveraging the appeal of two rituals at once).

As we mentioned, bookmakers cashed in on speculation about the newborn's name, turning it into a lucrative commercial opportunity. Indeed, it was their odds-on favorite name that won, as George Alexander Louis was announced, confirming a very traditional set of names most had anticipated in some permutation. After all, the third in line to the throne is unlikely to be called Brooklyn or Elton, and the choice needs to include at least three names to follow appropriate naming practices within the royal lineage. The

Queen herself has three names (Elizabeth Alexandra Mary), and her father, George VI, had four (Albert Frederick Arthur George). In choosing George as the baby's first name, William and Catherine referenced and reinforced the longevity of the monarchy, emphasized its continuity, and at the same time appropriately named their son after his much-loved great-grandfather who lives on in popular culture through the movie *The King's Speech*.* The baby's middle name, Alexander, is another suitably royal name (think "the Great"), once again signaling tradition and history, as well as echoing the Queen's middle name. Finally, his last name, Louis, is one of Prince William's names and also refers to Prince Charles's much-loved great-uncle, Lord Louis Mountbatten, who was tragically killed in an Irish terrorist attack.

Notably, however, Prince George not only reinforces the power and presence of the monarchy, but is already playing his part to support his consumer-culture link within the RFBC. As he takes his place as third in line to the throne, he becomes "a life-long British brand."[31] Although he will wait many more years to play his princely part in full, his commercial value is set to soar as many mothers (and some fathers) copy everything his parents choose for him. The UK baby market is worth £753 million ($1.1 billion). Furthermore, it takes an estimated £250,000 ($375,000) to raise a child to age twenty-one[32]—so parenthood is a costly business. The choices mothers make for their children are fraught with decisions about their own maternal identities and the type of parenting lifestyles they believe they should pursue. From "yummy mummy" to "eco mum," contemporary motherhood is an anxiety-provoking occupation, full of compromises and trade-offs against the ideals of motherhood portrayed in the media.

In short, the "Kate effect" is not only about many fans wanting to "touch greatness"[33] and be associated with Catherine's aura of royal style and glamour. It is also about helping parents (and especially mothers) make decisions in a marketplace where choice abounds. To decide which pram or cot to buy may take several weeks of perusing the available options and weighing the pros and cons of each. But if Catherine has bought the pram, it must be fashionable, it must be safe, it must be the best for her baby, and therefore, it must be the best for anyone's baby.

The first photos released to the world showing the proud parents with baby George were taken by Catherine's father, Michael Middleton, rather

* Not all King Georges were popular, as the comedy *Blackadder* reminds us in its merciless ridiculing of George IV.

than an official royal photographer. The photos show a relaxed and happy Catherine and William, with George and their dog Lupo. Set in the Middletons' garden, the photos reflect a typical middle-class English family on a summer day. The underlying message behind these photos, deemed to give them "a democratic charm,"[34] is that they are an ordinary family just like everyone else. Echoing their similarity to other families with newborns, and sounding like a typical new father in his first interview after the birth, William beguilingly described the new prince as "a rascal" and "a little fighter" who didn't want to sleep.*

In keeping with a less formal atmosphere around the birth, Prince George's christening on October 23, 2013, was a relatively low-key affair, a private ceremony at the Chapel Royal in London's St. James's Palace. Only twenty-two guests attended: the Queen and Prince Philip; Charles and Camilla; Prince Harry; Carole, Michael, Pippa, and James Middleton; and the seven godparents (including Princess Anne's daughter Zara Tindall) with six spouses. Honoring tradition, Prince George's flowing christening gown was a replica of that worn by Queen Victoria's firstborn in 1841. The original, designed in white silk satin with an intricate Honiton lace overlay to resemble Victoria's wedding dress, was worn by every monarch since Edward VII, as well as Prince Charles and Prince William. Prince Edward's daughter, Lady Louise Windsor, was the last royal infant to wear the original in 2003. Its century and a half of service had taken a toll on the delicate fabrics and lacework, and in 2008 the Queen's dressmaker handcrafted a new royal christening robe, faithful to the old in every respect, including the lace. The archbishop of Canterbury baptized George in a golden lily font commissioned by Queen Victoria, with water from the River Jordan. Based on Christians' belief that Christ was baptized in that river, the tradition of using water from that source dates from Richard I.

Christening gifts arrived from around the world for Prince George— some stranger than others. Topping the list for originality was a field of wildflowers in the Transylvanian hills, a present from Count Tibor Kálnoky, a Transylvanian noble who hosts Prince Charles when he visits the region. The symbolic intent of the gift was to raise public awareness and protect rare species in the area. Topping the list for "creepiness" (so deemed by the tabloids) was Pippa Middleton's gift, a life cast of George's hands and feet made of silver, which cost around £7,000 ($10,000). This gift caused much debate

* Aired on CNN on August 19, 2013.

in the popular press about the trauma George would have been forced to endure while the casts were made (apparently he would have had to keep his hands and feet still for thirty seconds in a jelly-like substance). Yet the gift is not as macabre as its modern-day audience may assume; it is actually rooted in royal tradition. Queen Victoria commissioned sculptor Mary Thornycroft to cast nine of her children's hands and feet, which were later sculpted in marble as enduring memories of their infancies.

For the first time in over a hundred years, official christening photographs depicted four generations of the Royal Family together. The most iconic picture was that of the eighty-seven-year old Queen with her son, grandson, and great grandson—the three kings-in-waiting, touting the symbolic strengthening of the Windsor line well into the future. This grouping echoed one taken in 1894 of Queen Victoria at Edward VIII's christening with Edward VII and George V. There is one subtle difference, however, between the two portraits. In Victoria's photo, she holds the baby on her lap, reflecting the expected assumptions of her era about the role of females in caring responsibilities. Significantly, in the current photo, it is William who holds baby George, indicating a more modern attitude to parenting, while symbolizing through this gesture the RFBC's willingness to adapt their traditions to the world about them.

From a branding perspective, then, William, Catherine, George, and the most recent addition to the family—Princess Charlotte Elizabeth Diana of Cambridge, the couple's second child, born on May 2, 2015—represent a highly successful commercial myth unfolding before our eyes, a myth that updates the monarchy for contemporary times. Its central narrative enshrines middle-class values and the social mobility espoused by Thatcher's Britain. Myths, by their very nature, hide as much as they reveal, and this narrative also masks the "bedrock of massive wealth and tradition" on which the RFBC is based.[35] Yet it is a happy and comforting myth in troubled economic and political times, one that people readily seek to embrace and identify with and, both literally and metaphorically, buy into. As William and Catherine remake the monarchy for the twenty-first century (and beyond), their challenge will be how they balance on the royal tightrope between majesty and ordinariness, between royal mystique and the bottom dollar. We examine this balancing act more closely in our next and final chapter, which ponders the future of the RFBC.

TEN

The Royal Family Brand

A RIGHT ROYAL FUTURE?

The previous chapters offer ample evidence that twenty years after many political and media pundits effectively sounded the death knell for the British monarchy, the institution is alive, well, and demonstrating more momentum than ever before in popular and consumer culture. We need look no further than the 2013 hit song "Royals" to reinforce this assertion. "You can call me queen bee," sings teenage singer-songwriter Lorde, as she confesses, "I'm in love with being queen," in a chart-topping single that reached the number 1 slot in eleven countries.[1] The memorable but simple chorus ("We'll never be Royals") helped make it the fifth best-selling song of 2013, with sales of over 4.4 million digital copies, and the highest seller by a female artist. Lorde, a New Zealander whose real name is Ella Marija Lani Yelich-O'Connor, admits to being "really into royals and aristocracy," and originally thought that adopting "Lord" as her stage name would be "super rad."[2] Ultimately, however, she added an *e* at the end to make it more feminine. This gesture of appropriation, in tandem with her song, beautifully illustrates how popular culture continually intertwines with royalty, updating and adapting it to new needs and new market segments (in this case, teen culture).

Provocatively, Lorde's lyrics address the gap between royalty and common people, raising the thorny issue of class consciousness and conspicuous consumption ("driving Cadillacs in our dreams"). Of special interest here is the confluence of royalty with the luxury goods she repeats in her lyrics. Cristal, Maybach, Grey Goose, Cadillacs, gold teeth, and "tigers on a gold leash" are all extravagant symbols of rap culture that emerged in New York City's South Bronx in the 1970s. In other words, they are culturally and symbolically about as far afield from the RFBC as one could get. After all, the Queen's favorite brands—Land Rover, Tupperware, the John Lewis department store, and Barbour (a Royal Warrant grantee for waterproof and protective outerwear)—are inconspicuous, even bland.[3]

"Royals" therefore offers an excellent illustration of the increasingly blurred boundaries of royalty and celebrity, and could even be interpreted as a signal that these boundaries have collapsed altogether. Increasingly, members of the Royal Family themselves contribute to blurring these boundaries as their interactions become more casual. The young royals often now pose for selfies on their walkabouts or sing onstage with celebrities, Prince Charles appeared on BBC Scotland to offer the weather forecast, and even the Queen photobombed a selfie at the 2014 Paralympic Games in Scotland in July 2014.

Reflecting on how the RFBC has evolved over the decade we actively studied them, we regard Lorde's hit song as a warning sign that the boundaries between royalty and celebrity may be becoming too fluid for the brand to retain its mystique. As we look to the future, we anticipate that the distinctions within the extraordinary social category of monarchy—which many in the world regard as aspirational—will erode further. Thus the balancing act required to deftly stem this erosion is likely to become increasingly difficult to manage for the RFBC. On the one hand, the Royal Family needs to maintain and manage its relationships with the media to communicate with its stakeholders and ensure its public still perceives the brand as relevant and accessible. But on the other hand, the RFBC may want to consider limiting its accessibility, exercising at least some degree of control over what is published and how royal images are (co)created and communicated.

For the RFBC to retain some of its mystique in an increasingly viral and volatile media environment, we believe it should attend to three key traits that distinguish this brand from other celebrities. First, it is important to note that its fame stems from heredity or "ascribed" status, rather than from achievement and recognition in culturally valorized endeavors such as the arts, commerce, or sports. (Of course, it is also true that like the famous eighteenth-century dandy Beau Brummell, some celebrities are simply "famous for being famous.") Arguably, in a world that increasingly values meritocracy over aristocracy, ascribed fame actually may place the Royal Family at a disadvantage. More than ever, monarchs and their kin must prove their mettle to Britain and the Commonwealth, as the entire institution is increasingly held up to public scrutiny.[4]

As crowd theorist Gustave Le Bon presciently claimed over a century ago, "The divine right of the masses is about to replace the divine right of kings."[5]

In short, it has become crucial that people perceive the Royal Family as making visible contributions to British commerce, heritage, industry, and tourism. For the moment, these contributions—which typically take the form of scheduled, publicized appearances and the propagation of customary and expected cultural rituals that stem from the institution of monarchy itself—help ensure that the Royal Family remains differentiable from other celebrities. Granted, Victoria and David Beckham once owned an English manor labeled "Beckingham Palace"—but it is doubtful they will ever participate in a cultural event that would spur a million people to line the streets of London, evoking collective (if imagined) memories of Britain in its heyday as the world's most powerful empire.

This brings us to the second aspect that we believe differentiates the RFBC from other celebrities. As we have observed, since Victorian times, the Royal Family consistently has chosen, and now seems expected, to serve as a moral template for family and civic values. Even as recently as December 2014, a YouGov survey reported that Britons rely more on the Queen and the Duke and Duchess of Cambridge for moral guidance than they do on the archbishop of Canterbury. Clearly, this requirement is not demanded of most celebrities, who are usually allowed to kiss and tell (or nowadays, to kiss and tweet) without public admonishment. In fact, the appeal of "trainwreck" celebrities often revolves around seeing exactly how far they will go in pushing the boundaries of decency and taste.

A crucial aspect of the Royal Family's ability to transcend the more salacious aspects of rubbernecking is its dedication to charity work. Between them, the current members have extended their patronage to around three thousand charitable organizations, some in place for several generations.[6] The Queen inherited various patronages from her father, George VI. She is also patron of the Mothers' Union, continuing a role first held by Queen Victoria in 1898. Marketers would label these efforts as core competencies of the RFBC, which enable it to differentiate itself from its competition and to justify its existence in a world where people increasingly are judged by their personal achievements. To act on behalf of others is one way the RFBC can embody the imperative to engage in meaningful duties and serve as symbolic figureheads and moral templates for Britain and the Commonwealth.

Members of the RFBC usually become patrons of causes consistent with their own interests and values. Prince Charles is patron or president of more than four hundred organizations; many reflect his interest in the environment, rural practices, and opportunities for young people. His wife is president of the National Osteoporosis Society, a cause that holds great significance for her, as her mother and grandmother both died from the disease. Securing a royal patron can considerably help raise public awareness of a charity, as evidenced by Diana's famous championing of controversial causes such as AIDS and land mines. There is also evidence that royal sponsorship encourages donations.[7]

Likewise, a growing hallmark of contemporary celebrity image management is increased participation in doing good works. Engagement with charitable causes enables celebrities "to raise their profile above the zone of the crudely commercial into the sanctified quasi-religious realm of altruism and charity."[8] We need look no farther than Angelina Jolie, who is a long-standing Goodwill Ambassador for the UN High Commission for Refugees, and who more recently has campaigned for the Preventing Sexual Violence Initiative. Likewise, actress Emma Watson of *Harry Potter* fame is also a UN Goodwill Ambassador, while the high-profile English pop star Robbie Williams is involved in Soccer Aid, which raises funds for UNICEF. Jon Bon Jovi, Paul McCartney, and U2 front man Bono are all successful celebrity fund-raisers.[9] Most large charities now retain a celebrity liaison officer to strategically manage links with the entertainment sector.

Yet it remains debatable how much celebrities actually contribute to raising the profile of their supported causes. A recent survey found that people are not really aware of the charities celebrities support and that their advocacy tends to promote the celebrity rather than the cause.[10] So although celebrities increasingly try to engage in good works that align with their values (further blurring the boundaries between royalty and other famous people), the RFBC remains unique in that it offers charitable causes the advantage of donors with a much higher profile. Of course, this pulling power is heightened when an event is hosted at Buckingham Palace or Clarence House, or at one of the carefully tended royal residences that HRP manages.

Our third key difference between royalty and celebrity entails a distinction between public and private. Celebrity culture thrives on the personal, private aspects of an individual's life; intimate revelations are its fodder. In contrast, most Royal Family members zealously guard their private lives and expect to be afforded respect and protection from the intrusive media. In the 1990s, when the world was made privy to taped phone conversations of Charles and Diana with their lovers, it may have seemed that these boundaries had well and truly dissolved. But since the motorcycle-pursuing paparazzi who chased Diana in the Place d'Alma tunnel were a core component of her death narrative, the British media have tried to act more responsibly toward the Royal Family, even if their actions stem as much from fear of a public opinion backlash as to any ethical sensibility.

Nor is it any secret that the Queen has personally intervened, asking editors to allow William, Catherine, and George to lead a life out of the limelight whenever possible. The desire for royal privacy was further facilitated by the dissolution of Rupert Murdoch's *News of the World* in 2011, when a hacking scandal proved to be the newspaper's downfall. In fact, the scandal began in 2005, when the publication paid a private investigator to intercept voicemail messages pertaining to activities of the Royal Family. But just as some countries do not honor UK or EU trademarks that ostensibly protect royal business ventures, the media in many countries likewise do not adhere to the same level of discretion as the British media now practice. This fact was brought home when the French tabloid *Closer* published photos showing Catherine sunbathing topless in a French chateau. British papers had been offered the photos but refused to run them. The couple subsequently filed a successful lawsuit against the tabloid to prevent any further publication, no doubt as a warning to other photographers and journalists.

Furthermore, well-known celebrity magazines, such as *Hello* and its down-market rival *Ok!*, continue to blur the boundaries between William and Catherine and other celebrities, even while respecting their privacy and refraining from idle speculation or gossip. The April 2014 cover of *Ok!* ran a headline claiming exclusive coverage of the couple's Australian tour; it was adjacent to promotion for a feature article on the marriage plans of Gary Lucy, star of *EastEnders,* a long-running British soap opera. The main front cover photos also featured Kerry Katona (a British singer best known for reality-show appearances) and her family. Similarly, the June 2014 issue of *Hello* claimed an exclusive with Catherine as she "maps out the future with her princes." Yet she is featured alongside Angelina Jolie, British actress and TV presenter Kelly Brook, and "Britain's ski sweetheart," Chemmy Alcott. Little wonder that many readers, especially younger ones, blur the boundaries between the RFBC and other celebrities as they flick through the pages of celebrity gossip magazines.

To maintain its distinction from ever-encroaching celebrity culture—and indeed, to continue to be perceived as above celebrity—it will be crucial for the RFBC to retain its aesthetic, cultural, historic, and touristic viability. In this respect, each of the five types of brands it contains will face challenges in the coming decades.

First, as a global brand, all signs point to expansion. The increasing growth of the middle class in highly populous countries, the democratization of travel and consumer culture in much of the world, and the continued expansion of traditional and new media that doubtless will perpetuate worldwide coverage of core RFBC activities should continue to fuel royal fever on the global scale. Yet this outcome cannot be taken for granted. Our approach throughout this book emphasizes the RFBC as a multifaceted cultural form and carrier of meanings. For some groups (e.g., British monarchists and royalists, Anglophiles, and especially American collectors), these meanings often go unquestioned. Most tap into shared traditions that assume a collective memory based on appreciating (or at least, understanding) the history and genealogy of the Royal Family. Yet we can expect these meanings to be less understood, and perhaps even challenged, as coverage and knowledge of the RFBC expands globally. For example, the French photographer who thought Catherine was fair game to be snapped topless clearly did not adhere to the same norms governing how to treat the wife of the future king of England as do photographers in her own country.

In fact, when seeking to understand the polysemy (or multiple meanings) that people attribute to the RFBC, we need look no farther than within Britain itself to grasp how the Royal Family can mean very different things to different people. In Northern Ireland, for instance, the Queen, Crown, and Union Jack are frequently displayed on walls to make political statements and mark out Protestant territory (figure 34). These often imaginative but overtly political murals—now themselves a tourist draw—convey menace to neighboring Catholic families, reflecting the long-running religious "troubles" in Northern Ireland.

The Queen's visit to Belfast in June 2014 was widely seen as a successful attempt to dilute such meanings. As part of her tour, she visited the notorious Crumlin Road Gaol* (closed in 1996 and now a dark-tourism attraction), which had housed many political prisoners. In a symbolic gesture of reconciliation, the Queen shook hands with Martin McGuinness, deputy first leader in the Stormont assembly, Northern Ireland's legislative council. McGuinness was allegedly an IRA commander in 1979, when a terrorist group murdered Earl Mountbatten, the Duke of Edinburgh's uncle. Nonetheless, as is often the case in Northern Ireland's strife-torn capital, protest was not far away even on this historic day. Irish Republicans had unfurled an enormous Irish

* In American English, "jail."

FIGURE 34. Loyalist mural, Shankill, Northern Ireland. Courtesy of John F. Sherry, Jr.

flag on Black Mountain overlooking Belfast. Its green, white, and gold stripes boldly visible below, the slogan painted above them challenged the Queen's authority to be there, claiming, "Eriu [Irish for Erin, a romantic name for Ireland used by nineteenth-century nationalists] is our Queen."[11]

Likewise, the lead-up to the Scottish vote for independence on September 18, 2014, raised many issues with respect to whether and how a relationship with the monarchy would continue should the referendum pass. Of course, the issue became moot when the referendum failed, with 55.3 percent voting "nae." A similar vote had failed in Australia in 1999, and in the aftermath of William and Catherine's successful royal tour of Australasia, it was reported that support for the monarchy in the country had doubled among Australians under the age of thirty.[12]

Another key pillar in the Royal Family's management of its global-brand dimension is its unofficial brand ambassadorship activities. However, the impact on the RFBC has not always been positive. In 2001, Prince Andrew officially began to act as the United Kingdom's Special Representative for International Trade and Investment. Nicknamed "Airmiles Andy" for his global jet-setting in the name of British business, he came under pressure to resign in 2011 after the criminal record of his American billionaire friend Jeffrey Epstein, who had served time for pedophilia, came to light. As 2014 came to a close, the impact of this relationship was exacerbated when a thirty-year-old woman included Prince Andrew as a party in a lawsuit against Epstein, for practices in which he offered underage women to his associates for sex. Andrew's ten-year career had been dogged with controversy and criticism over many dubious dealings; this was merely the final straw.[13] Yet in 2014, Andrew continued to engage in trade-related trips, prompting the government and the media to question why. For example, while visiting Bahrain on a trade mission, he praised its religious tolerance and diversity. His words baffled some reporters; the *Independent*'s headline read, "Prince Andrew Praises Bahrain, Island of Torture."[14]

The decision to (theoretically) phase out Andrew and provide the younger members of the Royal Family with more prominent international roles has boosted the global-brand component and rebranded the royal image. Unsurprisingly given their popularity, William, Catherine, and Harry have proven central to that effort. The princes have increasingly demonstrated their value to Britain, touring the world to raise money for charity (especially for their joint project, the Royal Foundation of the Duke and Duchess of Cambridge and Prince Harry) and promote British tourism and industry. Together and separately, the three leverage every opportunity to resonate in a world that finds the potent combination of youth and royalty hard to resist. As soon as the couple returned from their high-profile royal tour of Australia and New Zealand in May 2014, where they played a vital role in maintaining cordial Commonwealth relations, William was again making headlines for his charitable work. This time, his partner was David Beckham instead of Catherine, as prince and footballer teamed up to front an international wildlife crime campaign to stigmatize the purchase of ivory and rhino horn.

After a few false (but often entertaining) starts, Prince Harry is also proving his worth as an official ambassador for Britain. In 2013, he arrived at Milk Studios in New York City in a red double-decker bus to launch a global tour of the "GREAT Britain" campaign. The British government had initiated the effort to promote the nation internationally and to maximize the visibility and prestige gleaned from the one-two punch of the London Olympic Games and the Queen's Diamond Jubilee. Harry acted as an unofficial trade envoy, mixing and mingling with American and British companies from the creative and technological sectors to help cement business relationships between the two countries. In 2014, he launched the GREAT initiative in Brazil, encouraging its citizens to come to Britain to visit, study, and conduct business.

Harry's cousins (and Andrew's daughters), Princesses Beatrice and Eugenie, also have assisted with the campaign. In 2013, they drove around Berlin to launch the GREAT Britain MINI [Cooper] Tour, designed to promote British industry and tourism across Germany. Significantly, even the Queen lent her support to the initiative, allowing the government to commission a black-and-white photo portrait of her as the campaign included a celebration of her eighty-eighth birthday in 2014.

These good works by the young royals should ensure that their hard work will be rewarded on the global scale. Yet internal controversies and careful consideration of who will conduct brand-ambassador work for Britain and the RFBC, and how they will do it, demonstrate that alongside the Royal Standard, St. James's marketing professionals might consider raising a checkered caution flag as well. Those responsible for crafting the brand must consider how to make its narratives salient to an increasing sector of the British population whose roots stem from many regions of the globe, and for whom the historical significance of the Royal Family—its key point of differentiation from other complex human brands—may be minimal. Given the geographic scope of the Commonwealth, should the RFBC try to "bring home" more experiences that reflect the reach of the monarch's titular territory, rather than reserving the discourse of global diversity for its royal tours? In other words, should the monarchy strive to make the marketplace offerings and experiences that occur within Britain, including its traditional public rituals, more globally inclusive? Already, tourists can enjoy their visits to many royal residences in multiple languages. But in an increasingly hybridized world, these obvious but important nods to a global audience may need to be expanded. For example, actual product lines and experiences offered by the Royal Collection Trust and other monarchic stakeholders could revisit these offerings by adopting a global mindset (e.g., offering books in different languages or incorporating more aesthetic and historical elements of the Commonwealth realms into rituals that occur in the Mall outside Buckingham Palace and other tourist-heavy sites).

With respect to the second brand dimension, heritage, the RFBC is blessed with an abundance of narratives, repositories, and resources it can draw upon and embellish. The millions of pounds devoted to restoring and preserving ancient sites such as the Tower of London and Windsor Castle, as well as (relatively) more recent saga-steeped locales such as Balmoral, the Brighton Pavilion, Buckingham Palace, and Osborne House, allow the RFBC to satisfy visitors' desires and expectations within a variety of domains. These include aesthetics, co-creation, exhibits, food, generational and family appeal, shopping, and touristic pleasures, to name but a few. But as we demonstrate in our global discussion above, the RFBC needs to be increasingly concerned with the question "Whose heritage should the brand reflect?"

As a key royal stakeholder, Historic Royal Palaces positions itself squarely as an organization that tells stories linking the lives of past monarchs to those of contemporary visitors. Yet all British heritage-management organizations are well aware that macro-level initiatives such as the European Union have led to notable demographic shifts within Britain and Europe. Importantly, the United Kingdom's immigrants are increasingly different from each other as well. The 2011 census of England and Wales* reveals that Indian immigrants constitute the nation's largest ethnic minority group, and most new citizens come from that country. One in three London residents report being born overseas, and 24 percent of residents in the city are non-British nationals. The census also shows that Polish immigrants form the second-largest immigrant group, with Pakistan, Ireland, and Nigeria rounding out the top five sources of new residents.[15] Given the often dramatic cultural differences among these groups and the increasing size of the immigrant population, the RFBC and its partners will be challenged to create (or to facilitate the co-creation of) products, services, and experiences that resonate with these increasingly visible social groups.

Furthermore, controversies pertaining to the intersection of royalty and immigration may be brewing. The British oath of citizenship requires new citizens to promise "faithful and true allegiance to Her Majesty" and has become a point of contention in both Britain and Canada. In 2013, three Canadian immigrants filed a lawsuit to protest taking the oath as part of their path to citizenship; it was thrown out of court in 2014.[16] Likewise, British republicans argue that if new citizens need a British symbol to rally around, they can choose a "sports team, or [the actor] Stephen Fry."[17] On the

---

* Scotland and Northern Ireland conduct separate censuses.

other hand, some immigrants state that taking the oath makes them feel more emotionally connected to their new homeland.

Heritage is becoming an increasingly fluid and co-optable concept, as seen by the fact that other parts of the world now subsume British and royal heritage into their own cultures and for their own devices. Consider Thames Town, a replica English development nineteen miles from the center of Shanghai. Its architecture includes mock-Tudor buildings, Georgian terraces, and cobbled streets. It even boasts red telephone boxes and statues of Sir Winston Churchill and Princess Diana. Designed and developed by Atkins, a British engineering and design company, it opened in 2006. Often resembling a ghost town because buyers use the properties as investment purchases or second homes, one claim to fame is its popularity as a photographic venue for Chinese newlyweds. Its innovative location helps them fulfill a key norm of Chinese wedding rituals: staged photo shoots that present the couple as characters in exotic narratives. Nor does the Chinese passion for themed British icons stop there: Suzhou city, two hundred miles northwest of Shanghai, contains a reproduction London Bridge, along with other world landmarks.[18]

Doubtless, another pillar of support for the RFBC's heritage-brand dimension will be the activities that will mark the transition from Elizabeth II's reign to that of Charles III. It seems safe to predict that the outpourings of grief, respect, and reverence associated with the Queen's demise, as well as national and global grieving rituals laden with grandeur and even glamour, will eclipse the public mourning for Diana that captivated the world in September 1997. Indeed, it is highly likely that many of the Queen's subjects around the world, as well as millions of Anglophiles, will want to engage physically or psychologically in that historic cultural occasion. After all, over sixty (or perhaps even seventy) years will have elapsed since Britain last buried a monarch. As such, the Queen's funeral will possess two characteristics that contemporary global consumers find irresistible: novelty and scarcity.

Furthermore, the Queen's dutiful, faithful, moral, patriotic, and selfless persona leaves little doubt that her memory will be tangibilized in meaningful, permanent ways within Britain and around the world. Although we need not dwell on this inevitable outcome (and hope it is many years away), we believe it is safe to assume the British people and government will ensure that Elizabeth II's reign is historicized and honored across the world in accessible, aesthetically pleasing, and appropriate ways.

This point brings us to the next dimension of the RFBC, the human brand. Here, we focus on two key figures who play different but vital roles—Princes Charles and Harry. As we note above, the Queen is likely to be remembered as almost above reproach; her perceived mishandling of the Royal Family's response to Diana's death is generally regarded as one of the few missteps of her reign (perhaps even the only one). But Charles is decidedly different from his mother. Recalling our discussion in Chapter 1, it is fair to say he is likely the best exemplar of an ambiguous human brand within the RFBC.

As the cultural-heritage scholar Mike Robinson has pointed out, milestones such as the hundredth celebration of World War I often cause other entrenched social institutions to be brought into high relief, with cultural pundits reflecting upon and re-examining these institutions. This was the case when Charles turned sixty-five in 2013. The monikers the press and public generated to describe his past and present personas ranged from prescient environmentalist to royal style icon to good sport, on the positive side, to fastidious fussbudget, worrywart, lifelong "Nearly Man" (reflecting his long wait as heir apparent), loose cannon, and even "the Dork of England."*

In the late 1990s, after his marriage to Diana concluded, it was no secret that among the public, as well as within governmental and royal circles, Charles faced a serious image problem. His approval rating had dipped to 42 percent in 1996. Almost two decades later, after concerted efforts to craft and repair Charles's public persona, his rating had risen to 78 percent (the Queen's is 90 percent; Prince William's is 89 percent).

But Charles still ranks behind his mother and the triumvirate of William, Catherine, and Harry on the list of favorite Royal Family members.[19] As he moves ever closer to the time when he will be the focal face of the RFBC, there are still signs that he could prove problematic. His loose-cannon reputation surfaces with regularity, spurred by media reports that publicize controversial words and actions. In 2013, the British courts refused to release over two dozen "black-spider memos" (letters Charles had written to MPs in his scrawling longhand) to the liberal newspaper the *Guardian*. Charles had expressed his views on pressing political issues and even urged the MPs to take specific courses of action. The judicial system effectively prevented Charles from overstepping the established norm of royal neutrality on

* A label offered by a reader commenting on the online version of *Time*'s 2013 profile of Prince Charles.

political issues—in other words, from violating a core "brand promise" that the monarch would not interfere with governmental affairs.[20] Also that year, it was reported that the Duchy of Cornwall might be enjoying unfair tax advantages. In 2014, again violating the Royal Family's supposedly neutral political stance, Charles purportedly likened Vladimir Putin to Adolf Hitler as Russia made advances into the Ukraine.

Indeed, the reservations that many people share with respect to Charles's potential reign are dramatized in the quasi-Shakespearean tragedy *King Charles III,* a speculative play on the future of the monarchy, playing in London's West End when this book went to press.* The central plot thread revolves around the fact that after Charles ascends the throne, he almost immediately refuses to give royal assent to a parliamentary bill restricting press freedom. The play depicts the ensuing constitutional crisis his action provokes. In portraying Charles as a "tormented idealist,"[21] the drama cleverly exposes the underlying fear of many people: that although Charles may be well intentioned, his actions often seem to contain the seeds of disaster. A subplot of the play focuses on two key issues integral to the monarchy: the boundary between celebrity and royalty, and the tension between the monarch and the heir apparent, a saga that has afforded the Royal Family plenty of real drama over the centuries.

So how will St. James's Palace handle Charles III's image when he takes the throne? Clearly, the situation will be delicate, and the staff will have to both ratchet up reputational management and rein in his inclinations, without making the notoriously testy Charles feel handled. Crucial also to the RFBC is the fact that Charles will not automatically succeed as ruler of the Commonwealth; each nation will vote on whether to accept him in this role. In short, Charles's team will not market him in the same way as a premium brand of washing powder with a "special bluing agent," as he once feared. However, they must seek to create and leverage a persona that projects an able, accessible, and affable ambassador for Britain.

Even amid recent gaffes, Charles's rebranding has already begun in earnest. In 2013, one month before his sixty-fifth birthday, the cover of *Time* depicted a subdued, rather forlorn future king with the headline "The Forgotten Prince" (figure 35).[22] The substance of the sympathetic and somewhat laudatory cover story is that Charles is now understood as a man often

* It opened at the Almeida Theatre in April 2014, then moved to Wyndham's Theatre, where it proved so popular that its run was extended into 2015.

FIGURE 35. "The Forgotten Prince," *Time* cover reproduction.

ahead of his time, who has suffered ridicule for his once eccentric but now accepted opinions. Even his reported habit of talking to his plants to encourage growth has been vindicated. His role as royal activist, particularly in organic farming, architectural preservation, and environmental sustainability, represents a new persona among the RFBC stable. The article concludes that it is the right persona for the right time within the royal narrative.

The article also discussed Charles's softer side as husband and grandfather, bolstered a month later by the first interview his wife Camilla conducted with the press since their marriage.[23] The issue of Camilla's role as a human brand in the RFBC will soon come to the fore. When the couple married, it was implied that she would never be crowned as Charles's queen. Of course, such predictions and pronouncements are malleable, especially if careful and discrete polling indicates public approval of such an event.

From this sometimes error-prone prince, we now turn to the human brand in the RFBC who plays that role more consistently—Prince Harry. As we began this chapter, Harry was weeks from celebrating his thirtieth birthday on September 15, 2014. Building up to the day, some pundits began to emphasize his role as underdog in the royal narrative. William and Catherine's "heir and spare," Prince George and Princess Charlotte, make it highly unlikely that Harry will ever reign, nor has he married or started the family that the press reports that he desires.

In general, Harry's public persona is both that of a good bloke who possesses Diana's personal touch with people and a supportive sibling to the man who will one day be king. Since entering adulthood, his narrative has often stressed his unfettered masculinity, through persistent coverage of three themes: his love/sex life, his soldiering, and his swagger. Although he dated Chelsy Davy for six years, Harry rapidly acquired the playboy image his father once possessed—even as sources in the Royal Household note that Harry declared the summer of 2014 to be his last wild hurrah. His relative lack of responsibilities compared to William allows Harry's fun-loving nature room for many scrapes, as we have already documented. Yet it is precisely his conviviality that endears him to the public. As the wild child of the family, he keeps the RFBC from becoming too staid and remote.

At the same time, however, his advisers must ensure that Harry does not morph into his uncle Prince Andrew, whose high-life reputation and bad judgment in choosing friends and acquaintances have proved a liability. (Many argue that his bad judgment was in evidence in his choice of wife; Sarah Ferguson, Duchess of York, repeatedly embarrassed the Royal Family and provided regular fodder for the tabloids.)

In short, just as *Midsummer Night's Dream* needs Puck and *The Barber of Seville* needs Figaro, the Royal Family needs someone the public can count on to break up the monotony of a human brand primarily positioned around duty and morality. In other words, human-based brands need a relatively harmless fiasco every so often—one that is unorchestrated, so the brand does not seem inauthentic—to keep them interesting and spice up their core narratives. As Harry inevitably moves toward settling down, the question becomes where the RFBC will derive the unpredictability and comic relief that he, like his grandfather Prince Philip, sometimes provides.

Harry also plays a key role within the fourth component of the RFBC, the family-brand dimension. The quartet of William, Catherine, George, and "Uncle" Harry reinstated a much-needed symbol of family unity that Charles and Camilla, as heads of a blended family whose children have homes of their own, cannot provide. But although William and Catherine reinforce traditional family values, they also contemporize the monarchy's display of family by demonstrating a more intimate, emotional parenting style than their predecessors. (Diana, of course, was the exception.) It is no secret that Prince Charles felt his childhood was lonely. He was frequently left with a nanny while the Queen carried out her royal duties, which included embarking on long Commonwealth tours without her children. Charles shares little rapport with his father, the Duke of Edinburgh, who always failed to understand his most sensitive son and himself experienced a dysfunctional family upbringing.* The Duke's brusque, no-nonsense manner is thought to reflect the emotional void of his childhood.

By all accounts, Prince George's and Princess Charlotte's upbringings will be very different. William has been careful to demonstrate a modern, hands-on style of fathering, kissing and cuddling his children in public and even changing nappies in private. These actions contrast sharply with his father, who happily left daily household routines and child-raising to Diana and the staff, reflecting his generation's expectations of fatherhood. Contemporary fathers expect to take a more active role in their children's upbringing, and William's family involvement reflects that evolution in thinking. Significantly, however, it also symbolizes an evolving British monarchy, one more secure in expressing emotions.

All kinship circles, including royal ones, must flex and bend to accommodate the influx of new arrivals into the family fold. Many families find that in-law relationships are rarely simple and involve balancing loyalties and negotiating conflicting obligations. Whatever challenges the Middletons face as commoner in-laws engaged in trade, William and Catherine are determined that they will occupy a place of importance in the family dimension of the RFBC and "will not be airbrushed out of the picture as other royal in-laws have been."[24] William and Catherine spent their first Christmas as husband and wife at the Middleton home in Berkshire rather than attend-

* As chapter 8 notes, upon arriving in England as a child, Philip's care was left to generous relatives. His mother, Princess Alice of Battenberg, spent many years in a psychiatric asylum and subsequently entered a nunnery.

ing the customary royal gathering at Sandringham. Immediately after Prince George's birth, the family retreated to Berkshire while Catherine adapted to motherhood.

The Middletons' close family life appears to offer William a stable quality absent from his own upbringing, and he is said to be very comfortable calling his father-in-law either Mike or Dad. His in-laws exude an informality that is refreshing not only for William but also for the general public, many of whom identify with Carole's humble roots. Yet the middle-class values the Middletons infuse into the Royal Family, as well as the temptation to snub former friends and extended family, may risk compromising its mystique in the future. For if members of the Royal Family become too much like ordinary people, the question may arise—why do we need them?

Clearly, royal reproductive patterns have become more subdued in recent generations; compare George III's fifteen children or Queen Victoria's nine to the Queen's four. So it is likely that in-laws (especially photogenic ones like the Middletons) may prove to be more important and interesting to the media than in the past, since there are fewer actual royal progeny to write about. Some in-laws, like Catherine's siblings, Pippa and James, might only be peripheral players in the RFBC's core narrative—although recently, Pippa has shifted from activities that were potentially embarrassing to those revolving around charity work. Nonetheless, as with the Royal Family members themselves, these new relations can become sources of scandal or shame and damage the monarchy's mystique if their visible activities are not discretely managed and controlled.

We now arrive at the fifth and final dimension in the RFBC's crown—the luxury brand. The discourse that fuels the proliferation of these entities in contemporary consumer culture is that of entitlement—encapsulated succinctly in the slogan "I'm worth it," created in 1971 by L'Oréal, the world's largest cosmetics producer. The beauty of the slogan is that anyone—including an heir apparent who has waited to accede longer than anyone in his lineage—can explain why he or she deserves to indulge in the delights of the marketplace. (In *King Charles III,* the new monarch often argues that he is entitled to shape parliamentary policy, affirming that entitlement in contemporary society pervades politics as well as consumption.) This book presents a plethora of evidence that the RFBC's luxury dimension is highly seductive to consumers as well as stakeholders. In a recent survey, Chinese consumers ranked the Royal Family highest in terms of what they most associated with Britishness.* Leveraging this global-brand dimension, British luxury has become the epitome of high cultural capital that nouveaux riches around the world seek to emulate, a strong differentiating factor from other luxury European brands like Louis Vuitton and Prada.

As the most iconic symbol of British cultural capital, the fact that the RFBC often epitomizes British luxury in foreign markets may explain why many foreign brands outside the realm of EU and UK trademark law unabashedly name their products after Royal Family members. With the market for British luxury goods predicted to nearly double from £6.6 billion in 2012 to £12.2 billion in 2017, this sector's relationship with the RFBC is likely to strengthen in the future.[25] Middle- and upper-class consumers in emerging economies in Asia, the Middle East, and South America fervently buy top British brands such as Aston Martin, Rolls-Royce, and Burberry. As tourists, they flock to London's high-class department stores like Harvey Nichols and Harrods. In January 2014, the leading British luxury car manufacturer, Jaguar Land Rover, reported a sales increase of 39 percent in its Chinese market. Likewise, Burberry, synonymous with luxury British fashion, has enjoyed 20 percent annual sales growth in China in the past few years, boasts over seventy-eight stores in the country, and opened a stunning new flagship store in Shanghai in April 2014.

Paradoxically, however, while the RFBC's luxury dimension may provide both it and Britain with the winning edge among global consumers, ultimately this component may prove to be the most contentious to manage. As has always been the case, the Royal Family's lifestyle sharply illuminates and reinforces the difference between the haves and the have-nots. As such, it risks fueling antimonarchist sentiment by reminding people of an outdated class system that still exerts great economic, sociological, and political power in Britain. From 2013 to 2014, spending on upkeep of the royal residences increased by 45 percent. Likewise, Prince Charles's household has increased from 105 to 127 staff over the last six years.[26] Yet for much of the twenty-first century, Britain (and the world) endured a severe, multiyear recession, with the nation just beginning to see true signs of recovery in 2014. In prior years, Parliament slashed budget allocations for many key social programs, and the contrasting growth in the Crown's coffers fueled republican ire.

---

* David Beckham ranked second, exemplifying the rise of celebrity culture discussed earlier in this chapter.

Even the newest and most popular additions to the RFBC, William and Catherine, have not been spared criticism. In 2014, it was reported that £4 million ($6.5 million, four times the original estimate) was spent renovating Kensington Palace's famous apartment 1A. Though palace officials emphasized that these costs covered essential structural renovations and that the couple paid for interior decoration themselves, public skepticism was exacerbated by news that taxpayers had footed the bill for a second kitchen and several new bathrooms.

Prince Charles in particular has received much criticism over the years for his extravagant lifestyle. Sometimes referred to as the "pampered prince," with four valets to look after him and reputedly even a servant to squeeze toothpaste onto his brush, he likes to be fussed over. His public accounts in 2012 revealed that his personal spending had increased by 50 percent, provoking strong reactions from many quarters.*

Charles is an outspoken advocate of sustainability, at least in the area of land management. Paradoxically, he may increasingly find these values to be at loggerheads with his proclivity for indulgence, as the discourse that equates wastefulness with moral decrepitude is becoming more pervasive around the world. Another source of the luxury-goods critique stems from the wealthier "creative" segment of society—even from those producing such goods. British designer Jasper Morrison, whose style is described as utilitarian (but not inexpensive; his website offers a magazine rack for £210/$347), carped that the term *luxury* has "become an excuse for lack of common sense, and invariably stands for overpriced, poorly considered product."[27]

Despite the long list of extravagances that may attract some to the RFBC, contemporary Royal Family members will likely find themselves increasingly under pressure to curb their spending. Charles has been trying to overcome his spendthrift image for several years, and the Queen is notoriously cost conscious (it is rumored that she roams Buckingham Palace at night turning off lights). As early as 2002, the Lord Chamberlain's Office began to discuss staging a (relatively) scaled-down coronation ceremony for Charles. One recommendation under review is that he forgo the traditional elaborate coronation robes and "as an Admiral of the Fleet ... wear his full dress

* Of course, Charles follows a long line of monarchs and heirs apparent known for indulging their lavish tastes—including Henry VIII, Elizabeth I, Charles II, George IV, Edward VII, and the never-crowned Edward VIII.

uniform, though he will be crowned with St. Edward's Crown.... There will be fewer peers and peeresses in their robes, and a wider ethnic representation [among those] invited."[28]

Crucial to the RFBC's luxury-brand component will be how consumers continue to conceptualize and value luxury within this context and whether overall, the dimension will continue to be regarded as vital to the brand experience. Furthermore, it remains to be seen whether British manufacturers will regard as desirable royal promotion of luxury brands in their roles as institutional figureheads or grantors of the Royal Warrant. It will also be interesting to see whether and how Charles will reconcile his luxury-laden lifestyle with the increasingly fervent global discourse on sustainable consumption practices. In short, the RFBC cannot merely assume that consumers will continue to be grateful for exposure to or immersion in royal-controlled or preserved luxury goods or experiences. Instead, the RFBC must revisit the current perks and pitfalls of being a luxury brand in an increasingly resource-constrained world, and consider ways to adapt its narrative accordingly.

Our exploration of how the RFBC is manifest in (mostly) contemporary consumer culture is now at an end. At least in the foreseeable future, the trajectory of the brand's narrative seems to point steadily upward, as the two men and the toddler who are the three princes in the line of succession enjoy popularity within Britain and beyond. Furthermore, the brand's vitality seems to completely eradicate the pronouncement made by Tom Nairn 1994, that in any "spiritual or ideological sense . . . the House of Windsor is dead. It may continue in a moribund and more or less festering condition for as long as Queen Elizabeth lasts. But this only confirms the [assertion]."[29] Whatever side of the royal commemorative coin people may find themselves on with regard to the British monarchy, we are confident that the RFBC and its stakeholders will continue to offer a cornucopia of commercial and cultural touch points to captivate or challenge a variety of ideologies, imaginations, and itineraries.

Using the benchmark of William the Conqueror's coronation on Christmas Day 1066 as its "official" beginning, will the RFBC celebrate its thousand-year anniversary in approximately half a century? Although fifty years is a mere drop in the bucket for the lineage, it remains to be seen whether that commemoration will come to pass. Almost two decades into the twenty-first century, it seems almost a certainty that future generations will one day raise a glass to toast the new King George VII (if William and

Catherine's son chooses to be styled in that manner). Such is the power of a resilient brand like the RFBC, fueled as it is by almost ten centuries of compelling narratives that interlace family, globalization, heritage, humanity, and luxury—and the compelling core narratives that together constitute Britain's past, present, and future place on the world stage.

FIGURE 36. "A Right Royal Weekend," London bus ad. Photo by Cele Otnes.

Explanation of Fieldwork

Our fieldwork officially began in May 2005, when Cele Otnes met the manager of the former Hope and Glory commemorative store, located in the Kensington area of central London, and he encouraged her to contact Margaret Tyler. Over the course of nine years, we visited numerous royal-related sites and conducted formal interviews, informal conversations, and observations with dozens of people engaged in royal consumption, co-creation, and production. These included authors, educators, and employees of hotels, newspapers, magazines, museums, retail shops, restaurants, and tourist sites. The list of sites we visited include all five London-area Royal residences managed by Historic Royal Palaces (especially Kensington Palace and Hampton Court, which we visited multiple times), several multiday immersions in Windsor (where, besides the castle itself, we observed activities in souvenir shops, the Windsor Royal Borough Museum in the Guildhall, the Long Walk, and the Royal Farms Windsor Farm Shop), Buckingham Palace, multiple stays at Margaret Tyler's Heritage House Bed and Breakfast (and several of her royal-themed parties), trips to Althorp, the Wedgwood pottery in Stoke-on-Trent, the site of the excavation of Richard III in Leicester, various retailers in London and other parts of Britain, London's Jermyn Street, and exhibits in the National Portrait Gallery, the Queen's Gallery at Buckingham Palace, and the Museum of Advertising, Brands, and Packaging.

We also attended royal-related events such as the Trooping the Colour ceremony in 2012, royal wedding and birthday parties in London and Leicester, the annual commemoration of Princess Diana's death at the Kensington Palace gates, the Queen's visit to Royal Holloway University in the spring of 2014, and the final ceremony on Armistice Day at *Blood Swept*

Lands and Seas of Red, known colloquially as the "poppies exhibit" at the Tower of London. We also visited several royal exhibits outside of England, including the Diana traveling exhibit in Toronto and the Queen Mary in Long Beach, California. We taped and transcribed all formal interviews and made notes of conversations with those we met informally with their permission. We created extensive field notes for our observations; our data set comprises over 1,500 pages of text. We also took over one thousand photos and videoed select events.

In terms of archival research, we read extensively about the intersection of the monarchy and consumer/material culture in works by historians, journalists, biographers, and other popular and academic authors. We immersed ourselves in the ever-growing genre of royal documentaries. Pauline Maclaran watched all the key films containing royal figures made over the last twenty-five years (e.g., *Henry V, Elizabeth, The Queen,* and *The King's Speech*), as well as many historical ones (e.g., *Anne of the Thousand Days*). She also viewed all episodes of *The Tudors* and examined archival footage of popular British television shows that featured the Royal Family, such as *Spitting Image, Monty Python's Flying Circus,* and *Blackadder.* We also attended a production of *King Charles III* at Wyndham's Theatre in London in November 2014.

NOTES

PREFACE

1. Patrick Montague-Smith, *The Royal Family Pop-Up Book* (London: Crescent, 1988).

2. "How We Valued the Monarchy as a Brand: Public Opinion," *Brand Finance Journal*, May 27, 2012.

3. Alan Travis, "Support for Royal Family Falls to New Low," *Guardian,* June 11, 2000.

4. Tom Clark, "Queen Enjoys Record Support in *Guardian/*ICM poll," *Guardian,* May 24, 2012.

5. Maev Kennedy, "Duchess of Cambridge's Wedding Dress Draws Record Visitors to Palace," *Guardian,* Oct. 4, 2011.

6. See Kathryn Jones, *For the Royal Table: Dining at the Palace* (London: Royal Collection Enterprises, 2008); Charles Oliver, *Dinner at Buckingham Palace* (New York: Prentice-Hall, 1972); Ingrid Seward, *Royal Style* (New York: St. Martin's Press, 1988).

7. David Starkey, *Music and Monarchy* (London: BBC Digital, 2013), book with DVD; Mark Rankin, Christopher Highley, and John N. King, eds., *Henry VIII and His Afterlives: Literature, Politics and Art* (Cambridge: Cambridge University Press, 2013); Rufus Bird, Desmond Shawe-Taylor, Wolf Burchard, Kate Heard, and Kathryn Jones, *The First Georgians: Art and Monarchy 1714–1760* (London: Royal Collection Trust, 2014).

INTRODUCTION

1. Cele Otnes interview with John Pym, former manager of Hope and Glory commemorative store, London, July 2005.

2. Harry Mount, "Why the Queen Is Never Going to Abdicate," *Daily Telegraph,* Jan. 29, 2013.

3. Cannon and Griffiths, *Oxford Illustrated History,* 459–61.

4. Eleanor Beardsley, "Royalists Want Monarchy to Return to France," *NPR,* Jan. 27, 2010.

5. Lytton Strachey, *Queen Victoria* (New York: Harcourt, 1925), 311.

6. Kidlow and Gilbey, *The Really Useful Guide to the Kings and Queens of England,* 5.

7. Jane Johnson Lewis, "How Are Queen Elizabeth II and Prince Philip Related?" About.com Women's history.

8. Kidlow and Gilbey, *The Really Useful Guide to the Kings and Queens of England,* 5.

9. Cannon and Griffiths, *Oxford Illustrated History,* 40.

10. Robert Booth, "Secret Paper Shows Extent of Senior Royals' Veto over Bills," *Guardian,* Jan. 14, 2013.

11. John Cannon, *The Modern British Monarchy: A Study in Adaptation* (Reading, UK: University of Reading, 1987), 4.

12. Bagehot, *The English Constitution,* 64.

13. Bernard Nurse, "The Society of Antiquaries of London," *Making History,* www.history.ac.uk.

14. Kidlow and Gilbey, *The Really Useful Guide to the Kings and Queens of England,* 88.

15. "The Royal Household," Royal.gov.uk.

16. Vrushti Mawani, "Marriage Majestic: William-Kate Wedding to Cost $70 Million," *Industry Leader.*

17. Smith, *Elizabeth the Queen,* 506.

18. "Queen's Funding to Rise by £5m under New Sovereign Grant," *BBC News,* April 2, 2013.

19. Chris Kohler, "The Business of Royalty: The Five Richest Monarchs in the World," *Business Spectator,* April 24, 2014.

20. Smith, *Elizabeth the Queen,* 245.

CHAPTER 1

1. "The Brit List: Summer of London," *BBC America,* Aug. 16, 2012.

2. Stephen Bayley, "Queen of Cool: A Jubilee Tribute Like No Other You Will Read . . ." *Daily Mail,* May 26, 2012.

3. Andrew Rawnsley, "Diamond Jubilee: Congrats, Ma'am, on Preserving the Monarchy in a Populist Age," *Guardian/Observer,* June 2, 2012.

4. Richard Scully and Marian Quartly, *Drawing the Line: Using Cartoons as Historical Evidence* (Clayton, Australia: Monash University e-Press, 2009).

5. Smith, *Elizabeth the Queen,* 386.

6. Philip Hall notes in *Royal Fortune: Tax, Money and the Monarchy* (London: Bloomsbury Press, 1992) that Victoria, Edward VII, and George V all had paid taxes; the Queen's father, George VI, put a stop to the practice.

7. Cele Otnes interview with Margaret Tyler, April 7, 2005.

8. Dark tourism focuses on places where tragedies or deaths of historic merit have occurred; it has become increasingly popular in recent years. See Philip Stone and Richard Sharpley, "Consuming Dark Tourism: A Thanatological Perspective," *Annals of Tourism Research* 35, no. 2 (1998): 574–99.

9. Sharpe, *Selling the Tudor Monarchy,* 97.

10. Ackroyd, *London,* 146.

11. John Urry, *The Tourist Gaze* (London: Sage, 1990).

12. See Sharpe's *Selling the Tudor Monarchy* for an excellent, comprehensive discussion of how the Tudor monarchs, especially Henry VIII and Elizabeth I, used material culture to craft and control their image.

13. Cannon and Griffiths, *Oxford Illustrated History.*

14. "Coinage and Bank Notes," Royal.gov.uk.

15. "Secrets of the Royal Bedchamber," BBC4 documentary, August 5, 2013.

16. Ridley, *The Heir Apparent,* 155, 495.

17. Hywel Williams, "The Iron Queen," *Guardian,* June 22, 2000.

18. This tradition began with George III; Elizabeth II ended it in 1957.

19. Cele Otnes field notes, Windsor, England, April 9, 2005.

20. Except where permission was specifically given to use real names, pseudonyms are used throughout.

21. Cele Otnes interview with "Thomas," London, July 2007.

22. Cele Otnes interview with Margaret Tyler, July 24, 2005.

23. Cele Otnes and Pauline Maclaran, interview with "John," England, July 2007.

24. Born in 1927, he became King of Thailand in 1946.

25. Philip Long, "Introduction," *Royal Tourism,* 5.

26. Nairn, *The Enchanted Glass.*

27. Bernard Cova, Robert V. Kozinets, and Avi Shankar, *Consumer Tribes* (New York: Taylor & Francis, 2007).

28. Cele Otnes conversation with Sharon Shavitt, October 2012.

29. Long and Palmer, *Royal Tourism.*

30. Staff blogger, "On the Way Out, Like M&S Knickers," *New Statesman,* April 16, 2001, 4.

31. Julie Guérineau, "The British Royal Family: A Very Profitable Brand," *Pressbook de Julie Guérineau,* https://julieguerineau.wordpress.com/2012/04/27/the-british-royal-family-a-very-profitable-brand/.

32. Leslie de Charnatony and Francesca Dall'Olmo Riley, "Defining a 'Brand': Beyond the Literature with Experts' Interpretations," *Journal of Marketing Management* 14, no. 5 (1988): 417–43.

33. Marie-Agnès Parmentier, "When David Met Victoria: Forging a Strong Family Brand," *Family Business Review* 24, no. 3 (2011): 219.

34. John M. T. Balmer, "Corporate Heritage Identities, Corporate Heritage Brands and the Multiple Heritage Identities of the British Monarchy," *European Journal of Marketing* 45, nos. 9/10 (2011): 1386.

35. Ibid., 1396–97.

36. John M. T. Balmer, "Corporate Heritage Brands and the Precepts of Corporate Heritage Brand Management: Insights from the British Monarchy on the Eve of the Royal Wedding of Prince William (April 2011) and Queen Elizabeth II's Diamond Jubilee (1952–2012)," *Journal of Brand Management* 18, no. 8 (2011): 517–44.

37. "Fairy Tale Timeline," *SurLaLuneFairytales.com.*

38. Behice Ece Ilhan, "Transmedia Consumption Experiences: Consuming and Co-Creating Interrelated Stories across Media" (PhD diss., University of Illinois at Urbana-Champaign, 2011).

39. Matthew Thomson, "Human Brands: Investigating Antecedents to Consumers' Strong Attachments to Celebrities," *Journal of Marketing* 70 (July 2006): 114.

40. Ibid., 116.

41. Joe Hildebrand, "Etiquette: The Dos and Don'ts of Meeting Her Majesty Queen Elizabeth II," Mews Corp Australia Newspapers, June 2, 2012.

42. Stephen Brown, Pierre McDonagh, and Clifford J. Schultz II, "Titanic: Consuming the Myths and Meanings of an Ambiguous Brand," *Journal of Consumer Research* 40 (Dec. 2013): 595–614.

43. Ridley, *The Heir Apparent,* 353.

44. Danielle Sacks, "Chelsea Clinton Makes Her Move," *Fast Company* 185 (May 2014): 54+.

45. Parmentier, "When David Met Victoria," 219–20.

46. Sharpe, *Selling the Tudor Monarchy,* 189.

47. Ridley, *The Heir Apparent,* 36.

48. Cele Otnes interview with Margaret Tyler, July 24, 2005.

49. Balmer, "Corporate Heritage Brands and the Precepts of Corporate Heritage Brand Management," 529.

50. Dennis Rook, "The Ritual Dimension of Consumer Behavior," *Journal of Consumer Research* 12 (Dec. 1985): 252–64.

51. J. A. C. Roberts, *Coronation* (London: Ivor Nicholson and Watson, 1953).

52. Peter Pigott, *Royal Transport: An Inside Look at the History of Royal Travel* (Toronto: Dundurn, 2005), 138.

53. Caroline Tynan, Sally McKenchie, and Celine Chhuoun, "Co-creating Value for Luxury Brands," *Journal of Business Research* 63 (Nov. 2010): 1156.

54. Jean-Noël Kapferer, *The Luxury Strategy: Break the Rules of Marketing to Build Luxury Brands* (Philadelphia: Kogan Page, 2012), 13.

55. Sharpe, *Selling the Tudor Monarchy,* 412.

56. John Clarke, "George IV," in Antonia Fraser, ed., *The Lives of the Kings and Queens of England* (New York: Alfred A. Knopf, 1975), 287–88.

57. Luisa Kroll, "Just How Rich Are Queen Elizabeth and Her Family?" *Forbes,* April 22, 2011.

58. Lucy Cockcroft, "Buckingham Palace Valued at Close to £1 Billion," *Daily Telegraph,* Sept. 2, 2008.

59. Smith, *Elizabeth the Queen,* 513.

CHAPTER 2

1. Sue Shellenbarger, "When a Genealogy Hobby Digs Up Unwanted Secrets," *Wall Street Journal*, January 15, 2013.
2. Alan Farnham, "Who's Your Daddy? Genealogy Is 1.8 Billion Business," *ABC News*, Oct. 24, 2012.
3. Judi Hasson, "Are You Related to Royalty?" *AARP*, April 14, 2011.
4. Munich, *Queen Victoria's Secrets*, 26.
5. Ibid., 30.
6. Cannon and Griffiths, *Oxford Illustrated History*, 548.
7. Robert Lacey, *Majesty: Elizabeth II and the House of Windsor* (New York: Harcourt, Brace, Jovanovich, 1977), 181.
8. Arbiter, *On Duty with the Queen*, 62.
9. Lacey, *Majesty*, 187.
10. Caroline de Guitat, *The Royal Tour: A Souvenir Album* (London: Royal Collection Trust, 2009), 19.
11. Joanna Zelman, "Queen Elizabeth II Visits Ireland, First Trip by British Monarch in 100 Years," *Huffington Post*, May 17, 2011.
12. Lacey, *Majesty*, 184.
13. Pigott, *Royal Transport*, 52.
14. Hoey, *The Royal Yacht Britannia*, 26.
15. Nick Yaohnanen, "South Sea Tribe Prepares Birthday Feast for Their Favourite God, Prince Philip," *Telegraph*, Feb. 19, 2007.
16. Sharpe, *Selling the Tudor Monarchy*, 321.
17. Ibid., 362.
18. Ibid., 389.
19. Meyer, *The Tudors*, 436.
20. Sharpe, *Selling the Tudor Monarchy*, 430.
21. *Oxford Illustrated History*, 338.
22. John M. T. Balmer, "Scrutinising the British Monarchy: The Corporate Brand That Was Shaken, Stirred, and Survived," *Management Decision* 47 (2009): 649.
23. Ridley, *The Heir Apparent*, 427.
24. Ibid., 306.
25. Pearson, *The Selling of the Royal Family*, 30.
26. Ibid., 49.
27. Ibid., 46.
28. Smith, *Elizabeth the Queen*, 88–89.
29. "The Story of BBC Television—TV's Crowning Moment," *BBC—the BBC Story*.
30. *The Royals*, 213.
31. Hoey, *At Home with the Queen*, 239.
32. Smith, *Elizabeth the Queen*, 417–19.
33. Ibid., 342–43.

34. David Bowen, "Monarchs Without a Cause," *Financial Times,* May 31, 2002.

35. Arbiter, *On Duty with the Queen,* 89.

36. Ridley, *The Heir Apparent,* 563.

37. Edwards, *Royal Sisters,* 180.

38. Ibid., 128–29.

39. Harry Wallop, "Royal Wedding: Marriage Will Cost Economy £5bn," *Telegraph,* Nov. 23, 2010.

40. Patrick Barkham, "Royal Wedding Street Parties—an Endangered Species," *Guardian,* April 4, 2011.

41. The speech can be heard at http://www.youtube.com/watch?v= Bf30P_PbcZo.

42. Smith, *Elizabeth the Queen,* 140.

43. ABC's 'Concert for the Queen' Tops Premieres on NBC and FOX, *Tvbythenumbers,* June 6, 2012.

44. Cele Otnes interview with Mike Robinson, June 2012.

45. C. S. Lewis, *Mere Christianity* (New York: HarperCollins, 1980), xiii.

46. Nairn, *The Enchanted Glass,* xix.

47. Cannadine, *The Decline and Fall of the British Aristocracy.*

48. Hoey, *At Home with the Queen,* 217.

49. Ibid., 215.

50. "Firm Donates Royal Wedding Mugs to Children," *BBC News,* April 29, 2011.

51. Tamarkin, *Anglophilia,* 75.

52. Jones, *Accent on Privilege,* 142.

53. Prochaska, *The Eagle and the Crown,* 17.

54. Ibid., 28.

55. Ibid., 32.

56. Ibid., 45; for a pithy description of the debacle, see Balmer, "Scrutinising the British Monarchy," 649.

57. "Conserving Royal Wedding Dresses," *Royal Wedding Dress.*

58. Ridley, *The Heir Apparent,* 59.

59. Ian Radforth, *Royal Spectacle: The 1860 Visit of the Prince of Wales to Canada and the United States* (Toronto: University of Toronto Press, 2004), 313.

60. Ibid., 357–62.

61. Dana Bentley-Cranch, *Edward VII: Image of an Era 1841–1910* (London: Her Majesty's Stationery Office, 1992), 1.

62. Prochaska, *The Eagle and the Crown,* 151.

63. Michael O'Connell, "TV Ratings: 'Downton Abbey' Makes PBS Return to Record 10.2 Million Viewers," *Hollywood Reporter,* January 6, 2014.

64. "China Falls for Downton Abbey Effect," *Sunday Express,* Aug. 4, 2013.

65. "Hungry for Britain! UK Is Number One Vacation Spot for Americans," *Visit Britain Media Centre,* Oct. 1, 2010.

66. Cele Otnes interview with Bob Houston, July 2005.

67. Cele Otnes interview with Theodore Harvey, July 2014.

68. Cele Otnes interview with Andrew Lannerd, October 2014.

69. Sam Friedman, "The Cultural Currency of a 'Good' Sense of Humour: British Comedy and New Forms of Distinction," *British Journal of Sociology* 62, no. 2 (2011): 347.

70. Fox, *Watching the English*, 61.

71. Louis Cazmian, *The Development of English Humor, Parts I and II* (Durham, NC: Duke University Press, 1952).

72. Maev Kennedy, "Royal Wedding Cartoons Show William and Kate Are Lucky It's 2011," *Guardian*, April 2, 2011.

73. Colin Seymour-Ure, "What Future for the British Political Cartoon?" *Journalism Studies* 2, no. 3 (2001): 351.

74. Ibid.

75. "Cartoonists and the Royal Family, 1953–2003," April 1, 2009, https://www.cartoons.ac.uk/group/cartoonists-and-royal-family-1953–2003.

76. "ABC Forced to Pull Chaser Wedding Coverage," *Australian Broadcasting Corporation*, April 27, 2011.

77. "Kate and William Rule Out Souvenir Tea Towels on the Grounds of 'Taste and Decency'" *Hello*, December 9, 2010.

78. Leah Mclaren, "Welcome to the Silly Games," *MacLean's* 125, no. 31 (Aug. 13, 2012): 45.

79. "London Attracts Record Number of Visitor Arrivals in 2013," *ASIAtravel-tips.com*, May 9, 2014.

80. "The Queen Kicks Off Summer with First Garden Party at Buckingham Palace," *Hello*, May 21, 2014.

CHAPTER 3

1. Cele C. Otnes and Eliana N. Shapiro, "How Brand Collecting Shapes Consumers' Brand Meanings," in Russell W. Belk and John F. Sherry, Jr., eds., *Consumer Culture Theory: Research in Consumer Behavior* Volume 11 (Oxford, Elsevier, 2007): 401–19.

2. Cele Otnes Interview with Deirdre Murphy, July 2005.

3. Albert M. Muñiz and Thomas C. O'Guinn, "Brand Community," *Journal of Consumer Research* 27 (March 2001): 412–32.

4. Russell W. Belk, *Collecting in a Consumer Society* (New York: Routledge, 1995), 125.

5. Ibid., 94.

6. Ibid.

7. Russell W. Belk, "Possessions and the Extended Self," *Journal of Consumer Research* 15 (Sept. 1988): 139–68.

8. Rebecca English, "Just Like Windsor (Sort Of): Step Inside the B&B That Is Obsessed with the Royal Family," *Daily Mail*, May 9. 2012.

9. James H. McAlexander, John W. Schouten, and Harold F. Koenig, "Building Brand Community," *Journal of Marketing* 66 (Jan. 2002): 38–54.

10. Bernard Cova and Daniele Dalli, "Working Consumers: The Next Step in Marketing Theory?" *Marketing Theory* 9, no. 3 (2009): 315–39.

11. Meera P. Venkatraman, "Opinion Leaders, Adopters, and Communicative Adopters: A Role Analysis," *Psychology and Marketing* 6, no. 1 (1989): 51–68.

12. Philip Allen, "The Royal Baby: A Collector's Guide," *Telegraph*, July 20, 2013.

13. Christopher Wilson, "The Sun Goes Down on the Althorp Shrine to Diana, Princess of Wales," *Telegraph*, Aug. 13, 2013.

14. McAlexander, Schouten, and Koenig, "Building Brand Community."

15. Ibid.

16. Cele C. Otnes and Pauline Maclaran, "The Consumption of Cultural Heritage among a British Royal Family Brand Tribe," in Robert Kozinets, Bernard Cova, and Avi Shankar, eds., *Consumer Tribes: Theory, Practice, and Prospects* (London: Elsevier/Butterworth-Heinemann, 2007): 51–66.

17. M. Maffesoli, *The Time of the Tribes* (London: Sage, 1996).

18. Bernard Cova and Veronique Cova, "Tribal Marketing: The Tribalisation of Society and Its Impact on the Conduct of Marketing," *European Journal of Marketing* 36, nos. 5/6 (2002): 595–620.

19. Robert V. Kozinets, "E-tribalized Marketing? The Strategic Implications of Virtual Communities of Consumption," *European Management Journal* 17, no. 3 (1999): 252–64.

20. Michael Billig, *Talking of the Royal Family* (New York: Routledge, 1982), 1.

21. Muñiz and O'Guinn, "Brand Community."

22. Ibid.

23. Peyton, *Brilliant Britain*, 186.

24. Jennifer Smith, "A Throne Fit for a Pearly King: Fundraisers Descend on London Streets in Dazzling Procession to Mark the Beginning of Autumn," *Daily Mail*, Sept. 29, 2013.

25. Jasper Copping, "Morris Men Must Allow In Morris Women—but Not to Dance," *Telegraph*, April 24, 2011.

26. In *The Time of the Tribes*, Maffesoli describes the characteristics of neo-tribes as fluidity, the tendency to gather occasionally, and also a tendency to disperse.

27. Cele Otnes interview with Bob Houston, July 2005.

CHAPTER 4

1. Stephen Jeffreys made this comment after his presentation, "Writing Royalty: From Throne to Screen," at the Making of the Modern Monarchy Conference, Kensington Palace, London, June 2012.

2. Marilyn Morris, "The Royal Family and Family Values in Late Eighteenth Century England," *Journal of Family History* 21, no. 4 (1996): 519–32.

3. Tim Clayton and Phil Craig, *Diana: Story of a Princess* (London: Hodder & Stoughton, 2001), 1–14.

4. Ann Barr and Peter York, *The Official Sloane Ranger Handbook* (London: Ebury Press, 1982): 29.

5. Neeru Paharia, Anat Keinan, Jill Avery, and Juliet B. Schor, "The Underdog Effect: The Marketing of Disadvantage and Determination through Brand Biography," *Journal of Consumer Research* 37, no. 5 (2011): 775–90.

6. Beatrice Behlen, "'Does Your Highness Feel Like a Gold Person or a Silver One?' Princess Margaret and Dior," *Costume* 46, no. 1 (2012): 56.

7. Jacqueline E. Sharkey, "The Diana Aftermath," *American Journalism Review,* Nov. 1997, 3.

8. Raka Shome, "White Femininity and the Discourse of the Nation: Re/membering Princess Diana," *Feminist Media Studies* 1, no. 3 (2001): 323–42.

9. Marguerite Helmers, "Media, Discourse, and the Public Sphere: Electronic Memorials to Diana, Princess of Wales," *College English* 63, no. 1 (2001): 437–57.

10. Guy Debord, *The Society of the Spectacle,* trans. Donald Nicholson-Smith (New York: Zone Books, 1967); Jill R. Chaney, "Diana Doubled: The Fairytale Princess and the Photographer," *NWSA Journal* 11, no. 2 (1999): 163–75.

11. "Prince Charles and Lady Diana Spencer's Wedding," *BBC History,* June 21, 2014.

12. Cele C. Otnes and Elizabeth H. Pleck, *Cinderella Dreams: The Allure of the Lavish Wedding* (Berkeley: University of California Press, 2003).

13. Jeffrey Richards, Scott Wilson, and Linda Woodhead, *Diana: The Making of a Media Saint* (London: I. B. Tauris, 1999).

14. Helmers, *Media, Discourse, and the Public Sphere,* 437.

15. Clayton and Craig, *Diana,* 45.

16. Ibid., 79.

17. Michael Levine, *The Princess and the Package: Exploring the Love-Hate Relationship between Diana and the Media* (Los Angeles: Renaissance Books, 1998).

18. Ibid.

19. "Timeline: Diana, Princess of Wales," *Vogue,* www.vogue.co.uk/person /diana,-princess-of-wales/covers.

20. *Vogue,* Oct. 1997.

21. Andrew Morton, *Diana: Her True Story* (London: Michael O'Mara Books, 1998).

22. Jeremy Paxman, *On Royalty: A Very Public Inquiry into Some Strangely Related Families* (New York: PublicAffairs, 2007).

23. Rosalind Coward, *Female Desire: Women's Sexuality Today* (London: Paladin, 1984): 163–71.

24. Christine Geraghty, "Story," *Screen* 39, no. 1 (1998): 70–73.

25. Ibid., 71.

26. Ien Ang, *Watching Dallas: Soap Opera and the Melodramatic Imagination* (London: Routledge, 1985).

27. Coward, *Female Desire,* 163–71.

28. Robert Turnock, *Interpreting Diana: Television Audiences and the Death of a Princess* (London: British Film Institute, 2000): 40–41.

29. Morton, *Diana*, 335.

30. Jonathan Dimbleby, *The Prince of Wales: A Biography* (New York: William Morrow, 1994).

31. Sabine Kowal and Daniel C. O'Connell, "Theoretical Ideals and Their Violation: Princess Diana and Martin Bashir in the BBC Interview," *Pragmatics* 7, no. 3 (1997): 309–23.

32. Anna Pasternak, *Princess in Love* (London: Bloomsbury, 1994).

33. Kowal and O'Connell, "Theoretical Ideals," 309–23.

34. Ibid.

35. Julie Burchill, *Diana* (London: Weidenfeld and Nicholson, 1998); Beatrix Campbell, *Diana, Princess of Wales: How Sexual Politics Shook the Monarchy* (London: Women's Press, 1998).

36. Jude Davies, *Diana, a Cultural History: Gender, Race, Nation and the People's Princess* (Hampshire, UK: Palgrave, 2001): 49.

37. Rosalind Brunt, "Princess Diana: A Sign of the Times," in *Diana: The Making of a Media Saint,* ed. Jeffrey Richards, Scott Wilson, and Linda Woodhead (London: I. B. Tauris, 1999), 20–39.

38. Robert Lacey, "The Truth about Diana and the Queen: How Monarch Was Princess's Greatest Supporter . . . until THAT Martin Bashir Documentary," *Daily Mail,* January 28, 2012.

39. Chris Hastings, "Queen Sacked Us over Diana Interview, Says BBC," *Telegraph,* January 29, 2006.

40. Brunt, "Princess Diana," 20–21.

41. Clayton and Craig, *Diana*, 357.

42. Richards, Wilson, and Woodhead, *Diana*, 3.

43. Rosie Taylor, "The Ultimate Chart Rundown: Elton John's Candle in the Wind Diana Tribute Tops List of UK Best-Selling Singles," *Mailonline,* Nov. 5, 2012.

44. Turnock, *Interpreting Diana*, 7–31.

45. Frank Furedi, *Therapy Culture: Cultivating Vulnerability in an Uncertain Age* (London: Routledge, 2004): 18.

46. Jonathan Freedland, "Mourning Diana: A Moment of Madness," *Guardian,* Aug. 13, 2007.

47. A. N. Wilson, *Victoria: A Life* (New York: Penguin, 2014): 21.

48. Stephen C. Behrendt, "Mourning, Myth and Merchandising: The Public Death of Princess Charlotte," *Canadian Review of Comparative Literature* 30, no. 1 (2003): 75–95.

49. Ibid., 92.

50. Ibid., 90.

51. Dean and Cannons of Windsor, "The Funeral of Princess Charlotte," *Chapel Archives and Chapter Library,* April 2, 2012.

52. Helmers, *Media, Discourse, and the Public Sphere,* 437.

53. J. Gregory Payne, *An Era of Celebrity and Spectacle: The Global Rhetorical Phenomenon of the Death of Diana, Princess of Wales* (Boston: Emerson College, 1997), 1.

54. William J. Brown, Michael D. Basil, and Mihai C. Bocarnea, "Social Influence of an International Celebrity: Responses to the Death of Princess Diana," *Journal of Communication* 53, no 4 (2003): 587–605.

55. Ibid.

56. Richard Alwyn, "Modern Times: The Shrine," BBC4 documentary, Aug. 29, 2012.

57. Donald Horton and R. Richard Wohl, "Mass Communication and Parasocial Interaction: Observations on Intimacy at a Distance," *Psychiatry* 19, no. 3 (1956): 215–29; Cristel Antonia Russell, Andrew T. Norman, and Susan E. Heckler, "The Consumption of Television Programming: Development and Validation of the Connectedness Scale," *Journal of Consumer Research* 31, no. 1 (2004): 150–61.

58. Russell W. Belk, "Possessions and the Extended self," *Journal of Consumer Research* 15, no 2 (1988): 139–68.

59. Jane Parish, "The Age of Anxiety," in *The Age of Anxiety: Conspiracy Theory and the Human Sciences,* ed. Jane Parish and Martin Parker (Oxford: Blackwell, 2001), 1–16.

60. Ibid., 2–4.

61. Jon King and John Beveridge, *Princess Diana: The Evidence* (New York: SPI Books, 1999).

62. David Icke, *The Biggest Secret: The Book That Will Change the World* (Isle of Wight, UK: Bridge of Love, 1999).

63. Martyn Gregory, *Diana: The Last Days* (London: Random House, 2007).

64. Anita Singh and Gordon Raynor, "Unlawful Killing: Film about the Death of Diana Likens Prince Philip to Fred West," *Telegraph,* May 13, 2011.

65. Martyn Gregory, *The Diana Conspiracy Exposed: The Definitive Account of the Last Days and Death of Diana, Princess of Wales* (Milford, CT: Olmstead Press, 2000).

66. Nick Harding, "Truth and Lies: Conspiracy Theories Are Running Rampant Thanks to Modern Technology," *Independent,* Nov, 12, 2011.

67. Thomas Bloom, "Morbid Tourism: The Case of Diana, Princess of Wales and Althorp House," in *Royal Tourism: Excursions around Monarchy,* ed. Philip Long and Nicola J. Palmer (Clevedon, UK: Channel View, 2008), 142–58.

68. Elizabeth Bumiller, "Diana Cleans Out Her Closet, and Charities Just Clean Up," *New York Times,* June 26, 1997.

69. *Extreme Royal Collections,* Discovery Channel DVD, 2012.

70. Hilary Moss, "Princess Diana's Dresses Sell for $276,000 at Auction," *Huffington Post,* Sept. 5, 2011.

71. "Princess Diana Memorabilia: The Pinnacle of Royal Collectables," *Paul Fraser Collectibles,* Feb. 3, 2012.

72. "Diana's Back-up Wedding Dress and Shoes Sell for £84,000 at Auction," *Mail Online,* Dec. 1, 2011.

CHAPTER 5

1. Dan Falk, "William Shakespeare, the 'King of Infinite Space,'" *Telegraph*, Jan. 27, 2014.

2. Bill Bryson, *Shakespeare: The World as Stage* (New York: Atlas Books, 2007), 73.

3. Julian Bowsher and Pat Miller, *The Rose and the Globe—Playhouses of Shakespeare's Bankside, Southwark* (London: Museum of London, 2010), 19.

4. Bryson, *Shakespeare*, 78.

5. Edwin Wilson Alvin Goldfarb, *Living Theater: A History* (New York: McGraw-Hill, 2000), 185.

6. Saccio, *Shakespeare's English Kings: History, Chronicle, and Drama* (Oxford: Oxford University Press, 2000), 6.

7. Ibid., 4.

8. Michael Best, "The Tudor Myth," Internet Shakespeare Editions, University of Victoria, http://internetshakespeare.uvic.ca/Library/SLT/history/the%20histories/tudormyth.html.

9. All GBO figures are from *Box Office Mojo* (www.boxofficemojo.com) and include worldwide totals where given.

10. We could also have included *The Other Boleyn Girl* (GBO $77.7 million, 2008), but omitted it because the Boleyns, rather than Henry VIII, are its main stars.

11. Likewise we omitted *The Libertine* (2004), starring Johnny Depp, as it focuses on the Earl of Rochester rather than Charles II.

12. Robert A. Rosenstone, "The Historical Film: Looking at the Past in a Post-literate Age," in *The Historical Film: History and Memory in Media,* ed. Marcia Landy (New Brunswick, NJ: Rutgers University Press, 2001), 50.

13. Ibid., 53.

14. Ibid., 65.

15. Brown was featured in the June 30, 1866, edition of the satirical magazine *Punch.*

16. Alistair Jamieson, "Queen Not Amused by 'Inaccuracies' in *The Young Victoria* film," *Telegraph,* March 15, 2009.

17. *Monarchy,* a Channel 4 British TV series by British academic David Starkey that first aired in 2004–2006, charted the political and ideological history of the English monarchy from the Saxon period to modern times.

18. Nicholas Vincent, *Magna Carta: A Very Short Introduction* (Oxford: Oxford University Press, 2012).

19. Leger Grindon, "Drama and Spectacle as Historical Explanation in the Historical Fiction Film," *Film and History: An Interdisciplinary Journal of Film and Television Studies* 17, no. 4 (1987): 74–80.

20. Margaret Butler, "Costume Drama," *BFI Screenonline,* www.screenonline.org.uk/film/id/570755/.

21. Lara Stewart, "10 Best Costume Drama Movies," *Screenjunkies,* March 16, 2014.

22. Grant McCracken, *Culture and Consumption* (Bloomington: Indiana University Press, 1990), 11–15.

23. Alex von Tunzelmann, "Wild Liberties Take the Shine off *Elizabeth: The Golden Age*," *Guardian film blog*, Sept. 29, 2011.

24. Richard Rickett, *Special Effects: The History and Technique*, 2d ed. (New York: Billboard Books, 2007), 10.

25. Kara McKechnie, "Taking Liberties with the Monarch: The Royal Bio-Pic in the 1990s," in *British Historical Cinema*, ed. Claire Monk and Amy Sargeant (London: Routledge, 2002), 220.

26. Ibid.

27. Ibid., 218.

28. Martin Stollery, "London Can Take It (1940)," *BFI Screenonline*, www.screenonline.org.uk/film/id/443913/index.html.

29. McKechnie, "Taking Liberties with the Monarch," 221.

30. Susan Bordo, *The Creation of Anne Boleyn: A New Look at England's Most Notorious Queen* (New York: Houghton Mifflin, 2013).

31. McKechnie, "Taking Liberties with the Monarch," 221.

32. Ginia Bellafante, "Nasty but Not So Brutish and Short," *New York Times*, March 28, 2008.

33. Nicole Martin, "BBC Period Drama *The Tudors* Is 'Gratuitously Awful' Says Dr. David Starkey," *Telegraph*, Oct. 16, 2008.

34. Angela Mullin, "James Flyn Talks 'The Tudors,'" *IFTN*, Sept. 27, 2007.

35. John Plunkett, "TV Ratings: The Tudors Ends Reign with 1.4m," *Guardian*, Sept. 28, 2009.

36. Maria Puente, "The Tudors' Popularity Endures Past Showtime's Final Season," *USA Today*, Sept. 4, 2010.

37. Tracy Borman, "The Truth behind *The Tudors*," *BBC History Magazine*, Aug. 27, 2009.

38. Susan Bordo, "Anne Boleyn: A Cultural Timeline," *The Creation of Anne Boleyn*, https://thecreationofanneboleyn.wordpress.com/2013/02/17/anne-boleyn-a-cultural-timeline/.

39. Richard Alexander, *Aspects of Verbal Humour in English* (Tübingen: Narr Francke Attempto, 1997), 133.

40. Ibid.

41. British Comedy Guide, "Blackadder," www.comedy.co.uk/guide/tv/blackadder/.

42. "John Brown," *Undiscovered Scotland: The Ultimate Online Guide*, www.undiscoveredscotland.co.uk/usbiography/b/johnbrown.html.

43. Independent Online, "UK Royal Family Source of Comedy," *Tonight*, Sept. 25, 2011, www.iol.co.za/tonight/uk-royal-family-source-of-comedy-1.1144090.

44. Steven Felding, "Victoria on Screen: The Heart of a Heartless Political World?" paper presented at the Making of the Monarchy for a Modern World Conference, Kensington Palace, June 2012.

45. Ibid.

46. Ibid.

47. Bethany Latham, *Elizabeth I in Film and Television* (London: McFarland, 2011), 32.

48. Ibid., 34.

49. Ibid., 39.

50. Ibid., 270.

51. Ibid., 271.

52. Henry Hitchings, "*The Audience,* Gielgud Theatre, Theatre Review," *Evening Standard,* March 6, 2013.

53. Charles Spencer, "*The Audience,* Gielgud Theatre, Review," *Telegraph,* March 6, 2013.

54. Smith, *Elizabeth the Queen,* 217.

55. Ibid., 220.

56. Anita Singh, "Royal Family Documentary Revived Four Decades On," *Telegraph,* Jan. 13, 2011.

57. Smith, *Elizabeth the Queen,* 220.

58. Richard Tomlinson, "Trying to Be Useful," *Independent,* June 19, 2014.

59. Grant McCracken, "Who Is the Celebrity Endorser? Cultural Foundations of the Endorsement Process," *Journal of Consumer Research* 16, no. 3 (1989): 310–21.

60. Randee Dawn, "Elizabeth Hurley: New 'Royals' Series an 'Extreme, Sexy Adventure into Royalty,'" *Today,* Aug. 20, 2104, www.today.com/popculture/elizabeth-hurley-royals-extreme-sexy-adventure-royalty-1D80088359.

CHAPTER 6

1. Cotton Timberlake, "Britain's Royal Warrant Gives Snob Appeal but No Guarantees," *Associated Press,* April 31, 1988.

2. Geoffrey Jones, *Beauty Imagined: A History of the Global Beauty Industry* (Oxford: Oxford University Press, 2010).

3. Terence A. Shimp, *Advertising Promotion: Supplemental Aspects of Integrated Marketing Communications,* 5th ed. (Fort Worth, TX: Dryden Press, 2000).

4. Mark Tungate, *Luxury World: The Past, Present and Future of Luxury Brands* (London: Kogan Page, 2009).

5. John Crace, "Is the Royal Warrant Losing Its Appeal?" *Guardian,* Jan. 19, 2011.

6. "Al-Fayed Had 'Cursed' Harrods' Royal Warrants Burned," *BBC News UK,* Aug. 27, 2010.

7. Tim Heald, *A Peerage for Trade: A History of the Royal Warrant* (London: Royal Warrant Holders Association, 2001), 152.

8. Douglas Jones, "Architecture as a Discipline of the Humanities," *Journal of Architecture Education* 34, no. 4 (1981): 18–23.

9. A term for a heterosexual male interested in the consumption of fashion and beauty products. David Wiegland, "DVD Review: 'Beau Brummell: This Charming Man'" *San Francisco Chronicle,* July 27, 2008.

10. Heald, *A Peerage for Trade.*

11. Ibid., 44.

12. Rebecca English, "Kate and Wills Inc.: Duke and Duchess Secretly Set Up Companies to Protect Their Brand—Just Like the Beckhams," *Daily Mail,* Jan. 17, 2014.

13. Charlotte Higgins, "Buried Treasure," *Guardian,* April 20, 2006.

14. Annual Reports, Royal Collection Trust, www.royalcollection.org.uk /sites/default/files/Annual%20Report%202011 2012.pdf.

15. Jonathan Jones, "So People Want to Nationalise the Royal Collection? Off with Their Heads!" *Guardian,* Feb. 9, 2010.

16. Hoey, *At Home with the Queen,* 261.

17. Kathryn Jones, *For the Royal Table: Dining at the Palace* (London: Royal Collection Enterprises, 2008).

18. Lucille Grant, "British Royal Ceramics," *Antiques & Collecting Magazine* 106, no. 4 (June 2001): 27.

19. Ibid.

20. Eric Knowles, *Miller's Royal Memorabilia* (London: Miller's/Reed Consumer Books), 29.

21. Asa Briggs, *Victorian Things* (London: B. T. Batsford, 1988), 149. See Lucy Worsley, *A Very British Murder: The Story of a National Obsession* (London: BBC Books, 2014), for more on Britain's cultural preoccupation with crime, criminals, and detectives.

22. Michael Billig, "Stacking the Cards of Ideology: The History of the Sun Souvenir Royal Album," *Discourse & Society* 1, no. 17 (1990): 17–37.

23. Cele Otnes interview with John Pym, July 2005.

24. Peter Lockton, *Royal Commemorative Mugs and Beakers* (East Lothian, Scotland: Tuckwell Press, 2001), 117.

25. "Drcarrot" (seller), "Fab 1969 mug Prince Charles Investiture groovy fab font yellow orange," *Etsy,* https://uk.pinterest.com/jenncrabb/dr-carrots-etsy-offerings/.

26. Sarah Rainey, "Why Prince Charles's Duchy Originals Takes the Biscuit," *Telegraph,* Nov. 12, 2013.

27. Organic Food Industry Market Research and Statistics, *Report Linker,* www.reportlinker.com/ci02035/Organic-Food.html.

28. Rebecca Smithers, "Going Duchy: Waitrose and Prince Charles in Royalties Deal," *Guardian,* Sept. 10, 2009.

29. Steven Morris, "Welcome to UK's Poshest Veg Shop," *Guardian.* March 18, 2008.

30. Ibid.

31. "Branding That Is Fit for a Queen?" *Design Week,* Oct. 18, 2001.

32. Victoria Moore, "Royal Family to Produce Its Own Wine from Windsor Park Grapes," *Telegraph,* May 5, 2011.

33. Monica Rich Kosann, "The British Royal Family—They're Just Like Us!," *MRK-STYLE,*www.mrkstyle.com/archived/british-royal-family-auctions-heirlooms-at-christies/.

34. Hoey, *At Home with the Queen,* 257.

35. Ibid.

36. Michael Thornton, "Princess Margaret Jewellery Flogging Is So Very Vulgar," *Daily Mail,* June 15, 2006.

37. Andrew Alderson, "Queen Urges Margaret's Heirs to Avoid Another Royal Gift Scandal," *Telegraph,* June 16, 2006.

38. Ibid.

39. "Princess Margaret Auction: For Sale, the Crown Jewels," *Independent,* June 15, 2006.

40. "Ray Bellisario: the Photographer the Royals Hated," *AFP,* news.com.au, June 8, 2013.

41. Ibid.

42. "Royaltyac" (biography of Alicia Carroll), *ArtFire,* http://www.artfire .com/ext/shop/bio/royaltyac.

43. Alicia Carroll, "Everything Royal," *Everything Royal Catalog,* Sept. 9, 2003, 2.

44. "Royal Memorabilia for Sale," *CBS News,* Nov. 21, 2002.

45. Robert Opie, *Rule Britannia: Trading on the British Image* (Oxford: Past Times, 1985), 6.

46. Ibid., 8.

47. Ibid., 9.

48. Ibid.

49. Robert Opie, *Remember When: A Nostalgic Trip through the Consumer Era* (London: Bounty Books, 2007).

50. Ibid., 43.

51. "Royal Arms, Names, and Images," *Official Website of the British Royal Family,* www.royal.gov.uk/MonarchUK/Symbols/UseoftheRoyalArms.aspx.

52. Justin O'Brien, "Modalu: The Case of the Nearly Royal Brand Ambassador," case study for Entrepreneurial Marketing module, Royal Holloway University of London.

53. Opie, *Remember When,* 11.

54. Jamie Peck, "Meet the Woman Who Makes $1,000/Day as a Kate Middleton Impersonator," *Gloss,* Oct. 5, 2012.

55. "Pizza Hut Hires Royal Family Impersonators to Appear in Its 'Crown Crust' Advert (VIDEO)," *Huffington Post UK,* Jan. 6, 2012.

CHAPTER 7

1. Mike Robinson, "A World of World Heritage Seduction, Disenchantment, and New Imaginaries," presented at the University of Illinois at Urbana-Champaign, April 3, 2014.

2. Olga Khazan, "Is the British Royal Family Worth the Money?" *Atlantic,* July 23, 2013.

3. Evan Davies, quoted in Long and Palmer, *Royal Tourism,* 3.

4. Khazan, "Is the British Royal Family Worth the Money?"

5. Victor T.C. Middleton and Leonard John Lickorish, *British Tourism: The Remarkable Story of Growth* (London: Butterworth-Heinemann, 2007), 155.

6. They are the AJC Queen Elizabeth Stakes, Sydney, Australia; the Princess Elizabeth Challenge Cup, Henley, England (rowing); the Queen Elizabeth II Commemorative Cup, Kyoto, Japan; the Queen Elizabeth II Challenge Cup Stakes, Lexington, Kentucky.

7. Gwyn Topham, "Heathrow's New Terminal 2 Opens to First Passengers," *Guardian,* June 4, 2014.

8. "Diana Memorial—Liberty Flame, Paris," *Virtual Tourist,* www.virtualtourist.com/travel/Europe/France/Ile_de_France/Paris-99080/Things_To_Do-Paris-Diana_Memorial_Liberty_Flame-BR-1.html.

9. Mike Robinson and Helaine Silverman, "An Agenda in Heritage and Popular Culture," in *Encounters with Popular Pasts* (New York: Springer, 2015).

10. Bob Kampf, "Hot Dog! Hyde Park Train Station Anniversary Re-enacts Royal Visit," *Observer,* July 3, 2014.

11. "New Royal Heritage Route from the GNTO," press release, German National Tourist Office, London, Sept. 21, 2013.

12. Charles Phillips, *The Illustrated Encyclopedia of Royal Britain* (New York: Metro Books, 2009).

13 "Buckingham Palace Wins Award as Best Attraction for Group Visits," *Royal Collection Trust,* www.royalcollection.org.uk/news/buckingham-palace-wins-award-as-best-attraction-for-group-visits.

14 Steve Hawkes, "Buckingham Palace Takes Crown as Most Desirable 'Only in Britain' Destination for Tourists," *Daily Telegraph,* December 9, 2013.

15. Long and Palmer, *Royal Tourism,* 4.

16 "Thomas Cook's Royal Globetrotting Guide," *PR Newswire,* May 30, 2012.

17. Eamon Duffy, *The Stripping of the Altars: Traditional Religion in England, c. 1400–1580* (New Haven, CT: Yale University Press, 1992), 161.

18. John Towner, *An Historical Geography of Recreation and Tourism in the Western World, 1540–1940* (New York: Wiley, 1996).

19. Chloe Chard, "From the Sublime to the Ridiculous: The Anxieties of Sightseeing," in Hartmut Berghoff, Barbara Korte, Ralf Schneider, and Christopher Harvie, eds., *The Making of Modern Tourism* (New York: Palgrave, 2002), 47.

20. Cannon and Griffiths, *Oxford Illustrated History,* 261.

21. Chard, "From the Sublime to the Ridiculous," 33.

22. Allison Lockwood, *Passionate Pilgrims: The American Traveler in Great Britain, 1800–1914* (New York: Fairleigh Dickinson University Press, 1981), 458.

23. Ibid., 116.

24. Gilbert Sigaux and Joan Eveline Mabel White, *History of Tourism,* trans. Joan White (London: Leisure Arts, 1966).

25. Rob Shields, "The 'System of Pleasure': Liminality and the Carnivalesque at Brighton," *Theory, Culture and Society* 7, no. 39 (1990).

26. Irena Ateljavic, "From a 'Thermal Wonderland' to a Place 'Full of Surprises:' Reinventing the Destination of Rotorua, New Zealand," *Tourism* 50, no. 4 (2002): 383–94.

27. Phillips, *The Illustrated Encyclopedia of Royal Britain*, 456.

28. Ibid.

29. Ibid., 457.

30. Sue Berry, *Georgian Brighton* (West Sussex: Phillimore, 2006), xi.

31. Arbiter, *On Duty with the Queen*, 15.

32. "Conservation and Restoration," *Brighton and Hove City Council*, http://brightonmuseums.org.uk/royalpavilion/history/conservation-and-restoration..

33 "Saving the Saloon—Our Greatest Achievement," *Royal Pavilion Foundation*, http://brightonmuseums.org.uk/royalpavilion/history/conservation-and-restoration/.

34. N. C. Milne, *Scottish Culture and Traditions* (New York: Paragon, 2010).

35. Queen Victoria, *Leaves from the Journal of Our Life in the Highlands from 1848–1861*, ed. Arthur Helps (London: Smith, Elder, 1868), 16, 19.

36. David Duff, *Victoria in the Highlands* (New York: Taplinger, 1968), 13.

37. Richard W. Butler, "The History and Development of Royal Tourism in Scotland: Balmoral, the Ultimate Holiday Home?" in Long and Palmer, *Royal Tourism*, 58.

38. "Balmoral Castle in Scotland: The Queen's Private Vacation Home," *About-Travel*, http://gouk.about.com/od/royalty/ss/balmoral_about.htm.

39. Many are accessible at www.hrp.org.uk.

40. See Robinson, "A World of World Heritage Seduction, Disenchantment, and New Imaginaries."

41. Brett Dolman et al., *Experience the Tower of London* (Surrey, England: Historic Royal Palaces, 2011), 7.

42. *An Historical Description of the Tower of London and Its Curiosities* (London: Thomas Carnan, 1784), 59.

43. Ibid.

44. Ibid., 37.

45. Karla Adam, "Tower of London's Stunning Poppy Installation Creates National Sensation," *Washington Post*, Nov. 7, 2014.

46. Ibid.

47. Joe Murphy and Mark Blunden, "All-Night Vigil to See Poppies," *London Evening Standard*, Nov. 10, 2014.

48. Boris Johnson, "More People Will Now See the Awesome Poppies," *London Evening Standard*, Nov. 10, 2014.

49. Alistair Fox, *Politics and Literature in the Reigns of Henry VII and VIII*, quoted in Sharpe, *Selling the Tudor Monarchy*, 159.

50. "Royal Kitchen Garden at Hampton Court Palace," *Inside Story*, no. 21 (Autumn 2013): 11.

51. "The Next Chapter in Our Story," development brochure, Historic Royal Palaces, November 2014, 9.

52. Sharpe, *Selling the Tudor Monarchy,* 171.

53. Lucy Worsley, *Courtiers: The Secret History of Kensington Palace* (London: Faber, 2010).

54. Cele Otnes interview with Michael Day, June 2012.

55. Julian Hartman, Caitlin Carson, Cele C. Otnes, and Pauline Maclaran, "Contemporizing Kensington: Popular Culture and the 'Enchanted Palace' Exhibit," in Robinson and Silverman, eds., *Encounters with Popular Pasts,* 165–83.

56. Cele Otnes interview with Michael Day, June 2012.

57. Bagehot, *The English Constitution,* 76.

58. Cele Otnes interview with Deirdre Murphy, July 2007.

59. Cele Otnes interview with Michael Day, July 2005.

60. Ibid.

61. All HRP figures are from the 2012–13 annual report; references for other figures available from the authors.

CHAPTER 8

1. Hoey, *At Home with the Queen,* 61.

2. Bill Bryson, *Notes from a Small Island* (New York: Perennial, 1995), 55.

3. "Royal Tourist Walk for the Queen in 2015 Plans Revealed," *Royal Borough Observer,* June 24, 2013.

4. Edwards, *Royal Sisters.*

5. Ibid.

6. Robin Mackworth-Young, *The History and Treasures of Windsor Castle* (London: Pitkin Brittania, 1982).

7. Alfred Leslie Rowse, "Windsor Castle in the History of the Nation," *Journal of the Royal Society of Arts* (1975): 763–69.

8. Chris Greenwood, "Dig Unearths Round Table Evidence at Windsor Castle," *Independent,* Aug. 28, 2006.

9. Smith, *Elizabeth the Queen,* 40.

10. Mackworth-Young, *The History and Treasures of Windsor Castle,* 22.

11. Cannon and Griffiths, *Oxford Illustrated History,* 222.

12. Mackworth-Young, *The History and Treasures of Windsor Castle,* 42.

13. Ibid., 56.

14. John Baxendale, "The Constructions of the Past: The Origins of Royal Tourism," in Long and Palmer, *Royal Tourism,* 39.

15. Tim Lambert, "A Brief History of Windsor," www.localhistories.org /windsor.html.

16. Kelley, *The Royals,* 10.

17. "Timmy Mallett Rings in the Changes on His Windsor Phonebox." *Royal Borough Observer,* July 28, 2013.

18. Brown and Chapman, *Windsor Ablaze!,* 14.

19. Ibid., 20.

20. "1992: Blaze Rages in Windsor Castle," *BBC on This Day, 1950–2005,* http://news.bbc.co.uk/onthisday/hi/dates/stories/november/20/newsid_2551000/2551107.stm.

21. Brown and Chapman, *Windsor Ablaze!,* 5.

22. Richard Stevenson, "Most Art Safe in Windsor Castle Fire," *New York Times,* Nov. 22, 1992.

23. Adrienne Auslander Munich, "Queen Victoria, Empire, and Excess," *Tulsa Studies in Women's Literature* 6, no. 2 (1987): 272.

24. Munich, *Queen Victoria's Secrets,* 79.

25. Sonia A. Bedikian, "The Death of Mourning: From Victorian Crepe to Little Black Dress," *Omega* 57, no. 1 (2008): 40.

26. Liz Stanley and Sue Wise, "The Domestication of Death: The Sequestration Thesis and Domestic Figuration," *Sociology* 45, no. 6 (2011): 956.

27. Dilip Ramchandani, "Pathological Grief: Two Victorian Case Studies," *Psychiatric Quarterly* 67, no. 1 (1996): 79–80.

28. Munich, *Queen Victoria's Secrets,* 88.

29. Andrew Rose, *The Woman before Wallis* (New York: Picador, 2013), 302.

30. John Parker, *King of Fools* (New York: St. Martin's Press, 1988), 60.

31. Anne Sebba, *That Woman: The Life of Wallis Simpson, Duchess of Windsor* (New York: St. Martin's Press, 2011).

32. Ibid., 12.

33. Suzy Menkes, *The Windsor Style* (Topsfield, MA: Salem House, 1988), 152.

34. Ibid., 82.

35. Ibid., 136.

36. Ibid., 43.

37. "Person of the Year: A Photo History," *Time,* Dec. 16, 2006.

38. Sebba, *That Woman,* 217.

39. Menkes, *The Windsor Style,* 30.

40. Hannah Rand, "Wallis Simpson—Style File," *Vogue,* Sept. 8, 2011.

41. Elizabeth Large, "The Duchess of Chic," *Baltimore Sun,* Sept. 19, 1999.

42. Menkes, *The Windsor Style,* 104.

43. Ibid., 126.

44. Sebba, *That Woman,* 27.

45. Alice Furlaud, "Windsor's Paris Home to Become Museum," *New York Times,* Dec. 25, 1986.

46. Rita Reif, "Windsor Auction: $50 Million," *New York Times,* April 4, 1987.

47. "Royal Bracelet Breaks Record at Sotheby's Sale," *Reuters,* Dec. 1, 2010.

48. James Hardy and Catherine Milner, "Queen Bids for Duke of Windsor Heirlooms," *Sunday Telegraph,* Feb. 22, 1998.

49. *Property from the Collection of the Duke and Duchess of Windsor: Information,* exhibition catalog (New York: Sotheby's, 1997).

50. Charles Spencer, "*The Last of the Duchess,* Hampstead Theater, review," *Daily Telegraph,* Oct. 27, 2011.

51. "Royal Baby Gives Birth to Windsor Tourism Boom," *Royal Borough Observer,* July 26, 2013.

52. Paul Sonne, "In Her Majesty's Service, Loyal Minion Courts the Queen's Swans on Thames," *Wall Street Journal,* July 24, 2013.

53. Ben Arnoldy, "For Queen Elizabeth, a Google Doodle of Diamonds and Doggies," *Christian Science Monitor,* June 2, 2012.

54. Stephen Smith, "The Most Popular Dog Breeds in America," *American Kennel Club,* www.akc.org/news/the-most-popular-dog-breeds-in-america/.

55. Arnoldy, "For Queen Elizabeth, a Google Doodle."

56. Ann Hoevel, "Corgis Are 'the New Cats' of Internet Culture," *CNN,* Oct. 7, 2011.

57. Edwards, *Royal Sisters,* p. 41.

58. Caroline Davies, "Queen's Horse Estimate Wins Gold Cup at Royal Ascot Ladies' Day," *Guardian,* June 20, 2013.

59. Smith, *Elizabeth the Queen,* 186.

60. "Facts & Figures," *Ascot,* www.ascot.co.uk/facts-figures.

61. Smith, *Elizabeth the Queen,* 191.

62. "The Black and White of Royal Ascot," *Sports Illustrated,* June 30, 1958.

63. Ibid.

64. Belinda Goldsmith, "Royal Ascot Visitors Must Pay for Fashion Faux Pas," *Huffington Post,* June 20, 2013.

65. Sarah Ditum, "Royal Ascot's Dress Code Aims to Banish the Commoner Within," *Guardian,* June 19, 2012.

66. Smith, *Elizabeth the Queen,* 169.

67. Ibid., 171.

68. Prudence Leith-Roth, *The Florilegium of Alexander Marshall in the Collection of Her Majesty the Queen at Windsor Castle* (London: Royal Collection, 2000).

CHAPTER 9

1. Jen Doll, "The 7 Most Ridiculous Royal Wedding Products," *New York Village Voice Blogs,* March 21, 2011.

2. Eric Ives, "Marrying for Love: The Experience of Edward IV and Henry VIII," *History Today* 50, no. 12 (2000).

3. "Diana Tapes Broadcast in US," *Daily Telegraph,* Nov. 30, 2004.

4. Datablog, "Social Mobility: The Charts That Shame Britain," *Guardian,* May 22, 2012.

5. Jill Lawless, "Kate Middleton's Family Is a Close-Knit Clan with Humble Roots and Commercial Savvy," *Star Tribune,* April 28, 2011.

6. Claudia Joseph, *Kate: The Making of a Princess* (Edinburgh: Mainstream, 2010), 118.

7. Andrew M. Brown, "Kate Middleton Is a Typical St Andrews Girl," *Telegraph,* Nov. 16, 2010.

8. Belinda White, "Charlotte Todd Cashes in on Kate Middleton," *Telegraph,* Nov. 16, 2010.

9. Cele C. Otnes and Elizabeth H. Pleck, *Cinderella Dreams: The Allure of the Lavish Wedding* (Berkeley: University of California Press, 2003).

10. Lauren Milligen, "The Kate Effect," *Vogue,* July 22, 2011.

11. Olivia Bergin, "Demand for Duchess of Cambridge's Engagement Dress Almost Made Issa Go Bust," *Telegraph,* March 28, 2013.

12. Ashleigh Logan, Kathy Hamilton, and Paul Hewer, "Re-fashioning Kate: The Making of a Celebrity Princess Brand," in *Advances in Consumer Research* 41, ed. Simona Botti and Aparna Laproo (Duluth, MN: Association for Consumer Research, 2013), 378–83.

13. Brand Finance, "Brand Value: Catherine Duchess of Cambridge," *Brand Finance Journal: Special Jubilee Issue,* May 27, 2011.

14. Bianca London, "The Kate Effect Strikes Again! The Duchess of Cambridge's Love of Miniature Clutches Sees Size of Handbags Shrinking," *Mail Online,* May 7, 2013.

15. Thanks to Ashleigh Logan for this insight from her work on Catherine as a celebrity.

16. Hilary Mantel, "Royal Bodies," *London Review Podcast,* Feb. 21, 2013.

17. Centre for Retail Research, "The Royal Wedding—New Estimates of Forecast Retail Spending," www.retailresearch.org/royalwedding2011.php.

18. Harry Wallop, "Royal Wedding: Tea Towels Will Be Allowed," *Telegraph,* Jan. 11, 2011.

19. Tom Chapman, "2011 Royal Wedding—Will and Kate," *Royal Beer Collections,* www.royalbeers.co.uk/2011_Royal_Wedding_William_and_Kate.

20. Kimberly Sugden, "Cultural Marketing: Building Brands That Resonate," presentation, University of Illinois, College of Business, April 7, 2014.

21. BBC, "Royal Wedding: In Numbers," *BBC News UK,* May 1, 2011.

22. "The UK: Royal Wedding a Mixed Bag for the Economy," *Thomas White International,*www.thomaswhite.com/world-markets/the-u-k-royal-wedding-a-mixed-bag-for-the-economy/.

23. Christopher Wilson, "Royal Wedding of Prince William and Kate Middleton Has Created a New Beginning for the Monarchy," *Mirror,* May 1, 2011.

24. Nick Timmins and Emma Jacobs, "Britain: The Fairy-Tale Fantasy," *Financial Times,* April 25, 2011.

25. Daniel Dayan and Elihu Katz, *Media Events: The Live Broadcasting of History* (Cambridge, MA: Harvard University Press, 1992).

26. Marina Dekevella, "Constructing the Public at the Royal Wedding," *Media, Culture & Society* 34 (2012): 296–311.

27. "Royal Baby Hospital Is New Tourist Attraction, *Telegraph,* July 20, 2013.

28. Carolyn Folkman Curasi, Eric J. Arnould, and Linda L. Price, "Ritual Desire and Ritual Development: An Examination of Family Heirlooms in Con-

temporary North American Households," in *Contemporary Consumption Rituals: A Research Anthology,* ed. Cele Otnes and Tina Lowrey (Mahwah, NJ: Lawrence Erlbaum, 2004), 237–68.

29. Matt Chorley, "Welcome to Kate Britain: Tourism Bosses Launch Royal Baby Campaign to Promote UK as a Family-Friendly Destination," *Mailonline,* July 24, 2013.

30. Centre for Retail Research, "The Royal Baby Retail Estimates," February 2014, www.retailresearch.org/downloads/PDF/babygeorge.pdf.

31. "The Kate Effect," *ITN Tonight,* July 25, 2013,

32. Ibid.

33. Thomas C. O'Guinn, "Touching Greatness: The Central Midwest Barry Manilow Fan Club," in *Highways and Buyways: Naturalistic Research from the Consumer Behavior Odyssey,* ed. Russell Belk (Provo, UT: Association for Consumer Research, 2013), 102–11.

34. Jonathan Jones, "The Royal Baby Pictures Show Privilege Trying, and Failing, to Look Normal," *Guardian,* Aug. 20, 2013.

35. Ibid.

CHAPTER 10

1. Jeremy D. Larson, "Behind the Song: Lorde's 'Royals,'" *Radio.com,* Jan. 7, 2014, http://radio.com/2014/01/07/behind-the-song-lordes-royals/.

2. Lindsey Weber, "Lorde 101: Who Is This 16-Year-Old Singer?" *Vulture,* Nov. 6, 2013.

3. "All Her Majesty's Brands: 10 Brands the Queen Can't Live Without," *Marketing,* July 2, 2012.

4. "Special Jubilee issue," *Brand Finance Journal,* May 27, 2012.

5. Gustave Le Bon, *The Crowd: A Study of the Popular Mind* (New York: Viking, 1960 [1901]), 16.

6. "Royal Involvement with Charities," *Official Website of the British Monarchy,* www.royal.gov.uk/charitiesandpatronages/royal%20involvement%20with%20charities/royal%20involvement%20with%20charities.aspx.

7. Vanessa Barford, "Why Do Charities Want a Royal Patron?" *BBC News,* Jan. 5, 2012.

8. Jo Littler, "'I Feel Your Pain': Cosmopolitan Charity and the Public Fashioning of the Celebrity Soul," *Social Semiotics* 18, no. 2 (2008): 237–51.

9. Zack O'Malley Greenburg, "The Most Valuable Celebrity Charity Relationships," *Forbes,* Nov. 30, 2011.

10. Dan Brockington and Spensor Henson, "Signifying the Public: Celebrity Advocacy and Post-Democratic Politics," *International Journal of Cultural Studies,* May 8, 2014.

11. "Tricolour and Queen Sign Appears on Belfast Hillside," *BBC News,* June 26, 2012.

12. Luke Cooper, "How the Pretty Royals Are Turning Young People into Monarchists," *Crikey,* April 24, 2014.

13. Stephen Bates, "Prince Andrew to Step Down as Trade Envoy, Buckingham Palace Confirms," *Guardian,* July 21, 2011.

14. Patrick Cockburn, "Prince Andrew Praises Bahrain, Island of Torture," *Independent,* May 11, 2014.

15. Sudeshna Sen, "Indians Account for Highest Immigration into the UK: Polish Influx Up Tenfold," *Economic Times,* Dec. 13, 2002.

16. Emer O'Toole, "I Want to Be Canadian—But Why Should I Have to Swear Allegiance to the Queen?" *Guardian,* Aug. 14, 2014.

17. Ben Arnoldy, "On Diamond Jubilee's Eve, Diverse Britain Seeks Unity in Queen Elizabeth," *Chronicle of Higher Education,* June 1, 2012.

18. Lisa Miller, "Fake English Town in China: Deserted 'Thames Town' Is Abandoned . . . Minus the Newlyweds," *Huff Post Travel,* Sept. 14, 2013.

19. Olivia Goldhill, "Britons Want Prince Charles to Be Next King," *Daily Telegraph,* Nov. 14, 2013.

20. Rob Evans, "Prince Charles's Letters to Ministers Remain Private, Court Rules," *Guardian,* July 9, 2013.

21. Michael Billington, "*King Charles III* Review—a 21st-Century Shakespearean Tragedy," *Guardian,* Sept. 12, 2014.

22. *Time,* Nov. 4, 2013.

23. Gordon Rayner, "Camilla: Happy Birthday, Prince Charles, You're Exhausting," *Telegraph,* Nov. 14, 2013.

24. Allison Pearson, "Carole Middleton: The Grounded Granny Who Took Pole Position," *Telegraph,* July 24, 2013.

25. "UK Luxury Brand Benchmark Survey 2013," *Walpole,* July 29, 2013.

26. John Arlidge, "Because We're Worth It," *London Evening Standard,* July 11, 2014.

27. Jacob Davidson, "Even Kanye Thinks 'Luxury' Has Become Code for 'Rip-Off,'" *Time,* July 22, 3014.

28. Hoey, *At Home with the Queen,* 203.

29. Nairn, *The Enchanted Glass,* xxiii.

SELECTED REFERENCES

Ackroyd, Peter. *London: The Biography.* New York: Anchor, 2001.

———. *Thames: The Biography.* New York: Anchor, 2007.

Arbiter, Dickie, with Lynne Barrett-Lee. *On Duty with the Queen.* Deepdene Lodge: Blink, 2014.

Bagehot, Walter. *The English Constitution.* Oxford: Oxford University Press, 2001.

Brown, Alexandra M., and Charles Chapman. *Windsor Ablaze! The Windsor Castle Fire and Restoration Ten Years On.* Cambridge: Lutterworth Press, 2007.

Cannadine, David. *The Decline and Fall of the British Aristocracy.* New York: Vintage, 1999.

Cannon, John Ashton, and Ralph A. Griffiths. *The Oxford Illustrated History of the British Monarchy.* Oxford: Oxford University Press, 1998.

Clayton, Tim, and Phil Craig. *Diana: Story of a Princess.* London: Hodder and Stoughton, 2001.

Davies, Jude. *Diana, a Cultural History: Gender, Race, Nation and the People's Princess.* Hampshire: Palgrave, 2001.

Dayan, Daniel, and Elihu Katz. *Media Events: The Live Broadcasting of History.* Cambridge, MA: Harvard University Press, 1992.

De Guitaut, Caroline. *The Royal Tour: A Souvenir Album.* London: Royal Collection, 2009.

Edwards, Anne. *Royal Sisters: Queen Elizabeth II and Princess Margaret.* New York: Morrow, 1990.

Fox, Kate. *Watching the English: The Hidden Rules of English Behaviour.* Boston: Nicholas Brealey, 2008.

Garnett, Mark, and Richard Weight. *Modern British History: The Essential A-Z Guide.* London: Pimlico, 2004.

Heald, Tim, Jorge Lewinski, and Mayotte Magnus. *By Appointment: 150 Years of the Royal Warrant and Its Holders.* London: Queen Anne, 1989.

Hoey, Brian. *At Home with the Queen.* London: HarperCollins, 2002.

———. *The Royal Yacht Britannia: Inside the Queen's Floating Palace,* 3rd ed. Somerset: Haynes, 1999.

Jones, Katharine W. *Accent on Privilege: English Identities and Anglophilia in the U.S.* Philadelphia: Temple University Press, 2001.

Kelley, Kitty. *The Royals.* New York: Hachette, 2009.

Kidlow, Christopher, and Sarah Gilbey. *The Really Useful Guide to the Kings and Queens of England.* Surrey: Historic Royal Palaces, 2011.

Latham, Bethany. *Elizabeth I in Film and Television.* London: McFarland, 2011.

Lindsey, Karen. *Divorced, Beheaded, Survived.* Reading, MA: Addison-Wesley, 1995.

Long, Philip, and Nicola J. Palmer. *Royal Tourism: Excursions around Monarchy.* Clevedon: Channel View, 2008.

Meyer, G. J. *The Tudors: The Complete Story of England's Most Notorious Dynasty.* New York: Bantam, 2011.

Munich, Adrienne. *Queen Victoria's Secrets.* New York: Columbia University Press, 1996.

Nairn, Tom. *The Enchanted Glass: Britain and Its Monarchy,* 2nd ed. London: Verso, 2011.

Olechnowicz, Andrzej. *The Monarchy and the British Nation, 1780 to the Present.* Cambridge: Cambridge University Press, 2007.

Pearson, John. *The Selling of the Royal Family: The Mystique of the British Monarchy.* New York: Simon and Schuster, 1986.

Peyton, Jane. *Brilliant Britain.* Chichester: Summersdale, 2012.

Pigott, Peter. *Royal Transport: An Inside Look at the History of Royal Travel.* Toronto: Dundurn, 2005.

Prochaska, F. K., *The Eagle and the Crown: Americans and the British Monarchy.* New Haven, CT: Yale University Press, 2008.

Richards, Jeffrey, Scott Wilson, and Linda Woodhead. *Diana: The Making of a Media Saint.* London: I. B. Tauris, 1999.

Ridley, Jane. *The Heir Apparent.* New York: Random House, 2013.

Saccio, Peter. *Shakespeare's English Kings: History, Chronicle, and Drama,* 2nd ed. Oxford: Oxford University Press, 2000.

Sebba, Anne. *That Woman: The Life of Wallis Simpson, Duchess of Windsor.* London: St. Martin's Griffin, 2013.

Sharpe, Kevin. *Selling the Tudor Monarchy.* New Haven, CT: Yale University Press, 2009.

Smith, Sally Bedell. *Elizabeth the Queen: Inside the Life of a Modern Monarch.* New York: Random House, 2011.

Tamarkin, Elisa. *Anglophilia: Deference, Devotion, and Antebellum America.* Chicago: University of Chicago Press, 2008.

Wayne, Robert S., and Joel Godard. *Royal London in Context: The Independent Traveler's Guide to Royal London.* Decatur, GA: Independent International Travel, 2004.

INDEX

Anne, Princess Royal, 5; Bellisario transparencies, 184; divorce, xxiv, 114; as equestrian, 247; marriage, second, xxiv; and Order of Precedence, 260; philanthropy of, 12; as touristic ambassador, 198; wedding of, 58

Anne, Queen, xxii, 247

Anne de Boleyn (1914 film), 148*tab*.4

Anne of Cleves, 72

Anne of the Thousand Days (1969 film), 150*tab*.4, 153

Annus Horribilis, xxiv, 55, 114

anointing of the monarch, 3, 38, 53

Anonymous (2011 film), 152*tab*.4

anti-monarchists/anti-royalists, 41–42, 113

APL Anglesey, 170

appeal of, 46

Appleton, Tony, 278

Arbiter, Dickie, 34, 49, 56

aristocracy: country weekends, 23; decline of, 23–24; monarchy's reliance on, 60–62; rise of, 22

Armstrong-Jones, Antony, 108

Asda, British supermarket chain, 274

Asian cultures, middle class consumerism, 39

Astrakhan, 246

Atkins, British engineering and design company, 293

Atkinson, Rowan, 156

Attenborough, David, 161

auctions, 182–84, 242

The Audience (2013 play), 75, 160–61

Australasia goodwill tour, 11

Australia, 289

baby market, impact of "George effect" on, 280

Bagehot, Walter, 11

Bahrain, 290

balcony tradition, 57–58, 111

Balmer, John, 29–30, 31, 37

Balmoral: private mourning at, 122; restoring/preserving of, 292; royal residences, 205, 206*tab*.5; royal tourism and, 205, 208

Balmoral hampers, 180, 181*fig*.20

bank holidays, 58

Banqueting House, Whitehall, 206*tab*.5, 209, 218, 224

Barber, David, 244

Barbour, British brand, 284

Barker, William G., 146

Barmy Britain (stage show), 75

Bashir, Martin, xxiv, 117–18

Bath (spa town), 180, 201

BBC (British Broadcasting Corporation), xxiv, 53, 117–18

Beaton, Cecil, 58, 241, 248

Beatrice of York, Princess, xxiv, 62, 141, 271–72, 291

Beau Brummell (term), 40, 320n9

Beau Brummell (1954 film), 147, 149*tab*.4

Beau Brummell (TV biography), 169

Becket (1964 film), 150*tab*.4, 153

Beckham, David and Victoria, 170, 271, 285, 300

Bedikian, Sonia, 237

beers, Royal Wedding commemorative, 266–68, 267*tab*.6

Bellafante, Ginia, 154

Bellisario, Ray, 184

Benedict XVI, Pope, 1, 6

Bennett, Alan, 138

Bergoglio, Jorge Cardinal. *See* Francis, Pope

Bernhardt, Sarah, 146, 148*tab*.4, 159

Berry, Sue, 203

Bhumibol Adulyadej, King of Thailand, 14, 26, 309n24

Big Ben, 72

Bigge, Arthur, 232

The Biggest Secret (Icke), 124

Blackadder (TV show), 156, 280

Blair, Tony, 122, 140–41, 143

Blanchett, Cate, 140, 145, 151*tab*.4, 159, 160, 162

Bletchley Park, 74

Blois, House of, xx

Blood Swept Lands and Seas of Red exhibition, xxv, 215, 216*fig*.24, 305–6

Blue Almonds, 274

Blumenthal, Heston, 178

Blunt, Emily, 141, 152*tab*.4, 158, 162

Boisselier's Chocolates, 190

Boleyn, Anne, 74, 148*tab*.4, 150*tab*.4, 152*tab*.4, 153, 155

Bond, Samantha, 161

Bonham-Carter, Helena, 141, 150*tab.*4, 152*tab.*4
Bon Jovi, Jon, 286
Bono, 286
Bordo, Susan, 153, 155
Borman, Tracy, 155
Bowen, David, 55
Boyle, Danny, 71
Boyle, Richard, 200
Branagh, Kenneth, 138, 139*fig.*17, 150*tab.*4
brand, three dimensions in overarching narrative of (confusions, contradictions, cumulations), 35
brand ambiguity, 35
Brand Britain, Royal Family as representatives, 273
brand collector identities, 81*tab.*1
brand communities (tribes), unpaid labor, 86
brand components, global brand component, 30–31
brandfests, 85
branding, 29
brand repositioning. *See* rebranding
Brazil, 31
BRIC countries, middle class consumerism, 31
bridal traditions, 254–55
Bridgewater, Emma, 84, 274
Brighton, 202–4, 203*fig.*23
Brighton Pavilion, 292
Bring Up the Bodies (2015 film), 163
Britain's Worst Homes (TV show), 101
Britannia figure, 186
Britax, 279
Britcoms, and royal caricatures, 70
British Airways, 266
British Broadcasting Corporation (BBC). *See* BBC (British Broadcasting Corporation)
British Commonwealth. *See* The Commonwealth
British Empire, 11, 31, 202, 214, 215, 232
British fashion industry, 108, 112. *See also specific British designers*
British humor: as external aspect of RFBC, 69; in film and television, 155–57; *Handbagged* (2014 play), 161; humor products export, 70–71; *Punch,* 156; and royal baby marketing, 274–75; and royal weddings, 268

British identity, 72
British invasion, 66
British monarchy: appeal of, 45–75; costs of maintaining, 195; external characteristics, 45; glamour of backwardness, 27; internal characteristics, 45; longevity, 45; role of, 27
British Telecommunications Artbox projects, 232
British traits, stereotypical, 69
Brown, John, 137, 138–39, 143, 151*tab.*4, 153, 156, 208, 318n15
Brown, Stephen, 35
Brummell, George "Beau," 40, 149*tab.*4, 169, 284, 320n9
Brunei, 6, 41
Buckingham Palace: assessment value, 41; Changing of the Guard, 12, 73; Chinese Dining Room, 204; costs of maintaining, 195; gardens of, 74; opening to public, 73; protests, 251; public tours, xxiv, 43, 198, 234; Queen's Gallery, 87, 171; restoring/preserving of, 292; Royal Mews, 73, 171; royal residences, 206*tab.*5; special events, 286; State Rooms, 171
Buckingham Palace Port, 180
Bujold, Geneviéve, 150*tab.*4, 153
Burberry, 300
Burrell, Paul, 186
Burton, Sarah, 272
Bushmills, 191

Cadbury, 188, 188*fig.*21
Caernarfon Castle, Charles's investiture ceremony, 24
Cairns, Fiona, 269
Cameron, David, 265
Cameroon, 48
Camilla, Duchess of Cornwall, 75; adultery issue, 116; Camillagate, 114; image management, 56, 94; marriage of, xxiv, 63; *Spitting Image* mask, 82; tabloid industry and, 111
Campbell, Colin, 114
CAMRA (Campaign for Real Ale), 267
Canada, declaration of dominion, 11
"Candle in the Wind," 86, 119

consumer culture, 103–29; *Halo Trust,* 103; Heritage House, 110*fig.*13; Hewitt book, 117; hostility toward RF, 114; and human-brand component, 34; humanitarian causes, 103, 118; image management, 110, 113, 118, 119; impact on RFBC, 105; Kensington Palace tributes, 93, 124, 125*fig.*14; marriage, xxiv, 43, 81, 104, 113–14, 257, 258; media platforms, 105; memorials, 127; Memorial Temple, Althorp, 126*fig.*15; mental health issues, 114, 115*tab.*2, 117; as mother, 101, 113; nesting dolls, 26*fig.*3; philanthropy of, 12; popularity of, 75; portrayals of, 152*tab.*4; and press, 54; public mourning of, 119–20; public perceptions of, 104–5, 113–14; as Queen of Hearts, 109; sacralization of, 119; separation, 116–17; as "Sloane Ranger," 107; soap opera comparisons, 115–16, 115*tab.*2; and tabloid industry, 113; Tyler collection, 87, 104*fig.*12; underdog brand narrative, 107, 111, 116; wedding dress, 111, 125, 128; wedding of, 109, 111; as Woman of the Year, 117. *See also* Diana rooms

Diana, Princess of Wales Memorial Fountain, 74

Diana Circle, 93, 94

Diana fans, 88–89, 93–94

Diana: Her Last Love (Snell), 142

Diana: Her True Story (Morton), 114, 116

Diana: Her True Story in Her Own Words (Morton), 116

Diana in Private (Campbell), 114

Diana: Legacy of a Princess exhibit, 197

Diana memorabilia, investment in, 127

Diana Memorial Temple, 125, 126*fig.*15

Diana rooms, 88, 92, 95, 97, 128

Diana rose, 82, 86, 94, 103

Diana tours, 127

Dimbleby, Jonathan, 116

dimensions, eight *Rs* (Balmer), 30

dine and sleep events (Windsor Castle), 86, 250

Dior, Christian, 108

Disraeli (1916 film), 158

Disraeli (1929 film), 158

Ditum, Sarah, 249

divine right of kings, 38

divorces, royal: Charles, Prince of Wales, 258; Charles/Diana divorce mug and plate, 81; divorce commemoratives, 27; family brand dimension and, 37; and Margaret, 108; and RFBC, 105

Doctor Who (TV series), 158

dogs, royal, 244–45

dolls, Russian-Style wooden nesting, Diana, Princess of Wales, 25, 26*fig.*3

domestic tourism, 209

dorgies (Queen's breed of dogs), 245

Dorothy Vernon of Haddon Hall (1924 film), 148*tab.*4

Downton Abbey (TV series), 63, 66–67, 250

Dragons of Walton Street (furniture designers), 276

drama, 130–63

Drummond, Kent, 121

Duchy Originals, 164, 169

Dudley, Robert, 140, 148*tab.*4, 149*tab.*4, 151*tab.*4, 153

Duff, Anne-Marie, 137

Duffy, Carol Ann, 72

Dunkin' Donuts, 266

duties, monarchical, 10

dynastic narratives, 211

Earl of Snowdon, 182

East Enders (TV show), 55

Edgar, King, 38

Edinburgh, xxiv, 50

Edinburgh Castle, 198

Edison, Thomas, 146

Edward, Earl of Wessex, xxiv, 55, 89, 198

Edward I, xxi

Edward II, xxi

Edward III, xxi, 177

Edward IV, xxi, 8, 148*tab.*4, 149*tab.*4, 151*tab.*4, 153

Edward V, xxi, 8

Edward VI, xxi, 8, 172

Edward VII, 5; contradictions, 35, 47; coronation ceremonies, 176; death of, 57; entertainment cost of, 23; lying in state of, 57; mistresses, 53; portrayals of, 148*tab.*4, 157; public display, 52–53; Rotorua visit, 202; royal patronage of,

Ernst August of Hanover, Prince, 197

Essex and Elizabeth (1939 film), 149*tab.*4, 160

Eton College, 243, 244

Eugenie of York, Princess, xxiv, 62, 271, 291

European roots, 9–10

European royal families, commoner wives, 33

European royal houses, website comparison, 55

European Union, trade barriers, 48

Everything Royal (website), 184

exception, luxury of, 39

The Execution of Mary, Queen of Scots (1895 film), 146, 148*tab.*4

exemption, luxury of, 39

external aspects of RFBC, 60. *See also* Anglophilia; British humor; commercial offering in the marketplace; nobility/aristocracy

fairy tale narrative: and Catherine, Duchess of Cambridge, 271; and Diana, 104, 106, 111, 113; global aspect of, 32–33; and royal portrayals, 143; and royal weddings, 273; Walt Disney Company, 33, 111

family, as key social structure, 36

family brand dimension (of RFBC), 35–37

family dynasties, 36

family narratives, and longevity characteristic, 46

fanfare dimension (of RFBC), 37–38, 246

fashions, royal: Catherine, Duchess of Cambridge, 263–65, 272; and Diana, 107; Diana, Princess of Wales, 39–40; and Edward VIII, 241; Elizabeth, Queen Consort, 66; Elizabeth I, 40; and Elizabeth II, 108; and goodwill tours, 49–50; and Margaret, 108; and Royal Ascot, 248–49, 249*fig.*29; royal weddings, 271–72; and Simpson, Wallis, 241

Fawcett, Michael, 186

Fawlty Towers (TV series), 70

Fayed, Dodi, 118–19, 124, 142, 242

Ferguson, Sarah "Fergie," 141, 190; divorce, xxiv; portrayals of, 155; scandals, 114; TV show participation, 55

fiascos: and brand ambiguity, 35; Diana, Princess of Wales, 116; Elizabeth II, 122; Harry, Prince, 34–35, 49; Margaret, Princess, 108; and Royal Family Brand Complex (RFBC), 35; Royal Standard issue, 54; and tabloid industry, 113; William I (the Conqueror), 35

fieldwork, authors' description, 305–6

50,000 Miles with the Prince of Wales (1920 film), 148*tab.*4

Fiji, 50

film appearances, 19; Elizabeth II, 19, 161; Victoria, 157

films, 130–63; and Anglophilia, 67; coronation ceremonies, 54; historical drama, 144; James Bond film series, 67; Royal Film Productions, 148*tab.*4; wartime films, 147. *See also specific films*

Fire over England (1937 film), 147, 149*tab.*4, 159–60

Firth, Colin, 141, 152*tab.*4

"Fitz" children. *See* illegitimate children

Fitzherbert, Maria, 204

The Florilegeum of Alexander Marshall, 251

Flynn, Barbara, 161

Flynn, Errol, 146, 149*tab.*4

folktales, as universal form of narrative, 32

foreign tourism, 198

Forever Amber (1947 film), 149*tab.*4

"The Forgotten Prince," 296*fig.*35

Forsythe, Blanche, 148*tab.*4, 158

Fort Belvedere, 66, 237, 238

Fortnum & Mason, 87, 179, 276, 276*fig.*33

fount of honour, 11

Fox, Emilia, 161

Fox, Kate, 69

Francis, Pope, 6

Franklin Mint, 265

Freud, Lucian, 72

Frogmore House, 171, 237

Furedi, Frank, 119

Gambia, goodwill tours, 50

Gatcombe Park, 180

Geller, Uri, 242

Thegenealogist.com, 46

genetic connections, 45

gentleman, defined, 60

George, Duke of Cambridge, 61
George, Duke of Kent, 183
George, Prince: birth of, xxv, 244, 277–79; christening of, 281–82; commemorative china, 174; first photos, 280–81; naming of, 279–80; Prince George effect, 190; and RFBC branding, 280–81; William's involvement, 298
George I, xxii, 5, 197
George II, xxii, 12, 21, 183, 197
George III, 105, 138; auctioned items, 183; Hanover, House of, xxii; lying in state of, 57; madness of, 120, 153, 169; portrayals of, 149*tab*.4, 151*tab*.4, 157; progeny of, 9; and royal tourism, 200–201; traditions, 309n8
George IV, 13, 138; and Ascot, 248; and Brummell, 147, 169; and Caroline, 253; and Fort Belvedere, 238; Hanover, House of, xxii; lifestyle of, 40, 120, 203–204; portrayals of, 149*tab*.4, 150*tab*.4, 156, 280; Royal Pavilion, 202–4, 203*fig*.23; and royal tourism, 201, 205
George V: burial site, 230; Chinese Dining Room, Buckingham Palace, 204; death of, 239; and Fort Belvedere, 238; introversion, 53; portrayals of, 152*tab*.4; *Royal Cavalcade* (1935 film), 147; Saxe-Coburg and Gotha, House of, xxii; stability of, 47; taxes, 308n6; Windsor, House of, xxiii
George VI, 53; coronation ceremonies, 53; coronation souvenirs, 239; family branding of, 37; and Logue, 141; patronage of, 285; portrayals of, 141, 147, 149*tab*.4, 152*tab*.4; quote, 13; Rhodesia goodwill tour, 48; South Africa goodwill tour, 48; taxes, 308n6; and Townsend, 108, 257; US royal tour (1939), 66, 197; wedding of, 255; Windsor, House of, xxiii. See also *The King's Speech* (2010 film)
Geraghty, Christine, 114–15
Germane, Charlotte, 254–55
German National Tourist Office, 197
G. H. Hurt and Son, 279
gifts, as luxury brand aspect, 50

Gilbert, E. W., 202
Gilbey, James, 114
glamour of backwardness, 27
global brand component, 30–31, 32
global consumer culture, 24, 32, 87
global goodwill ambassador, 13
global tourism, 30–31, 196
Gloriana image, 52
"God Save the Queen," 59–60
Golden Jubilees: Elizabeth II, xxiv; George III, 175; royal concerts, 60, 157; Victoria's, 52
Goldsmith, Carole, 259
Goldsmith, Ron, 259
goodwill tours, 11, 49, 50
Grand Tour, 199–201
Granger, Stewart, 147
Great Britain, 4
GREAT Britain campaign, 290–91
GREAT Britain MINI [Cooper] Tour, 291
Great Exhibition, 175, 189, 190
The Great McGonagall (1971 film), 158
Green, Milly, 277
Grey, Jane, lady, 149*tab*.4, 150*tab*.4
Groom, Suzanne, 70
Guérineau, Julie, 29
Gwyn, Nell, 148*tab*.4

Hall, Edward, 132
Hall, Philip (Phil), 109–10, 308n6
halo effect, 210
Halo Trust, 103
Hamad of Bahrain, King, 251
Hampton Court, 74
Hampton Court Palace, 155, 206*tab*.5, 209, 216–17, 224
Handbagged (2014 play), 161
Hanover, House of, 197; George I, xxii; George II, xxii; George III, xxii; George IV, xxii; stability factor, 47; Victoria, xxii; William IV, xxii
Hanoverian Crown Jewels exhibition, 197
happy snaps, 17, 58
Harald V, King of Norway, 44, 270
hardest-working Royal. *See* Anne, Princess Royal
Harold II, 4
Harrison, Dorothy, 259

Harrison, Jane, 258

Harrods Diana and Dodi memorials, 127

Harry, Prince, 75, 273; as ambassador for Britain, 290–91; birth of, xxiv, 113; christening, Prince George's, 281; as Diana's story, 129; Eton College, 243; as family-brand dimension, 298; fiascos of, 34–35; as human brand, 297; image management, 56; Las Vegas fiasco, 49; rebranding royal image, 290; Tsessebe, 170; US goodwill tour, 49

Harry Potter (film series), Alnwick Castle, 62

Hartnell, Norman, 40, 49, 108, 112

Harvey, Theodore (American consumer), 45, 68, 137

Hastings, Battle of, 4

Hawthorne, Nigel, 138

Hayes, Helen, 66

The Heart of a Queen (1940 film), 149*tab*.4

heir apparent, 257

heir presumptive, 257

Hello (periodical), 113, 287

Helmers, Marguerite, 111

Henry, Prince of Wales. *See* Harry, Prince

Henry I, xx

Henry II, xx, 150*tab*.4

Henry III, xxi

Henry IV, xxi

Henry IV Parts 1 and 2 (Shakespeare), 132

Henry IV Parts 1 and 2 (TV production), 133

Henry V: Agincourt victory celebration, 21, 133; Lancaster, House of, xxi; portrayals of, 138, 149*tab*.4, 150*tab*.4

Henry V (1944 film), 133, 147

Henry V (1946 film), 149*tab*.4

Henry V (1989 film), 137, 138, 139*fig*.17, 144, 150*tab*.4

Henry V (2012 TV production), 133

Henry V (Shakespeare), 132

Henry VI, xxi, 199, 243

Henry VII, xxi, 137

Henry VIII, 8, 153, 172; Anglican Church establishment, 20, 199; armor, suit of, 232; burial site, 230; and Catherine of Aragon, 253; cumulations (multiple meanings within a brand narrative), 35;

family narratives, 46; human branding of, 36; portrayals of, 148*tab*.4, 149*tab*.4, 150*tab*.4, 152*tab*.4, 154–55, 157, 163; reign of, 39; Tudor, House of, xxi

Henry VIII (1911 film), 146, 148*tab*.4

Henry VIII (1979 film), 150*tab*.4

Henry VIII (Shakespeare), 133

Henry VI Parts 1, 2, and 3, 132

Hepburn, Katherine, 146, 148*tab*.4, 150*tab*.4

hereditary monarchies, 4–5

hereditary peerages, 61

hereditary revenues, veto power, 10

heritage brand dimension (of RFBC), 73; and Balmer, 37; and consumption practices, 97–98; and fanfare dimension, 37–38; and social networking, 90–91

heritage caretaking, 63

Heritage House, 76–77, 77*fig*.9; *Britain's Worst Homes,* 101; Diana, Princess of Wales, 110*fig*.13

heritage management, 209

heritage tourism, defined, 194

Herleva, 9

Her Majesty, Mrs. Brown (1997 film), 137, 138–39, 141, 143, 144, 151*tab*.4, 153, 154, 158

Hewitt, James, 117

Highclere Castle, 63, 69, 250

Highgrove, 87, 164, 169, 177, 179–80

high tea, as endangered cultural practice/ experience, 29

Hilary (Tyler RFBC tribe member), 95–96

Hill, William, 250

Hilliard, Nicholas, 145

Hillsborough Castle, 209

Hindoo style, 202–4, 203*fig*.23

Hirst, Michel, 154

historical costumes, 144–45

historical drama, 131, 137, 143–45

Historic Royal Palaces (HRP), 194, 207*tab*.5, 209–24; brand visibility, 211; and management issues, 292; persona distinction, 223–24; purposes of, 209–10; royal residences, 206*tab*.5

Hitler, Adolf, 239; Putin comparison, 295

magazines, royalty, and US, 67

Magna Carta, 72, 142, 181

"Making of the Modern Monarchy Conference" speech, 314n1

male primogeniture, 4–5

A Man for All Seasons (1966 film), 150*tab.*4, 153

Mantel, Hilary, 163, 264–65

Margaret, Princess: burial site, 230; Christie's auctions, 182–83; death of, xxiv, 37; Diana comparison, 109; divorce, 108; dorgies, 245; family branding of, 37; as fashion icon, 108, 112; fiascos of, 108; Margaret set, 108; and paparazzi, 108–9; portrayals of, 152*tab.*4, 155; and Townsend, 108, 257

Margaret set, 108

Margrethe II of Denmark, 270

Maria (Diana collector), 128

Marienburg Castle, 197

Marina, Duchess of Kent, 183

marketing concepts, brand (branding), 29–30

marketing strategies, 164–93; dimensions of, 30; Elizabeth II, 54; internet commerce, 184; and touristic experiences, 198

marketplace: choices, 24; RFBC intersection with, 63; role of, 74; royal representations of, 27

market researchers, Way Ahead Group, 55

Marks & Spencer, 269

Marmite theory of monarchy, 55

Marr, Andrew, 161

Mary, Queen Consort: burial site, 230; dollhouse of, 232; lace trimmings of, 111; pomp and popularity, 53; portrayals of, 152*tab.*4; reputation for mooching, 23; stability of, 47

Mary, Queen of Frocks (TV show), 264

Mary, Queen of Scots, 72, 148*tab.*4, 150*tab.*4, 151*tab.*4, 208

Mary, Queen of Scots (1971 film), 150*tab.*4, 153

Mary I, xxi, 8, 153

Mary II, xxii

Mary of Scotland (1936 film), 148*tab.*4

Mary Quant, 66

mass-media era, 51, 56

matroshka collections, Diana, Princess of Wales, 25, 26*fig.*3

Maundy coins, 59

McCartney, Paul, 286

McCracken, Grant, 145

McGonagall, William, 158

McGuinness, Martin, 288

McQueen, Alexander, 272

media coverage: and Diana, 116, 121–22; of Royal Family, 113; of Royal Family events, 88; Tyler on, 90

media images, marketing strategies, 130

media industry: and consumer tribe relationships, 98; and Diana, 107, 116

media platforms, 130–63; broadcast industry, 53–54, 88; and conservatives, 54; drama, 87; films, 148*tab.*4; television broadcasts, 53, 55, 59, 98. *See also* films; paparazzi; tabloid industry

media products, Royal Film Productions, 148*tab.*4

media representations, RFBC, 130

media saturation, 20

media sources: Tyler as, 86, 86–87; Tyler referrals, 89–90

mediated experiences, 43

medieval era: drama, 131, 132; and humor, 69; religious pilgrimages in, 199

Melbourne, 143

Mette-Marit, Crown Princess of Norway, 33

micro-rituals, anointing of the monarch, 3

middle class consumerism, 31, 39

Middle East, 39

Middleton, Carole, 259–61, 281, 299

Middleton, Catherine. *See* Catherine, Duchess of Cambridge

Middleton, James, 259, 299

Middleton, Michael, 259

Middleton, Noel, 259

Middleton, Philippa "Pippa," 191, 259, 272, 281, 299

Middleton family, 87, 190–91, 259–61, 281, 299

Milligan, Spike, 158, 162

minglers, consumer tribe, 91

Minton pottery commemoratives, Thomas (American consumer), 25

ritual experiences: and consumer tribes, 92–93, 99–100; locales, 72. *See also* cultural rituals

ritualized cultural practices, 56–57

RMS *Queen Elizabeth,* 209

RMS *Queen Mary,* 209

Robert I, Duke of Normandy, 9

Roberts, Monty, 246

Robinson, Mike, 60, 194, 211, 294

Robson, Flora, 147, 149*tab.*4, 159–60

role conceptualization, 63

Rolls-Royce, 39, 272*fig.*31

Roosevelt, Franklin D., 66, 152*tab.*4, 197

Rosenstone, Robert, 137–38

Rowntree, 188

Royal Archives, 250

Royal Ascot, 24, 181, 247–48, 249*fig.*29

royal assets, 41, 49

royal babies: Fortnum & Mason display, 276*fig.*33; "Keep Calm" signage, 275*fig.*32; naming of, 279–80; pregnancy announcements, 274; Throne Up sick bag, 28

Royal Baby Collection, Huddle and Bliss, 274

royal baby items, 87

royal baby marketing: commemoratives, 275–77, 276*fig.*33; merchandising, 274

royal baby-watch, 197

royal baby-watching, 277

royal beds, 23

royal births, as public affairs, 277–79

"Royal Bodies" lecture, 264–65

royal branding practices, 170, 171

royal caricatures, seventeenth century, 70

Royal Cavalcade (1935 film), 147

Royal Collection Trust, 12–13, 164, 171–75, 250; auction bids, 182; commemorative china, 174, 279; commemoratives, 265, 276; and Edward VIII, 241; exhibitions, 172; Queen's Gallery exhibits, 87; and Windsor Castle fire, 233–34

royal commemorative candy boxes, 188, 188*fig.*21

royal commemoratives, in warrior king era, 22

royal concert, 60

royal consumer culture: and Anglophilia, 67; and economic downturns, 67

royal consumption spectrum, 20–21; aspects of, 43; dark tourism, 21; viability factors, 21–22

Royal Courts, and humor, 69

royal cultural rituals: ancient roots, 38; modernization of, 38

Royal Deeside, 205

royal dimension of marketing strategy, (eight Rs), 30

royal duties, global goodwill ambassadors, 13

royal events, 58; and touristic experiences, 199; annual garden party, 74

Royal Family: as brand, 30; consumption practices, 41; cost of, 13–14; duties, monarchial, 10; endurance of, 1–2; as icons of British culture, 28; marketplace representations, 27; motorcycle caricature, 25; as object of consumer/tourist gaze, 29

Royal Family, criticisms of, 19, 90, 234

Royal Family (1969 film), 161–62

Royal Family Brand Complex (RFBC): accessibility of, 34, 122, 162, 173, 243, 284; as addiction, 43; advertising portrayals, 189–93; ambiguities, 38; and aristocracy, 62–63; brand components, 30; brand types, 287–88; British humor, 69; and changing values, 238–39; and collecting, 43; and commemorating, 43; and commemoratives, 63; consumer culture experiences/outlets, 43; consumer gains, 21; and consumer tribes, 91–102; contemporary media representations, 130, 133, 142, 162; contributions to Britain, 285; defined, 30, 31*fig.*4; and Diana, 107; Diana's impact on, 105; establishment of, 105; and European countries, 197; evolution of, 284; family brand dimension, 298–99; family narratives, 46, 105; fanfare dimension, 37–38; and fiascos, 35; future of, 283–303; global brand component, 288–91; global comparison, 44–45; and Harry, 105; heritage brand dimension, 37–38, 73, 96, 292–93; human brand dimension, 294–97; and humor, 69; image management, 105; interactions, member, 68–69; interest increase, 31; internet channels, 184–85; and London, 71–72; luxury brand dimension, 39, 210, 299–302; and Margaret, 108; marketing channels, 182; marketing strategies, 184; marketplace intersections, 63; and mediated experiences, 43; Middleton family and, 260; persona change, 55; public perceptions of, 105; royal branding practices, 164; and royal divorces, 105; royal future, 283–303; royal staff sales, 185–86; and Royal Warrants, 164–69; and Shakespeare, 130; shape consumer experiences, 43; shape producer offerings, 43; stability factor, 47; and temporary touristic offerings, 196; and tourism, 279; and touristic experiences, 43; and Tyler brand tribe, 100–101; underdog brand narrative, 111; visibility of, 48; and William, 105; and Windsor, 234–35; and Windsor Castle, 231–32. *See also* Tyler, Margaret

Royal Family narrative, soap opera comparisons, 114–16, 115*tab*.2

Royal Family narratives, contemporary media representations, 162–63

Royal Family phrase, first use of, 37

Royal Family textiles, 127–28

Royal Farms, 180, 180–81

royal fever, roots of, 44–75

Royal Film Productions, 148*tab*.4

Royal film productions, 148–50*tab*.4

Royal Foundation for the Duke and Duchess of Cambridge and Prince Harry, 290

royal genealogy, 46

Royal Heritage Route, 197

royal historical film genre, evolution of, 145–47, 153–55

Royal Household: annual holiday party, 235; branding efforts, 56; Clarence House, 171; costs, 13–14; Frogmore House, 171; Holyroodhouse, Palace of, 171; scope of, 62–63, 171; unofficial merchandising by staff, 186; Windsor Castle, 171

royal images, Tudor era, 22

royal image usage, 187, 189–90

royal impersonators, 191–92

royalists/monarchists: Tyler as loyalist, 76; in US, 67–68

royal kitsch (tat). *See* Tyler, Margaret; collectors, Royal, 25

Royal Library, 233, 250

royal luxury-brand dimension: fashion source of, 39–40

Royal Marriages Act of 1772, 108

royal mascots, Elizabeth II, 54

Royal Maundy service, 59

royal memorabilia market, 184–90, 186–90

royal merchandising, and royal weddings, 268–70

Royal Mews, 73, 171

Royal Mile, 198

The Royal Nappy, 274

royal narrative, and temporary tourist sites, 197

A Royal Night Out (2015 film), 152*tab*.4, 162

Royal Paintbox exhibition, 172

Royal Palace, Oslo, Norway, 44

royal palaces. *See* Historic Royal Palaces (HRP)

Royal Palace Shops' Coldstream Guards, royal baby items, 87

Royal Pavilion, 202–4, 203*fig*.23, 207*tab*.5; Brighton, 203*fig*.23

royal privacy, 287

Royal Procession at Ascot, 247–48

royal progresses, Elizabeth I, 52

royal protocol, and human-brand component, 34

royal representations, range of, 25–27

royal reproductive patterns, 299

royal residence narratives, 222–23

royal residences, 194–251; Althorp, 87–88, 106, 125, 126*fig*.15, 206*tab*.5; Balmoral, 205; Banqueting House, Whitehall, 206*tab*.5, 209, 218, 224; Historic Royal Palaces (HRP), 194; Osborne House, 204–5; Royal Pavilion, 202–4, 203*fig*.23; tours of, 200; Windsor Castle, 225–51. *See also* Buckingham Palace; Windsor Castle

royal rituals, 21; coronation ceremonies, 38

"Royals" (2013 single), 283

The Royals (2015 TV drama), 162–63

Shy Di hairstyle, 109
Sigaux, Gilbert, 201
signature colors, Elizabeth II, 54
Silver Jubilees, George V, 176, 232
Silverman, Helaine, 27
Simmons, Jean, 149*tab*.4, 159, 160
Simpson, Wallis, 51, 66, 152*tab*.4, 238–43
sixties pop culture, 66
The Six Wives of Henry VIII (1971 TV
    miniseries), 154
Sixty Glorious Years (1938 film), 147,
    149*tab*.4
Sixty Years a Queen (1913 film), 148*tab*.4,
    158
The Sloane Ranger Handbook (York), 107
Sloane style, 107, 112, 156, 261
Smith, Peter, 186
Smith, Sally Bedell, 41
Snell, Kate, 142
Snow White and the Seven Dwarves (1937
    film), 33
soap opera narrative, 114–16, 115*tab*.2, 123
Soccer Aid, 286
social class interactions, 24
social networking, 56, 90–91, 128
social roles: Brand Collector Identities,
    81*tab*.1; of brand collectors, 81; and
    RFBC, 90–91; and Tyler collection,
    81*tab*.1
solar queens, 16*fig*.1
Somer, Paul van, 173
Sonja, Queen of Norway, 270
Sophie, Countess of Wessex, 190
Sotheby's, 182, 242–43
South Africa, 25, 27, 48
South America, middle-class consumerism,
    39
souvenirs, 63, 64*fig*.7. See also
    commemoratives
Sovereign Grant system, 14
spa industry, 201–2
spa-based tourism, 201–2
speeches, Edward VII, 52
Spencer, Charles, 9th Earl, 88, 106, 125
Spencer, Diana. *See* Diana, Princess of
    Wales
Spencer, Jane, 106
Spencer, Johnny and Frances, 106

Spencer, Sarah, 106, 112
Spencer, Warfield, 66
Spitting Image (TV series), 130, 155–56
Spitting Image mask, 82
Spitting Image slippers, 130, 131*fig*.16
Squidgygate, 113–14
stability factor, 47, 54
staff costs, 14
stakeholders (in RFBC), 29–30, 34
St. Andrew's University, 260
Starkey, David, 142, 154, 277, 318n17
State Apartments, 233–34
State Dining Room, 250
State Opening of Parliament ceremony, 11
State Rooms, 171
St. Dunstan, 38
Stephen, Blois, House of, xx
Stern (German periodical), 117
St. George mascot, 54
St. George's Chapel, 121, 199, 230, 240
Stirling Castle, 207*tab*.5
St. James's Palace: and branding, 29, 190;
    Chapel Royal, 281; marketing strategies,
    198; public relations, 56; and Royal
    court, 73; and Victoria's wedding,
    253–54
St. Mary's Hospital, 197, 277
stoicism, and humor, 69
Stoke-on-Trent, 175
Stonehenge, as endangered practice/experi-
    ence, 29
St. Paul's Cathedral, 111, 127, 207*tab*.5, 208
Straubenzee, Thomas van, 62
street parties, 58
Stuart, House of, xxii. *See also* Anne;
    Charles I; Charles II; James I; James II;
    Mary II; William III
Stylist.com, 109
succession, royal: elected systems, 2, 4, 6;
    hereditary systems, 4–5; policies of, 4
Succession to the Crown Act (2013), 5
Summer of London, 19
Sun (tabloid), 113, 113–14, 277
supporters, consumer tribe, 92
Susan (royal corgi), 245
"Swan Upping," swan census, 244
Swaziland, 6
Swedish Royal Family, 30, 33

Sweyn Forkbread, 10
Sydney, Australia, AJC Queen Elizabeth
    Stakes, 323n6

tabloid industry, 51; antimonarchism and,
    113; and Diana, 118; Ferguson, Sarah
    "Fergie," 155; and Margaret, 108; privacy
    request, 56; and Windsor Castle fire,
    234
Taggesspiegel (German periodical), 117
Tapley, Rose, 158
taxes, income, monarchs payment of, 20,
    234, 308n6
Taylor, Elizabeth, 147, 149*tab*.4, 242
Team GB, 273
telephone box, Royal, 233*fig*.27
television programs, 153–54; *Fawlty Towers,*
    70; *Monty Python's Flying Circus,* 70;
    Mr. Bean, 71; "Pantomime Princess
    Margaret," 70
Terrabona Tea & Coffee, 191
Tesco, 269
Thailand, 26, 41
Thatcher, Margaret, 11, 161, 282
Theatre Royal Windsor, 235
Thomas (American consumer), 24–25
Thompson, Emma, 138
Thomson, Matthew, 33–34
Throne Up sick bag, 28
Tigrett, Pat Kerr, 127–28
Tindall, Zara, 247, 281
T-Mobile video, 268
Todd (Tyler RFBC tribe member), 91,
    93–94, 96
To Kill a King (2003 film), 151*tab*.4
Tonga, 49
tourism research, 194
tourist gaze, 21, 196
touristic experiences, 198, 199
touristic practices, Royal, 43; Diana
    tours, 127; foreign tourism, 67,
    198; Scottish Highland region,
    205; Transcendent (tour operator),
    69
tourists, consumer tribe, 91
tourist sites, Royal Tourism, 206*tab*.5
tourist souvenirs, 44–45

Tower of London, xxv, 21, 207*tab*.5, 208–
    10, 211–15, 224, 292
Townsend, Peter, 108, 257
trade ambassador role, 273
Transcendent (tour operator), 68
transmedia consumption, Walt Disney
    Company, 33
travel costs, 13, 14
Travolta dress, 127
Treacy, Philip, 271
Treaty of Waitangi, 202
tribes. *See* consumer tribes
Trooping the Colour: ceremony, 12, 198;
    Elizabeth II, 57*fig*.6; protests during,
    42, 42*fig*.5; resisting at, 42*fig*.5; as ritual-
    ized cultural practices, 57, 246
T-shirts, 71
Tudor, House of, xxi, 39, 70, 137. *See also*
    Edward VI; Elizabeth I; Henry VII;
    Henry VIII; Mary I; War of the
    Roses
Tudor era, 22, 154–55
Tudor Myth, 137
Tudor Rose (1936 film), 149*tab*.4
The Tudors (TV series), 154–55, 163
Twiggy, 66
Tyler, Margaret, 76–102, 77–78; acquisi-
    tions methods, 77–78, 92; brand collec-
    tor identities of, 81, 81*tab*.1; *Britain's
    Worst Homes,* 101; Charles and Camilla
    wedding, 234–35; on Charles/Camilla
    marriage, 90; collection items,
    80*fig*.10^11, 81–82, 131*fig*.16, 253*fig*.30;
    collection organization, 78, 82, 101;
    collection style, 79, 81; collective sup-
    port, 95–96; consumer brand tribe,
    91–102; consumption fantasies, 96–97;
    on Diana, 101; Diana, Princess of Wales,
    104*fig*.12, 110*fig*.13; Diana Room, 88, 92,
    95, 97, 103, 110; Diana rose, 82, 86, 103;
    Diana tributes, 93–94; heritage brand
    dimension, 96; Heritage House, 77*fig*.9;
    as historian, 81–82; image management
    quote, 20; as loyalist/royalist, 101; as
    media expert, 86–87; media representa-
    tions, RFBC, 130; memorabilia sanctu-
    ary, 83–84; personal momentos, 79;

as public mourner, 122; and RFBC, 85–90, 89–90; royal baby memorabilia, 87; royal baby-watch, 278; on royal criticism, 90; on royal divorce, 37; *Royalty A to Zed* appearance, 89; Sandringham Room, 84; social facilitator role, 84; special events, 84–85, 98–100; *Spitting Image* mask, 82; *Spitting Image* slippers, 130, 131*fig.*16; supporters of, 92; as tourist attraction, 88–89; TV media coverage, 85; ugliest thing quote, 25

UK Trade and Investment (UKTI), 273
underdog brand narrative, and Diana, 107, 111, 116
UNESCO World Heritage Sites, 211
UN Goodwill Ambassadors, 286
UN High Commission for Refugees, 286
UNICEF, 286
Union Jack flags, 58
The Union of the Two Noble and Illustre Famelies of Lancastre & Yorke (Hall), 132
United Kingdom, 3, 31, 257
United States, Anglophilia in, 64–65
Unlawful Killing (2011 documentary), 124
Untitled (2008 play), 87
Upstairs Downstairs (TV series), 67
Ustinov, Peter, 147, 149*tab.*4

valorization, celebrity, 45
valorized character traits, and humor, 69
Vatican City, 1, 6
V-E Day, Royal Family balcony appearances, 57–58
Versace, Gianni, 118
veto power, 10
Victor (Tyler RFBC tribe member), 91, 94
Victoria: accession, 8; annual garden parties, 74; bridal traditions, 255; and Brown, 138–39, 143, 153, 208; china sets, 174–75; commemoratives, 175; coronation ceremonies, 65; death of, 205; Diamond Jubilee, 157, 157*fig.*18; family narratives, 46, 208; fashion, 65, 145,

236–37; film appearances, 157; hand/feet casting, 282; Hanover, House of, xxii; Jack Daniel's Tube ad, 192*fig.*22; *Leaves from the Journal of Our Life in the Highlands,* 208; as moral compass, 13; Mothers' Union, 285; portrayals of, 141, 147, 148*tab.*4, 149*tab.*4, 151*tab.*4, 152*tab.*4, 157, 158; progeny of, 9; and RFBC, 105; and Royal Pavilion, 204; and royal tourism, 204–5; seclusion of, 52, 236; stability factor, 47; successor, 5; taxes, 308n6; Thornycroft, 282; wedding dress, 254; wedding of, 65, 253–54
Victoria, Crown Princess of Sweden, 33
Victoria, Princess Royal, 5
Victoria and Albert (TV miniseries), 158
Victoria and Albert Museum, 72, 250
The Victoria Cross (1912 film), 158
Victoriana, 65
Victoria Regina (1936 play), 66
Victoria the Great (1937 film), 147, 149*tab.*4, 158
Vincent (Tyler RFBC tribe member), 92, 93–94, 96, 100, 101
The Virgin Queen (1923 film), 148*tab.*4, 159
The Virgin Queen (1955 film), 149*tab.*4
Virgin Queen persona, 52, 140, 159
Vogue, Diana covers, 113

Waitrose, 178–79
"Waity Katie" nickname, 32
Wakeley, Amanda, 112
Walker, Catherine, 112
Walt Disney Company, 33, 111
Ward, Freda Dudley, 67
Warhol, Andy, 72
War of the Roses, 62, 137. *See also* Lancaster, House of; York, House of
warrior king era, 20, 21–22
Wars of the Roses, 137
Watson, Emma, 286
Watts, Naomi, 78, 105, 142, 152*tab.*4
Wax Museum, Madame Tussaud's, 75
Wax Work, Fleet Street, 75
Way Ahead Group, 55
W.E. (2011 film), 152*tab.*4

websites: *City Discovery,* 127; official British monarchy, 12, 13, 55–56; Stylist.com, 109; www.princeofwales.gov.uk, 55; www.royal.gov.uk, 12, 55; www.royaltymonarchy.com, 68
weddings. *See* royal weddings
Wedgwood, 175
West End theater district, 75
Westling, Daniel, 33
Westminster, Palace of, 74
Westminster Abbey, 75, 207*tab.*5; Diana, funeral of, xxiv; Diana tours, 127; Elizabeth II wedding crowd, 270; as iconic cultural contributions, 72–73; royal tourism and, 208; William and Catherine wedding, 271
Westwood, Vivienne, 264, 271
What Kate Wore website, 264
Whitehall Palace, 218
Who Are You? exhibit, 72
Widow of Windsor, 7, 236
Wilde, Oscar, 19
Wilhelm II, Kaiser of Germany, 10, 231–32
William, Duke of Cambridge, 252; after wedding kiss, 38; APL Anglesey, 170; birth of, xxiv; courtship, 261–62; as Diana's story, 129; effect on consumer culture, 263; engagement, 262–63; engagement representations, 27; Eton College, 243; fathering style, 298; goodwill tours, 49; hereditary title, 61; image management, 56; Madame Tussaud's Wax Museum, 75; marriage, xxv, 29; marriage of, 72; pregnancy announcements, xxv; rebranding royal image, 290; role of, 273–74; St. Andrew's University, 56; Tyler table, 253*fig.*30; wedding of, 58, 252–53, 258; wedding toilet paper, 25. *See also* Catherine, Duchess of Cambridge; Charlotte, Princess; George, Prince; George, Prince of Wales; Royal Wedding
William I (the Conqueror), 4, 8; coronation ceremonies, 72; fiascos of, 35; and humor, 69–70; illegitimacy of, 9; and nobility/aristocracy, 60; Normandy, House of, xx; and warrior king era, 21; White Tower, 211

William II, xx
William III, xxii, 59
William IV, xxii, 8, 13, 152*tab.*4, 204
William the Conqueror. *See* William I (the Conqueror)
Wimbledon, 24
Wimdu, German lettings company, 84
Windsor, 225, 233*fig.*27
Windsor, House of, xxiii; as brand repositioning, 10, 232; as dead, 302; key events (1981-present), xxiv–xxv; as luxury-brand house, 39; and marriages, 257. *See also* Edward VIII; Elizabeth II; George V; George VI
Windsor Castle, 74, 171, 225–51; 1992 fire, 114; Changing of the Guard, 232, 236*fig.*28; and Charles II, 230; China Corridor, 174; dine and sleep events, 86; early history, 228–29; and Elizabeth II, 225, 227–28; family narratives, 105; fire, xxiv, 232–34; Garter ceremony, 229; and George IV, 231; and Henry VI, 230; and Henry VIII, 230; Long Walk, 230; public tours, 232; redesign of, 231; renovations, xxiv, 198, 292; Royal Collection, 230–31; *Royal Paintbox* exhibition, 172; souvenirs, 232; St. George's Chapel, 121, 230; telephone box, Royal, 233*fig.*27
Windsor City Sightseeing Bus tour, 181
Windsor Farm Shop, 164, 169, 179, 180, 181*fig.*20
Windsor Great Park, The Long Walk, 226*fig.*26
Windsor Green, 54
Windsor Royal Station, 231
winter season, 234–36, 236*fig.*28
Wisteria Sisters, 261
Witan council, 4
Wittstock, Charlene. *See* Charlene, Princess of Monaco
Wolf Hall (2015 film), 163
World War I: Armistice Day poppies, 215; effects on aristocracy, 23; hundredth celebration, 294; and public spirits, 255
World War II, declaration of war speech, 141
Worshipful Company of Dyers, 244
Worshipful Company of Vintners, 244